PENGUIN HANDBOOKS

The Penguin Guide to the Railways of Britain

Edgar Jones was born in 1953 in Beckenham, Kent, and was educated at St Clement Danes Grammar School in London and Oriel College, Oxford, where he read modern history. He held a Research Studentship at Nuffield College and is now completing doctoral research there on transport and the Industrial Revolution. He has worked as a cataloguer at Sotheby's and as company historian to a well-known accountancy firm, and he is currently writing a history of British industrial architecture.

The Penguin Guide to the Railways of Britain

Edgar Jones

CONSULTANT EDITOR: CHRIS COOK

Penguin Books

Penguin Books Ltd, Harmondsworth, Middlesex, England
Penguin Books, 625 Madison Avenue, New York, New York 10022, U.S.A.
Penguin Books Australia Ltd, Ringwood, Victoria, Australia
Penguin Books Canada Ltd, 2801 John Street, Markham, Ontario, Canada L3R 1B4
Penguin Books (N.Z.) Ltd, 182–190 Wairau Road, Auckland 10, New Zealand

First published 1981
Published simultaneously by Allen Lane
Copyright © Edgar Jones, 1981
All rights reserved

Made and printed in Great Britain by
Hazell Watson & Viney Ltd, Aylesbury, Bucks
Set in Monotype Baskerville

Except in the United States of America, this book is sold subject
to the condition that it shall not, by way of trade or otherwise, be lent,
re-sold, hired out, or otherwise circulated without the
publisher's prior consent in any form of binding or cover other than
that in which it is published and without a similar condition
including this condition being imposed on the subsequent purchaser

To the Great Central

Contents

List of Plates	xiii
List of Text Figures	xv
List of Maps	xvi
Preface and Acknowledgements	xvii
Abbreviations	xix

1 THE COMING OF THE RAILWAYS — 1

2 THE PATH OF TECHNICAL IMPROVEMENT — 15
The steam locomotive	16
Electric railways	29
The diesel locomotive	37
Carriages and wagons	42
Tracks, signalling and general engineering	49

3 THE RAILWAYS OF LONDON — 55
The Metropolitan Railway	56
The District, Circle and later extensions	58
The Bakerloo, Northern, Piccadilly and Central Lines	60
The suburban system and 'Metroland'	67
Broad Street and the North London Railway	71
Fenchurch Street	81
Marylebone	82

4 THE GREAT WESTERN	83
Paddington	83
The suburban service to Reading	85
Reading to Didcot	89
Swindon, Bath and Bristol, Cheltenham	90
Didcot to Hereford	97
Routes to the south-west	101
Preserved steam railways	110
The Dart Valley Railway (p. 110) – The Torbay Steam Railway (p. 111) – The West Somerset Railway (p. 112) – The East Somerset Railway (p. 112)	
5 THE SOUTHERN REGION	113
Victoria	114
The 'Golden Arrow' and the Dover lines	117
The 'Brighton Belle' and the Brighton line	121
Waterloo	125
Waterloo to Exeter	130
Suburban Services	134
Charing Cross	137
London Bridge and the London to Greenwich line	137
Holborn and Blackfriars	141
Nine Elms and Clapham Junction	142
Preserved steam railways	143
The Bluebell Railway (p. 143) – The Kent and East Sussex Railway (p. 144) – The Romney, Hythe & Dymchurch Railway (p. 145) – The Isle of Wight Steam Railway (p. 146) – The Mid-Hants 'Watercress' Railway (p. 147)	
6 THE RAILWAYS OF EASTERN ENGLAND	148
Liverpool Street	149
Colchester to Norwich	151
Cambridge, Ely and King's Lynn	155

CONTENTS ix

King's Cross 157
King's Cross to Doncaster 158
Suburban Services 161
The Great Eastern: Liverpool Street to Hertford East 161
The Central Line: Stratford to Ongar 165
The Great Northern: King's Cross to Stevenage 167
Fenchurch Street to Southend 168
Preserved steam railways 170
  The Bressingham Live Steam Museum (p. 170)
  – The North Norfolk Railway (p. 170) – The Peterborough
  and Nene Valley Railway (p. 171) – The Stour Valley
  Railway (p. 171) – The Colne Valley Railway (p. 172)

7 THE MIDLANDS 173
Euston 174
Euston to Birmingham 175
Birmingham 178
Wolverhampton, Stoke, Stafford and Crewe 181
St Pancras 187
St Pancras to Leicester, Nottingham, Sheffield and
Derby 190

Suburban Services 200
St Pancras to Luton and Bedford 200
Euston to Northampton 203
Marylebone to Banbury and Aylesbury 206
Preserved steam railways 209
  The Birmingham Railway Museum, Tyseley (p. 209)
  – The Main Line Steam Trust, Loughborough Central
  Station (p. 210) – The Quainton Railway Society
  (p. 211) – The Midland Railway Centre, Butterley
  Station (p. 211)

8 RAILWAYS IN WALES AND THE BORDERS 212
Coastal main lines 213

Internal upland railways 224
The Welsh Borders 226
Narrow-gauge railways 229
The Festiniog Railway (p. 230) – The Talyllyn Railway (p. 230) – The Vale of Rheidol Railway (p. 231) – The Welshpool & Llanfair Railway (p. 231) – The Snowdon Mountain Railway (p. 232) – The Fairbourne Railway (p. 232) – The Llanberis Lake Railway (p. 233) – The Bala Lake Railway (p. 233) – The Severn Valley Railway (p. 233) – The Llangollen Railway Society (p. 235) – The Caerphilly Railway Society (p. 236) – The Gwili Railway (p. 236)

9 THE NORTH-WEST 237
The Liverpool & Manchester Railway 238
Manchester 241
Liverpool 249
Blackpool 254
Lancaster and the route to Carlisle 257
Carlisle 259
Barrow and the Furness Railway 261
The Lake District 263
The Isle of Man's Railways 264
Preserved Steam Railways 265
The Lakeside & Haverthwaite Railway (p. 265) – The Ravenglass & Eskdale Railway (p. 267) – Steamtown, Carnforth (p. 268) – Dinting Railway Centre (p. 270) – Steamport, The Southport Locomotive and Transport Museum Society (p. 270)

10. THE NORTH-EAST 272
The 'Race to the North' 273
York 276
Darlington 279
Newcastle 282
Newcastle to Berwick and Carlisle 287
Leeds and south-west Yorkshire 290

CONTENTS xi

Sheffield 295
Hull and the Humber 298
Scarborough 303
Middlesbrough 304
Sunderland 305
Preserved steam railways 305
The North Yorkshire Moors Railway (p. 305)
– *The Keighley & Worth Valley Light Railway* (p. 306)
– *The Yorkshire Dales Railway* (p. 307) – *The Middleton Railway* (p. 309)

11. SCOTLAND 310

The Southern Uplands 311
Glasgow 314
Edinburgh 323
Perth and Dundee to Aberdeen 326
Aberdeen 330
The Highlands: West Coast 332
The Highlands: East Coast 336
Preserved steam railways 340
The Glasgow Museum of Transport (p. 340) – *Falkirk Railway Museum* (p. 341) – *The Strathspey Railway* (p. 341)

12 CONCLUSIONS: THE NEW AGE OF RAILWAYS 343

APPENDIXES 353
1. Steam, Diesel and Electric Wheel Arrangements 353
2. Railway Company Liveries 355
3. Railway Museums 359

GLOSSARY OF ARCHITECTURAL TERMS 361
GUIDE TO FURTHER READING 363
INDEX 367

List of Plates

1. 222 Marylebone Road, headquarters of British Rail. (*British Rail*)
2. The replica of the *Rocket* in Kensington Gardens. (*Author*)
3. No. 60022, *Mallard*. (*British Rail*)
4. No. 71000, *Duke of Gloucester*. (*British Rail*)
5. No. 92220, *Evening Star*. (*British Rail*)
6. A City & South London Railway electric train, 1922. (*London Transport Executive*)
7. A class 87 electric locomotive. (*British Rail*)
8. The Advanced Passenger Train. (*British Rail*)
9. A class 47 diesel-electric locomotive. (*British Rail*)
10. High Speed Trains at the Bradford Exchange terminus. (*British Rail*)
11. Dining saloon, West Coast Route, c.1912. (*British Rail*)
12. A L.N.E.R. semaphore signal gantry. (*British Rail*)
13. Birmingham New Street's computerized signal box. (*London Midland Region, B.R.*)
14. The Metropolitan Line's No. 12, *Sarah Siddons*. (*London Transport Executive*)
15. District Line R stock. (*London Transport Executive*)
16. R stock interior. (*London Transport Executive*)
17. The Bakerloo Railway's prototype all-steel motor car, 1906. (*London Transport Executive*)
18. Gloucester Road Station, 1916. (*London Transport Executive*)
19. Acton Central Station. (*Author*)
20. Notting Hill Gate Station, 1863. (*London Transport Executive*)
21. Chiswick Park Station. (*Author*)

22. Interior of a Metropolitan Railway Pullman car of the 1930s. (*London Transport Executive*)
23. Circle Line C69 stock. (*London Transport Executive*)
24. Victoria Line stock. (*London Transport Executive*)
25. A King class locomotive at Teignmouth, 1937. (*British Rail*)
26. No. 35012, *United States Lines*, hauling the Devon Belle, 1950. (*National Railway Museum, York*)
27. A 'Great Northern' suburban electrical multiple unit. (*British Rail*)
28. King's Cross Station, designed by Lewis Cubitt and completed 1852. (*British Rail*)
29. The G.W.R.'s Cambrian Coast express. (*N. G. Stead*)
30. A Great Western 28xx class freight 2–8–0 locomotive. (*British Rail*)
31. The Irish Mail, hauled by Royal Scot class No. 46164, *The Rifle Brigade*. (*British Rail*)
32. St Pancras Station. (*British Rail*)
33. No. 506, *Butler-Henderson*. (*British Rail*)
34. The Midland Hotel, Manchester. (*British Rail*)
35. No. 46236, *City of Bradford*. (*British Rail*)
36. Robert Stephenson's Royal Border Bridge at Berwick-on-Tweed. (*British Rail*)
37. York Station. (*British Rail*)
38. Newcastle Station, *c.* 1860. (*National Railway Museum, York*)
39. The first 4-6-0 class, designed by David Jones in 1894. (*British Rail*)
40. A three-car d.m.u. crossing the Forth Bridge. (*British Rail*)
41. The Princes Street Station Hotel in the 1920s. (*British Rail*)

List of Text Figures

1. William Hedley's *Puffing Billy* colliery locomotive, built in 1814 — 17
2. David Joy's *Jenny Lind* locomotive, built for the Midland Railway in 1847 — 20
3. James Stirling's first bogie locomotive, completed in 1873 — 23
4. Matthew Kirtley's goods 0-6-0 locomotive, designed for the Midland Railway in 1869 — 24
5. Cross-section through a typical 4-6-2 express locomotive — 28
6. A Deltic diesel-electric locomotive — 40
7. A mail coach, built for the Grand Junction Railway in 1837 — 43
8. Diagram of railways through the North Downs — 124

Figure 5 is adapted from *Main Line Steam* (Main Line Steam Trust, 1978).

Figure 6 is taken from *British Rail Main-Line Diesels*, compiled by S. W. Stevens-Stratten, with drawings by R. S. Carter (Ian Allan, 1975).

List of Maps

1. British Rail's principal passenger network — 4–5
2. The North London Line — 72
3. The railways of West London — 74
4. The route of the Kensington & Richmond Railway (L.S.W.R.) — 76
5. Railways through the Cotswolds — 91
6. Exeter, Plymouth and Barnstaple — 106
7. The railways of South London — 115
8. Southampton, Portsmouth and the Isle of Wight — 129
9. East Anglia's present railway system — 152
10. The Great Eastern's suburban network — 162
11. The Great Northern suburban — 166
12. Birmingham's railway network — 180
13. Stoke's railways — 185
14. Leicester's railways — 192
15. The Great Central Railway and its survivals — 197
16. The railways of North Wales and Anglesey — 215
17. The present railways of South Wales — 219
18. Manchester's railways — 242
19. Liverpool's railways — 248
20. Newcastle's railways and the Metro — 284
21. Sheffield's railways — 296
22. Glasgow and its present railways — 315
23. The railways of North-East Scotland — 329
24. The railways of North-West Scotland — 334

Preface and Acknowledgements

This guide is principally designed to serve the traveller using British Rail and accordingly is concerned with the present railway network. The country has been divided into nine separate districts based on B.R.'s Regions and the earlier company territories. Within this framework, the main lines to London and the cross-country routes between the other major settlements (the Inter-City service), together with the most interesting branch lines, are examined. The guide does not cover Northern Ireland, as its railway system is both historically and operationally distinct. By way of introduction, the chronological evolution of Britain's rail network is described, while the associated technical developments are traced from the days of the *Rocket* to the Advanced Passenger Train.

The guide is not a comprehensive history of British railways (a thirteen-volume history under the editorship of D. St John Thomas and J. A. Patmore is now nearing completion), although the historical and preservation aspects are discussed. It is essentially concerned with the surviving national network, and is designed to serve as a passenger's companion to be consulted when travelling over the system. Like the late nineteenth-century travel guides and Baedekers, it provides a brief history of a line's construction, information about any special trains which have operated along the route and details of its railway architecture and engineering achievements. It is hoped that the guide will be revised in the future to take account of new timetables, locomotives and rolling stock, together with improvements in the permanent way and signalling.

The author wishes to acknowledge the valuable help and advice offered by all those who have been connected with this guide. Thanks are due to British Rail, who have answered many questions with great patience, explained their policies and provided much practical assistance. A debt of gratitude is owed to John Griffiths, Nigel Bowles, Christopher Hall, Nicholas Jones, Graham Baird and Christine Thomson for contributing their comments or valuable knowledge of Britain's railways. Further information has been provided by London Transport, British Transport Hotels, Merseyside County Museums and the National Railway Museum, York, and this has been most gratefully received. A special note of thanks is due to Chris Cook, whose idea the book originally was, and who encouraged and shaped the guide throughout its writing.

The author also wishes to thank Reginald Piggott, who drew the maps and Figure 8, and Raymond Turvey, who drew Figure 2 (also used on the title page) and Figure 5.

Abbreviations

A.P.T. Advanced Passenger Train
B.R. British Rail
B.T.C. British Transport Commission
B. & T.R. Blythe & Tyne Railway
C. & H.R. Chester & Holyhead Railway
C.K. & P.R. Cockermouth, Keswick & Penrith Railway
C.L.C. Cheshire Lines Committee (Midland, G.N.R. and G.C.R.)
C.L.R. Central London Railway (now the Central Line)
C.R. Caledonian Railway
d.m.u. Diesel multiple unit
E.C.R. Eastern Counties Railway
E. & G.R. Edinburgh & Glasgow Railway
E.U.R. Eastern Union Railway
F.R. Furness Railway
G.C.R. Great Central Railway
G.E.R. Great Eastern Railway
G.J.R. Grand Junction Railway
G.N.R. Great Northern Railway
G.N. of S.R. Great North of Scotland Railway
G. & S.W.R. Glasgow & South Western Railway
G.W.R. Great Western Railway
H. & C.R. Hammersmith & City Railway
H.R. Highland Railway
H.S.T. High Speed Train
I. & B.R. Ipswich & Bury Railway
K. & W.V.L.R. Keighley & Worth Valley Light Railway
L. & B.R. London & Birmingham Railway
L.B. & S.C.R. London, Brighton & South Coast Railway
L.C. & D.R. London, Chatham & Dover Railway
L. & C.R. Lancashire & Carlisle Railway

ABBREVIATIONS

L. & M.R.	Liverpool & Manchester Railway
L.M.S.(R.)	London, Midland & Scottish Railway
L.N.E.R.	London & North Eastern Railway
L.N.W.R.	London & North Western Railway
L.P.T.B.	London Passenger Transport Board
L. & S.R.	Leeds & Selby Railway
L.S.W.R.	London & South Western Railway
L.T.	London Transport
L.T. & S.R.	London, Tilbury & Southend Railway
L. & Y.R.	Lancashire & Yorkshire Railway
M.C.R.	Midland Counties Railway
M. & C.R.	Maryport & Carlisle Railway
M. & L.R.	Manchester & Leeds Railway
M.E.R.	Manx Electric Railway
M.R.	Midland Railway
M.S. & L.R.	Manchester, Sheffield & Lincolnshire Railway
N.B.R.	North British Railway
N. & C.R.	Newcastle & Carlisle Railway
N.E.R.	North Eastern Railway
N.L.R.	North London Railway
N.S.R.	North Staffordshire Railway
N. & S.W.J.R.	Northern & South Western Junction Railway
N.W.R.	North Western Railway
S.A. & M.R.	Sheffield, Ashton-under-Lyne & Manchester Railway
S. & D.R.	Stockton and Darlington Railway
S.E. & C.R.	South Eastern & Chatham Railway
S.R.	Southern Railway
S.W.R.	South Wales Railway
W. & P.R.	Whitby & Pickering Railway
W.L.E.R.	West London Extension Railway
W.L.R.	West London Railway
Y. & N.M.R.	York & North Midland Railway

1 The Coming of the Railways

Britain's railways have experienced a concertina-like development over the last 150 years of their history. With the success of the Stockton & Darlington and the Liverpool & Manchester schemes, there was a rapid burst of construction lasting until the mid-1850s. Almost 5,000 miles were constructed between 1845 and 1855. This was followed by an initial deceleration in the rate at which lines were being projected and laid down. However, mileage continued to rise steadily and consistently, at about 2,000 miles per decade, until the First World War. A peak was reached at around 1925, when there was a total of 20,400 miles in Britain. The number of passengers and the volume of freight carried by the railways paralleled this development, with both mileage and receipts subsequently falling. Closures were slow at first, picking up momentum in the 1930s as a result of the depression and the rationalization encouraged by grouping. The rate accelerated through the 1960s as a result of the Beeching Report. Since 1970 the situation has stabilized, and although there is still a slight downward trend, a few lines and stations have been re-opened, as on Merseyside.

Partly as a result of the exceptionally varied terrain and partly because Britain was the pioneering railway nation, the country has produced a number of outstanding achievements. The Severn Tunnel, 4 miles 628 yards long, the Forth Bridge, 1 mile 1,006 yards long, and the $3\frac{3}{4}$-mile brick viaduct supporting London's first railway to Greenwich (since widened) are the longest structures of their kind in the country. The world's first underground railway was opened between Bishop's Bridge (Paddington) and Farringdon in 1863 and survives as part of the present Metropolitan Line. The world's first deep electric railway was the City & South London, opened in 1890 (it now forms part of the Northern Line from Monument to Stockwell, the tunnels having been widened). The Liverpool Overhead was the first high-level electric railway. St Pancras held the record for the largest single-span building, its train shed being 243 feet across. Clapham Junction developed as the busiest station in the world. Euston possessed the world's first station hotel, opened by the London & Birmingham in 1839.

With locomotives and trains, Britain's achievements are equally impressive. *Mallard* holds the world's steam speed record at 126 mph. More recently, in June 1973, the prototype High Speed Train broke the world record for a diesel train when it clocked up 143 mph. It also gained the title of Britain's fastest train ever. Presumably, the electrically powered Advanced Passenger Train, which is said to be capable of cruising at 150 mph, will smash this second record. In the late 1920s and early 1930s, the Great Western fought a protracted battle with the Canadian Pacific for the fastest train service and their 'Cheltenham Flyer' captured the title twice. On the second occasion, No. 5006, *Tregenna Castle*, hauled a train from Paddington to Swindon in 56 minutes 21 seconds at an average speed of 81.6 mph. The L.N.E.R.'s London to Edinburgh service, introduced in May 1928, was the world's longest nonstop run.

The earliest railways were built in industrial areas primarily to transport freight. The first train on the Stockton & Darlington, in September 1825, was largely composed of mineral wagons filled with coal, and it remained a colliery line for fifteen years. The Liverpool & Manchester, which followed in 1830, owed its existence to the agitation of merchants and manufacturers frustrated by the Bridgewater Canal's inability to cope with an increasing volume of goods and its monopolistic charges. In the event, it proved so popular that freight trains

THE COMING OF THE RAILWAYS

were delayed or cancelled to allow extra passenger trains to run. However, the railway schemes which immediately followed – the Leicester & Swannington (1832), Leeds & Selby (1834), Newcastle & Carlisle (in part 1835) – all had a distinctly industrial character.

Once the railways had established themselves as a safe and economically viable means of transport, more ambitious projects were attempted. The Grand Junction between Birmingham and Warrington, completed in July 1837, was Britain's first trunk railway. The first section of the London & Birmingham Railway, from Euston to Boxmoor, was opened in the same year and extended to Curzon Street in September 1838. Generally, trunk routes were constructed from the capital and radiated to important centres of business. The London & Southampton Railway was opened on 11 May 1840. The G.W.R.'s line from Paddington reached Maidenhead in June 1838 and Bristol in 1841, while lines were laid throughout the north and Midlands to link up the growing manufacturing and mining districts.

So by 1855 England's railway network in its essentials was largely complete. It had taken only thirty years from the opening of the Stockton & Darlington to lay a comprehensive system of trunk routes centred on London. From this time forth railway construction was a matter of filling in the gaps and duplicating routes. There were a few exceptions. For example, the Settle and Carlisle line was not completed until 1876 and the Severn Tunnel, providing a direct route to South Wales, was constructed as late as 1880. These anomalies were the result of engineering difficulties and the high cost that their solution demanded.

Wales and Scotland exhibited a different pattern. Both areas were far from London and the other expanding manufacturing centres. Their industrial potential was as yet undeveloped, while their upland character also tended to make directors wary. It was not until easy opportunities in England had been exhausted that engineers and investors turned their attention to

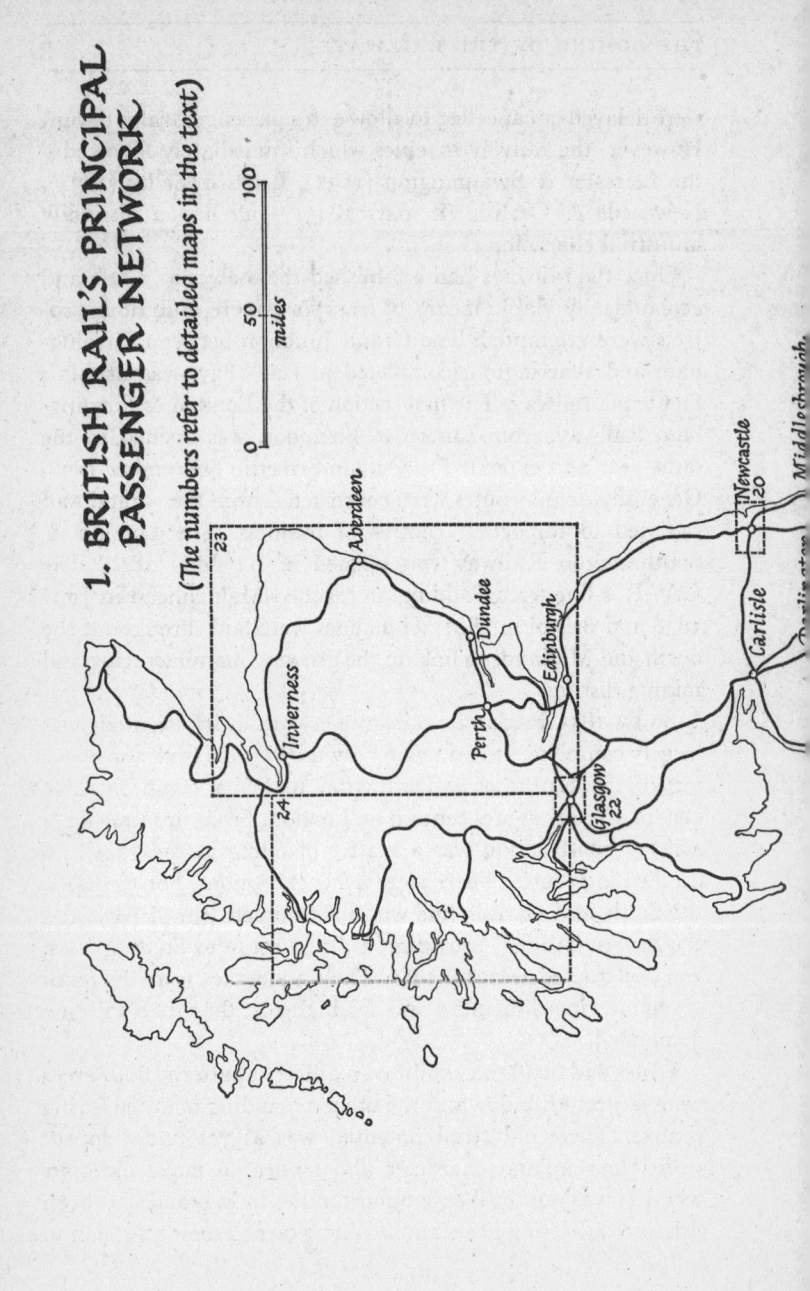

1. BRITISH RAIL'S PRINCIPAL PASSENGER NETWORK

(The numbers refer to detailed maps in the text)

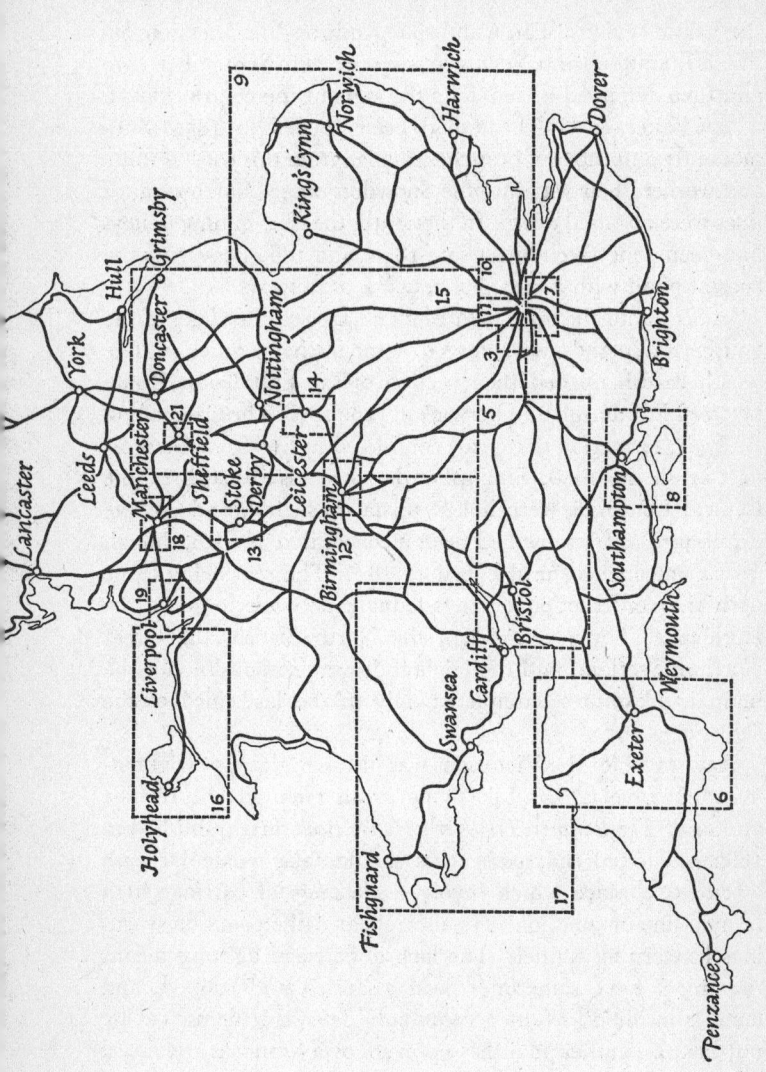

the Celtic regions. The Cambrian Railways' first section between Llanidloes and Newtown was opened in September 1859 and then extended its tentacles throughout the central massif. The Chester & Holyhead had been opened in 1850. Subsequently a number of branches divided from this coastal route and worked their way into the Snowdon range. Narrow-gauge lines were also laid down. In the south, the coal-mining valleys had been penetrated in the late 1850s and 1860s, covering the coastal plain with a complex network of railways.

In Scotland, the links with England around the edges of the Southern Uplands were forged comparatively quickly. The North British opened their section of the East Coast Route between Edinburgh and Berwick in June 1846. The Caledonian Railway, formed in that year, completed its line from Glasgow to Carlisle in 1848. Similarly, the business districts of the Central Lowlands were linked up fairly swiftly. Indeed, the Edinburgh & Glasgow had been incorporated in 1838, though it was not opened until February 1842. The real delay came with the construction of an adequate network to serve the Highlands. Three companies, the North British, the Great North of Scotland and the Highland, were responsible for the main trunk routes, completed only in the last third of the century.

Rail travel for the Victorians was just as exciting or frightening as air travel is to us. Like flying, it was a real adventure. The author of *The Railway Traveller's Handy Book*, first published in 1862, suggested that passengers should take particular care when at 'a place which involves a change of carriage at a branch line or junction'. He also repeated the common warnings concerning tunnels. The lack of carriage lighting meant that men 'have sometimes been assaulted and robbed, and females insulted'. Women commonly defended themselves by putting pins in their mouths to prevent over-amorous advances. Soccer hooliganism is not the only form of lawlessness to have occurred on trains.

As with the canals, it was often the last railways to be built which were the first to close. Mostly constructed on a wave of speculative mania, these schemes had been projected and carried through without a proper appreciation of the trade they might attract. Branch lines were laid to remote areas, or popular routes were unnecessarily duplicated, in the hope that their very existence would encourage new levels of business. The closures suggested by the Beeching Report enveloped these railways and many more which had become under-used as the motor car gained popularity.

In the East Midlands, for example, there had been a dramatic growth in the number of stations between 1840 and 1855. Until 1910, the rate of increase slowed but remained quite steady. Then there was a levelling until the depression and grouping, when more were closed. Again the situation stabilized, until 1950. Nationalization brought more station closures and a dramatic drop in numbers throughout the 1960s, but since 1970 there has been little change.

From the outset there has been a desultory move towards centralization. Initially each line was constructed by a completely independent body. Then companies widened their operations, building branches or extending their original routes. In 1844 George Hudson took the unprecedented step of amalgamating several adjacent companies into one body, the Midland Railway. This encouraged others to merge. The L.N.W.R., a combination of the London & Birmingham, the Manchester & Birmingham and the Grand Junction (which had absorbed the Liverpool & Manchester), was founded in July 1846. The L.B. & S.C.R. (from the London & Brighton and the London & Croydon) followed eleven days later.

Other companies, like the Great Western, which had grown in size, took over smaller railways on their borders. The North Eastern was founded in July 1854, taking in the Stockton & Darlington in July 1863. The Great Eastern was the last of the major companies to be set up when on 7 August 1862 the Eastern Counties, Eastern Union, East Anglian, Newmarket and Norfolk Railways merged.

Both world wars produced demands for post-war nationalization, which succeeded after the Second. But the First World War did have an effect. Under state control between 1914 and 1918, the railway system had never been so unified. However, the Liberal–Conservative coalition resisted demands for government purchase, though they did form a Ministry of Transport in 1919 which formulated the new Railway Act (1921). The railway companies were combined into four 'groups' – the Great Western, the Southern, the London, Midland & Scottish and the London & North Eastern. The Act came into effect from 1 January 1923 and met with little determined opposition. A few companies were exempted: the Cheshire Lines Committee (a marvellously English name for a railway company) and the Midland & Great Northern Joint were two of the largest.

This was a preliminary to nationalization and the creation of a single governing body. On 1 January 1948 British Railways was formed with its headquarters in London at 222 Marylebone Road, in the former Great Central Hotel. To avoid the remoteness often associated with centralization, the grouping divisions were retained in a modified form. Western, Eastern, Southern and Midland Regions and a separate Scottish Region were created, with their respective offices at Paddington, York, Waterloo, Euston and Buchanan House, Glasgow.

The whole period of railway development has been accompanied by a corresponding growth in government control. As early as the 1840s, politicians perceived just how important railways were for the economy and society as a whole. Peel instructed Gladstone, in view of the massive speculation in railway shares, to consider nationalization. This would have been a bold step in an age of unparalleled *laissez-faire*. This radical suggestion was never acted upon, but Gladstone did introduce a Cheap Trains Act in August 1844, ordering every company to run at least one train along each line (in each direction) for third-class passengers every day, at a maximum fare of one penny per mile. The Act was designed to help the poor to travel to work and to ensure that the social benefits of the railways were not confined to the better-off.

In 1846 Peel's Conservative government passed the Gauge Act, another early example of state intervention in the workings of the economy. In future all railways had to be constructed with a 'standard gauge', 4 feet 8½ inches. One important exception was made, for the Great Western, which was permitted to continue to lay its lines with Brunel's seven-foot track, though in practice a third rail was fitted to accommodate other companies' locomotives and stock. The government had recognized the need for a truly national network. Smooth transference from one railway's territory to its neighbour's could follow only if gauges were the same. The canal system had suffered in the previous century because locks, bridges and aqueducts had not been built to standard widths, hindering the transshipment of freight throughout the country.

Successive governments made legislation to ensure that railways were safe and efficiently operated. A terrible accident on the Great Northern Railway of Ireland in 1889 prompted the government to introduce the Regulation of Railways Act, which made continuous automatic brakes and absolute block working (see p. 52) compulsory on all lines. However, such acts were designed to protect the public and did not directly interfere with the financial operation and independence of the companies.

Full governmental control was not imposed until 1948, when the Labour administration created British Railways and placed the whole system under state control. In fact, this move was not as unprecedented as might be supposed. Apart from the consolidation of 1923 and the creation of the Ministry of Transport, London's railways had been placed under a single government-supervised authority in 1933, when the London Passenger Transport Board was formed.

During the seven years of war the government had taken over much of the overall running of the railways. The service was cut – in terms of both trains and facilities – and staff were reorganized, many being sent to join the forces. New 'Austerity' locomotives were designed, trains were taken over for troop movements and special supply consignments, while many locomotive workshops were diverted to produce armaments. So it was quite natural for a Labour government to consider continuing state control after 1945, especially with the prevailing demands for nationalization. In 1946 the Bank of England, cable and wireless, coal, electricity and civil aviation were taken over by the state. Railways, roads and canals followed in 1947.

British Railways (since 1964 British Rail) then settled down under the management of the British Transport Commission. In the late 1960s and 1970s, there has been a trend away from government interference as British Rail has asserted itself. Sir Richard Marsh successfully resisted governmental pressure to trim the railway network still further and headed off the misguided attempts to make it profitable. He secured the admission that the railways perform a valuable social function and that it is impossible for a substantial railway system to make a profit in present economic circumstances. Sir Peter Parker has developed these arguments. No longer does the state 'subsidize' the railways. Rather, British Rail has a 'contract' with the government to provide a service for which it then pays an agreed sum, and as a sign of efficiency and good faith British Rail returns some of the government's cash every year.

Finally, developments in railway traffic, both passenger and freight, and the facilities which have been offered over the last hundred and fifty years, must be considered. In 1845, 30 million passengers were carried by the railways. As the network expanded and as improved locomotives were built permitting more frequent and longer trains to be run, so the number of people using the railways rose. In 1855, 111 million passengers were carried; by 1885, this figure had risen to 687 million, a sixfold increase; ten years later, 1,115 million journeys were made.

The major growth area in the second half of the nineteenth century was in third-class travel. This was a period of economic prosperity and continued growth. Standards of living did rise for the population as a whole, while Factory and Shops Acts meant that people generally worked shorter hours and were given more days' holiday. The railways took advantage of the fact that the bulk of workers were both better off and had increased leisure time, the number of third-class carriages increasing dramatically. Indeed, in April 1872 the Midland Railway took the step of introducing third-class coaches on all their trains; in January 1875 they abolished second class altogether, re-classifying it as third and improving the quality of their original third-class stock. Not every company followed suit. Consequently British Railways inherited in part a three-class system and it was not until June 1956 that all third-class travel was designated second.

Growth was also encouraged by the provision of special trains. Holiday excursions were regularly advertised by companies fortunate enough to possess resorts within their network. The L.N.W.R. publicized North Wales, the N.E.R. Scarborough and Bridlington, the G.W.R. Torquay and the south-west, while the L.B. & S.C.R. encouraged Londoners to visit Brighton. Poor Law guardians, trades unions and Friendly Societies all hired special trains for days out. Football clubs also took advantage (not then to the detriment of other passengers) of this new cheap and quick form of travel.

The number of travellers using the railways reached a peak in the early inter-war years, when in 1920 1,579 million journeys were made throughout Great Britain. By 1930, almost in the depths of the depression, the figure had fallen to 844 million, and it never recovered. The Second World War caused further disruption. Although the closures of the fifties and sixties reduced Britain's rail mileage from 20,000 in 1938 to 12,400 in 1968, the number of passengers has not shown a corresponding decline, because, of course, the least used lines were the ones shut down. 837 million passengers were carried in 1967, by 1976 this figure had fallen to 701 million, in 1977 there were 702 million and in 1978 there was an impressive increase to 724 million, mainly due to the introduction of the popular High Speed Train.

The real reason for the general decline in the number of rail travellers has nothing to do with Dr Beeching's closures, but lies in technology's provision of other means of transport. The aircraft has creamed off continental passengers and businessmen journeying long distances. For example, the 'Golden Arrow' between Victoria and Paris was discontinued because too many people now fly to Europe. The car and the motorway captured many regular and holiday travellers.

The number of passengers demanding the most luxurious rail services has fallen, many executives and richer families preferring to drive or fly to distant destinations. The Pullman Company, originally a privately owned organization providing luxurious accommodation for a supplementary charge, was absorbed into British Rail in January 1963. The last Pullman train left Paddington on 4 July 1973 and the only remaining Pullman service is from Euston to Manchester, a twice-daily businessman's train. The eventual obsolescence of its stock and the introduction of the Advanced Passenger Train on the West Coast Route presumably means that this service has a limited life, and the Pullman will soon be history.

The range of meals provided on trains has been reduced, manning levels have been cut and there has been a move towards convenience foods. The following culinary choice, offered by the L.N.E.R. in 1937, illustrates the change:

Grapefruit or lentil soup
Boiled turbot, shrimp sauce or pickled fresh herring
Minced turkey and poached egg, or roast shoulder of mutton, onion sauce, brussels sprouts, jacket and mashed potatoes
Gooseberry pudding, meringue chantilly, or stewed figs and cream

There were cheeses as well. Tea or coffee was 4d. extra. The total cost was a mere three shillings and sixpence ($17\frac{1}{2}$p.).

Nevertheless, the scale of catering on British Rail is still far larger than in any other European country. The proportion of trains with buffet or restaurant cars is greater, while 183 stations provide a catering service. There has, however, been a reduction in the number of dining carriages, from 480 in 1967 to 387 in 1977, though British Rail has recently reduced prices to encourage people to use their facilities. The service makes a loss. No train catering operation anywhere in the world pays its way, but the deficit is considered worthwhile as a means of attracting passengers who might otherwise travel by air or car.

The introduction of the High Speed Train and the advent of the Advanced Passenger Train, with their shorter journey times, has also reduced the necessity for sleeping cars. Here too there has been a reduction in numbers, from 447 in 1967 to 365 in 1977.

So far we have concerned ourselves with passenger services. But, as we have seen, the railways were originally built to carry freight, and that is an important role which they have continued to perform. Throughout the nineteenth century the volume of goods shipped by rail increased: 88 million tons were carried in 1860, 232 in 1880 and 508 in 1910, receipts rising in step with this upward trend. Unfortunately, the First World War caused much disruption and pre-war levels were never regained. The depression hit the railways' freight business hard and only 318 million tons were carried in 1920, falling to 264 by 1938.

The Second World War caused even greater disruption; industrial centres, marshalling yards and stations were bombed, and the post-war years did not see a return to former levels of activity. There has been a steady decline in the volume of traffic going by rail in the last fifteen years. The completion of the motorway network and the introduction of larger trucks and trailers encouraged businesses to take to the road, and only 170 million tons of freight were carried by British Rail in 1977. Freight revenues have declined accordingly: £348 million in 1977 as against £195 million in 1967 (£570 million at 1977 prices). However, motorway building is at an end and public pressure resists the spread of the juggernaut. The railway has a powerful environmental argument on its side. It is to be hoped that more firms will take advantage of the government's offer to pay half the cost of a new siding and tonnages will start to rise again. The freightliner and speedlink services are both excellent ways of shifting goods quickly and efficiently.

There is much hope for the future of the railways. The High Speed Train has proved very popular and is being introduced as quickly as it can be produced. The Advanced Passenger Train came into service in 1980. The electrification of the suburban services on the former Great Northern has proved successful and is being extended to the St Pancras–Bedford route. If British Rail can solve their problems on Southern Region, then the next decade should be one of growing prestige and popularity, a new age of railways.

2 The Path of Technical Improvement

While the English railway system had been laid down in its essentials by 1855, after a mere thirty years of building, its engineering and mechanical aspects have continued to evolve over a far longer period. Locomotives, carriages and wagons, together with signalling methods and track design, have been improved out of all recognition. Steam engines of a stationary sort had been in existence since the early eighteenth century. Watt's invention of rotary motion in 1781 paved the way for the steam locomotive. *Locomotion* and Robert Stephenson's *Rocket* of 1829 were almost unrecognizably different beings from the engines of the Pacific (4–6–2) type such as Gresley's streamlined A–4s, Stanier's Coronation class and Bulleid's Merchant Navy expresses. British Rail's *Duke of Gloucester*, a 4–6–2, produced in the final days of steam, was said to have the potential to eclipse them all.

Carriages began as stage-coach bodies attached to wagon bases. They were small, cramped, unlit and generally uncomfortable, without heating or travel facilities. In time, coaches were lengthened and designed with corridors. Oil lamps, replaced first by gas lamps and then by electric lights, steam heating and comfortable seats were features of the late nineteenth century. The 1880s saw the introduction of kitchens with purpose-built dining cars for passengers travelling long distances. The luxuries of the Pullman carriage, now almost defunct, offered a sharp contrast to the open wagons which operated on Britain's earliest lines.

Track for the Liverpool & Manchester Railway, opened in 1830, was of a very basic design. Short lengths of wrought-iron rail were attached to square stone blocks, while on earlier tramways the flanges had been attached to the rails rather than to the wheels. The improved manufacture of steel and the adoption of the wooden sleeper and iron chair made for stronger tracks and faster, smoother rides. Today reinforced concrete sleepers, supporting continuous welded rails, permit High Speed Trains to operate at well in excess of 100 mph without damaging the track itself. Coloured light signals have replaced the mechanically operated semaphore arms on most main lines throughout the country, and computerized signal boxes have superseded their manually operated predecessors, bringing greater efficiency, reliability and safety. Although the geographical shape of Britain's railway system has not altered appreciably since 1855, except for the Beeching closures, it has experienced a mechanical and technological revolution. George Stephenson would not recognize the trains of today, nor would he know how they worked.

THE STEAM LOCOMOTIVE

Stationary steam engines were widely in use by the end of the eighteenth century. They were employed to pump water from mines, to haul wagons by ropes along tramways and to operate machinery in factories and foundries. However, it was not until the first decade of the nineteenth century that steam power was successfully applied to a self-propelling vehicle. Richard Trevithick, the Cornish engineer, was responsible for the design and construction of four locomotives, for Coalbrookdale in 1803, Penydarren in 1804, Gateshead in 1805 and London in 1808. They were pioneering engines without safety valves, featuring a single vertical cylinder, connected by complicated gearing to the left-hand-side wheels. The first two and probably the third were able to work as stationary engines when not running along a trackway. The last was more advanced, and has been suggested as the world's first passenger locomotive. This 2–2–0, featuring a direct-drive mechanism, was run round a circular track. It operated on the site of the present London University Senate House between July and September 1808, with passengers being charged for short rides. Although these locomotives had a curiosity value and performed some good work, conditions in the economy had not yet ripened for their full exploitation.

Steam locomotives continued to be constructed throughout the early years of the nineteenth century. They were experimental machines, adopting various types of drive gearing and different cylinder and boiler designs. A fine example of one of these engines is *Puffing Billy* (Fig. 1). Now preserved in the Science Museum, the locomotive was completed in 1814 and

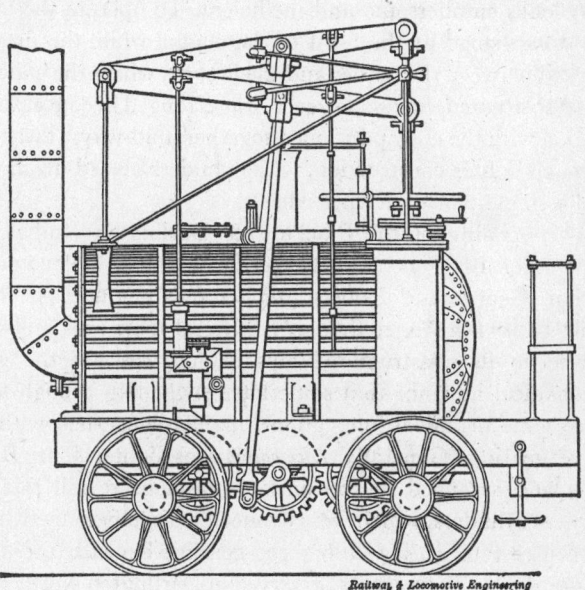

Fig. 1. William Hedley's *Puffing Billy* colliery locomotive, built in 1814.

set to work at the Wylam Colliery hauling coal wagons. It was designed by William Hedley and said to be the first locomotive to have a wrought-iron boiler and two outside cylinders. In addition, it used the exhaust steam to increase the draught through the firebox, thereby raising the machine's efficiency. Constructed on a solid wooden frame, the boiler and probably the cylinders were lagged with wooden strips, while the remainder appeared as black metal. Like all early locomotives, *Puffing Billy* was distinguished by the delicate array of rods, beams and shafts which formed an iron framework over the boiler. Stationary pumping engines were designed with vertical cylinders – locomotive engineers had yet to make the imaginative leap needed to adopt the horizontal cylinder, with its more direct drive motion.

In contrast to *Rocket*, completed fifteen years later, *Puffing Billy* looks cumbersome and inefficient. To operate the latter the driver stood at the front of the engine while the fireman worked between the tender and the firebox, where the chimney was also situated. *Rocket*, however, was arranged in conventional fashion with the crew positioned together, mid-way. It was also of much lighter construction, with cylinders placed diagonally and a single pair of driving wheels.

The opening of the Stockton & Darlington Railway in September 1825 encouraged the development of locomotive design. George and Robert Stephenson's engineering works built *Locomotion No. 1*, though neither of them was really involved in its construction. This engine was not the great mechanical advance that some have suggested, though there were some technical innovations, mainly concerned with the drive gearing. Generally *Locomotion* was lighter than *Puffing Billy* and arranged in conventional fashion. It still retained vertical cylinders, which were connected directly to the wheels, in contrast to *Puffing Billy*'s cog-gearing beneath the main frame. Today *Locomotion* is preserved at Darlington North Road Railway Museum.

An innovation visible on later Stockton & Darlington locomotives was the use of the iron tyre. Previously, wheels had been constructed from either solid iron or wood, both of which wore out fairly quickly, requiring the whole to be replaced. In 1816 Losh and Stephenson took out a patent on a central iron wheel fitted with a malleable tyre, but the design was not in fact adopted until the later 1820s.

A further development followed with the introduction of the *Royal George* in 1827. Early sketches reveal that it was fitted with separate tyres, though more important were the advances made in the gearing. There were no crossheads or sidebars, the six wheels being driven by connecting rods from the two driving wheels at the rear end. In addition, the engine was sprung. *Royal George*, now in the Science Museum, had about 50 per cent more tractive capacity than *Locomotion* and the other four-wheelers on the Stockton & Darlington Railway.

The construction of the Liverpool & Manchester Railway as a medium-distance passenger line created a further incentive to improve locomotive design. Originally it was felt that trains should be hauled by ropes worked by stationary engines. Then, in 1829, it was suggested that trials should be held to select a strong and reliable engine which could be used as the basis of their locomotive stock. The conditions included a minimum running speed of 10 mph, smokeless combustion and good suspension to avoid track and wheel damage. Only three engines fulfilled these requirements, *Rocket*, *Sans Pareil* and *Novelty*. The first two are now in the Science Museum. *Sans Pareil* was too heavy, was unsprung and retained outmoded vertical cylinders. *Novelty* was designed with speed in mind, and maintained 28 mph for over a mile, yet its lightness meant that it lacked both power and adhesion. *Rocket* not only won the competition but was also the engine with the greatest potential for mechanical improvement.

Robert Stephenson's engine was fitted with good suspension. The cylinders had been moved to a diagonal position on either side of the firebox, so that the pistons could drive the wheels directly. For the trial the angle was surprisingly steep (35°), producing an uneven, bouncing motion. The original engine shows the cylinders as modified, being almost horizontal. Unfortunately many parts are now missing and some are modern replacements. There is also an exact reconstruction of the first design, cut away to reveal internal working parts, easily distinguished by its bright yellow livery. Other important innovations were the multitubular boiler with separate firebox and blastpipe exhaust, features which were taken and developed by the most advanced steam engines. *Rocket* proved to be the most reliable of the three competitors and ran at over 30 mph with the lowest fuel consumption.

So by 1830 the essentials of steam locomotive design had been laid down. The design of the boiler, firebox and exhaust equipment, the construction and positioning of the cylinders, the type of wheels and the general layout of engine and tender were established. However, *Rocket* was not a powerful locomotive by late-nineteenth-century standards, developing a tractive effort of only 825 lb. Collett's Castle class, introduced in 1923, produced 31,625 lb. The history of locomotive design from 1830 to the 1950s was one of continual modification to increase power and raise running speeds. For example, *Jenny Lind* (Fig. 2), a 2–2–2 constructed for the Midland Railway in 1847, had a tractive effort of 4,900 lb. and could run at 50 mph.

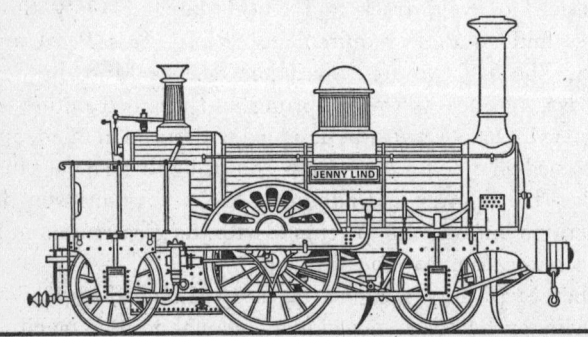

Fig. 2. David Joy's *Jenny Lind* locomotive, built for the Midland Railway in 1847.

THE PATH OF TECHNICAL IMPROVEMENT

Like *Rocket*, she could pull around three times her own weight.

After *Rocket*, the next major development was to place the driving wheels at the back and put the cylinders at the front under the smokebox. Outside frames were employed for the first time. The original engine in this standard form was built by Robert Stephenson for the Liverpool & Manchester Railway, and called *Planet*. Many variations were constructed around this theme. For example, it became common practice to replace the front set of carrying wheels by a second pair of drivers linked by a connecting rod.

The adoption of an outside frame, to support boiler, firebox and wheels, also encouraged the transfer of cylinders from under the smoke box to outside the frame. Forrester of Liverpool was the first to build 2-2-2 engines to this design. However, these locomotives had a tendency to shake and were nicknamed 'boxers'. The fault was cured in 1839 with the adoption of counter-balancing, which involved placing a metal weight inside the rim of the driving wheel to counteract the thrust of the piston.

By the late 1830s the 2-2-2 arrangement had been established as the standard locomotive form for the next thirty years. For example, Sir Daniel Gooch produced the famous Iron Duke class for the Great Western using this model. A replica of *North Star*, a prototype built by Robert Stephenson for Brunel and developed by Gooch, is on display at Swindon Railway Museum. Sturrock, working for the G.N.R., designed a 4-2-2 along these lines. Throughout the 1840s and 1850s, the Crewe locomotive works were responsible for nothing other than standard 2-2-2s or 2-4-0s. David Joy, who created the Jenny Lind class, advanced valve motion design, but persevered with the 2-2-2 arrangement. These engines were also noted for their high-pressure boilers (120 lb. to the square inch). Another popular locomotive built to the same specifications was the Lady of the Lake class by John Ramsbottom, a classic midcentury design given a typically Victorian name. There are a number of this type at York, including *Columbine*, No. 49, from the G.J.R. (later the L.N.W.R.), a 2-2-2 constructed in 1845.

In the 1860s and 1870s there were a number of important technical breakthroughs. Many experiments were carried out to find a satisfactory method of burning coal rather than coke, which was twice as expensive. McConnell of the L.N.W.R. and Beattie on the L.S.W.R. both tackled the problem, but it was the Midland and Taff Vale Companies who first overcame the difficulties. The answer lay with the provision of a larger firebox, specially sloped to aid the intermixing of air and fuel without creating thick clouds of stifling smoke.

The cheaper and more effective production of steel, created by the Bessemer converter, enabled engineers to replace many of the weaker iron parts. Steel tyres began to be fitted in the late 1850s, becoming general in the following decade, and Crewe produced over a thousand a year after Ramsbottom had speeded up the manufacturing process with the introduction of powerful horizontal steam hammers to prepare ingots for the rolling mill. Large parts, including axles, reversing shafts and cylinders, were increasingly made from steel. The manufacture of rolled steel plates meant that boilers could be made to withstand higher pressures and hence generate greater power.

The introduction of the bogie also permitted faster speeds and indirectly encouraged more powerful locomotives. In 1870 Patrick Stirling, the Great Northern's engineer, built a new express engine with a 4-2-2 wheel arrangement. The locomotive, No. 1, now at York, propelled by a pair of huge drivers, was guided and supported by a truck containing four carriers, which meant that longer engines could be built and still cope with sharp curves, while the pivoted bogie made for greater stability at speed on the straight. In fact bogies had been in use throughout America for several years, suggesting something of British engineers' conservatism. This was all the more serious as a single overloaded front axle, resulting in breaks, had been the cause of many accidents.

As bogies were more generally adopted, the driving wheels

THE PATH OF TECHNICAL IMPROVEMENT 23

were often doubled. The classic British passenger locomotive – borrowed from American examples – emerged in the 1870s as the 4–4–0; less common was the 4–4–2 Atlantic design. These formed the basic Victorian express stable. Generally they were finely proportioned engines, with a long slim boiler running into a short curved cab. The neat arrangement of wheels, forming a solid base, balanced the composition, which the low tender completed. Examples of the 4–4–0 class can be seen at York, including L.S.W.R. No. 563 (1893) and N.E.R. No. 1621 (1893), while the G.N.R. has provided the two 4–4–2s on display, No. 990, *Henry Oakley* (1898), and No. 251 (1902).

Fig. 3. James Stirling's first bogie locomotive, completed for the Glasgow & South Western Railway in 1873.

The 4–4–0 and Atlantic arrangement was taken up by engineers as the basis for their larger tank engines. The original stock for the underground railways, 4–4–0Ts built from 1864 onwards by Beyer, Peacock of Birmingham, were among the earliest designs to use a bogie. No. 23 is preserved in the London Transport Museum. The first batch of tank engines for the London, Tilbury & Southend Railway, with outside cylinders and the last pair of wheels supporting the coal bunker at the rear, were 4–4–2Ts (see p. 170).

However, the classic Victorian goods locomotive developed as an 0–6–0 tender engine. The advantage of this design was that it afforded the maximum adhesion on all six driving wheels without putting too much weight on any single axle. The earliest 0–6–0s were turned out by Timothy Hackworth for the S. & D.R. between 1827 and 1830 – the first being *Royal George*. This class was usually manufactured with inside cylinders, the argument being that they were warmer here and so prevented condensation. Among the best known 0–6–0s were those designed by Matthew Kirtley for the Midland Railway in 1869 (Fig. 4). Built in large numbers by Dübs of Glasgow, they soon came to be regarded as the standard goods engine, being noted for their efficiency and reliability.

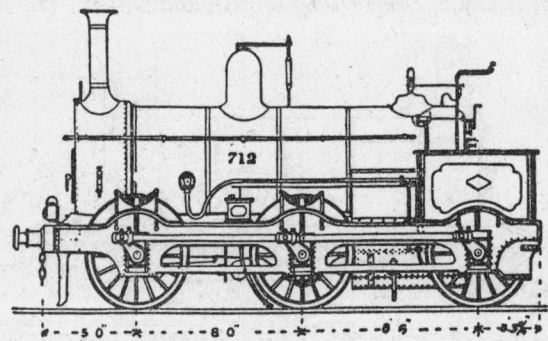

Fig. 4. Matthew Kirtley's goods 0–6–0 locomotive, designed for the Midland Railway in 1869.

Like the 4–4–0, this wheel arrangement was then selected for tank engine design, when smaller goods trains were needed. The tank locomotive is a more compact version of its larger counterpart for use where loads are lighter and distances shorter. Accordingly, the 0–6–0T was often used as a shunter. Good examples of these hard-working engines at York include No. 82, *Boxhill* (1880), from the L.B. & S.C.R., and No. 87 (1904) from the G.E.R. This basic design continued to be adopted until the end of steam, as manifested by the ubiquitous industrial and Great Western pannier tanks.

The next major breakthrough came in the first decade of the twentieth century. With the continued growth of passenger traffic and the demand for faster and more luxurious trains, pressure was placed on company engineers to produce more powerful locomotives. The answer came in the form of the 4–6–0. George Churchward, chief mechanical engineer to the Great Western between 1902 and 1921, was the first to come up with a really successful locomotive, the Star class in 1907. David Jones had already produced a 4–6–0 for the Highland Railway in 1894, though these engines were designed for goods trains. Churchward studied French plans and eventually created a very advanced locomotive, with four cylinders (two internal and two external), a superheater, and a tapered boiler to provide maximum heating at the firebox end. As a result the Star class proved to be a powerful and reliable engine, stable and smooth at speed. The only survivor, No. 4003, *Lode Star*, is preserved in the Great Western Museum, Swindon.

From this basic design, Churchward proceeded to draft a series of engines, which meant that standardized parts could be exchanged, reducing maintenance and manufacturing costs. Collett, his successor, followed this principle. His Castle, Manor, Hall and King classes, though twenty or thirty years later, bore a strong resemblance to Churchward's seminal locomotive designs. Although companies took up the 4–6–0 arrangement (C. J. Bowen-Cooke, engineer to the L.N.W.R., produced an initially troublesome four-cylinder version, the 'Claughton', in 1913), the G.W.R. remained far in advance of its rivals and only in the inter-war years did the other three really grasp the secret of his success and manufactured comparable engines.

The ultimate development of the steam engine came with the Pacific class, the 4–6–2. The first Pacific to run on British railways, *The Great Bear*, a huge engine distinguished by an enormous smoke box, was designed by Churchward in 1908. Such a large locomotive was not really needed and it remained the G.W.R.'s only Pacific. Nigel Gresley was responsible for the Great Northern's first 4–6–2s: the A–1, a three-cylinder locomotive, introduced in 1922. They were not very successful, but he persevered, and as engineer of the newly formed L.N.E.R.

produced some of the world's finest express engines. With higher boiler pressures and a revised valve gearing, he produced the Flying Scotsman class in 1923, and then in 1935 the more powerful and streamlined A-4s with their aerodynamic casing designed for fast running. They developed a tractive effort of 35,455 lb. *Mallard* (now at York) is, of course, the most famous of these, and holds the world's steam speed record, at 126 mph.

The Great Western, now under Collett's control, evolved the King class. Although only 4-6-0s, they had all the power and potential of the new Pacifics and were intended as their rivals, but not being streamlined never reached the high speeds of Gresley's expresses. For the L.M.S., Sir William Stanier in 1933 introduced his Coronation class, a Pacific designed to tackle Pennine gradients with heavy trains. These successful locomotives recorded some impressive times between Euston and Carlisle on the West Coast Route.

The Southern Railway was the last of the big three to enter the Pacific era. O. V. Bulleid did not introduce his 4-6-2 Merchant Navy class until 1941, while the slightly smaller West Country and Battle of Britain engines followed in 1945. These were partially streamlined – in Bulleid's phrase, 'airsmoothed'. (A number of these had their casings removed under British Railways to facilitate maintenance.) They featured a number of technical innovations, including specially constructed wheels to withstand the thrust against the flanges when taking curves at speed (see p. 131). The Merchant Navy class No. 35029, *Ellerman Lines*, has been preserved at York, one side of the engine having been dissected to reveal internal working parts.

Under British Railways one further Pacific class was produced, the Britannia. Designed by R. A. Riddles in 1951, they were a practical two-cylinder type which proved to be an excellent general-purpose passenger engine. A more powerful three-cylinder variant, No. 71000, *Duke of Gloucester*, was completed in 1954. Then the decision was made to switch to diesel and electric traction, and no further locomotives were manufactured. No. 71000 remained unique, and at present is under restoration in Loughborough, though its highly original valve gearing has been preserved at the Science Museum.

The last steam engine manufactured by British Railways was No. 92220, *Evening Star*, completed at Swindon in March 1960. To mark the occasion, this powerful 2–10–0 was painted in lined green livery rather than the usual plain black. This Standard 9 class was B.R.'s basic locomotive for heavy goods trains, though *Evening Star* successfully worked passenger services. In 1968 steam running ended on British Rail. Although capable of further development, the steam locomotive has clearly reached the end of its history, and not even the exhaustion of oil supplies is likely to produce a recall. Electric locomotives (the electricity supplied by atomic power stations) are then most likely to take over throughout the country. The Advanced Passenger Train is electrically powered, and the routes at present worked by diesel will be gradually converted to overhead cables. It is logical to look next at the development of electric traction, the motive power which will eventually supersede all others.

But before considering the electric train, we shall pause to look at the working of a modern steam engine (Fig. 5). In a typical 4–6–2 express locomotive (not of any particular class), water, stored in the tender, is fed into the boiler by an injector, a device which by projecting a mixture of water and steam through a series of cones, propels the water into the boiler with such force as to overcome the considerable pressure inside – often as much as 250 lb. per square inch. The water circulates around the boiler, where it is heated by contact with the metal firebox and by the many tubes which convey smoke and hot gasses from the fire. The lighter ashes are collected beneath the chimney in the smokebox, while the smoke itself is forced upwards by the blast pipe below, which, at the same time, increases the draw on the fire. Steam is collected at the top of the boiler in the dome where the regulator valve, operated from the cab, lets it into the superheater, which dries and re-heats the

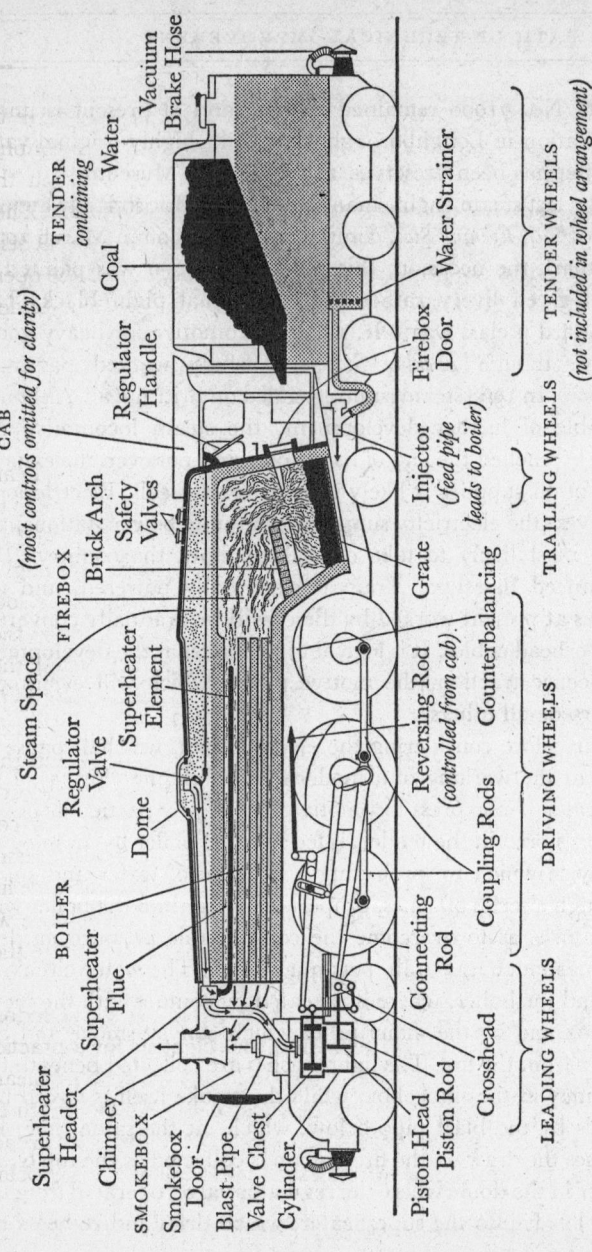

Fig. 5. Cross-section through a typical 4–6–2 express locomotive.

steam before it is fed into the pistons. They in turn drive the wheels through the crosshead, connecting rods and coupling rods. The reversing lever simply switches the direction that steam enters the cylinders, thereby reversing the motion. There are, of course, no gears on a steam locomotive, speed being generated by the pressure of steam in the boiler and the operation of the regulator which governs its passage into the cylinders.

ELECTRIC RAILWAYS

While the steam locomotive was the product of the technological and mechanical revolution of the late eighteenth and early nineteenth centuries, the electric train owed its existence to the scientific revolution which followed in Victoria's reign. L. T. C. Rolt[1] has recently demonstrated that engineers working by trial and error were initially responsible for progress in locomotive design. Scientists followed behind, theorizing their achievements. With the development of electrical power their respective roles were reversed. The scientists were now at the forefront of research and the engineer was forced to wait outside the laboratory to pick up the results of their studies and then incorporate them into his mechanical world. By 1880 most of the great engineering difficulties associated with railway construction had been solved. The new element was the harnessing of electricity to drive the beast along. Electrical knowledge had advanced so far that in 1881 an international conference was held in Paris so that physicists could pool and synthesize their discoveries.

Engineers faced with the need to solve central London's growing traffic problem turned to the scientists for a practical solution. The capital lacked a radial railway system. Clearly any new lines would have to be constructed deep beneath the ground to avoid any disruption to existing businesses and roads. Weighty steam engines with their choking exhausts were useless,

[1] In *Victorian Engineering*, London, 1970, pp. 211–12.

so that even the shallow well-ventilated tunnels built for the Circle, District and Metropolitan Lines soon became filled with a thick, unpleasant gas. An electric train was the obvious answer. Though there had been several short electric railways opened at Brighton, Blackpool and Ryde between 1883 and 1886, the City & South London was the first to operate beneath ground. Authorized in 1886 and opened by the Prince of Wales on 4 November 1890, it ran from King William Street (near London Bridge) to Stockwell, three miles south (see pp. 62–3).

The motors were housed in separate locomotives, each of which hauled three carriages. The first engine is preserved in the Science Museum and one passenger car is on display at the London Transport collection. These locomotives continued in service until 1923, when the railway was closed so that the tunnel could be enlarged and incorporated within the Northern Line.

Although British engineers had been responsible for this pioneer electric railway, they failed to exploit their advantage, so that when Liverpool decided to build an overhead line along the Mersey, they turned to an American company to supply them with rolling stock (see p. 252). Indeed, the further construction of underground railways was largely American financed and equipped. The present 600-volt d.c. system adopted by London Transport originated in the United States, and the ancestors of the present multiple-unit trains were imported complete from America to run on the Bakerloo Line.

However, after the City & South London the next major electric undertaking was the Liverpool Overhead Railway, opened in 1893 and extended in 1896. The rolling stock was purchased from the Electric Construction Corporation and a motor car, No. 3 (1892), is preserved in the transport section of the County Museum. The success of this and London's early electric railways encouraged the construction of a complete network of underground lines across the capital. In 1900 the first section of the Central Line between Shepherds Bush and Bank was completed, the Bakerloo and what is now the Piccadilly followed in 1906, and the Northern, then called the Charing Cross, Euston & Hampstead Railway, in 1907. By this time the District system had been electrified, as well as all the Metropolitan except for the suburban arm to Harrow and Aylesbury.

The appearance of the underground train has changed as its technology has developed. First, an important distinction should be made between the smaller 'tube' trains which run far beneath the surface, and the more spacious sets which operate in the earlier shallow trenches. As we have seen, engine and carriages were entirely separate on the City & South London Railway. Initially this practice was adopted on the Central, and thirty locos were ordered from the General Electric Company of Schenectady, America. They were triangular-shaped, with a central cab. Weighing 44 tons largely unsprung, they set up heavy vibrations and as a result were replaced from 1903 onwards by carriages fitted with motors situated behind the driver's cab, an innovation first developed by Sprague at Chicago in 1898.

Henceforth 'tube' trains were operated by cars containing a motor section, rather than by a separate engine. However, the earlier practice was retained on the longer suburban lines of the Metropolitan to Aylesbury and Amersham. For this service the well-known Bo-Bo electrics were used, of which twenty were built between 1904 and 1906. Modified in 1922, they proved a successful and long-lived locomotive – four survived into the early 1970s. One, No. 5, *John Hampden*, is preserved in the London Transport Museum.

Contemporary photographs of carriage interiors on the Central Railway reveal that they were similar in plan to today's coaches. Seats with arm-rests were arranged along the sides, and benches fixed laterally to the gangway, while advertisements and route maps were pasted on the roof and sides above the windows. Entry was by means of lattice gates at each end of the car. In 1914 central doors were provided, though as yet they were manually operated with electric locks. In 1919, the Piccadilly Railway was the first to introduce air-operated doors, manufactured by Cammell Laird. A motor car No. 3327 (built for the Piccadilly Line in 1927) has been restored and is on display in the Science Museum. Part of the bodywork has been cut away to reveal the engine compartment.

The next noticeable development arose as a result of the 1935-40 New Works Programme, when 1,121 advanced cars were ordered. This modern stock was introduced from 1938 (it is still running today on the Bakerloo Line) and gave a fresh look to tube trains. The motor compartment was discarded and the engine, contractor bank (replaced by a control unit), generators and batteries were now fitted below the frame, allowing extra seating in the car itself. A braking retardation unit was added to the Westinghouse brakes and dead man's handle. These trains, still in their bright red livery, are easily distinguished by the viridian green interiors, and the V-shaped ventilators over the driver's cab.

Since then there have been two major introductions of tube stock, in 1959-62, and in 1967 for the Victoria Line. The first phase was based on the experimental cars, produced in 1956, which had witnessed the beginning of the 'silver era'. Introduced and still running on the Central and Northern Lines, these trains have simpler, cleaner lines, conventional interiors and an improved technology. However, more startling innovations were made with the Victoria Line stock, which have even smoother lines, the driver's cab windows curving round the corners for wider, uninterrupted vision. They are one-man trains, with the driver taking on the guard's duties, though his job is made easier by the automatic controls – for safety a manual alternative is always available. The doors have been fitted with angled glass to enable passengers to look out without stooping.

The development of London Transport's surface stock naturally follows a similar pattern. Steam was retained until 1905, when the District and Circle Lines were converted to electric traction. The Metropolitan from Baker Street to Uxbridge followed in the same year, and with the exception of outlying suburban lines, was completely electrified by November 1907.

Although these steam companies had been experimenting with electric traction as early as 1900, American influence was clear from the outset. Vehicles were called 'cars' rather than carriages and bogies were termed 'trucks'. The practice, prevalent in New York, of having only one motor truck per car was initially adopted by the District Railway. Convinced of the electric train's efficiency, in 1903 they ordered 420 cars for their system. Called 'B' stock, they were mostly built in France at Blanc Misseron, to an American design. The transatlantic influence was obvious from their clerestory roofs, square lines and vestibule entrances. At first they were fitted throughout with longitudinal seats and rattan upholstery, but later the central bays were redesigned with latitudinal benches and trimmed in traditional moquette. They were, of course, lit by electricity.

Although the new Metropolitan stock exhibited substantial technical differences, the general look of their trains was not so dissimilar. They too had clerestory roofs and vestibule entrances. Westinghouse also supplied most of the mechanical equipment. However, inter-war designs lost their American appearance, and of these the 'F' stock cars were among the most distinctive. Turned out in 1920 by the Metropolitan Carriage, Wagon and Finance Company in Birmingham, they were soon nicknamed 'dreadnoughts' or 'tanks'. This was either because they were constructed from steel or because the firm had till then been manufacturing parts for armoured vehicles. The driver's cab and trailer ends were fitted with twin oval windows, reminiscent of Pullman carriages. About 100 were completed, and in 1938 they were fitted with sliding doors which were air-operated, with passenger push-button controls.

As was the case with tube stock major innovations came from the 1935–40 New Works Programme. As a result 573 cars were ordered, giving rise to the familiar 'O', 'P' and 'Q' designs. Although the three divisions reflected certain technical differences, the basic design was much the same, 'O' cars being purchased to replace Hammersmith & City stock, 'P' Metropolitan and 'Q' District. They became the classic surface stock and the last still run today on the District Line. Painted bright red, they are distinguished by a flared base accentuating their U-shaped profile, while their windows have the characteristic diamond-shaped covers. Internally the conventional arrangement of seats was followed. Famous artists, including Paul Nash, Enid Marx and Marion Dorn, were commissioned to design the moquette patterns for the upholstery.

'Q' stock, introduced from 1938, were the last to be put into service, corresponding with an important technical advance, the metadyne system – a rotary transformer placed between the supply line and the motor itself, replacing the older less efficient control system. It had several advantages, being much smoother and permitting a more economic regenerative braking unit. As a result, trains were slowed down by their motors acting as generators and thereby creating power during deceleration, though the final force was provided mechanically by conventional brake shoes. Once they had proved reliable, metadyne machines were fitted to existing 'O' and 'P' stock. The other early silver trains on the District are 'R' stock, a similar but later design introduced from 1949.

In 1968 an order was placed with Metro-Cammell of Birmingham for 212 cars to run on the Metropolitan and Circle Lines. Called 'C69' stock because they were due to enter service in 1969, they were not in fact introduced until the following year and have since replaced all other trains on both lines. The flared contours have been discarded, giving them a clean, simple finish. New features include the provision of four sets of double doors, while the number of seats has been reduced to thirty-two because they are mostly used for short journeys with many interchanges. There have been considerable technical modifications, evident from the truck design, affecting the suspension and braking qualities of these trains.

The latest addition to Underground stock is on the District

Line. In January 1980 the first of seventy-five D78 trains were introduced and the remainder will follow over the next two years, replacing the District's mixed red and silver fleet. For the passenger their most novel feature, encouraged by energy conservation, is the return to push-button doors. Individual doors (now four wide single doors per car in place of the mixture of double and single doors on existing trains) can be operated only by pushing the lit buttons, situated inside and outside the train, when activated at stations by the guard. As in the 'Great Northern' electric stock designed for B.R., the guard alone can close the doors. The new cars are eight feet longer than existing stock and as a result trains consist of six-car rather than seven-car sets. The extensive use of aluminium alloy in place of steel has reduced their weight by about 60 per cent, while the improved rubber suspension provides a smoother ride. The interior colour scheme – yellow and brown panels with yellow check moquette seat covers – marks a departure for the Underground, though the exterior conforms with the plain aluminium silver finish adopted for all new stock.

It is often forgotten that a number of pre-grouping companies had implemented electrification schemes. The Lancashire & Yorkshire Railway had converted their line between Liverpool and Southport in 1904, the N.E.R. similarly switched to electric traction for services between Newcastle and Tynemouth, and the L.B. & S.C.R. had begun a modernization programme in 1909. In addition, the L.S.W.R. had electrified their line from Waterloo to Wimbledon in 1915. Unfortunately these sporadic changes produced a multitude of different technical systems, though a measure of standardization was introduced to parts of the Home Counties with the formation of the Southern Railway in 1923. Seven years later almost all of its network within twenty miles of London had been converted to electric traction.

Trains followed the general pattern of London Transport's surface stock. Sets of coaches were hauled by a car with a motor compartment, one at each end, which meant that turntables could be discarded when steam had been completely replaced. However, early motor coaches were often uncomfortable when the vibrations and noise mounted, and even the new all-steel stock introduced in the 1930s was not trouble-free. Only the separate electric locomotive entirely eliminates this problem.

In fact the N.E.R. (later the L.N.E.R.), the other major company particularly involved with electrification, designed a number of electric locomotives. One of their 'camel' Bo-Bos, No. 1, completed in 1904, is preserved at York. The L.N.E.R.'s most ambitious scheme, finally completed in 1954, was to electrify the line from Sheffield Victoria to Manchester London Road, which involved the construction of a new Woodhead tunnel to accommodate the overhead cables. An experimental engine, No. 6000 (B.R. 26000), built in 1941 for the L.N.E.R., is also preserved at York. It has been restored to its B.R. colours – black, with white, grey and red lining.

From the point of view of standardization, it was fortunate that electrification did not proceed very far under the independent companies. The real era of conversion came in the 1960s, when British Railways set out to modernize the main lines between Euston, Liverpool, Manchester and Birmingham. Work was completed in 1966. The system had first been tested on the route from Colchester to Clacton and Walton, and was later extended to Liverpool Street. After some teething troubles the new inter-city service proved to be a success, and it was carried northwards to Glasgow in 1974.

Since then the 'Great Northern' suburban service has been electrified between Moorgate, Hertford North and Welwyn Garden City. This has witnessed the introduction of a new type of stock, consisting of three-car units, powered by electric motors supplied through a pantograph from overhead cables. The interior arrangement of seats is similar to that of surface Underground trains, and carriages are fitted with semi-automatic sliding doors. This system is at present being extended to the St Pancras–Bedford service.

The Advanced Passenger Train represents the latest development in electric rail transport. The prototype was initially driven by gas turbine engines (generating power for the electric bogie motors) situated, as in the H.S.T., at each end of the train behind the driver's cab. It was originally planned that the pantograph and electrical equipment would be similarly placed in the A.P.T., but tests have shown that the A.P.T. runs most efficiently with the power cars located in the centre of the train.

While the H.S.T. is an example of the considered extension of existing technology, the A.P.T. represents the outcome of a period of long-term research into a number of novel areas. One of the results of this experiment was the development of a new bogie with certain self-steering characteristics which do not occur in conventional designs and which place the axles on the radius of the curve, eliminating 'hunting' as the train corners at high speed. This allows the A.P.T. to tackle bends 20–40 per cent faster than conventional trains. However, this advance meant that it was then necessary to offset the powerful pressures acting on the passenger and the coach body was designed to tilt into curves, balancing any unpleasant centrifugal forces.

In addition, the A.P.T. is aerodynamically shaped – to a greater extent than the H.S.T. – to reduce wind resistance and aid stability. The coaches are constructed from an aluminium alloy, lightening them by as much as 40-per cent in comparison with conventional steel carriages. The main doors are power-operated and designed to close flush with the body sides. In June 1978 the first power car built for passenger service was named *City of Derby*, to commemorate the association with the town where the A.P.T. was designed and constructed. It is possible that a diesel-powered version of the A.P.T. will be developed for use on non-electrified lines.

THE DIESEL LOCOMOTIVE

At this moment 60 per cent of trains are diesel-powered. With the progressive introduction of the H.S.T. – the most advanced diesel-electric in the world – it is fair to say that this form of power has reached its apogee in Britain. Since electricity holds the key to the future, when these expresses become obsolete it is probable that the diesel, like steam, will disappear.

Although the diesel engine was invented at the end of the nineteenth century, there was a considerable time lag before it was successfully applied to the railway locomotive. In 1893 W. D. Priestman had developed an oil-engined shunter for the N.E.R. to haul trains at the Alexandra Dock, Hull, while a number of similar engines were purchased by the War Office between 1898 and 1904 to work in the Woolwich Arsenal. However, these were limited affairs and could have achieved neither the power nor the speed required of a main-line express. The difficulty associated with the diesel engine lies in finding an efficient means of transmission. It is not possible to run a motor directly on to the driving wheels. A lorry can use a clutch and gear-box, but the weight of a whole train and the effort required to haul it rule out this method.

Diesel power may be transmitted in one of three ways: electrically, hydraulically and, in more limited circumstances, mechanically. The first has proved the most successful. It consists of connecting the main engines to a generator which in turn drives a number of electric traction motors located in the bogies. As the diesel revs faster, so the generator produces more energy and the greater is the force applied to the motors. The hydraulic system works on the principle that liquids are almost incompressible and so can be used to transmit power along defined channels. The mechanical process is complicated, but results in the diesel building up pressure which is then transmitted by hydraulic fluids to the wheels.

The Great Western was the first company to pioneer the use of diesel-powered trains, though they were limited in scale. Introduced in 1934, they consisted of single railcars operating a regular local schedule from Oxford to Kingham and Princes Risborough, with a faster service from Birmingham to Cardiff. They were not true diesel locomotives, in the sense that

THE PATH OF TECHNICAL IMPROVEMENT 39

they were really road coaches adapted to run on rails. Like the present day d.m.u.s, they had a mechanical transmission and a gear-box like that of a charabanc. So it was not until the post-war period that main-line diesels started to appear.

The L.M.S. were the first to experiment with a large diesel-electric locomotive. In 1947 at their Derby works they completed No. 10000, a Co-Co class 5P/5F with a tractive effort of 41,400 lb., and a second, No. 10001, followed in 1948. While the steam engine remained more efficient and less expensive, there was little incentive to develop their design, though they continued to be used, often in conjunction, for freight trains until the 1960s, when they were scrapped.

The first really successful main-line locomotive was the Deltic class (Fig. 6). English Electric completed a prototype in 1955. It had a distinctly American appearance with its high curved ends, drivers' cab mounted above, and central lamp and horns. The original Deltic was never owned by British Railways and so was painted in the livery of the English Electric Company, powder blue, light-grey, with cream and black lining. The multiple 'V' symbol at front and rear added to the transatlantic impression, mimicking the eagle which usually decorates American diesels. The stripes along the sides were intended to reduce its apparent height and the chevrons to disguise the bulk of the bonnet casings. The Deltic was powered by two patrol-boat engines originally designed by Napier for the Royal Navy, and it was the triangular arrangement of the pistons, forming the Greek letter 'delta', which gave the engine its name. Six electric traction motors, creating a tractive effort of 60,000 lb., located in the bogies each drove a pair of wheels. After extensive trials, twenty-two engines were ordered in 1958 and were introduced from May 1961. The prototype is now on display in the Science Museum, South Kensington.

The Deltics proved to be exceptionally reliable and popular locomotives. They are powerful and capable of sustained running at 100 mph and after certain modifications are still hauling

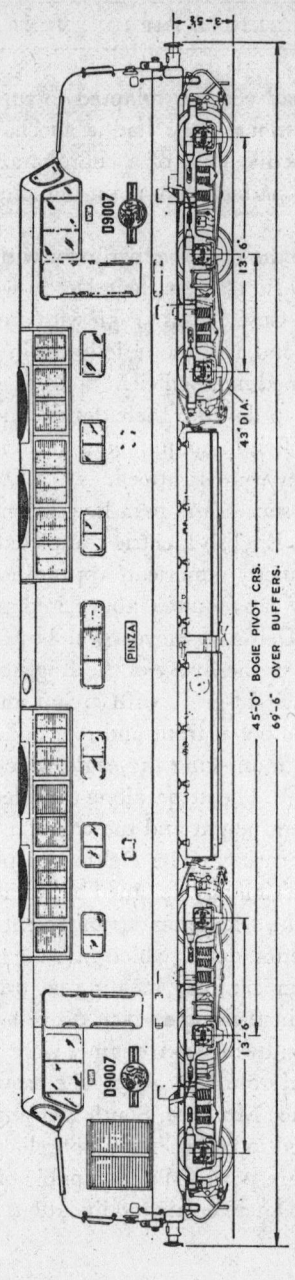

Fig. 6. D 9007 (now 55 007), *Pinza* (1961), a Deltic diesel-electric locomotive.

expresses today. In common with other early diesels they were named, in their case after famous racehorses and regiments of the British Army.

Apart from shunters, the class 47 is now the most numerous diesel-electric in service with British Rail. They were introduced in 1962 to work fast passenger and freight trains. Powered by a single Sulzer 12 LDA 28C engine, they have a Co-Co wheel arrangement and six traction motors. Only sixteen were originally named. The other numerous group of diesel-electrics includes the classes 45 and 46, which closely resemble and are based on the class 44 Peak locomotives (named after mountains in England and Wales). Unlike their predecessors only a few have been given names. They are capable of speeds up to 90 mph and develop a tractive effort to 55,000 lb. They can be distinguished by the unusual pair of carrying wheels at each end of the locomotive, and by the class number which always prefixes the engine's individual number.

The diesel-hydraulic has fallen from favour, so that there are none operating today on British Rail. The first to be introduced was the Warship class, which came into service in 1958. They were a Bo-Bo type and produced a tractive effort of 52,400 lb. Unfortunately, they were not very reliable and were quickly withdrawn, becoming extinct by 1972. No. D821, *Greyhound*, has been preserved but is not yet on public view. Much more successful were their successors, the Western class, which started running in 1962. With their Co-Co arrangement and sleek lines, these were particularly distinguished by their maroon livery, but worked entirely on the Western Region, like the Warships, and were all given names prefixed with the word 'Western'. They were very powerful, developing 72,600 lb., and proved to be more reliable. The class has now been withdrawn, but a number have been restored.

There was one further class of diesel-hydraulic, the Hymek. Manufactured by Beyer, Peacock, they were not as powerful as the other two, developing a tractive effort of 49,700 lb. Often used in pairs, they were all allocated to the Western Region, but have now been scrapped, though one has been preserved at Didcot.

The ultimate development in diesel-electric traction, is, of course, the High Speed Train. Designed as a complete whole, with engine and driving units at each end, the H.S.T. is based on the Pullmans of the 1960s. These too were multiple units with specially produced coaches. The motor carriages were partially streamlined and had a similar appearance to the modern trains, though their livery was slightly different – Nanking blue with a white stripe and the Pullman name and coat-of-arms. They were particularly luxurious and used only for special services.

The H.S.T. is a more advanced train, running at much higher speeds, with many improved technical features. Powered by two Paxman 'Valenta' engines, it is driven by eight electric traction motors located in the bogies. There are disc brakes to stop it efficiently and smoothly. The train is sleek and well designed (outwardly the carriages resemble something of the Silver Jubilee stock of 1935), and distinguished by the bright yellow cab and the words 'Inter-City 125' along the sides.

Finally something ought to be said of the ubiquitous class 08 shunters which pervade the whole B.R. network. They stem from a standard design produced in 1945 by English Electric for the L.M.S. They were an efficient, compact and reliable locomotive producing a tractive effort of 35,000 lb. The type was taken up by the G.W.R. and L.N.E.R. companies and subsequently modified under B.R. It is surprising that they have hardly changed in their external appearance since 1945. The front radiator, the enclosed rear cab and the engine side panels mark them out, while they are one of the few locomotives today still using coupling rods.

CARRIAGES AND WAGONS

Railway carriages have undergone a startling transformation in the last 150 years. Originally they were little more than open

THE PATH OF TECHNICAL IMPROVEMENT 43

Fig. 7. A mail coach, built for the Grand Junction Railway in 1837.

trucks on wheels. For the better-off, stage-coach bodies or complete carriages were attached to flat trucks. The early first-class coaches on the Liverpool & Manchester Railway (there are replicas on display in the Merseyside County Museum) appear as three stage-coach bodies placed back-to-back on a sprung chassis with buffers at each end. Again stressing their historical continuity, they were painted in traditional coaching colours, black and yellow. There was space on the roof for luggage, while certain companies still provided a seat here for the guard. Queen Adelaide's coach, built in 1842 and on display at York, is a good example of an early luxury railway carriage. Divided into three compartments, with a coupé at the front, it is a fine piece of craftsmanship, reminiscent of an expensive road vehicle and featuring gilded, carved ornaments, hand-painted monograms and arms, while the interior is a mixture of watered-silk upholstery and polished wood. At this stage second- and third-class accommodation consisted respectively of covered and open trucks with bench seating of varying quality.

As railway travel became more popular and more widely accepted so the design of the carriage evolved and lost its traditional associations with the road. The history of its design is essentially one of continuous development to improve facilities and quality, by incorporating advances in technology. For example, the cheap production of steel from the 1870s enabled engineers to design much longer and more stable carriages. Although the modern High Speed coach may not be more comfortable than the late-nineteenth-century Pullman car, it is certainly technically more sophisticated, with its automatic doors, sound-proofing, air-conditioning and disc braking.

The trend in the nineteenth century was for railway carriages to become larger and better appointed. Four wheels gave way to six, then eight. In 1852 the Great Western introduced the first eight-wheeled coaches, nicknamed 'Long Charlies'; unsuccessful as express stock, they were later relegated to the Metropolitan Railway. They were not fitted with independent bogies and were thereby limited in their turning capacity. This idea, well developed in America, was not adopted in England until the Midland Railway's Pullman cars had proved their worth in the 1870s.

In 1872 the Midland Railway took the important step of introducing third-class carriages on all their trains – hitherto fast services had been entirely first and second class. Indeed, third-class passengers had been poorly treated by most companies, and though their coaches were now covered, most had uncomfortable seats and some none at all. Henceforth there was a dramatic growth in the number of thirds, as the standard of living for the mass of the people rose and they were able to afford the fares.

Technical improvements multiplied after 1870. The first Pullman car, a sleeper, was introduced in 1874 on the Midland Railway, and in the following year the M.R. ran the first six-wheel bogie carriage. The Pullman Company, originating in America, was responsible for producing a number of mechanical innovations and it remains an unfortunate fact that in this period most new railway ideas came from the United States. Their bogie design was copied and adopted for most express stock. Their Pullman cars were heated and well-ventilated, while British railway companies merely provided 'footwarmers' – tin cans filled with hot water or acetate of soda. The Great Western had only introduced these meagre facilities for first-class passengers in 1856, though, in 1891, they were the first to run a train heated entirely by steam (supplied by the locomotive). Pullmans also offered superior lighting. When electric lighting was fitted to the Pullman car 'Beatrice' (run from a battery located beneath the frame) on the L.B. & S.C.R., Stroudley, the company's engineer, decided to extend the system to his regular stock from 1883. Carriages on the N.L.R. were lit by gas from bottles replenished at Broad Street terminus. A few gas-lit coaches survived into the British Railways era, finally disappearing with the introduction of Mark I stock in 1951.

In 1879 the first dining saloon, called a 'hotel car', was operated by the G.N.R. between King's Cross and Leeds. For long journeys it was clearly desirable not only to reduce the number of stops, but also to provide refreshments. Passengers customarily alighted at stations for meals, delaying the train's progress. The Great Northern's service was adopted in 1882 by the Midland, which had gained a reputation for luxuriously high standards, and in 1889 by the L.N.W.R. The Great Eastern served third-class passengers in a dining car from 1891 – the first company to do so.

The Great Northern was responsible for the earliest corridor coach, though the corridor did not extend to other carriages, merely permitting passengers to reach the toilets at each end. In 1892, the Great Western introduced the first all-corridor train, which ran on their service from Paddington to Birkenhead and consisted of a first, second and third, with a brake third (a passenger carriage whose latter part is occupied by a luggage section and a guard's compartment from which the brakes may be applied in an emergency), plus a non-corridor van.

By 1900 carriage lengths had generally reached 65 feet for

twelve-wheelers, with an average of 45 feet. Churchward surprised the railway world in 1904 when he revealed a 70-foot 'Dreadnought'. They were huge coaches designed to combine maximum seating with minimum weight, and one, No. 3299 (a corridor third built in 1905), is now being restored at Didcot.

There are some fine examples of carriage design at York. For unparalleled luxury, there are the various royal coaches. The L.N.W.R.'s saloon designed for Queen Victoria was completed in 1869. It is carpeted throughout and the chairs and walls are upholstered in blue watered silk and the ceiling in cream, a richness which is matched by the range of facilities. There are also two carriages dating from 1903 used by Edward VII. The L.N.W.R. first-class dining saloon, No. 76 (1900), shows that elegant and expensive interiors were not confined to royal coaches – it features a decorated clerestory ceiling, much marquetry work and richly patterned moquette. The standard of craftsmanship at the turn of the century was probably at its height in the field of carriage construction.

In 1921 Gresley introduced an articulated dining-car set on the Great Northern – two linked coaches with three bogies in total. He had previously experimented with these carriages before the First World War but with limited success. This second trial consisted of a brake third, third diner, kitchen, first diner and brake first, while in 1924–5 Gresley extended the principle under the L.N.E.R., introducing three- or four-car sets on expresses and suburban units comprising eight or ten carriages. The idea of the articulated coach has most recently been adopted by the new A.P.T.

In 1928 the L.M.S. ran the first all-steel train with their 'Queen of Scots' Pullman. With the speed rivalries of the 1930s much new stock, characterized by fine interiors and colourful liveries, was built by most of the major companies. Initially British Rail continued with established designs, producing their Mark I coaches in 1951. These were corridor compartment carriages with Pullman bogies and distinguishable from pre-nationalization stock by their cream and maroon livery. In

1962 an important break was made with the introduction of the first of their Mark IIs, open coaches with wide vestibule entrances, air-conditioning and an end to steam heating. The Mark III (the carriage for the High Speed Train) is a refined version of its predecessor. This is a longer coach with improved sound-proofing, suspension and running abilities. It might be argued that although it is a technically sophisticated carriage, the quality of the interior is not as high as before, since first class is no longer divided into compartments, and in second class some of the seats are slightly cramped, with a poorer range of vision. Open seating has also been adopted on the Advanced Passenger Train.

Until 1965, and British Rail's adoption of a 'corporate identity', carriages were a source of interest not simply as examples of advancing design but for their display of company liveries and devices. The Pullman cars were among the best liked. Painted in chocolate and light cream, lined in gold, they were some of the most magnificent coaches ever constructed. In addition, all the first-class diners and saloons were named. The Midland also gained a reputation for splendid exteriors, as their carriages were painted in a deep rich red lined in black and gold, while the company's shield decorated each side. Some of the better-known liveries included olive green on the Southern, dark brown and white on the L.N.W.R., and chocolate and cream on the Great Western. In 1935 Gresley introduced his 'Silver Jubilee' stock which was finished throughout in that colour. The L.M.S. replied in 1937 with the 'Coronation Scot' painted in garter blue and Cambridge blue above the waistline. In a sense the L.N.E.R. was different in that it had no carriage livery, Gresley favouring teak, an exceptionally tough and hard-wearing wood, for his coach building. This was varnished, and lined in red and gold.

The development of wagon design naturally follows in the path of advances in carriage building. The earliest wagons were very basic and of two types: the chaldron for coal, and

the flat truck. The first persisted late into the nineteenth
century – in 1872 nearly two thirds of mineral wagons on the
N.E.R. were chaldrons, without suspension or buffers. Three
are preserved at York and may be distinguished by their
tapered profile. These were slowly replaced by the straight-
sided truck, still common today. Covered and cattle wagons
were introduced and, later in the century, oil and refrigerated
varieties. Other specialized wagons were constructed to hold
bullion, gunpowder and even corpses.

As carriages generally grew larger, so did wagons. In 1871
the Great Western built four 20-ton wagons (six-wheelers).
Later, bogies were fitted to trucks to enable them to manage
longer loads, and today much of B.R.'s new goods stock is designed with bogies. Car transporters and freightliners are both
examples of their adoption. However, British railway companies only slowly equipped their goods vehicles with continuous brakes, and those that were fitted were often of a simple
kind, independent and hand-operated. Hence heavy freight
trains, which could be stopped only by the locomotive assisted
by the guard's brake van, remained potentially dangerous and
accordingly were not operated at express speeds. Eventually
companies started to furnish wagons with continuous brakes.
The Great Western began in 1903, but even by nationalization
not all had been converted, and two fifths of B.R.'s entire in-
heritance was scrapped. Even by 1959, after heavy expenditure,
only one third of their wagons had been fitted with an efficient
braking system.

Since then B.R. has done much to encourage its freight-
carrying. Speedlink and the freightliner are both efficient
responses to the demand for high-speed goods trains. The
freightliner is a long truck on to which containers can be easily
loaded, while Speedlink provides fast, selective freight transport
in modern wagons hauled by express locomotives. There has
been a broadening in the range of specialized vehicles: hoppers
for minerals, special tanks for chemicals, with pressurized
varieties for cement powder which can then be pumped out

THE PATH OF TECHNICAL IMPROVEMENT 49

like a liquid into railside silos. B.R. has long-term contracts with the major oil companies and operates a fleet of 100-ton wagons for them.

Although the volume of freight transported by British Rail has fallen by 15 per cent, from 200 million tons in 1967 to 170 million in 1977, this does not take account of the reduced mileage, and in fact represents a very real increase in productivity. There are 40 per cent fewer locomotives and 60 per cent fewer wagons today. In addition, the government has offered grants to firms which have a railway siding built to their works. Since B.R. have improved their organization and stock, this further incentive may well encourage the continued growth of freight traffic. The railways themselves can do little more. It can only be hoped that this side of their business develops, since there are very sound economic and environmental reasons why it is desirable.

TRACK, SIGNALLING AND GENERAL ENGINEERING

Trackways were in existence before the first steam engine was invented. They were used in England throughout the eighteenth century to guide simple wagons hauled by men or horses, though the rails were usually constructed from stone or timber. Cast-iron and then wrought-iron rails were encouraged by the introduction of the locomotive, as they alone were capable of bearing the weight of an engine. In 1797 Thomas Barnes laid down a colliery line from Walker to the River Tyne using wrought-iron rails fixed to stone blocks by 'chairs', his method of construction becoming the norm for the next fifty years.

The track laid for the Liverpool & Manchester Railway (a short section is on display under *Sans Pareil* at the Science Museum) was of this type. Diagonally set stone blocks supported short lengths of fish-bellied rails. The early practice of fitting the flange to the rail rather than the wheel had been rejected. From the 1830s timber instead of stone was being adopted for sleepers, as it gave smoother riding and better service.

Both the Stockton & Darlington and the L. & M.R. laid their lines on what came to be known as 'standard gauge', 4 feet 8½ inches. Brunel, engineer to the Great Western, had different ideas, setting his rails 7 feet apart. In addition, they were supported on longitudinal timbers, held together by transoms at intervals of 15 feet. He argued that such an arrangement made for smoother running and potentially faster speeds, while permitting more spacious and comfortable carriage design. His practice was not copied and the Great Western remained the only major company not to adopt standard gauge. An Act was passed in 1844 forbidding the construction of any new lines with unusual widths, though it was not until 1892 that Brunel's broad gauge was entirely converted. For this reason bridges often appear unreasonably wide on Western Region, while platforms appear to be generously spaced apart, occasionally permitting the insertion of one or two extra lines. Even today some tracks inside Paddington are laid on longitudinal timbers supported by transoms.

Until the mid-1860s rails were constructed from wrought iron and were prone to breakage under stress. They were considerably shorter than today's. Bessemer's steel-founding process made it possible to produce good-quality steel rails at competitive prices. Although companies were at first reluctant to adopt them, their clear advantages in strength made them a necessity with the introduction of heavier and faster trains, and by 1878 four fifths of the Great Western's main line had been converted to steel. The classic track, still used in essence by B.R. for branch lines and sidings, was developed by the L.N.W.R. in 1894 – timber sleepers fitted with chairs and wooden keys supporting regular lengths of steel rail, joined together by fishplates, leaving small expansion gaps. The whole was laid on a bed of stone chippings, regularly replenished and kept clear from weeds. By 1900 the standard length of rail had risen from 30 to 45 feet, and in some cases 60. A fine display of

THE PATH OF TECHNICAL IMPROVEMENT   51

the evolving shapes of track in cross-section, and the various types of chairs, can be seen in the transport galleries of the Science Museum.

British Rail have since introduced important changes in track design. Reinforced concrete sleepers have replaced timber and continuous welded rails have superseded shorter lengths and fishplates, while chairs and keys have largely been replaced by springs or plates, pressing between sleeper and rail. These three improvements have been essential in view of the regular operation of High Speed Trains. There can be no doubt that the new track is both harder-wearing and gives a smoother, quieter ride, though it has yet to bear the forces of the A.P.T. running at speeds of 150 mph plus.

The safety of rail travel depends not only on the skill of the driver and the efficiency of the engine and rolling stock, but also on the reliability of the signals. Early signalling was simply a matter of hand or flag waving. The first fixed signals were probably installed on the L. & M.R. in 1834 and consisted of boards on pivots, turned at right angles to halt the progress of a train. With the rapid growth of the railway system, producing junctions, cross-overs, complex sidings and many-platformed termini, the necessity to devise safe and efficient signalling codes was paramount. Initially each company produced its own solutions.

A wide range of different types of signals was developed. The Great Western adopted a coloured ball with a lantern suspended below, the whole being raised or lowered to indicate the state of the line. The L.S.W.R. used a revolving disc symbol with red and green lights for darkness. After 1860 the semaphore signal – horizontal for danger, raised or lowered for go, balanced so as to return to danger should a cable break, with different coloured arms to provide advance warnings – gained general acceptance. They were mounted on tall masts, often 40 or 60 feet high, so as to be visible from great distances. A number of Victorian photographs of signal gantries survive; one depicting the great assembly of arms, mounted above 'A' signal box over the approaches to Waterloo, provides a majestic sight. Through the drifting locomotive smoke they resembled line upon line of masts and sails of ships slipping into battle.

Probably the most important signalling innovation was the introduction of block working in the 1840s and 1850s. Essentially, lines were divided into sections controlled by a signalman, who reported the progress of a train by telegraph to the next box, setting points and signals accordingly. The first railway worked completely by the block system was the Yarmouth & Norwich, opened in 1844. Although highly successful, there was still resistance to change until a terrible accident in 1861 on the Brighton main line at Clayton tunnel, resulting in the deaths of twenty-three people, caused companies to abandon hand signalling based on time-intervals. Henceforth, signalmen could direct operations with a high degree of certainty instead of relying on what they could see and guess.

With points and signals becoming more sophisticated throughout the nineteenth century, the signal box itself became an increasingly technical place. Rows of coloured levers, clocks, varnished boxes with brass controls, bells and dials created an impression of a Victorian attempt at space travel. The telegraphs are splendid pieces of highly finished machinery. Charles Dickens was moved to write a number of evocative and slightly chilling short stories about signalmen. The first, entitled 'Mugby Junction, No. 1 Branch Line' (1866), concerned a railwayman confined to a signal box situated in a remote cutting at the entrance of a haunted tunnel. He was tormented by a spirit which affected his instruments and bells, enticing him to the tunnel opening by its mysterious form, where he was finally run down by an emerging train.[1]

When British Railways was formed it continued with the mechanically operated semaphore signals and points, but there was room for modernization. B.R. installed an automatic warning system (pioneered by the Great Western since 1906)

---

[1] Charles Dickens, *Selected Short Fiction*, ed. D. A. Thomas, Harmondsworth, 1976, p. 78.

THE PATH OF TECHNICAL IMPROVEMENT 53

which rang a bell in the driver's cab before a danger signal and operated the brakes if he failed to respond. Semaphore signals are slowly being replaced by coloured lights, which can be operated by much larger signal boxes located at greater distances. Computers are now used to assist in setting points and monitoring the progress of trains. While this has produced a significant gain in efficiency and a reduction in the number of men employed, it has also resulted in the demise of the traditional British signal box, and the signalman's job is now one of reduced personal responsibility, but greater overall control.

Each railway company had its own distinctive style. The L.N.W.R. constructed fortress-like boxes from brick at important junctions, though most featured weatherboarded walls, painted in the railway's livery. The Midland decorated their roofs with ornate finials, and such boxes may still be seen in operation on the main line from St Pancras to Sheffield. No one could deny the beauty of a rural signal box sited amongst lineside trees, a trickle of smoke from its single chimney indicating a kettle on the boil.

The railways probably exerted the greatest stimulus on the development of civil engineering in the nineteenth and early twentieth centuries. Following advances made by canal engineers, they evolved techniques for tunnel and bridge design. A body of experience had already been laid down by waterway builders, such as Brindley, Rennie and Telford, based on their aqueduct, embankment, lock and tunnel construction. Railway engineers went on to tackle larger and more ambitious projects. In 1845 the Woodhead tunnel (three miles long) was completed, coming after such achievements as Box, Glenfield, Kilsby and Summit.

Viaducts covering considerable distances at spectacular heights were also built – Stockport, Ouse, Hanwell and Harringworth are among the finest. Brunel's Royal Albert Bridge at Saltash, opened in 1859, illustrates a remarkable episode in railway engineering construction, which culminated in the mammoth Forth Bridge, designed by Sir John Fowler and Benjamin Baker and completed in 1890. Much less spectacular is the viaduct supporting the London & Greenwich Railway, finished in 1838 after three years' work and running for almost four miles. Built from grey Kentish brick, the arches beneath were let out as shops, warehouses and dwellings.

Railways were instrumental in advancing the design of large halls for their termini. St Pancras held the record for the widest single-span arch in the world. The architects they employed for their hotels and offices were selected from the best – Dobson at Newcastle, the Hardwicks for Euston, Scott for St Pancras and E. M. Barry for Charing Cross – and have produced some of the finest domestic buildings of the period.

Railway companies were not simply responsible for grand station buildings. At Crewe, Swindon, Wolverton and Barrow-in-Furness they planned whole towns, and there are few cities which do not possess a district comprising 'railway cottages'. In London, the Great Western's 'Garden Village Society' was responsible for developing most of West Acton, where semi-detached houses were offered for rent or mortgage to their employees. At Fishguard, 100 cottages were built for railway-men. The railways have thus played a major part in moulding the landscape of present-day Britain.

3 The Railways of London

In any consideration of the capital's railway network, the Underground must occupy a prime place. Except for the Waterloo & City Line, it is now entirely owned by London Transport, which is also responsible for buses and coaches. In most of the central districts, the system is completely beneath ground, and many lines are very deep down, the tight, circular shape of the tunnels earning them the nickname 'tubes'. Through the suburbs of Greater London, trains run largely overground. In many ways the present system belies its origins, as it was not constructed by a single body to a unified plan. Lines were built, piecemeal, by independent railway companies looking for profit. Originally the Underground was like any other railway network in a large city, except that it ran in places below street level, though only just. For the earliest lines were laid in trenches beneath the surface, so that buildings could then be constructed on top. Later, electrification encouraged the digging of proper tunnels, which proceeded to go deeper as the system became highly connected and complex. In the inter-war years the Underground was amalgamated and eventually given state assistance.

At first, there was no real difference between the railway companies which were later taken over by London Transport and those taken over by British Rail, though these two operating bodies now appear quite distinct. Suburban trains run by the Great Eastern, L.S.W.R. and Great Western often used the same stations as Underground trains. For example, the London,

Tilbury & Southend Railway owned the tracks later used by the District to Upminster, the line to Richmond was shared by the L.S.W.R. and the District Railway, and today Ealing Broadway is a part of both the Central Line and Western Region, though they use separate platforms.

This chapter also deals with a number of London's suburban railways now under British Rail's control, which are not so very dissimilar in function and history from the Underground, though the design and livery of their rolling stock is an obvious surviving difference. In addition, a number of commuter termini and important London Transport stations are examined.

THE METROPOLITAN RAILWAY

The first underground railway in the world was the Metropolitan. It was built in 1863 and ran between Paddington and Farringdon, via Baker Street, Euston and King's Cross. The names of its stations give the clue to its function, as it was designed to link up the various north London termini, each then independently owned and operated. The Marylebone Road was an important highway not only for passengers wishing to change lines, but also for Londoners on their daily journey to work. It was popular and soon became very congested. The obvious solution was to lay a railway line below street level to reduce the crowding above. The scheme was developed by Charles Pearson, a City solicitor, and effected by John Hargrave Stevens, a surveyor, and John Fowler, the engineer.

There had been many abortive attempts to build lines through the capital in the 1840s and 1850s, so that it was not without a struggle that Pearson gained parliamentary consent. One of his early supporters was Sir Rowland Hill, who backed the railway on the grounds that it would benefit his postal services, while Brunel, as an engineer, also gave his support. Though the Act was passed in 1854, a lack of funds and the economic disruption caused by the Crimean War meant that the railway was not completed until 1863, the actual construction having started only three years before. The Great Western, with its own terminus at Paddington, saw the obvious advantages of such a line, and subscribed to the Metropolitan. The Great Northern was also to have access to the tracks. Because these companies operated on different gauges, it was agreed that the new railway was to have three rails so that both standard-gauge and broad-gauge locomotives could operate along its length. In fact, most of the later extensions were built to accommodate standard-gauge engines alone, thereby reducing the area of land to be purchased.

To commemorate the line's opening on 10 January 1863 a special train was run. Photographs had been taken of an earlier official inspection, and one of the best known features Gladstone sitting in an open carriage wearing a high top hat. The Metropolitan was a great novelty, and twenty-nine thousand passengers were carried in the first three weeks, its traffic soon expanding as the usefulness of the trains became clear. It must have been a thrill to have travelled beneath the streets and offices of London, in smoky, ill-lit coaches, while the exhaust beats of the steam engine echoed round the brick-lined tunnels.

Engineers soon appreciated the problem of running locomotives in a confined space. There was no fresh air to dilute the soot, smoke and noxious fumes. Sir Daniel Gooch, locomotive superintendent to the Great Western Railway, asked to suggest a solution to these problems, designed a 2-4-0 steam engine fitted with a special condensing tank, holding 420 gallons of water. Yet there was soon a disagreement. The Great Western refused to continue to provide locomotives and the Metropolitan was forced to order its own engines. These were 4-4-0 tank engines, designed and built by Beyer, Peacock in Manchester, and distinguished by curved copper pipes leading from the cylinders to water condensing tanks, an extremely successful design which continued to operate until electrification. No. 23 (1866) has been repainted in its 1903 maroon Metropolitan livery and is preserved in the London Transport Museum at Covent Garden. The first eighteen locomotives all had titles of classical origin, and included *Jupiter*, *Mars*, *Medusa*, *Aurora*, *Ixion* and *Daphne*. No. 8 was aptly named *Pluto*, god of the underworld. A later Metropolitan Railway design, the 0-4-4T E class, has one representative, at present under restoration. No. 1, built at Neasden in 1898, is being repainted in its London Transport livery and number, L44, at present being shedded at Quainton Road, near Aylesbury.

In a sense the Metropolitan was not an underground railway. The line was not constructed by tunnelling far below the surface; rather a trench was dug sufficiently deep to accommodate a train. Brick arches were then constructed and buildings or thoroughfares laid on top, concealing the railway beneath – the classic 'cut-and-cover' method. It was employed for the District Railway and its and the Metropolitan's later extensions. This explains how in Conan Doyle's mystery 'The Bruce Partington Plans' the villains were able to deposit the body of the murdered man on the roof of a train, which had stopped beneath their back-stair window. His body eventually toppled off outside Aldgate Station when the train swayed over a particularly complicated set of points. Sherlock Holmes was left to puzzle why the man had no ticket.

Though the Metropolitan Railway solved the problem of traffic congestion in the short term, the gradual expansion in the size of the capital and the Underground's growing popularity encouraged its extension. In its first year of operation over nine million passengers were carried and in 1868 the line was carried eastwards to Moorgate. The obvious development was to extend the line from each end southwards to form a complete circle linking up the major termini at Victoria, Charing Cross, Blackfriars and Cannon Street.

THE DISTRICT, CIRCLE AND LATER EXTENSIONS

In April 1868 the Metropolitan had already agreed to a new branch, running north from their Baker Street Station to Swiss Cottage. Unfortunately both financial difficulties and company wrangles led to a much reduced service. In 1864 two Acts had been passed which laid the foundation for the Inner Circle service. They permitted an extension from Paddington south to South Kensington, via Notting Hill Gate, and another from Moorgate to Minories (now Tower Hill). As the Metropolitan was being extended, so the District Railway was also being laid down and opened. One interesting feature of the latter's extension to Gloucester Road was the cutting of Leinster Road at right angles. Its stately, stuccoed terraced houses would have been spoiled had a gap been created by a new railway bridge, so the façade was deliberately preserved, leaving Nos. 23 and 24 (as they remain today) with false fronts as in a film set.

The District Railway was planned to run along an east–west axis linking up the two extensions from the north. But it, too, encountered difficulties from existing housing patterns and, in addition, had to negotiate the many rivers flowing into the Thames. The River Westbourne had to be captured and confined within a pipe – which can still be seen above the platforms – to avoid its emptying into Sloane Square Station. There was a frantic rush to open the line to Westminster Bridge to be ready for the Christmas traffic of 1868, 3,000 navvies being employed around the clock to complete the digging and lining. The trains connected with the Houses of Parliament, and Gladstone is reported to have said in 1871 that the line 'had an influence of remarkable efficiency in removing members of the House of Commons from their seats'.

It follows that the oldest stations to be seen on the present Underground system are not actually at its core, but are to be found around its first circle. Though they are below street level, they tend to be open-air, featuring lofty vaulted train-sheds, and, where still visible, arcaded brick walls. Even Westminster Station, which gives every appearance of being below ground, is in fact open to sunlight. Notting Hill Gate, Paddington, Kensington High Street, Gloucester Road, Earls Court, South Kensington and Sloane Square were all constructed to a very similar design. Arcaded brick walls supported a curved iron and glass roof, with platforms on each side. Unfortunately, most of the roofs have been replaced or removed, and much of the ornate brick and iron work has been covered over by advertisement-hoardings, although South Kensington Station provides a fine view of the arcaded side walls and brick cuttings. Baker Street and the first northern stations do not quite conform to this pattern. They have wide arched brick roofs, with curved shafts let into the structure, in order to light and ventilate the platforms. Though they have subsequently been blocked up, the openings at Baker Street are still plainly visible. The Inner Circle was actually completed in October 1884 with the linking of Tower (Hill) and Mansion House Stations, the service being operated jointly by the Metropolitan and District Railways.

THE BAKERLOO, NORTHERN, PICCADILLY
AND CENTRAL LINES

The Inner Circle service had filled a real transportation need in the capital, providing a link between the various termini and additional communication from the expanding residential areas of Paddington, Bayswater and Kensington to central London. Thus much of its early traffic was local. The great increases which came in the twentieth century generally resulted from the suburban services which were built from this basic system. One of the first lines to be tunnelled through the centre of the city and extended into the suburbs was the Central London Railway, opened from Bank to Shepherds Bush in July 1900. The Bakerloo followed, then the Piccadilly and the Northern, while the post-war period has seen the Victoria and Jubilee Lines, with the Piccadilly extended to Heathrow in 1977.

The Bakerloo is said to have originated with the wish of City businessmen to enjoy the last hour's cricket at Lord's without leaving their offices unduly early. There certainly existed an urgent need for an efficient north–south connection across the capital. A Bill was originally put forward in 1891 to construct a proper tube line from Waterloo to Baker Street (later the two names were conflated to form 'Bakerloo'). Money was not immediately forthcoming and it was not until 1898 that work actually began. In the following year parliamentary powers were obtained to extend the line southwards, under the Thames, to the Elephant and Castle, and north-westwards to Paddington. In March 1906 the first section, between Baker Street and Lambeth North, was opened, while the extension to the Elephant and Castle followed in August.

The construction of this line, in contrast to that of earlier ones, was a dangerous and difficult process. First a shaft had to be sunk so that a pressurized shield could be placed at right angles to the line which the tunnel was to take. This was a solid circular framework, supporting the roof and sides while the digging was under way. As it moved forward so the tunnel was lined with cast-iron sections. A repeated problem working at such depths was the seepage of water from underground streams, necessitating continual pumping.

The stations themselves were, of course, of a very different design from those on the Metropolitan and District. The platforms were merely extensions of the tunnels and the surface buildings simply consisted of an entrance hall and ticket office for the lines below. Designed by Leslie W. Green, they were of a standard and distinctive type. There was a spacious ground floor, part of which was let out as shops, surmounted by a mezzanine floor, in which the windows formed a series of broad arches, while the level roofs enabled offices or flats to be built above. The stations can easily be distinguished today by their glazed ruby-red tiles. The exterior was then lit by lines of gas lamps, suspended by wrought-iron brackets from the upper floor. Oxford Circus survives in its original form. Though the title 'Baker Street and Waterloo Railway' has been removed from beneath the frieze, the company's monogram survives on a scalloped shield. The old Euston underground station in Cardington Street is another example of this design, as are the disused stations at Hyde Park Corner (next to St George's Hospital) and by the Brompton Oratory in Cottage Place.

The platforms themselves were decorated with different-coloured tiles so that passengers could easily recognize their destination. The Northern Line also adopted this principle. The following stations still have coloured glazed bricks to distinguish stops: Goodge Street (light green), Camden Town (light blue), Kentish Town (raw sienna), Tufnell Park (yellow ochre), Archway (dark brown) and Euston (dark blue). These new deep stations encouraged a further innovation. Passengers of all ages and sizes needed to be conveyed in large numbers to and from the platforms, and lifts were installed by the famous American company Otis, with large cages designed to hold seventy passengers. The greatest descent was 80 feet at the Elephant, while Trafalgar Square was only 39 feet. The escalator was a later development, the first being introduced on the Piccadilly Railway at Earls Court in October 1911.

Not only did these tubes inspire further improvements in technology but they, in their turn, had resulted from previous advances. They could never have operated without the developments which had taken place in electric traction. Steam engines would have been impractical in these confined spaces far below the ground, their bulk and exhaust fumes creating innumerable problems. In fact, the Bakerloo was constructed after the successful electrification of earlier underground lines.

The first 'tube' railway proper was the City & South London, opened in 1890. After the various changes of plan the scheme was designed to run from the northern end of London Bridge, in King William Street (now Monument Street), under the Thames to Stockwell, three miles south. The tunnels, constructed by Edmund Gabbutt of Liverpool, were wide enough to accommodate standard-gauge track. Although it was originally planned that the trains should be operated by cables, the success of other electric-powered railways turned the directors' minds in that direction. The stations were gas-lit and had island platforms, with hydraulic lifts to transport passengers from ground level. Fourteen electric locomotives were ordered from Mather & Platt at their Salford Iron Works to the designs of Dr Edward Hopkinson. They had two electric motors which picked up current from a third rail placed just inside the left-hand track, and were fitted with air brakes whose reservoirs had to be topped up at Stockwell on each trip. They were originally painted dark red-brown, though chrome orange panels were later painted along the sides and lined out in yellow and black. One locomotive, No. 1, still survives and is on display at the Science Museum, South Kensington.

There were three carriages to a train. The coaches themselves were quite unlike any operating on the Underground today. Their ends were open but protected by lattice gates which were opened by attendants who rode on the cars and had to tell passengers where they were, as the upholstery was carried up to the roof, leaving only slit windows for ventilation (they were lit electrically). The carriages were soon nicknamed 'padded cells', suggesting that early tube travel must have been a rather claustrophobic experience. One of these, No. 3, is preserved at the London Transport Museum, Covent Garden.

The Bakerloo and District Railways independently drew on this experience, while adopting an improved automatic signalling system. The passing train triggered an arm alongside the rails which then operated a signal and could operate the brakes should the driver run past without noticing. The rolling stock also took a step forward. No longer was the engine a separate vehicle, motor and driver's cab being incorporated into the leading coach, as they are today. These first sets were built in America and assembled in Manchester. In all there were thirty-six motor coaches and seventy-two trailers, brightly painted in the Bakerloo's scarlet and white livery. Henceforth, the American term 'car', rather than carriage, was adopted.

The Metropolitan Line, however, continued to operate some trains hauled by separate electric engines. Their round-fronted, squat Bo-Bo locomotives, rebuilt in 1922, continued to haul trains into the 1950s, while four continued to perform depot duties in the mid-1960s. They were reconstructions of two earlier series, Nos. 1–10, which had been built in 1904, and 11–20, completed in 1906. Named after famous people associated with the areas which the Metropolitan served, they included *Sherlock Holmes* (No. 8), *W. E. Gladstone* (No. 10), *George Romney* (No. 11), *Wembley 1924* (No. 15) (to commemorate its being displayed at the Empire exhibition there), and aptly No. 18, *Michael Faraday*. One, No. 5, *John Hampden*, has been restored and is kept at Covent Garden. They were originally painted in the Metropolitan's livery of maroon with black and yellow lining, with vermilion solebars, buffer beams and window linings, and the company's name and coat-of-arms on each side. These powerful and speedy locomotives, capable of 65 mph, originally worked all parts of the railway, being confined in later life to the longer-distance runs from Baker Street to Aylesbury.

An interesting change occurred in the Metropolitan Railway's coat-of-arms when they switched from steam to electric traction. Initially it consisted of the City's arms placed over the front and rear views of two steam-hauled trains in separate brick tunnels. In 1905 the new shield reflected the company's geographical expansion and technical advances. The City's arms were quartered with those of Middlesex, Buckinghamshire and Hertfordshire, surmounted by a clenched fist radiating sparks of electrical energy.

The Piccadilly Railway was opened in 1906, with a formal ceremony to celebrate the completion of the section between Hammersmith and Finsbury Park. It had its origins in a scheme devised in 1897 to provide a railway between Piccadilly Circus and Earls Court. Although part of the route was already served by the District Railway, it had become so congested that it had ironically been nicknamed 'the Daylight Route'. For part of its course the Piccadilly ran parallel but beneath the District Railway, but because the two lines were independently owned, separate stations were constructed. Gloucester Road still provides an excellent example of this duplication. The District Line station is a simple building constructed in light-yellow bricks, and the upper floors still display the original white and green mosaic sign announcing the station's name, with the proclamation 'Trains to all parts of London'. It is a neat symmetrical edifice with round arches and uncomplicated windows, offering a sharp contrast to the Piccadilly station next door. This is a typical Green building, with broad expansive windows, ornamental shields and a decorated frieze constructed from glazed ruby-red tiles.

The Science Museum, not so far away at South Kensington, has a Piccadilly Line motor car, No. 3327. Designed in 1927 and built by Metro-Cammell, this carriage was completed in 1929 and worked on that line until 1931, when it was transferred to the Bakerloo, moving to the Central in 1939. It has been restored to the bright red London Transport livery of 1961, while parts of the bodywork have been cut away to reveal the details of the motor compartment set behind the driver's cab.

An interesting station saga has played itself out on the Central London Railway. The line was extended from Shepherds Bush to Wood Lane Station in 1908 to serve the Franco-British Exhibition opened that year on the site of the present B.B.C. studios. Another station, also called Wood Lane, was opened on the Metropolitan Line at the end of Macfarlane Road, where a number of timber platform supports survive. When the 1928 Olympic Games were held at White City Stadium, a special movable platform was added at Wood Lane (C.L.R.) to accommodate the six-car trains used to transport the large crowds. The platform was electro-pneumatically operated from the signal box as it fouled a branch line to the depot when in position and for safety its working was incorporated with the signals and points.

However, in 1920 the Central Line had been extended beyond Wood Lane to Ealing Broadway and this meant that there was an awkward delay while trains reversed in and out of the terminus. It made sense to build a new through station near by. In 1947, to coincide with the completion of the branch to Greenford, the present White City station was opened and Wood Lane closed. The new building is pleasantly designed in the pre-war tradition with ample space for crowds attending the stadium. It was given a Merit award in 1951 by the Festival of Britain committee and this fact is commemorated by a blue plaque at the entrance. Wood Lane terminus is extant several hundred yards to the south and though its mosaic signs have been painted over, their message is still quite clear.

The Underground system developed throughout the twentieth century, the Victoria and Jubilee Lines being simply the latest phase in this general expansion. However, this continued growth has been accompanied by a move towards centralized control. In 1910 the Piccadilly absorbed the Bakerloo and Hampstead Companies, while in 1915, the Central, the District and the City & South London joined them, retaining their legal identity. The headquarters of the group (now called the 'Underground') was at 55 Broadway, where a skyscraper block was constructed. Completed in 1929, it was designed by Charles Holden as a central tower with four radiating wings, which were decorated with sculptures representing the winds, day and night. They were executed by various artists, including Henry Moore, Jacob Epstein and Eric Gill. 55 Broadway, as a functional building advanced for its time, stands today as an impressive tribute to Frank Pick, who as Managing Director argued for its construction and commissioned so many of the eminent artists connected with London Transport.

In 1933 the London Passenger Transport Board was formed, incorporating the Metropolitan Railway and bringing trains, buses and trams under a single authority. The development of London Transport's roundel device, used to display station's names, paralleled this gradual centralization. Originally each company possessed their own motif. The District's circle, the Metropolitan's lozenge and the General Bus Company's symbol all contributed to the 'bull's eye' device adopted by the L.P.T.B. in 1933.

In 1948 the newly created British Transport Commission placed the Underground system under the control of London

Transport and, though the B.T.C. was dissolved in 1962, L.T. has remained. The government has subsequently provided financial assistance for the replacement of stock and the construction of new lines. However, since 1970 the Greater London Council has exercised supreme control of the Underground (and L.T. buses), severing the traditional link with the Ministry of Transport.

THE SUBURBAN SYSTEM AND 'METROLAND'

Leaving London's central districts and the development of their underground railway system, let us move to the suburbs. These lines are generally more modern and were constructed from the inner network, gradually cutting their way outwards as the capital grew in the inter-war years. Other parts taken over by London Transport were steam-operated branch lines which had changed their character as London enveloped their villages and fields. Most of the system was, of course, overground.

The first extensions into suburban London were in the west. In 1872 an Act was obtained to lay a line from Earls Court to join the L.S.W.R. at Barnes. In 1874 the District was extended from Earls Court to Hammersmith. Having demonstrated their firm intention to build a line to Richmond and Kew, and hence compete with the existing L.S.W.R. service, the latter agreed to let the District operate trains along their rails. Hammersmith junction was completed in 1877, allowing District trains to run from Mansion House direct to Richmond. The line continued to be shared after nationalization and, until recently, Kew Station, a neat symmetrical brick building, featured Southern Region green and white signs. These have been replaced by the simpler, standard British Rail name plates rather than L.T.'s bird's eye signs.

Encouraged by the success of this undertaking, the District Railway embarked on another westward extension. In July 1879 a line was completed between Turnham Green and Ealing Broadway involving an agreement with the Great Western

Railway to use their station there. Finally, in 1880, the District completed their third and last extension, south from West Brompton to Putney Bridge, the line eventually being connected to Wimbledon by agreement with the L.S.W.R. nine years later. Richmond, situated on the Thames, and Kew, with its fine botanical gardens, were favourite weekend haunts for Londoners, while Wimbledon's annual tennis tournament was also an attraction. However, their staple revenue came from local residents who worked in the City and travelled regularly to work on the lines.

Baker Street Station, noted the 1896 *Baedeker*, 'practically ranks among the London termini since the extension . . . to Rickmansworth, Chesham and Aylesbury' (p. 56). It has developed into an important junction, with stops on the Circle, Metropolitan and Bakerloo Lines. When the Metropolitan Company adopted its policy of developing suburban sites in the early twentieth century, it was decided that the London end of the line was capable of similar improvement. Their architect, C. W. Clark, was commissioned to build a block of flats at Baker Street above the subterranean complex of tracks. The high, stately stone edifice, completed in 1929, was called Chiltern Court, and still stands today with its pub, cinema and shops, as a gateway to Metroland.

The Metropolitan Railway was not slow to perceive the advantages of extending their network into the expanding suburban districts. In the 1880s they operated a line to Swiss Cottage, via St Johns Wood. They had meantime taken over part control of the Kingsbury & Harrow Railway, which in 1874 was authorized to lay a further five and a half miles, taking in Harrow-on-the-Hill, where a fine Queen Anne style station was erected. This project also included a new connection with the Midland Railway at Finchley Road. As the Underground network grew, so it doubled its connections with the main-line companies. This was simply good sense, as the latter's long-distance passengers and the former's commuters would often wish to use the other's services.

Still the Metropolitan pushed outwards. After its amalgamation with the Harrow & Rickmansworth Company, it reached Pinner in 1885 and Rickmansworth in 1887. 'What could be the object of carrying the line through a district consisting of only farms and fields?' asked a contributor to a local paper. As many contemporary photographs demonstrate, much of this far-flung building was indeed speculative. The Bakerloo extension to Stanmore in the 1930s involved laying a line through fields, not housing estates filled with potential customers. The railways were deliberately encouraging builders to buy land in these now well-connected sites, and relying on the continued expansion in London's population. Previously the Great Eastern had encouraged the middle classes to move to the suburbs by offering free season tickets to house builders in their areas. In 1889 the Metropolitan reached Chesham and two years later took over the Aylesbury & Buckingham Railway, until then part of the Great Western. Clearly the company potentially saw itself in main-line terms.

Indeed, the Metropolitan Railway differed in many respects from its modern counterpart. Not only was it steam-operated in these districts, it also fulfilled some of the functions of a conventional railway company. It operated freight services to London, running milk trains every morning from outlying districts to supply the capital. A Metropolitan milk van, No. 3, has been restored, lined out in yellow, decorated with the company's shield and put on display at Covent Garden. In addition, the Metropolitan ran trains akin to the expresses of the other major companies. For the Aylesbury schedule there were two Pullman coaches, 'Mayflower' and 'Galatea', both put into service in 1910 and operating until 1939. In common with other Pullmans they remained the property of the Pullman Car Company, passengers being charged a supplement of 6d. between London and Rickmansworth, and 1s. further north. It is odd to think of these luxurious chocolate and cream cars working over parts of the present Underground. The Metropolitan also had a number of 'Dreadnought' coaches, long compartment carriages similar to some suburban stock operating from the various London termini.

Having constructed their lines into the countryside, the Metropolitan began encouraging the development of these well-connected fields. With peace restored in 1919, low fares were introduced and an expensive advertising programme initiated. A Metropolitan Railway Country Estates Committee was formed to sell land and build houses. An advertisement published in the 1930s for new houses built on Cuckhoo Hill Estate, Pinner, 'the City man's ideal suburb', proclaimed that it was only eight minutes' walk from the station, while schools, tennis courts, bowling greens and spacious gardens were provided. By 1939, 4,600 homes had been constructed on their lands. The new suburban areas were christened 'Metroland' after the railway company which had deliberately fostered their growth. Wembley, formerly a hamlet, grew after the iron rails had touched its borders. Its population rose from 10,277 in 1881 to 31,217 in 1911, and by 1961 had reached over 124,000.

Among the lasting and interesting features of Metroland and the other inter-war suburbs are the novel station designs which these inter-war years produced, offering a sharp contrast to the earlier Victorian brick edifices and the Edwardian exuberance of Green's buildings. They were simple clean-lined structures, exploring unusual shapes and the latest engineering possibilities. Those of the 1920s tended to be plain, symmetrical buildings with few outstanding features, often finished in stone and incorporating shops or small confectioners in their overall plan. Morden, opened in 1926, is a good example. The stations of the 1930s tended to be more adventurous and were generally constructed from brick with generous areas of glass. Arnos Grove (designed by Adams, Holden and Pearson in 1932) on the Piccadilly Line has a high oval booking hall with columns of windows breaking up the central brick rotunda, topped by a level roof. A low flat frontage, forming a horizontal foundation, completes the design. Other stations constructed in a similar style included Chiswick Park, Rayners Lane, Uxbridge, Cockfosters, Park Royal and West Acton. Taking an electrical conductor as the basis for its design, Southgate Station also boasts a shopping precinct. Dollis Hill, completed in 1949, transported these principles into the post-war era. With the use of large areas of glass divided into smaller panes, a strong stress on horizontals and an obvious use of brick and concrete with little adornment, it offers an example of continuity.

There are three London termini whose almost total reliance on commuter traffic has set them apart from their main-line counterparts. They are Broad Street, Marylebone and Fenchurch Street. Each formerly offered express services to distant towns, but these have since been re-routed or abandoned as a result of nationalization or post-war closures.

BROAD STREET AND THE NORTH LONDON RAILWAY

The first of these three is probably the saddest. Broad Street Station is the very model of decaying and faded elegance, as its truncated train-shed encloses a despondent though still inspiring scene. The building was constructed from light grey-ochre bricks, and patterned with red and dark blue. The massive roof columns taper to reveal delicate leaf scrolls at their capitals, which seem to reflect the overgrown sections of disused line, for only five platforms remain in use, about half the original number.

The whole building was constructed in Lombardic style by the North London Railway's engineer William Baker and completed in 1866. The administrative assistance rendered by the London & North Western Railway is reflected in the terminus's decorative monograms, the N.L.R.'s on the right and the L.N.W.R.'s on the left. From the outside, the twin mansard roofs balancing a higher, central clock tower, still decorated with bands of ornate ironwork, create a splendid impression. A fine arched staircase climbs up the east side taking passengers from street level to the concourse. The station was constructed

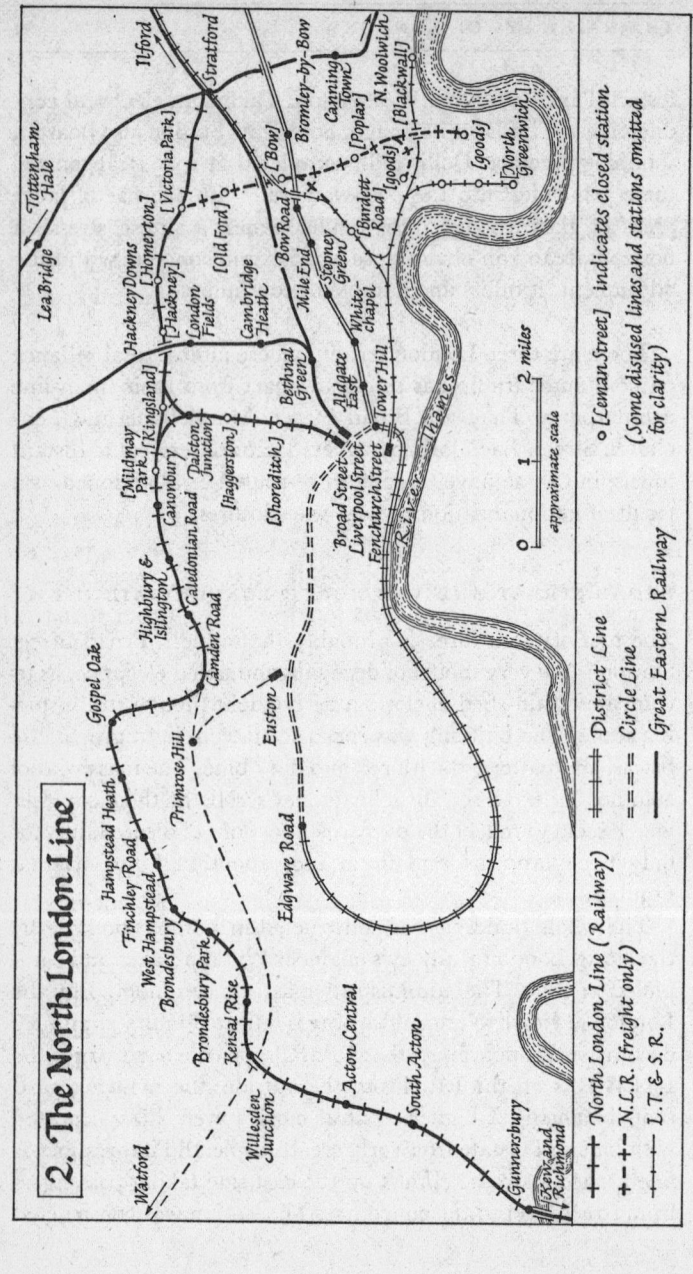

2. The North London Line

on two levels. The area beneath the platforms and to the west was used as a goods station. Massive Doric cast-iron pillars supported the upper section while hydraulic lifts were installed to lower wagons from the main line to the ground-level sidings below the main train-shed.

Broad Street Station, though dirty and in poor repair, has remained an impressive structure, dominating the adjacent Liverpool Street terminus. It is surprising that the latter has continued to be an important and busy station, while Broad Street has declined, belying its outward appearance. In the first year of its operation (1865), 14 million passengers passed through its entrances. After Liverpool Street and Victoria, it was the third busiest terminus in London. Today it merely offers two services – a regular twenty-minute schedule to Richmond and a rush-hour service to Watford. Formerly, there was an eastward extension from Dalston Junction to Hackney, Homerton, Victoria Park, Old Ford, Bow and Poplar, while from 1910 to 1915 a businessman's special was operated daily to Wolverhampton via Birmingham. A luxurious dining car and typists were among the facilities offered by the L.N.W.R.

There was also a southern branch, the West London Railway, from Willesden Junction which ran to St Quintin Park and Wormwood Scrubs Station, Uxbridge Road and Addison Road (now called Kensington Olympia) and joined the District Railway at Earls Court and West Brompton. From here trains travelled over the Inner Circle to Mansion House, not more than a couple of miles from their departure at Broad Street. Unfortunately the line ceased regular passenger operation in October 1940, though there is an early morning and evening service from Clapham Junction to Kensington Olympia along the former West London Extension Railway. (Like the W.L.R. it was jointly owned by the L.S.W.R. and the L.N.W.R.) In addition, District Line trains run on the W.L.R. from Kensington Olympia via Earls Court to High Street Kensington during exhibitions. The track north to Willesden Junction is only used for motorail, special and freight trains, as both Uxbridge Road

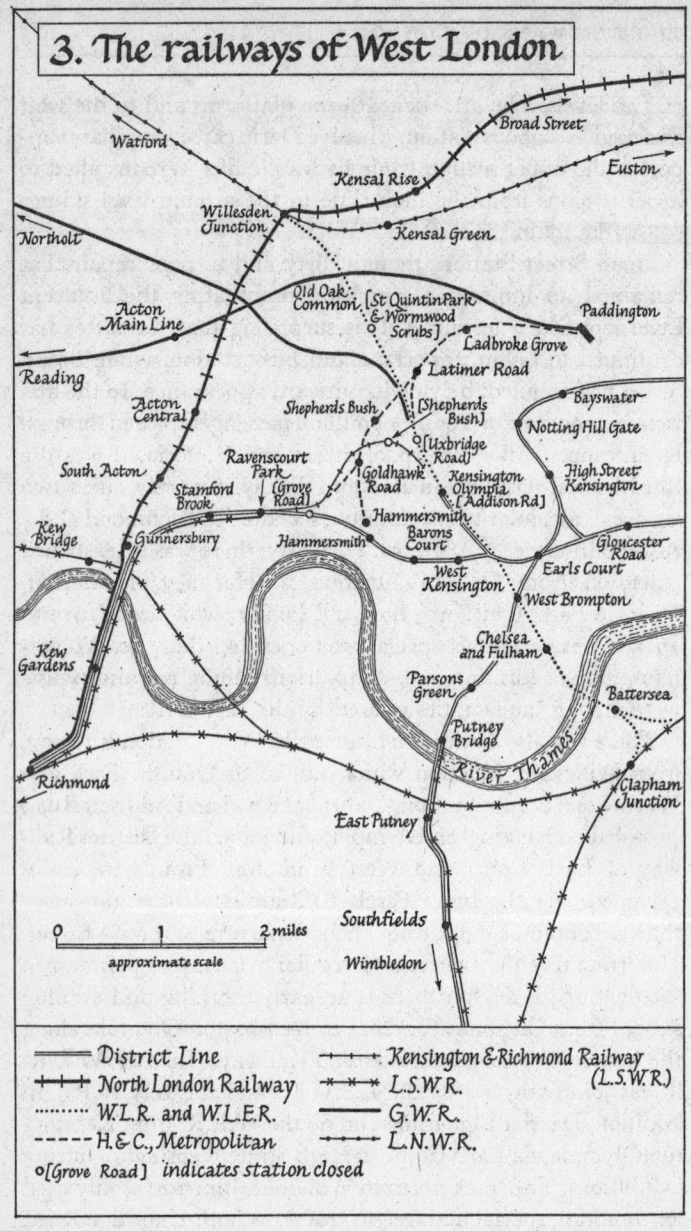

and St Quintin Stations have been demolished. Similarly the stations on the W.L.E.R., at West Brompton, Chelsea & Fulham (lying between the King's and Fulham Roads, with an entrance in Wandon Road), and Battersea have been pulled down, though there are a few archaeological remains.

There was an extension from the Hammersmith & City Railway (now the Metropolitan from Paddington to Hammersmith Broadway) at Latimer Road to the West London line. The spur (see Map 3) is still visible at the far end of the station, where the brick viaduct divides and runs for ten yards in the direction of Shepherds Bush. For the first year of its life, 1864-5, the Hammersmith & City was worked by Great Western broad-gauge locomotives, but the Metropolitan took control in 1868 and the third rail was lifted.

There was another spur from the viaduct section between Goldhawk Road and Hammersmith, which connected with the Kensington & Richmond Railway, just before the now demolished Grove Road station. This divide is also visible at the north end of the engine sheds at Hammersmith, and is marked by a dilapidated wooden signal box. Down below in Trussley Road there remain the brick bridge foundations and embankment which formerly carried the Kensington & Richmond Railway to its junction with what is now the Metropolitan, which meant that it was possible to travel direct from Paddington to Richmond. To complete the picture, the Kensington & Richmond Railway was operated by the L.S.W.R., and ran south-west from here to share the route with the N.L.R. and District to the Thames at Richmond. East from this junction (see Map 4) the line cut under the Metropolitan and continued to Shepherds Bush Road, where there was a station. Then the line curved south to join the W.L.R. just north of Addison Road (Olympia) Station. The route is easily distinguished by the modern buildings which have been constructed along its former trackbed, and in Richmond Way there is a former L.S.W.R. sign proclaiming a three-ton weight restriction for vehicles crossing the bridge. In fact, the brick supports and the

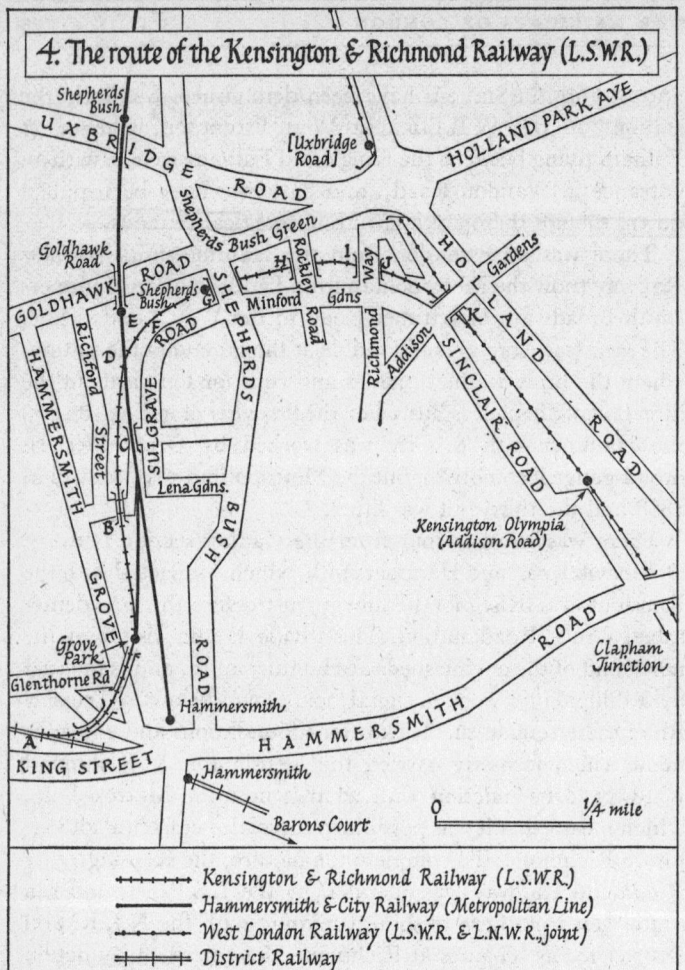

4. The route of the Kensington & Richmond Railway (L.S.W.R.)

++++++ Kensington & Richmond Railway (L.S.W.R.)
──────── Hammersmith & City Railway (Metropolitan Line)
·········· West London Railway (L.S.W.R. & L.N.W.R., joint)
≠≠≠≠ District Railway

A Brick viaduct, partially demolished
B Brick foundations of a railway bridge
C Disused signal box
D Viaduct opening filled in
E London Transport Bus garage on site of line
F 'Railway cottages' in Sulgrave Road
G Remains of railway bridge and hump in road
H L.S.W.R. weight restriction sign
I L.S.W.R. sign and bridge remains
J Office block on former trackbed
K Junction under Addison Gardens Road bridge, now a car park

main iron girders are still visible from the entrance to Kensington House. These B.B.C. offices stretch from here to the junction with the W.L.R. under the Addison Gardens road bridge. It was possible, therefore, to take a single train from Richmond to Waterloo, via Shepherds Bush and Clapham Junction. The intricacy and very comprehensiveness of the late-nineteenth-century rail network reveals how heavily Victorians relied on trains for their daily transport.

The North London Line, as it is now called, provides one of the most interesting rides across some of the most diverse areas of the capital. Indeed, it was originally built by the North London Railway Company, supported by the L.N.W.R., to capture the increasing numbers of commuters travelling into the centre from their suburban homes. Consequently it cuts a somewhat circuitous route, taking in the richest and poorest districts. From Broad Street the line passes north over arched brick viaducts through the now disused stations at Shoreditch and Haggerston to Dalston Junction, the first stop. There is a Dickensian flavour about this section of the line. Large Victorian warehouses, factories and offices dominate the scenery, while soot-blackened brick cuttings alternate with chimney-lined roofs, back walls and blocks of flats. There is a magnificent high-level crossing after Caledonian Road Station, where the N.L.R. runs at right angles to the main line from King's Cross. The Gothic outline of St Pancras stands out against the misty London panorama.

Camden Road (formerly called Camden Town) is one of the largest high-level stations. It was one of those rebuilt in 1873 to the designs of E. H. Horne. Selecting the Venetian Gothic, a style made popular by Ruskin, he constructed a number of confident structures in light-ochre Suffolk brick dressed with white Portland stone. Camden Road is an important junction on the North London line, controlling the branch to Primrose Hill and Watford and constituting the western terminus of the Stratford and North Woolwich d.m.u. service. Even so only two of the four platforms are used today. Platform 1 has retained its original cast-iron columns and brackets together with the decorative valancing.

At Camden the line runs parallel to the Regent's Canal and the locks are visible. There are semaphore signals in use throughout the route, their red and white arms and lattice structures offering a fine sight. These are much in evidence at Gospel Oak junction where the line circles round the base of Parliament Hill, a short but pleasant stretch of green before Hampstead. A tight, vertical brick cutting funnels the train out of Hampstead Heath Station into a long dark tunnel. On emerging, the passenger is presented with a new and refreshing type of scenery, as the Brondesbury and Kensal Rise area boasts detached Victorian villas with generous gardens. Tree-lined leafy banks present a pleasant view. Looking back from Kensal Rise, the rural scene is more akin to a countryside branch line than a bustling City-commuter route.

The character of the line becomes more industrial near Willesden. Here the tracks are lifted over the main line from Euston and the busy junction with its depots and sidings is left for suburbia again as the train swings south-west to Acton. From Gunnersbury the trains use the same tracks as the District Line, crossing the Thames and passing on to Kew and Richmond. The bridge over the river is an interesting structure. Although almost entirely of iron, it has been designed as if it were constructed from carved stone, featuring decorative pillars with foliated capitals and intricate scroll work. The picture here is similar to that at Brondesbury, large detached houses with green spaces and quiet tree-lined streets.

Acton Central (formerly plain Acton) has recently been cleaned and renovated. Strictly speaking, it is on the Northern & South Western Junction Railway which was laid from Willesden to join the L.S.W.R.'s line at Gunnersbury – now imperceptibly part of the North London Line. The present station was also built in the latter part of the nineteenth century by the N.L.R. to the design of Horne. Constructed from light-ochre brick in a restrained Italianate manner, Acton Central has survived almost unchanged. Situated adjacent to a park, with original columns and valancing, it has the timeless, relaxed atmosphere of an authentic Victorian suburban halt. This short railway also had a short branch from South Acton to a terminus called Hammersmith and Chiswick, on the Chiswick High Road. Though the grassy trackbed survives for most of its course, the latter section which runs under the District Line from Stamford Brook is now a car park, and the terminus has recently been demolished.

The eastern half of the North London Railway was entirely closed to passenger traffic, while continuing to be used for goods trains. In May 1979 the section from Dalston Junction to Stratford was re-opened so that the service from North Woolwich could be extended to Canonbury and terminate at Camden Road. Hackney Station (re-named Hackney Central) has re-opened, and a new halt near Victoria Park, now called Hackney Wick, has been built. Hackney Central, which survives virtually intact, was another of the stations, rebuilt by Horne in Venetian Gothic and said to be the only British stations executed in this style.

Homerton Station in Barnabas Road is not so well preserved. All that remains are the brick foundations, an ornate gas lamp bracket with the stanchions and hand rails guarding the pavement edge outside the former entrance. Victoria Park has disappeared with the construction of a dual carriageway, as has Old Ford Station, though a new footbridge over the line offers a bleak view of the latter's brick platform supports. Bow Station and the locomotive works to the south have been pulled down. The railway passes beneath Bow High Road, so the buildings were constructed across the lines, with flights of steps leading down to the platforms. The broad brick cutting suggests that there were sidings here as well. Only a few stone capitals, the cobbled driveway and substantial blocks of wall and bridge remain. Devons Road survives as a footbridge over a grass-covered island platform, while the final stop, Poplar, is just as dilapidated. The entrance buildings in East India Dock Road have been demolished and the frontage partially covered by advertisement hoardings, and the platforms below are covered in a jungle of bushes.

The murder of Thomas Briggs by Franz Müller when travelling on the North London Railway in 1864 aroused great agitation, as the victim might have been saved if he had been able to summon help. Coaches on the line were fitted with separate compartments without a communicating corridor, as are some Southern Region carriages today. Following the outcry, some companies pierced the wall between compartments with a circular window, these holes being nicknamed 'Müller's lights'. A contemporary cartoon in *Punch* showed a woman about to adjust her hat, thinking the window to be a mirror, while 'an impertinent young man' on the other side grins at her surprise and embarrassment. A N.L.R. six-wheeled carriage has been restored by the Quainton Road Society, near Aylesbury, while the company's Directors' Saloon (1872) is on display at York. The only N.L.R. locomotive to be preserved is on the Bluebell Railway, No. 116 (L.N.W.R. No. 2650), an 0-6-0T built in 1887.

Although the Camden Town to Victoria Park (now Wallis Road) section is over N.L.R. metals, the second half of the service to North Woolwich, from Stratford, is in former Great Eastern territory. The stations at Canning Town, Custom House and Silvertown have been tastefully rebuilt, while a new island platform and connection with the District and Metropolitan Lines has been opened at West Ham. Stratford Market (in High Street) is the red-brick station lying disused after Stratford itself. However, North Woolwich terminus is the pride of the line. A splendid Italianate building completed as early as 1847, it is a symmetrical two-storey structure with rusticated round-arched windows and Tuscan columns, topped by lighter tri-partite windows. North Woolwich is unusual in that the tracks end at a depressed circle (which presumably once held a turntable) rather than at a rectangular buffer stop. Most of the route is through dockland, beside the Lea Navigation, along the Royal Victoria, Royal Albert and King George V Docks, offering a varied panorama of refineries, cranes, warehouses, power stations and rows of Victorian terraced housing.

FENCHURCH STREET

One of the oldest and least changed of London's termini is Fenchurch Street. The original building, completed in 1840, served the broad-gauge London & Blackwall Railway though eight years later its cable trains were replaced by standard-gauge steam locomotives. The station's catchment area was progressively extended eastwards. In the 1850s a line was laid to Southend and Tilbury, while connections were also made with the Eastern Counties' routes. Throughout the latter part of the nineteenth century, the docks were being enlarged and the construction of new warehouses and factories along the river added to the business of the London, Tilbury & Southend Railway. As a result Fenchurch Street developed as one of London's busiest stations, handling around 24 million passengers annually at the turn of the century. Unfortunately, the post-war period has witnessed the progressive closure of the Port of London and a reduction in the number of commuters using the railway.

The building itself largely dates from 1853 and was designed by George Berkeley, the L.T. & S.R.'s engineer. It is a simple, symmetrical structure, which, like King's Cross, reflects its function. A row of tall windows, interspersed with pilasters, are topped by a curved clock pediment, while below this a wooden zig-zag canopy provides last-minute shelter for passengers leaving the booking hall. The ticket offices are at street level and on each side attractive cast-iron flights of steps lead upwards to the concourse and platforms. The whole building was constructed in grey-ochre bricks with cream stone adornments. It has recently been cleaned and repainted and so presents a pleasant sprightly gateway to London's eastern suburbs and its traditional holiday resort, Southend.

MARYLEBONE

Marylebone completes the trio of London suburban termini and is the most recent, having been built in 1899 by the Great Central. Originally the railway had its terminus at Canfield Place, near Finchley Road. The two-mile extension to Marylebone was bitterly opposed by the residents of St John's Wood and the M.C.C., forcing the company to construct three lengthy tunnels. Although it handled expresses from Manchester, Sheffield and Nottingham, Marylebone seemed destined to become a commuter station. It was planned that its three platforms should be doubled (hence the wide concourse) but lack of cash prevented this expansion. Today there are only suburban and local d.m.u. services to Aylesbury, High Wycombe and as far as Banbury (see p. 206).

The Great Central Hotel, which was built to face the Marylebone Road and is still linked to the station by an attractive glazed awning, has since become the main offices for British Rail. The railings outside the terminus continue to display the company's monogram cleverly worked into their design. These initials were often adapted to express their railway's supposed characteristics and in view of the speculation in their shares, the Manchester, Sheffield & Lincolnshire Company was said to have stood for Money, Sunk and Lost, while G.C. meant Gone Completely. Marylebone's station bar has a finely preserved interior, retaining the original moulded ceiling, panelling and ornate mirrors.

4 The Great Western

Although this chapter covers part of the territory formerly operated by the L.S.W.R., it is primarily concerned with those routes belonging to the Great Western. The L.S.W.R.'s lines to Devon are discussed in the next chapter. Of course, the G.W.R. extended its tentacles well beyond the south-west of England, an important area of its business being in Wales and the Borders. The company also ran trains into the Midlands and had stations at Birmingham and Wolverhampton, while one of its lines reached Nantwich, via Market Drayton.

The Great Western was not noted for its commuter services. It was primarily a main-line company operating expresses to the holiday, sporting and business centres of the south-west. In addition, it was responsible for a large number of rural branch lines. Many of these have been closed, but a few (the Dart, Torbay and West Somerset Railways) have been re-opened by preservationists, and together with those still run by Western Region they offer a splendid way of viewing a variety of picturesque scenery.

PADDINGTON

Paddington Station is a building of considerable interest, little having changed since it was completed in the mid nineteenth century. It is a terminus which has witnessed much history. Special trains left Paddington for royal functions at Windsor, Londoners travelled from here in their droves to the new

Cornish resorts, troops in both world wars used it as an embarkation point, while more recently the first High Speed Trains were operated from this terminus. The three-sided clock mounted above Platform 1 has seen all these developments.

The station's essential structure and fittings have scarcely altered since the completion of the train-shed in 1854. It was designed by Brunel, assisted by his friend Matthew Digby Wyatt, who had been closely involved with Joseph Paxton, the architect responsible for the Crystal Palace. His influence is apparent. It is a light, airy structure originally consisting of three glass-filled iron vaults. The roof has been subsequently modernized, though early photographs and engravings give very much the same overall impression. Brunel's original terminus, near Bishop's Bridge, no longer exists. It was sited on a line with the old goods depot – the long dun-coloured building visible to the right as trains depart.

In 1839, from the first terminus, there were only fourteen departures a day. By 1855 this had risen to twenty and in 1903 there were thirty-nine local and sixty-four main-line trains daily running from Paddington. Consequently the station was progressively enlarged. There were extensions in 1878, 1884 and 1893, and in 1915 another vault containing a further three platforms was added. One of the best ways to try to imagine a Victorian Paddington, when Sir Daniel Gooch's broad-gauge locomotives were heading expresses, is to look at W. P. Frith's famous picture *The Railway Station* (1862), in Royal Holloway College. Frith shows the clamour of an important terminus in 1862. A husband and wife, escorted by relatives, depart for their honeymoon, schoolboys are packed off by their mothers, two Bow Street runners arrest a suspect, an army sergeant says goodbye to his daughter, while a foreign visitor puzzles over a tip for a cabbie. The impressive roof is captured in detail, and its appearance only differs from today's in its gas lamps.

Today the station's façade is an uninspiring sight. Even the hotel in Praed Street, built between 1851 and 1853 by P. C. Hardwick, is a restrained symmetrical structure. When opened it was one of the largest in the country and was significant architecturally in being one of the first buildings to exhibit a French Renaissance influence, particularly in the mansard roof. The pediment sculpture is by John Thomas and illustrates peace, plenty, industry and science. The road entrance to the train-shed from Praed Street is brightened by the company's coat-of-arms placed at the top of the archway, and the shields of London and Bristol placed side by side serve as a reminder of the Great Western's first trunk route.

Until 1892, when the third rail was lifted, Paddington contained both broad-gauge and standard-gauge tracks. It is also an Underground station; the very first service of the Metropolitan Railway ran from here to Farringdon (see pp. 56–8). When in October 1868 the Metropolitan completed its southern extension from Edgeware Road to the District Railway at High Street Kensington and Gloucester Road, a new station called Praed Street (now Paddington) was connected to the terminus by a passageway.

THE SUBURBAN SERVICE TO READING

Although the railways were originally conceived in order to link major towns, they soon came to perform a different though related function. Brunel's original brief was to construct a line joining London to the port of Bristol. A fast and efficient transport system would, the directors believed, earn good dividends from freight and passengers. But as events proved, the places which the rails touched en route came to have unforeseen value. Between Paddington and Reading a string of smaller (though not always tiny, as in the cases of Slough and Southall) stations were built to cope with the growing demands of commuter passengers. Historical research has shown that railways were usually a response to the growth of suburban England and not initially its cause. Stations were constructed where Victorian builders had already laid down villas for the increasingly prosperous middle classes. These travellers preferred to live away from the soot and grime of the expanding metropolis, and to spend their leisure hours in a rural setting. Those who could afford the price of a season ticket, and the higher cost of these houses, were the mainstay of the Great Western's customers between Paddington and Reading.

However, as Francis has pointed out in his early *History of the English Railway* (1851), Brunel's task in constructing this section of line was not a simple one. In addition to engineering difficulties, there was opposition from local vested interests. An unusual source of protest was Eton College. The masters believed that it would be injurious to the discipline of the school and dangerous to the morals of the pupils, and, it was added, 'anybody who knew the nature of Eton boys, would know that they could not be kept from the railway'. Others argued that passengers might be suffocated in tunnels or burned in carriages. Slopes were magnified into precipices, engines likely to be upset and necks sure to be broken. In fact, this stretch of line is one of the smoothest in Europe, with only the very slightest gradients. Eventually the opposition was allayed and the railway painstakingly constructed by gangs of navvies. It is paradoxical that they should have been given this name, as they were originally called 'navigators' for their work on the canals. The new railways, faster, more efficient and initially cheaper, were to prove to be the instrument of death for a number of waterways.

Travelling from Paddington to Reading there are many stations of note. First is the now disused Hanwell. It serves as a slightly dilapidated reminder of what a Great Western station looked like. Built on the famous Hanwell viaduct, it is still painted in the company's livery of chocolate and cream. Edward Churton, author of the *Railway Book of England* (1851), described this viaduct as 'a noble piece of architecture'. His work traces the routes of the major railways for the traveller and describes points of historical interest along the line. Pausing at Slough, he noted, 'although in the immediate vicinity of numerous wonders of nature and art, this spot has no remarkable feature beyond the station...'. His comment is an indication of the railway's importance in Victorian England, not only as a means of transportation.

The Great Western generally favoured the Italianate style for their stations and good examples survive at Taplow, Maidenhead and West Drayton. When Slough Station was rebuilt in 1879 the company experimented with the French Renaissance manner with splendid results. Two sets of red brick buildings were constructed on either side of the line, the southern being a smaller version of the main entrance opposite. They each feature three curved mansard roofs with elaborately framed bull's eye windows and decorated with ornate ironwork. The original glazed awnings are supported by slender foliated columns. The broad platforms illustrate Slough's continuing importance as a commuter station, while one serves as the terminus for the branch to Windsor.

'Just after passing the Slough Station,' Churton continued, 'is a short branch to Windsor and Eton.' In contrast to the L.S.W.R.'s Riverside royal station (1851), constructed by William Tite in Gothic style, the Great Western replaced its original train-shed in 1897 by a much grander French Renaissance building. The western side of the building was reserved for royal visits, and a luxurious waiting room was constructed solely for this purpose. The rooms featured a stained-glass cupola, panelled walls and a finely carved chimney breast, being furnished with a writing desk and comfortable sofas. Unlike most waiting rooms, their purpose was for people to await the arrival of passengers rather than a train. When Slough telegraphed that the train had switched on to this branch line, the officials would prepare to receive the monarch and guests with due ceremony. During Edward VII's reign the station was constantly in use as he entertained at Windsor Castle to repay the hospitality he had received in European courts.

The telegraph was first operated on the Great Western in 1843 between Paddington and Slough. A series of wires was run through iron pipes laid at the side of the line. The device, having proved successful, was extended and improved, the company being the first to appoint a telegraph superintendent – in 1855. Stations were also constructed at Maidenhead on the Thames, and at Twyford. Turner's famous painting *Rain, Steam and Speed* (in the National Gallery) depicts one of Gooch's Firefly class engines racing over Maidenhead viaduct through sleeting weather.

A few of the engines which worked these suburban trains from Paddington to Reading have been preserved. The classic design first produced by G. J. Churchward (Chief Mechanical Engineer for the G.W.R. between 1902 and 1921), and then modified by his successor C. B. Collett, was the 2–6–2 tank engine. It was a compact and efficient engine, designed specifically for short-distance runs, but powerful enough to haul crowded commuter trains at good speeds. The Great Western Society based at Didcot has one 61xx class locomotive, No. 6106, built in 1931. A selection of the less luxurious second- and third-class carriages used on these runs may also be seen restored to their fine chocolate and cream livery at this depot.

Nowadays, of course, these trains are operated by British Rail's diesel multiple units, based at Southall. In fact, the Great Western experimented with diesel-powered coaches in the inter-war years. Their first 'autocar' was introduced in December 1933. They were partly built by the A.E.C. company, builders of London's buses, at the Park Royal Coachworks. The first were designed as single-car units with a streamlined bodywork and curious dummy buffers. These trains were remarkable in that they had a buffet, toilets, luggage compartment and forty-four seats all in the one carriage. Railcar No. 4, which had been used between Cardiff and Birmingham, is preserved at Didcot. A more adventurous type, consisting of two motor cars attached at either end to a regular carriage, was introduced in 1941. After tests between Southall and Westbury (with stops at Slough, Reading, Newbury, Bedwyn and Patney), they continued to operate into the 1950s with a good deal of success, and may be seen as precursors of the modern diesel multiple units.

THE GREAT WESTERN   89

There are two branch lines running from the main line between Slough and Reading: from Maidenhead to Marlow; and from Twyford to Henley. The second is a particularly pleasant route, calling at Wargrave and Shiplake, while Henley is a delightful red-brick terminus situated by the river and in the town itself. The train-shed was designed by Brunel and the brick offices were added in 1857, though it has since been partially modernized. These two services are worked by diesel multiple units and connect with suburban schedules from Paddington.

READING TO DIDCOT

Reading is the first major station encountered by the traveller out of Paddington. Sited close by the River Thames it has developed into a complex junction of lines. The Southern Region connects here with a branch from Guildford and Reigate. This line is now electrified and its multiple units are easily distinguished from the Western Region's diesel-powered engines. The station buildings themselves, built in the less ostentatious Italianate style from sienna and light ochre-coloured bricks, are not particularly distinguished. Reading, as well as being a major passenger and goods transfer point, has extensive marshalling yards for the suburban services. Outside the station the main line divides, one section heading south to Taunton and the West Country (to which we shall return), the other, Brunel's original project, proceeding along the Thames valley to Didcot and thence to Bath and Bristol.

The line then passes through Pangbourne, another station situated on the banks of the meandering Thames, to Goring. This area is the point where Brunel dug into the white limestone of the Chilterns to form an impressive steep-sided cutting. Cholsey, in Oxfordshire, soon follows, with its single-track line to neighbouring Wallingford (now closed).

Didcot is the next station on the line. It is an important junction, linking the former Great Western routes west to

Bristol and north to Oxford, Worcester and Hereford. Consequently, the area has a triangular configuration, with a central locomotive depot situated to the north of the station. Though the old watertower was in use in the latter part of the nineteenth century, the depot itself is relatively new, having been laid down in 1932. It was used by the Great Western and then British Railways as a locomotive storage and maintenance yard until 1967 when the conversion to diesel power rendered Didcot obsolete.

Since then the Great Western Society has taken over many of the sidings and buildings for the preservation of former G.W. engines and rolling stock. From their foundation in 1961, they have built up an impressive collection of locomotives, No. 6998, *Burton Agnes Hall*, No. 5900, *Hinderton Hall*, and No. 7808, *Cookham Manor*, completing their medium-powered engines. In addition, there are two Castle class locomotives in the process of being restored, No. 5029, *Nunney Castle*, and No. 5051, *Earl Bathurst*. There are a number of goods and suburban or local engines of which No. 5322, a 2-6-0 dating from 1910, is the oldest. The Society also possesses a broad range of G.W. coaches and freight vehicles. The splendid rakes of chocolate and cream carriages are passed by Oxford-bound trains which by-pass Didcot Station. A turntable has recently been installed and the sidings have been extended. Situated in the centre of this B.R. triangle, the Society has direct access to the main line and has been able to run steam excursions to Worcester.

SWINDON, BATH AND BRISTOL, CHELTENHAM

Twenty-four miles of fast straight running separate Didcot from the famous railway town of Swindon. Early in the Great Western's history, 'the necessity of providing an increased stock of locomotive engines, carriages and wagons', together with 'large repairing shops', gave rise to Swindon's prominence. Operations on this scale called for an expansion in the town's workforce, and hence the company's willingness 'to arrange for

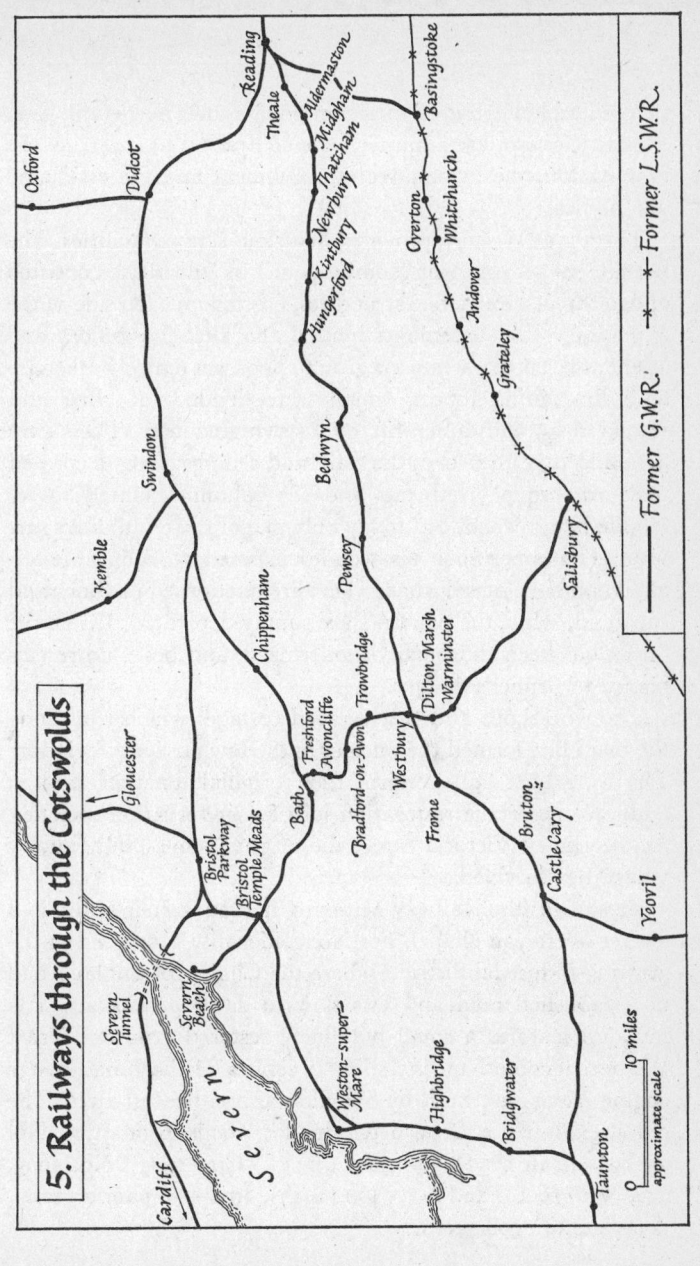

the building of cottages' to accommodate their new employees. Messrs Rigby of Westminster were contracted to construct the new station, the locomotive establishment and the estimated 300 houses.

The Great Western provided luxurious station facilities. The permanent refreshment rooms, opened in July 1842, consisted of two three-storey stone structures, erected on each side of the main line. The basements housed the kitchens, offices and attendants' rooms, while the ground floor was entirely taken up with the dining rooms, which were divided into first and second class, with a central, oval serving counter. They were magnificently furnished, the walls and ceilings being decorated with arabesque ornaments and the columns painted to resemble inlaid wood, but today only one of these buildings survives. The upper floor has been left exposed, revealing the original honey-coloured stone. There are unadorned pediments at each end, while the windows are simply decorated. Inside the buffet has been thoroughly modernized, and bears no resemblance to Brunel's designs.

The workshops and the terraced cottages which run along the main line formed the nucleus of the town of New Swindon. The workshops still perform their original function, and in addition undertake restoration jobs for preservation societies. At the end of Victoria Street the original stone-built railway village has survived.

Close by is the Railway Museum, housed, rather aptly, in a former Wesleyan chapel. For Nonconformity prospered in the growing industrial districts where the Church of England had no established hold and was slow to develop missions. The museum features a small but finely restored group of Great Western locomotives, including a replica of the broad-gauge engine *North Star*, built by Swindon apprentices in 1925. The oldest exhibit is a Dean 0–6–0 tender, goods locomotive, No. 2516, built in 1897. No. 3717, *City of Truro* (1903), No. 4003, *Lode Star* (1906), and No. 9400 (1947), an 0–6–0 pannier tank, complete the collection.

City of Truro has been the centre of a controversy for many years. The Great Western, and subsequently its enthusiasts, claimed that it was the first steam engine to run at over 100 mph (in 1904 while travelling between Plymouth and Bristol), predating the *Flying Scotsman*. The recording was made by a specialist on the train. Unfortunately it is an unconfirmed timing, and must in the light of similar experiences remain an unlikely suggestion. There is no doubt, however, that this journey was completed in exceptionally fast time for the period.

The museum has more to offer than just locomotives. There are G.W.R. ticket machines and the company's distinctive black and white signs. Lamps, models and signalling equipment make up the collection. There is a coffee pot designed as a scale reproduction of a Gooch engine, with the percolator ingeniously situated in the firebox. It was once used in the refreshment rooms, where it is said to have served unpleasant-tasting coffee. Brunel himself is reported as saying, 'I have long ceased to make complaints at Swindon. I avoid taking anything there when I can help it.' Clearly part of British Rail's catering reputation is based on a historical tradition.

The line divides at Swindon. Travellers for Gloucester and Cheltenham have to take the local train via Kemble, Stroud and Stonehouse. Kemble, constructed in Cotswold stone and featuring bay windows and Gothic arches with the original iron columns and valancing, is an exceptionally attractive station. The route between Kemble and Stroud is delightful. After Sapperton tunnel, the line winds down the valley, along tree-lined slopes, through the villages of Lynch, Chalford and Thrupp. In winter, after snowfalls, long icicles hang from the tunnel roof. Here the line has been converted to single track so that on one side these stalactites of ice, no longer disturbed by passing trains, form a ghostly stretch of sparkling light. The Cotswold scenery and the domestic architecture are an additional attraction, while the Thames & Severn (or Stroudwater) Canal runs by the side of the railway through the hills. Stroud has a stone engine shed which still proclaims an advertisement for the Great Western.

The other line from Swindon proceeds westwards to Chippenham. Because the Cotswolds lie in its path, this section has been the subject of considerable engineering works. Scarcely one of its thirteen miles is within ten feet of the original surface of the ground. Viaducts, tunnels, cuttings and embankments were Brunel's solution to this most difficult stretch. The most impressive engineering feature is probably Box tunnel. Work was begun as early as 1836. As in so many of these enterprises, the excavation was hampered by underground streams, pumping engines having initially proved inadequate. Box tunnel was finally completed in August 1840 and the whole section of line opened in June of the following year. It is 3,212 yards long and many have claimed that the sun shines along its full length on Brunel's birthday. This seems unlikely, though it might occasionally be a happy coincidence.

The entrance to Bath, along a curving viaduct over the River Avon, is impressive. The station and its approaches, situated at the foot of the town, provide a splendid view of Bath's Regency terraces as they rise steeply up the valley side. Great efforts were made by both the Kennet & Avon Canal and Great Western Railway to soften their intrusion. The Kennet & Avon Canal was later purchased by the G.W.R. and subsequently neglected. The proximity of canal and railway is particularly apparent between Reading and Pewsey, on the line to Exeter, where the two often take parallel courses, demonstrating why the Great Western should wish to take over their competitor. The bridges, cuttings and the various buildings were carefully designed to blend with the surrounding architecture, and were constructed, at some expense, from local stone. There is a fine walk along the canal tow path under its company's offices and past the locks which bring the cut down to the Avon itself. The railway skirts the grounds of the Holburne Museum, from which many photographs of Great Western locomotives have been taken. The grounds are now part of a public park, making for the easy viewing of modern diesels as they race past.

Brunel's station at Bath was originally a covered affair, built in Gothic style. The roof resembled a Tudor baronial hall, rather like his station at Bristol. It had a span of 50 feet, covered four rails, and was supported on each side by a row of cast-iron columns, inconveniently placed within four feet of the platform's edge. However, most of the station has since been rebuilt in a more conventional fashion.

Bristol Temple Meads is not far up the line. Brunel's station, much smaller and less grand than its successor, stands at right angles to the present entrance. This was a larger version of Bath Station, having a false 'hammerbeam' roof with a span of 72 feet and covering seven tracks. A sector-table was provided at the end of the arrival line to release the incoming engines, and there was also a traversing frame inside and several turntables outside the terminus. The west end in Temple Gate, still visible, has an ornamental Gothic façade, behind which was situated the boardroom, the offices of the Bristol committee and a residence for the station superintendent. Towards the close of the nineteenth century increased traffic necessitated the rebuilding and expansion of this station. This larger addition was designed by Sir Matthew Digby Wyatt (Brunel's assistant at Paddington) and completed in 1878. Temple Meads was constructed from local stone in Tudor style with a central and highly ornate clock tower, to blend with the more restrained Gothic of Brunel's first terminus. Inside the long curved platforms are reminiscent of York.

In addition to Temple Meads and Parkway, Bristol has its own local service with a number of suburban stations. The railway to Severn Beach (originally called Avonmouth Town, a terminus with a through line, now lifted) takes a circuitous route through east and north Bristol, calling at Lawrence Hill, Montpelier, Redland and Clifton Down, the last being the most impressive, with Gothic stone buildings and an ornate iron footbridge. Avonmouth and St Andrew's Road serve the docks, mills and refineries which lie along the estuary. Severn Beach, like Southend or Tynemouth, was a resort for day trippers with its own funfair and amusements, but has recently declined.

Bristol, as the terminus of the Great Western's first trunk route from London, has strong associations with Isambard Kingdom Brunel. It was here in their docks that the S.S. *Great Britain*, now salvaged from the Falkland Islands, was constructed and is now undergoing extensive restoration. No. 5069, a Castle class locomotive, was named after Brunel, but because his three names took up so much space on the name plate it was decided to cast a special large-radius board. This was fitted at Swindon and the experiment was photographed. Unfortunately the design looked ungainly, contrasting strongly with the gently curved lines of the splashers. The letters were removed and fitted to a longer version of the traditional plate and the photograph was filed away marked 'not to be published'.

The 'Cheltenham Flyer', which operated between Paddington and Cheltenham, via Swindon, was the Great Western's fastest train. The inaugural run on 9 July 1923 was hauled by No. 2915, *Saint Bartholomew*, an engine which continued to be selected for this famous speed run. The service's selling point, aimed at the racegoers who regularly travelled on the train, was that it was then 'the fastest train in the world'. There were various specially staged runs to secure record-breaking times. One in 1932 was designed to cover the 77.3 miles between Paddington and Swindon at an average of over 69 mph. In 1929, the Great Western had succeeded in getting the average speed for the journey up to 66 mph. But then in 1931, the Canadian Pacific timed a crack train at 68.9 mph and the Great Western felt impelled to reply to this challenge. They succeeded in July 1932 in producing an average of 69.2 mph for the journey, while in the following September, to emphasize the point, No. 5006, *Tregenna Castle*, hauled a train of 190 tons in just 56 minutes 21 seconds, at an average speed of 81.6 mph. Consequently, the schedule was revised to operate at over 70 mph and stay well ahead of their Canadian rivals. Towards the end of the decade the Great Western lost supremacy in speed when the streamlined engines of the L.N.E.R. and the L.M.S. closed for battle in the 'race to the north'.

DIDCOT TO HEREFORD

The line north to Hereford via Oxford and Worcester was completed comparatively late in the Great Western's history. This was due not to any lack of enterprise on the railway company's part, but to the natural conservatism of the university town. It is difficult to appreciate today how novel the railways were for the Victorians. Not only were they a dynamic element in their economy, but they also exerted a powerful influence on the whole fabric of society and became popular symbols of progress. To the reformers they were instruments of improvement (their construction, for example, through older industrial towns often resulted in the destruction of slums), and to one eminent thinker, Dr Arnold, they were 'destroying feudality for ever'.

To Oxford's city fathers and college fellows they were viewed as a damaging influence. They might destroy the cloistered calm regarded as essential for this studious city. Though plans for a branch line from Didcot to Oxford were published as early as 1833, it was not until 1843 that parliamentary consent was secured. There was still opposition from the Corporation and 300 inhabitants, but this was said to have been organized by the canal company, which rightly feared railway competition. Accordingly, the new station was an unimpressive affair. Constructed in wood, it was sited out to the west, well away from the university and town centre. A newer station was completed in 1852. This too was a rather dull building, again constructed largely from timber, and has since been replaced by a standard British Rail design. Seasoned travellers will no doubt remember the former station's exceptionally low platforms, making disembarkation a tricky maoneuvre.

In fact, the first line to the city, opened in June 1844, was constructed by the Oxford Railway Company, a protégé of the

G.W.R. This was developed by the Oxford, Worcester & Wolverhampton Railway (nicknamed the 'Old Worse and Worse'), which was eventually absorbed by the Great Western in 1863. In addition, the L.N.W.R. had laid a branch to Oxford from Bicester, Bletchley and Bedford. Though closed in October 1951, their original timber terminus, situated parallel to the present station down the slope towards the city centre, is still extant. Painted blue and white, it is now a garage, serving the form of transport which captured so much business from the railways in the post-war era.

Once the line from Didcot to Oxford was open, the logical move was to extend it to Worcester, Birmingham and Wolverhampton. It was not without a struggle that the Great Western was able to link the three cathedral cities, Hereford, Worcester and Oxford, to the metropolis and introduce the service which operated on this line, 'The Cathedrals Express'. Having agreed to buy out the projected Oxford, Worcester & Wolverhampton Railway in 1844, Brunel and the directors set about raising the cash to build the line. It was not a simple matter. The country was still in the grips of the deep depression of 1842 and money for new enterprises was difficult to procure. Disagreements and wrangles were the pattern for the next six years, so that it was not until October 1850 that the first section was opened linking Worcester with the Midland Railway at Abbot's Wood. In fact the line was not completed until June 1853, though the opening had been celebrated by the directors in the previous May when they had travelled along the railway from Dudley for a champagne lunch at Evesham, ending the day with a sumptuous dinner at Oxford.

Worcester is a city with strong Great Western associations. It was here that Sir Daniel Gooch, Brunel's first locomotive superintendent, spent much of his time, as his uncle lived in Worcester and his father was buried just outside the town in a country churchyard at Claines. Gooch was selected at the early age of twenty-one to be Brunel's locomotive designer. The gamble paid off and he produced the highly successful Firefly class engines. With the establishment of Swindon works, under his supervision the Company was able to produce the engines it needed and became noted for its reliability and speed running.

As we have seen, the new railways were important in moulding the shape of Victorian society. The county cricket championship, for example, could never have developed without their ability to transport large numbers of people quickly and cheaply around the country. Until the railway era sport had remained largely a local matter, with neighbouring villages competing against each other. It is no coincidence that the establishment of a host of county cricket and divisional football clubs corresponded with the multiplication of train services and stations between the late 1850s and the 1870s. Excursion trains were an essential element in nationwide sports championships and one of the reasons why Worcester has a county cricket ground. Areas well served with train services – Lancashire, Derbyshire, Nottingham and Yorkshire, all regions noted for their railway history – have first-class sides. Hereford, late to obtain a railway connection, is not included in these fixtures.

Today the line between Oxford, Worcester and Hereford is one of the prettiest in the country. Worcester Shrub Hill Station is a pleasant railway junction. The main buildings, completed in 1865, are faced in hard blue-black bricks and cream stone dressings, while a long, curving drive leads up to the *porte cochère*. There is a splendid cast-iron Victorian waiting room on Platform 5, patterned with a broad range of decorative tiles. The line to Hereford is carried by a high embankment and viaduct to Worcester Foregate Street Station in the city centre. The train then crosses the River Severn, offering a fine view of the cathedral, the city itself and the distant cricket ground.

The line then runs on to the Malvern hills, skirting round their edge to Great Malvern Station. This is constructed from local purple-brown Malvern rag and is dressed in a lighter honey-coloured stone. Designed by E. W. Elmslie in 1862, its style was described as 'French Gothic'. The columns have highly detailed, floriated capitals and brackets, while its outstanding feature is the clock tower and delicate spirelet, mounted on the slate roof. The adjacent road bridge is constructed in the same manner, as is the Imperial Hotel, which was connected to the station by a covered way, visible on the 'up' side. Great Malvern must be among the most attractive branch stations in England.

Though Hereford (see p. 228) was one of the last major towns in the country to be connected to the railway network, it is now a centre for steam preservation. Bulmers have established an impressive depot here. Their railway centre is part of the Midland Railway's Moorfields depot, and connects with the first two lines to be laid to the city. The first was from Newport and Abergavenny, operated by the Great Western and opened in 1853, while the second, constructed in 1864, was part of the Midland system and ran west to Wales and east to Worcester.

The pride of Bulmers' collection is the ex-Great Western express locomotive No. 6000, *King George V*. Completed in July 1927, this engine was the first of the King class designed by Collett. The ever faster running times achieved on the East and West Coast Routes created great pressures on mechanical engineers to produce quicker and more powerful designs. This class was the Great Western's bid for a share of this prestige. Within a few weeks of leaving Swindon, *King George V* was shipped to America to represent Britain in the centenary celebrations of the Baltimore & Ohio Railroad. The brass bell and medallions on the cab sides are mementoes of this visit. After a total of thirty-five years' service comprising nearly 2 million miles' running, No. 6000 was withdrawn from service in 1962. Bulmers undertook its restoration in 1968.

There are two other main-line locomotives on show here. There is No. 35028, *Clan Line*, a Merchant Navy class engine from the Southern Railway. *Clan Line* was actually built under British Railway's auspices in 1948 and so has been restored to that livery. Each of the Merchant Navy class was named after a shipping line and features their flag on each side of the boiler,

An interesting feature of these modern steam engines is the amount of cab protection which they offered the crew. As we have seen, Victorian locomotives at first had no covering at all, but then developed a small cab with open windows. These later engines have a tender with a roof which extends over the coupling to give all-round coverage for the driver and fireman.

The third express locomotive at Hereford is No. 6201, *Princess Elizabeth*, from the L.M.S. Built in 1933, this engine was restored and repainted in crimson-lake livery in 1969. There is also a former G.W.R. pannier tank, No. 5786 (1930), one of a number of 0–6–0Ts purchased from London Transport, where she had been numbered L.92. There are five Pullman carriages preserved here, which formerly worked 'Golden Arrow' and 'Bournemouth Belle' trains.

ROUTES TO THE SOUTH-WEST

The railways had an important impact on the use of leisure in Victorian Britain. For they made it easy for people in large and growing numbers to travel away from their homes. Trains were quick, and Peel's 1844 Act, enforcing the operation of a regular third-class service, made them cheap as well. The novelty, the association with progress, the wonder of the steam engine itself, encouraged the growth of the system. Railway companies saw the financial possibilities. County newspapers in the 1860s and 1870s regularly advertised special trains running to well-known resorts, such as Scarborough, Blackpool, Harrogate, York, Brighton and Windermere. Much of this section, therefore, is concerned with the rise of Devon and Cornwall as tourist centres, and the development of the Great Western's services throughout these areas. The company eventually came to operate some of the best-known and most prestigious holiday trains, taking Londoners to the beaches and sun of the south-west.

The 'Cornish Riviera' was the G.W.R.'s outstanding express and today is the best-known on Western Region. The service was originally conceived in 1904, when a train was planned to run from Paddington via Bristol to Plymouth, some 246 miles in 265 minutes. To achieve these swift times a certain amount of modification to existing tracks was required. The G.W.R. route to the south-west had been nicknamed the 'Great Way Round', suggesting that efficiency was not always the governing factor. So strong was the demand for a quick train to the resorts that the directors began the new service before all the modernization had been completed. The first express left Paddington at 10.10 on the morning of 1 July 1904.

The *Railway Magazine* latched on to its popularity and set up a competition to select a name for the new service. 1,286 entries were received. The G.W.'s General Manager, James Inglis, judged the winner. He chose the title 'Riviera Express', which had been suggested by two entrants. Other names included 'Cornish Riviera Ltd' and 'The Royal Duchy Express', while one contributor to the magazine humorously proposed 'The Inglisman'. It is not certain whether the title 'Riviera Express' was ever actually used, as the present name was quickly adopted for the official nameboards on the carriage roofs. In the first timetables, the train was booked as 'The Plymouth, Falmouth and Penzance Special', but to the railwaymen who operated the service it was known as the '10.30 Limited', from its new departure time – today it leaves almost an hour later, at 11.25.

The train originally consisted of six coaches, including a dining car, but with its growing popularity and the technical advances made in locomotive design, the number of carriages was increased, rising to seven or eight in the first summer of operation. Fortunately the 4-4-0s and Atlantics heading the 'Cornish Riviera' were still able to haul its weight to Exeter unassisted, while the heavier gradients past Newton Abbot demanded a further engine. The service was noted for its luxury and smartness, the engines being specially prepared, and cleaned to a high standard.

In fact, the 'Cornish Riviera' was all part of a deliberate plan by the Great Western to profit by the growing popularity of the south-west as a holiday area from the latter part of the nineteenth century onwards. As the general rise in the standard of living had given more people the cash, and factory legislation had given them the opportunity, so city dwellers generally were able to take longer and more expensive breaks in the summer. People of middling wealth could now afford a week or a fortnight in the hotels of the south-west. As the Great Western's publicity programme of the inter-war years shows, this was still an area of growth. One slightly spurious poster compared the geographical shapes of Cornwall and Italy, and suggested that there was an even greater similarity in their climates. The 'Cornish Riviera' captured the popular imagination. A stylized poster entitled 'Speed to the West' depicted a King class racing against a backcloth of sunny clouds, with a number of the luxurious 'Ocean Specials' behind – a stirring and striking picture designed to appeal to the contemporary spirit.

To encourage this interest the G.W.R.'s publicity department published a number of magazines and guides. Their *Holiday Haunts* was produced from 1906 to 1947, being halted only by wartime. It contained over 300 pages in 1906 and over 1,000 at its peak in 1927. Sales were large – 100,000 copies were sold in 1908, 200,000 between 1928 and 1931. It was never dearer than 6d. and provided holidaymakers with details of where to go, which hotels to stay in and what to see. In addition, the company published a number of serious books designed to encourage interest in the area, including Sir Charles Oman's *Castles*, M. R. James's *Abbeys* and S.P.B. Mais's *The Cornish Riviera*.

From 1900 a whole series of guides had been published by Baedeker, Nelson and Murray. These handy, compact books, each covering a specific region, took railway routes as a basis for their visits and tours. The intricacies of the various company timetables, hotel facilities, and historical and scenic points of interest were all discussed. Folding maps indicated the whereabouts of stations and cross-country walks for the holidaymaker. The entry for Plymouth in the 1901 *Thorough Guide* to South Devon and Cornwall, for example, lists stations and cab fares and provides a street plan. Excursions to near-by villages, coves and market centres were described, with road distances and their railway connections. In the pre-car age these books must have been invaluable to the inexperienced tourist.

An interesting but not unique feature of the 'Cornish Riviera' was its use of a 'slip' coach. This was the means by which passengers could travel to intermediate stations without hindering the progress of an express. Carriages, specially designated, were detached as the train travelled at speed, being brought to a halt by the guard. For its non-stop run between Paddington and Plymouth, slip coaches were provided on the 'Cornish Riviera' for connections to Westbury and Weymouth. Further carriages allowed passengers to alight at Taunton, Minehead, Barnstaple, Exeter and stations on the Torquay line. In addition, this arrangement had the fortunate consequence that the load the engine had to pull became progressively lighter as the steeper gradients of the west were approached.

Other holiday expresses included the 'Cornishman', the 'Torbay Express' and the 'Bristolian'. The last was introduced in 1935 and left at 10 am daily, returning from Temple Meads at 4.30 pm. Specially prepared engines of the King and Castle class were used for these runs. The first of the latter, No. 4073, *Caerphilly Castle*, has been restored to its Great Western livery and is now on display in the Science Museum, South Kensington.

Exeter is the railway centre of the south-west peninsula and has retained all four of its stations: St David's, St Thomas (both G.W.R.), Central and St James' Park (both L.S.W.R., see p. 132). St David's is the most important and has been rebuilt several times to take account of its growth. In 1911–14 the train-shed was removed, leaving only the façade, which has since been obscured by a more recent G.W. canopy and offices. Constructed from local stone with ashlar dressings, it consists of a row of recessed Italianate arches with a disc frieze above. The station lies on a north–south axis, trains for Paddington and Barnstaple leaving from the north and those for Waterloo, Newton Abbot, Paignton and Plymouth from the south.

Exeter St Thomas is the saddest of the town's stations, being the oldest, the most attractive and the one in greatest need of attention. It was designed by Brunel and completed in 1846. It consists of a delightful, two-storey Italianate building which leads up to the stone viaduct carrying the railway through the surrounding district and over the River Exe. Unfortunately the station is obscured by temporary buildings and part has been let out as workshops. The train-shed has been removed and the buildings are in desperate need of attention, though there is a splendid view of the cathedral from the exposed high-level platforms. St James' Park (on the Waterloo line, just outside Exeter Central), situated in a deep grassy cutting, is merely a halt designed to serve the near-by football ground.

The railway between Exeter St David's and Barnstaple Junction is the only remaining example of a rural branch line in Devon. It was constructed by the North Devon Railway (later part of the L.S.W.R.) and completed in August 1854. The line is double-track as far as Crediton, where the original Brunel-designed station buildings survive. Crediton is a pleasant red-brick Gothic 'cottage', with a small signal box and level crossing set away from the town centre. Generally the more substantial station buildings have survived, as at Copplestone, Morchard Road, Lapford, Umberleigh, King's Nympton and Eggesford, which also serves as a passing point. They all had double platforms, but today most have been reduced to one and the second track has been lifted, though the sidings at King's Nympton have steel sleepers with welded chairs. Yeoford formerly commanded Coleford Junction and the route west around the northern edge of Dartmoor to Okehampton and Plymouth, but this line has been closed.

The line now ends at Barnstaple Junction, which as its name indicates was not originally a terminus. The tracks actually

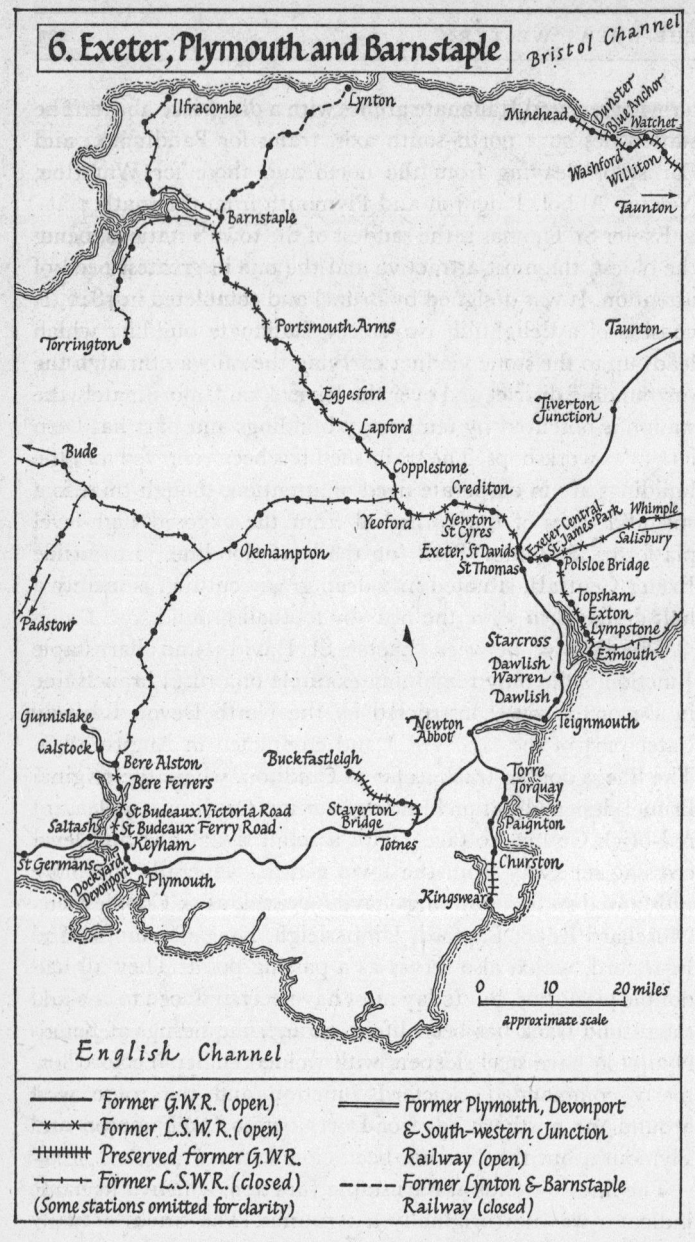

continue (to reverse engines) for half a mile along the former L.S.W.R. route to Bideford and Torrington. The adjacent road bridge spans the disused trackbed, which continued across the River Taw to Town Station. The buildings with their sole platform and awnings still stand in Castle Street, while railings and level crossing gates mark off the gravel trackbed from the quayside. The line ran north to Ilfracombe with another branch to Lynton. A car park has been laid over the northern exit from the station, though the railway's route may be sighted from the disused gantry solitary in the distance. In addition, there was a Great Western station opposite Barnstaple Junction, the terminus for their line from Taunton. The single-track bridge over the Taw stands to the east just outside Barnstaple Station and is clearly visible from the train.

Probably the most memorable stretch of the main line in the south-west is between Exeter and Plymouth. The railway avoids Dartmoor and makes its way around the coast. From Dawlish to Teignmouth horizontal beds of red sandstone have met the sea as impressive steep cliffs. To take his line as far as Newton Abbot, Brunel was forced to construct a stone embankment at their base and tunnel through the largest headlands. It is a spectacular journey of alternating empty darkness and bright waves crashing against a dark red coast.

It was here that Brunel experimented with his atmospheric railway. A tube was laid between the rails and pressurized by stationary pumping engines built at the lineside. The locomotives had a piston which was inserted in the tube and held in place by leather seals. The train was drawn forward by the vacuum in front of the piston and the inrush of air behind. Unfortunately the seals decomposed and frequently tore, causing the tubes to leak. The railway, opened in September 1847, was discontinued in the following year when conventional locomotives were introduced. An original locomotive shed and engine house survives just south of Starcross Station. Adjacent to the main line, this substantial red stone building with Bath stone dressings features an Italianate tower and office buildings. Today it serves as a builder's yard and appears to be all that remains of Brunel's atmospheric railway.

The outstanding engineering feature of the line to Penzance remains Brunel's Royal Albert Bridge at Saltash (just after Keyham Station), spanning the River Tamar. There are two sections, each 455 feet wide, supported on tapered stone pillars. The bridge is carried by suspension chains counter-balanced by the tubular arches above. Unfortunately, cost dictated that it should be single-track. Saltash was opened on 2 May 1859 – one of the last sights viewed by Brunel before his death. Indeed he was so ill that he could only manage to inspect his masterpiece lying on his back while being drawn across it in an open wagon. Once across the bridge, the line curves southwards for St Germans and offers a splendid sight of the Royal Albert Bridge and the naval ships moored at Devonport.

Although Newton Abbot Station lacks architectural interest, it is considerably enlivened by No. 151, *Tiny*, a vertical-boilered 0–4–0WT displayed on Platform 1. No. 151 is the only surviving Great Western broad-gauge locomotive. The branch line to Paignton leaves the main line outside Newton Abbot, swings south through the disused station at Kingskerswell and runs on to Torre.

Torquay is the finest station on the line. Constructed in local grey granite with ashlar dressings, it has retained the original ridge-and-furrow glazed awnings and much decorative ironwork. These elegant buildings are brightened by the carefully laid-out gardens. There is a fairly steep descent to Paignton, the railway running down to the sea, parallel to rows of colourful bungalows. Paignton Station is divided between British Rail and the Torbay Steam Railway (see p. 111), which operates the line south to the original terminus at Kingswear. Paignton is a popular holiday resort, a fact which is reflected in the summer Saturday timetable: there are trains to Sheffield, Derby, Birmingham, Liverpool, Manchester, Nottingham, Leeds and Bristol with a connecting service to London.

Because of Cornwall's thriving tourist industry, the county's principal railways have survived the closures well, though many rural branch lines have been axed. The main line from Plymouth to Penzance is partly operated by H.S.T.s, while the branch lines from Liskeard to Looe, Par to Newquay, Truro to Falmouth and St Erth to St Ives continue to support local d.m.u. services.

An early feature of Cornish railways were Brunel's timber trestle viaducts, which were cheap to build and intended only as temporary measures to serve as long as the line's viability was in doubt. When routes had proved their financial worth, more solid stone structures were erected in their place. For example, the seven-arched Liskeard viaduct (one mile west of the station) runs beside the original ivy-covered Gothic piers. When the timber bridges were demolished, expense again dictated that their stone foundations remain and many late Victorian viaducts still overlook them today. Between 1859 and 1863, there were as many as forty-two timber trestle bridges constructed on the Cornwall Railway from Plymouth to Falmouth and it took a considerable time to rebuild them. The last, the College Wood viaduct at Penryn, was not replaced until 1934.

Liskeard, though a small station, has two separate parts: the through platforms on the Penzance main line, and the terminus buildings for the branch line to Looe. The latter can be a source of confusion to passengers. For although Looe is situated on the south coast, the terminus is placed to the north of, and at right angles to, the main line – pointing in the opposite direction. The explanation is that the branch line curves south-eastwards and passes under the main line before travelling to Coombe, St Keyne, Causeland, Sandplace and Looe.

The railway from St Germans to Lostwithiel was particularly expensive to build. The hilly terrain is dissected by swift-flowing streams, which necessitated the construction of the many viaducts and embankments. For example, Bodmin Road has a picturesque position on a tree-lined valley side. It is a particularly pleasant stretch of railway characterized not only by its viaducts, but by the yellow gorse bushes and rhododendrons which flower along its side. At Par the china clay works and their plateau spoil-pits dominate the landscape, while St Austell must be one of the few British stations to have palm trees growing in its platform beds. It also features an ornate G.W. lattice footbridge dated 1882. Truro, one of Cornwall's largest stations, is approached by the county's longest viaduct (443 yards), which presents a clear panorama of the city, dominated by its spired cathedral. Again the character of the area changes near Redruth. Still a tin-mining region, the scenery is divided up by the tall stone chimneys of disused engine houses.

St Erth commands the junction to St Ives and by contrast has pleasant stone, slightly Italianate station buildings – most of Cornwall's smaller stations are weatherboarded, again a feature determined by cost. Cutting across the narrow peninsula, the railway reaches the southern coast at Marazion (the disused stone station still stands), where there is an uninterrupted view of St Michael's Mount. The approach to Penzance is flanked on the northern side by extensive sidings, sheds and British Airways' heliport and on the south by the sandy sweep of beach which leads around to Penzance harbour. The terminus consists of an unadorned granite-sided train-shed (c. 1865) covered by a shallow crescent iron roof. Longer platforms extend eastwards to accommodate lengthy holiday trains, while semaphore signals still control its operation.

PRESERVED STEAM RAILWAYS

The south-west is an area of picturesque and unusual branch lines, alas now much reduced in number. Many of these local railways were closed after the Beeching Report in the mid-1960s. Fortunately a few have been re-opened by enthusiasts, one of the earliest enterprises being the Dart Valley scheme.

The Dart Valley Railway

This line was closed down by British Railways in 1958. A great deal of work has been undertaken to re-open the railway for passenger operation. The track had to be cleared and repaired, stations renovated, and not least the locomotives and rolling stock restored to sound working order. Today it is largely single-track and runs from Totnes Station to Buckfastleigh.

The Dart Valley Railway relies on auto-coaches and pannier tanks for its basic operation. There are three of the latter: Nos. 6430 and 6435, built at Swindon in 1937, and No. 1638, completed to a Hawksworth design under B.R. in 1951. Another pannier tank, No. 1369, has outside cylinders and was specially produced to work on routes where the curves were too sharp for the larger inside-cylinder variants. Two Collett 0-4-2 side-tank engines (Nos. 1420 and 1450), have been restored, while No. 4920, *Dumbleton Hall*, is being renovated. The railway also possesses two Ocean Saloons, the Great Western's luxury carriages, No. 9111, 'King George', and No. 9116, 'Duchess of York'.

The Torbay Steam Railway

The Torbay Steam Railway runs from Paignton to Kingswear, via Goodrington Sands and Churston. Paignton is now the southern terminus for the B.R. line from Exeter St Davids and Newton Abbot, calling at Torre and Torquay. Closed in 1971, the line was purchased by the Dart Valley Railway in the following year and progressively re-opened. Their finest engine, used for the heaviest of the seasonal summer traffic, is the 4-6-0 No. 7827, *Lydham Manor*. At other times the service is operated by two Prairie 2-6-2 tank locomotives, Nos. 4555 and 4588. It is an exceptionally picturesque railway, running along the coast from Paignton, inland through Greenway tunnel to the Dart valley and Kingswear. Opened in 1864, it was not among the earliest schemes, initially because of its geographical remoteness and later because of the high cost of construction. Viaducts were needed at Broadsands and Hookhills, while the marshy land at Goodrington presented further problems. Improvements were made during the 1920s, when the popularity of Torquay and Brixham as holiday resorts encouraged the strengthening of the track to accommodate King and Castle class locomotives hauling the 'Torbay Express'. However, the post-war era saw a decline in the numbers of tourists travelling to the area by rail and the branch from Churston to Brixham was closed in 1963, the remainder following in 1971.

The West Somerset Railway

Another holiday line re-opened by enthusiasts is the West Somerset Railway, which operates from Minehead to Williton. British Rail ran their last d.m.u. in January 1971, but a preservation society was formed and the line was acquired in 1975. The official re-opening followed in March 1976. The West Somerset Railway is steam-operated from Minehead to Williton and it is hoped to open the remaining section from Norton Fitzwarren for a d.m.u. service.

A G.W. pannier tank, No. 6412, has been purchased from the Dart Valley Railway. In addition, there are two Bagnall 0–6–0 saddle-tank engines, *Victor* and *Vulcan*, while three 'small Prairies' purchased from Barry scrapyards, Nos. 4561, 5521 and 5542, are being restored. The Mark I coaches have been repainted in the company's maroon and cream livery. The line had originally been opened in 1874 and serves as a reminder of the important connection between the railway, increased leisure opportunities and the rise of Victorian holiday resorts.

The East Somerset Railway

The East Somerset Railway is situated at Cranmore, several miles from Frome, a station on the Westbury–Taunton section of the main line to the West Country. Witham, the next station (now closed), commanded the G.W. branch line to Cranmore, Shepton Mallet, Yatton and Bristol. The E.S.R. has purchased about a mile of track towards Doulting, restored the station buildings and constructed an engine shed to Victorian specifications. No. 928, *Stowe*, a Southern Railway Schools class, and two B.R. locomotives (No. 92203, a Standard 9F now named *Black Prince*, and No. 75029, a 4–MT class now named *The Green Knight*) have been preserved and are steamed here.

5 The Southern Region

The area now encompassed by the Southern Region contains one of the most complex railway networks in Europe. Clapham Junction is still the busiest station in the world, though closures have recently affected the system which in its heyday was even more intricate and comprehensive than at present. For example, Crystal Palace, the great exhibition centre of mid and late Victorian England, was served by two stations and connected by lines coming from five directions. Of course, the existence of four major companies competing for traffic produced an unnecessary duplication of routes, which has since been rationalized by British Rail. Yet one of the reasons why the Underground has barely touched south London (the lines to Wimbledon, on L.S.W.R. tracks, and to Morden are the exceptions) is the wide coverage provided by the electric suburban network.

Though the Southern is primarily known today for its commuter services, it does have a fine tradition of express running. Continental boat trains and holiday Pullmans to the south-west were important features of former timetables, and even if motorways and cheap flights to Europe have undermined this aspect of the region's working, these distinguished passenger trains are worth recalling.

The Southern remains a curious mixture of old and new. It has an impressive range of Victorian and Edwardian stations, tunnels, viaducts, cuttings and junctions which preserve much of the atmosphere of the old steam service. However, it was the first of the post-1923 companies to adopt electric traction. The application of electricity was the really modern feature of the inter-war years. As steam power had symbolized progress in the Victorian age, so electrical energy suggested modernity in the 1930s. In tune with this, the Southern Railway proceeded to electrify its suburban network. By 1939 their task was virtually complete, while many trunk routes to the coast had also been converted. Today the Southern's system and stock appears dated when set beside the new 'Great Northern' trains operating from Moorgate, or against the main-line services from Euston to Manchester and Scotland. Hence, the region remains one of interesting contrasts.

VICTORIA

The imposing, though somewhat discontinuous, buildings which confront the traveller at Victoria today are not the earliest which have stood on this site. The first station, opened in 1860, a timber and brick structure with a wooden palisade in front, was built with economy in mind. The expense of extending the existing lines from the south over the River Thames, and enclosing them in a tunnel to prevent pollution, cost the L.B. & S.C.R. and L.C. & D.R. (London, Brighton & South Coast Railway, and the London, Chatham & Dover Railway) so much that an expensive stone and steel structure was out of the question. Though this building was described as 'temporary', it did in fact last some forty years. The station was divided in two, with separate entrances for the Brighton and the Chatham services. The former was considered superior because it had associations with the Royal Pavilion and the Regency spa, while Chatham was a naval dockyard. Wilde, in *The Importance of Being Earnest*, mitigated Worthing's shame at being found in a handbag at Victoria by the fact that he had been found on the Brighton side, and hence was probably of middling status.

In 1899 the two railway companies combined, though they retained their outward distinctions. By the early 1900s it had

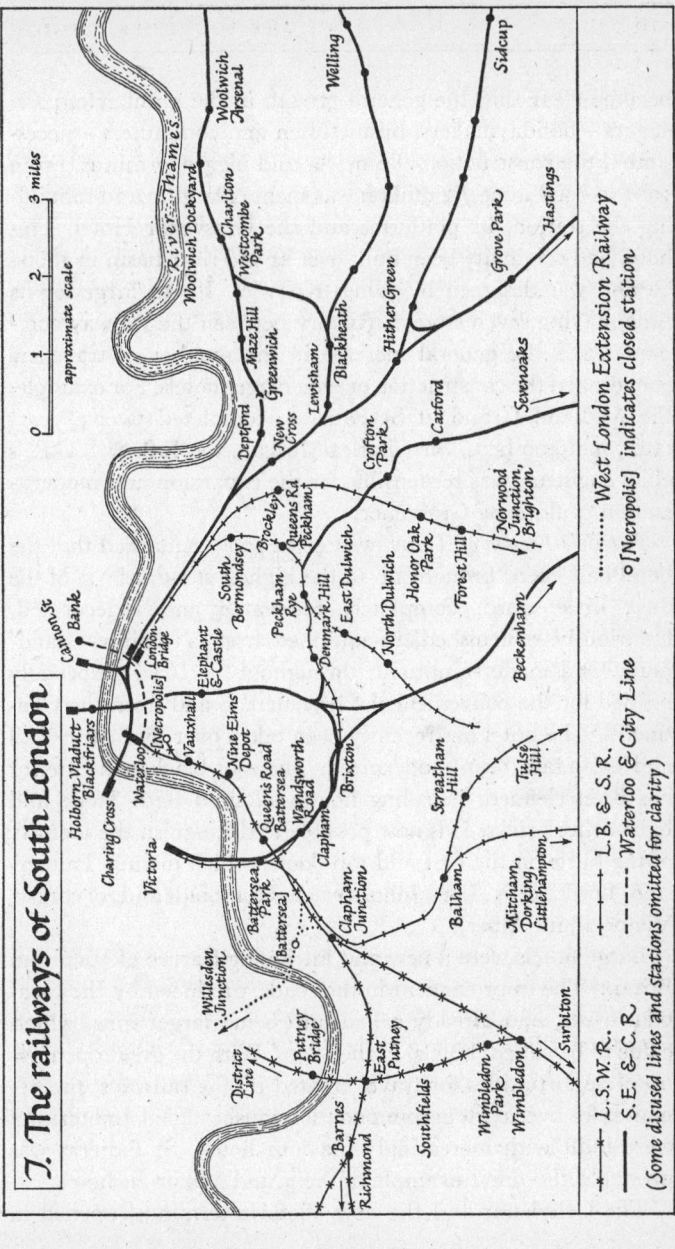

become clear that the general growth in the number of passengers – holidaymakers, businessmen and commuters – necessitated the construction of a newer and bigger terminus. From 1902 to 1908 some £2 million was spent enlarging and rebuilding the station, its platforms and the Grosvenor Hotel. This hotel had originally been built over an old river basin in 1860–62 and was designed by James Knowles. It was large for its time, having seven storeys. Rivalry between the railway companies and the general increase in the number of travellers encouraged the construction of even bigger hotels. For example, the Midland Grand at St Pancras, completed twelve years later, had 400 beds. Sir Charles Morgan, the L.B. & S.C.R.'s chief engineer, was responsible for the expansion and modernization of the new Grosvenor.

Pascoe's *London of Today*, written in 1903, remarked that the hotel had been 'brought up to the highest standard . . . of the day; in a word, completely renovated and redecorated, luxuriously refurnished, re-equipped from a sanitary standpoint, and made sumptuous throughout . . . It was especially needed for the convenience of travellers to and from the Continent.' The hotel has recently been taken over by British Rail and has again been modernized. The soot-blackened exterior has been cleaned, revealing honey-coloured Bath Stone and light-ochre bricks. It is now possible to distinguish the identity of the busts on the first and top floors, which include Palmerston, Lord Derby, Lord John Russell, Humboldt and, of course, Victoria and Albert.

Large hotels were a new and intriguing feature of Victorian Britain. The improvement in the roads, produced by the turnpike trusts, had already called into being larger inns, which came to be called 'hotels' in the 1830s. With the great opening-up of opportunities for travel created by the railways, the demands for overnight accommodation mushroomed and termini were built with increasingly spacious hotels. St Pancras was probably the finest example of the grand Victorian hotel.

The Grosvenor and the new Victoria terminus, opened in

July 1908, presented a varied and imposing sight to Edwardian London. It is a structure which has hardly been altered since. To commemorate the event a new Pullman service was inaugurated, christened the 'Southern Belle', operating between London and Brighton and timed for exactly an hour. The train is now more familiar to travellers as the 'Brighton Belle', the name adopted in 1934. With the national grouping of railway companies in 1923 and the formation of the Southern Railway, the distinction between the two halves of the station was officially dropped. The booking offices and two departure boards continued to preserve this tradition, much to the confusion of travellers, until recently, when they were modernized.

THE 'GOLDEN ARROW' AND THE DOVER LINES

The best known of all the express services which have operated from Victoria must surely be the 'Golden Arrow'. It was an extremely luxurious, fast boat train, running between London and Paris and distinguished from Southern stock by its distinctive chocolate and cream Pullman cars. Indeed, the service's origins lay with the introduction and early appeal of Pullman cars. They were the brainchild of an American, George M. Pullman, who hit on the idea of designing and building exceptionally comfortable luxury coaches and then hiring them out to existing railway companies. So successful was his scheme in the United States that he exported the venture to Britain.

With the growing numbers of well-to-do Londoners taking holidays on the Continent and the south coast, the demand for stylish travel increased throughout the latter part of the nineteenth century. The L.B. & S.C.R. seized on Pullman's American scheme and ran their first carriage in 1875. In 1881 the first train composed entirely of Pullman coaches was operated, while the notion of extending their range to the Continent was debated. In the following year the L.C. & D.R. ran the Pullman carriage 'Jupiter' on its line to Dover, but the experiment was not a success. But 1889 saw the opening of the International

Exhibition in Paris and the matter was raised again. However, the service was not operated with English stock and 'Wagons-Lits' were used on the new trains to Europe. Yet even this extra demand was not sufficient to justify the expense of running such a luxurious train, and it was discontinued after four years.

Meanwhile, the L.B. & S.C.R. had started operating a series of boat trains from Victoria to Newhaven. These were composed of Pullman carriages and proved financially successful, encouraging their rivals to use them on more of their schedules to the south coast. The introduction of a prestige train, consisting in part of Pullman cars, running from London to the Continent was held up by the First World War, and it was not until after the groupings of 1923 that the new Southern Railway could consider the introduction of this now famous boat train. In November 1924 the company began a new Pullman service from Victoria to Dover. This first train consisted of seven Pullmans together with one or two regular first-class carriages and a brake van. It was timed to leave Victoria at 10.50 am and reached Dover at 12.32. The new King Arthur class (4-6-0), designed by R. Maunsell, were used to haul the trains. It had been decided that they should be named after personalities and places connected with King Arthur and the knights of the Round Table. The decision having been made by the board, Maunsell, the designer of this N. 15 class, had to be informed, and Sir John Elliot, the Southern's chief public relations officer, broke the news to the engineer. Maunsell, on hearing the announcement, remarked with fine Irish humour, 'Tell Sir Herbert I have no objection, but I warn you it won't make any difference to the working of the engine.' These original names proved popular and became firm favourites with the travelling public. Some of the more stirring and unusual included: 736, *Excalibur*; 739, *King Leodegrance*; 754, *The Green Knight*; 745, *Tintagel*; 785, *Sir Mador de la Porte*; and 788, *Sir Urre of the Mount*.

In September 1926 the Pullman service was extended to Paris and the French section was christened the 'Flèche d'Or'.

The train left London at 10.45 and reached Dover at 12.23; passengers crossed the Channel to board the 'Flèche d'Or' at 2.10 pm and arrived in Paris at 5.40. In May 1929 the name 'Golden Arrow' was officially adopted for the Victoria to Dover run. The Second World War witnessed the service's suspension and it was not until October 1946 that the train was reintroduced. No. 35001, *Channel Packet*, a Merchant Navy class Pacific, hauled the inaugural train. Initially the service was hampered by the after-effects of the blitz, while the growing popularity of air travel drew away Continental passengers. On 12 June 1961 the first electric-hauled 'Golden Arrow' left Victoria. However, the continuing attractions of the aircraft resulted in a reduction in the number of Pullman cars as the green-liveried Southern carriages occupied an increasing proportion of the train. Finally, on 30 September 1972 British Rail withdrew the 'Golden Arrow', though a number of its Pullmans have been preserved.

Today there are two principal routes to Dover, the first from Charing Cross via Sevenoaks, Ashford and Folkestone, and the second from Victoria via Chatham and Canterbury East. Both lines were part of the S.E. & C.R. network, which spread almost exclusively throughout Kent. Waterloo East, situated at the opposite end of Hungerford Bridge, is the first stop on the Charing Cross route. Its blackened brick viaduct dissects the South Bank between County Hall and the Festival Hall, offering one of the best views of Waterloo's memorial entrance. Chislehurst, where these two routes cross (Charing Cross over Victoria, with connecting spurs between), is an important junction. The station itself is a substantial, Italianate, red-brick structure – the style most commonly selected by the S.E. & C.R. during the nineteenth century.

After tunnelling through the North Downs, the train runs over pleasant countryside to Sevenoaks and Tonbridge, where the line divides, continuing south to Hastings and east to Ashford. Battle (1852) is probably the best-known station on the former. Designed by William Tress in the Gothic manner and inspired no doubt by the proximity of the medieval abbey, it was faithfully executed in dark stone, with light Caen dressings and featured lancet windows, a belfry and exposed rafters in the booking hall. The diesel-electric four-car sets (class 202) which work the Charing Cross–Hastings line were built in 1957 for the special loading gauge and survive as some of the oldest stock on Southern Region. They are distinguished by their straight sides and the louvred engine compartments situated behind the driver's cab at each end of the train.

Ashford Station has been rebuilt, though most of the locomotive sheds remain. Once the site of the S.E. & C.R.'s works, the extensive sidings and yards bear witness to its continuing importance as a maintenance depot. Folkestone still has three stations, Central, West and Harbour, but Junction has been closed; the first, and its viaduct, provide a panoramic view over the town, its martello towers and the distant docks. The journey to Dover is particularly picturesque, offering a largely unspoilt view of the high chalk cliffs, as the line is constructed on a narrow embankment set at their base above the sandy beaches, while a series of short tunnels take it through the headlands – like Brunel's railway between Teignmouth and Dawlish. Finally the line curves around the harbour and cuts north through the cliffs to the town centre and Priory Station.

Dover Marine Terminus (originally called Pier) is the more architecturally distinguished of the two remaining stations. First opened in 1915 for military traffic, its northern elevation is executed in light grey stone on a grand scale. Massively rusticated blocks form the entrance to the light, airy train-shed, still proudly displaying the S.E. & C.R.'s initials. Inside there is a large war memorial (both plaque and statue) to commemorate the company's staff who fell in the First World War. The quay, which lies parallel to the terminus, was designed so that carriages could be shunted directly on to the ferries from the main line.

Returning by the Victoria route, trains climb out of Dover to Kearsney, cut through the scarp slope of the North Downs by

Lydden tunnel and ascend to Shepherds Well. A station was built at Snowdown to serve the local collieries, whose shafts, winding gear and coal tips make an unexpected appearance in the Kent countryside. Canterbury East offers a view of the cathedral, while Faversham, a light-yellow brick structure, is a more interesting station. Here trains from London are divided (and vice versa), one portion continuing to Margate and the other to Dover Marine. A similar process takes place at Ashford, where trains are split between Dover Priory and Margate, via Canterbury West and Broadstairs. Neat apple orchards and hop fields decorated with rows of poles and a network of supporting wires form much of Kent's characteristic scenery in this area. By contrast, Chatham and Rochester, soon after Faversham, provide a panorama of docks, warehouses, timber yards, cranes and boats, while from Bromley South the housing thickens into the dense Victorian suburbia which surrounds central London.

THE 'BRIGHTON BELLE' AND THE BRIGHTON LINE

From January 1933 the 'Brighton Belle' was officially operated as an all-electric train. The opening of this modern service included a civic visit to Worthing by a Pullman unit and a luncheon with the Mayor of Brighton at the Royal Pavilion, while the Pullman Car Company provided a madrigal concert for passengers to mark this special occasion. It was a scheme which had taken three years to complete. In 1929 Sir Herbert Walker (later General Manager of the Southern Railway) had declared, 'Gentlemen, I have decided to electrify to Brighton.' On the face of it, this seemed no great task, as most of the suburban system had already been electrified and was working successfully. However, the significant difference lay in the provision of electrical power over long distances.

A technical solution was found. Engineers designed substations which would work automatically, being overseen by larger units set at greater distances, as the expense of manning each sub-station would have proved prohibitive. The greater cost of electricity, as against coal, was offset by greater efficiencies and the ability to operate longer or more frequent trains. As with the earlier suburban changeover, the opportunity was taken to tailor the track layout to the needs of multiple-unit operation. Stations were lengthened (as at Brighton Central and Hove), and in certain cases rebuilt. Taking advantage of the new electric current, colour signalling was installed over the thirty-six miles from Coulsdon North to Brighton – then a record length for Britain. In the Brighton area six signal boxes with 582 levers were replaced by one electrically interlocked box with a mere 225 levers. Automatic devices were used wherever possible, and a total of twenty-two manual boxes were abolished. In fact, Britain was experiencing something of an 'electrical revolution'. In 1914 electricity was still in a very experimental stage. By 1946 its use had become widespread, and electric heating, lighting and transportation had all become established.

The 'Brighton Belle' and the regular Southern electric stock which also worked the new system were of high quality. The Pullman Company provided first, second and third class carriages. In all thirty-eight cars were needed and these were ordered from Metropolitan-Cammell (makers of London's Underground stock) at a cost of £205,000. Even the kitchens were now operated on electric power. The scheme was a success. Receipts were up by 78 per cent over the Easter holidays in 1933, rising to a peak on the Bank Holiday Monday to 127 per cent. Even the new Southern coaches which ran along this line were well appointed. Contemporary photographs show a plush first-class compartment with well-padded seats, a thick carpet and polished wooden doors. The third-class compartments were not of immensely lower standard. The continued success of the scheme led to the continued electrification of inter-city routes out of Victoria.

Today the L.B. & S.C.R.'s London to Brighton main line still supports a busy and frequent service. The first section from

Victoria to East Croydon is largely through late-nineteenth-century and inter-war suburbia, ending in a complex triangular junction which extends from Selhurst, Norwood and East Croydon itself. This is the omphalos of the L.B. & S.C.R. commuter network. Trains from Charing Cross, London Bridge and Victoria are ensnared in its web of cross-overs, viaducts and branches. The broad areas of rough grass which surround the rising and falling lines complete the railway wasteland – a farm devoted to the cultivation of electric trains. The suburban system is monitored and controlled by the many signal boxes erected by the Southern Railway in the 1930s, and there are good examples at Purley, Balham, East Croydon and Gloucester Road Junction, which serve as distinctive memorials to that period's 'cinema' style of building. The rectangular blocks of light-red brick and concrete have gently curved ends with broad windows on the upper floor, topped by an overhanging flat roof.

The major obstacles to railway construction in the south-east are the Downs. Generally engineers preferred to ascend the gentle 'dip' slope by long, deep cuttings and then tunnel through the sharp 'scarp' slope (see Fig. 8). Accordingly, the railway runs through a series of dark tree-lined cuttings as it makes the easy ascent from Croydon to Coulsdon, entering the Merstham tunnels to pass through the southward-facing scarp. The Charing Cross to Tunbridge Wells line similarly climbs the North Downs by a series of cuttings from Petts Wood to Knockholt, negotiating the escarpment by Polhill tunnel (almost a mile and a half long) to Dunton Green and Sevenoaks.

Special trains are timetabled to serve Gatwick Airport. A new station consisting of three broad island platforms, linked directly to the airport buildings by overhead bridges, was opened in 1958. Although these modern stations have little to commend them architecturally, they are functional and better suited to passengers' needs than many of their Victorian predecessors (other examples are Birmingham International, Heathrow Underground and Tees-side Airport Stations).

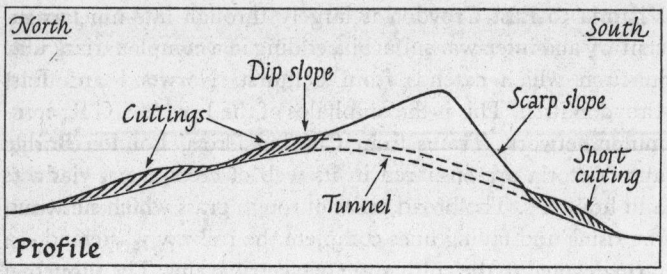

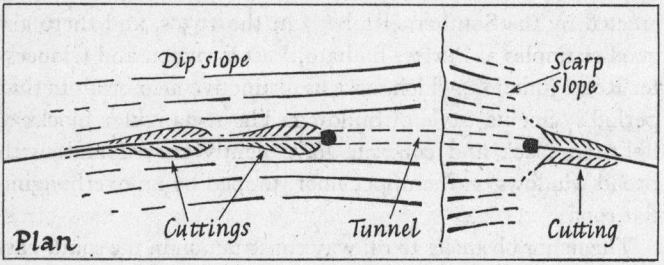

Fig. 8. Diagram of railways through the North Downs.

The finest railway feature in this central area of farmland is the Ouse viaduct (1841), designed by David Mocatta, the distinguished architect, and J. U. Rastrick, the L.B. & S.C.R.'s engineer. Situated between Balcombe and Hayward's Heath Stations, it is a light stone structure consisting of thirty-seven arches adorned in the Italianate style, with four mock pavilions at each end. The scarp slope of the South Downs faces their northern counterparts, so that railway tunnels are sited furthest from Brighton, which lies at the end of the dip slope. Unlike the Ouse viaduct, the northern portal of the Clayton tunnel (scene of a terrible accident in 1861 – see p. 52) was executed in the Gothic manner with battlements and twin castellated turrets.

Brighton was the L.B. & S.C.R.'s southern headquarters. The car park immediately to its west was once the site of the company's locomotive works, while the extent of the sidings and sheds on the approach to the station indicate the former scale of their operations. Rastrick's first Brighton Central was rebuilt in 1883, when H. E. Wallis constructed a curved, double train-shed over the original platforms. The ornate cast-iron columns and brackets bear the Company's arms, and the large four-sided clock suspended over the concourse still carries the L.B. & S.C.R.'s initials. The stately timber tobacconist between Platforms 6 and 7 also dates from the rebuilding.

Brighton Central is an important terminus, commanding the 'east-coast' and 'west-coast' routes across the South Downs to Eastbourne, Hastings, Worthing, Littlehampton, Bognor Regis and Portsmouth. First stop on the east-coast line, London Road, is reached by a curving, round-arched viaduct, which offers a splendid view across the town's terraced streets as they slope down to the seafront. The station itself is a characteristic Italianate design completed in 1877. Lewes, rebuilt in 1889 on the earlier triangular plan, has its Italianate yellow-brick buildings set between the Brighton–Eastbourne line and the branches north to Hayward's Heath and south to Newhaven and Seaford. Polegate (1889) is a sad sight, as the delicate, Italianate station has been isolated by the lifting of the tracks between the island platforms and the entrance buildings. Eastbourne terminus has been restored to its original condition. Constructed from clear yellow brick with red brick and cream stone dressings, it is a substantial structure dominated by a heavily dentilled clock tower and an imposing lantern (as at Lewes). The confusion of scales and styles is unified to a degree by the materials and exuberant treatment.

WATERLOO

Situated on the South Bank of the Thames, Waterloo is one of London's largest and most imposing stations, though it is not one of the earliest. The London & Southampton Railway had originally built its terminus at Nine Elms in 1838, but the gradual extension of its tentacles and the amalgamation of 1845 to form the London & South Western Railway made it clear that Nine Elms was no longer capable of serving the growing volume of traffic. A two-mile extension on a long curved viaduct was completed and Waterloo Bridge Station was opened in 1848.

Throughout the latter part of the nineteenth century the station expanded in a haphazard fashion as more lines were laid and new schedules initiated. When two extra platforms were added in 1879 they were christened 'Cyprus', as Disraeli had just annexed the island for the British Empire. Again in 1885, the new Windsor platforms were nicknamed 'Khartoum', a town then in the news.

In 1899 the L.S.W.R. decided that a more modern station had to be built. Some 700 trains were being handled daily and the crowded system was no longer working efficiently. The viaduct to Vauxhall was widened to accommodate additional tracks, and the new station, designed by J. R. Scott, was finally completed in 1922, the First World War having interrupted the work. Constructed in the grand manner, Waterloo suffers, as Pevsner has noted, from a lack of space, making it impossible to appreciate the majesty and scale of the façade while the line from Charing Cross to Waterloo East runs so close. Inside, the huge sweeping concourse linking up the twenty-one platforms, still dominated by the large four-sided clock suspended from the train-shed, has retained something of its dignity. There were two splendid manually operated departure boards, with impressive columns of destinations. But in the interests of efficiency they have recently been replaced by computer-controlled boards. There were also decorative wrought-iron ticket barriers, featuring moulded hands each with a downward pointing finger to direct doubting travellers to the platform entrances.

An unusual feature of Waterloo's work was its connection with the graveyards near Woking. In 1852 the London Necropolis Company opened a large cemetery at Brookwood. A special station and branch line were provided, the former being paid for by the company in 1864. In addition, they opened their Necropolis Station (the name derives from the Greek '*nekros*', meaning corpse) adjacent to Waterloo in Westminster Bridge Road, where mourners could gather with the coffin for conveyance by special train to the cemetery. With the growth of London's population, the venture proved highly successful. In 1902 a new and grander Necropolis Station was constructed at No. 121. It was a solid four-storey structure, featuring broad Edwardian arches and curiously indistinct *art nouveau* decorations. Contemporary photographs reveal it to be an eerie building, fitted for its purpose. Unfortunately it was bombed in May 1941, though Brookwood, substantially rebuilt at the end of the century, survives.

Waterloo is the only London terminus to operate its own tube. The Waterloo & City Electric Railway, a two-mile underground route to the Bank of England, was opened on 8 August 1898. Naturally the L.S.W.R. were anxious to gain control, and absorbed the line in 1907. Sir Herbert Walker was determined that London Transport should not infiltrate his suburban network south of the Thames. He retained control of the Waterloo & City even though it connected with the Underground. The distinction is still preserved and the rolling stock is painted in B.R. blue with Southern Region numbers, while the ventilators at each end of the carriages proclaim the words 'Southern Railway'. The trains' age – they were introduced in October 1946 – is further indicated by their tiny windows and the dated practice of placing the motors in a separate compartment behind the driver rather than in the bogies themselves.

Waterloo has been the terminus for an impressive number of express services – boat trains to Southampton for the Continent, to Weymouth for the Channel Islands, and the 'Belles' to the south-west and coastal resorts. The 'Bournemouth Belle', running at first only on Sundays, but later on weekdays throughout the summer season, was introduced in 1931. From 1936 its popularity was such that it was operated all the year around. It was usually composed of ten Pullman carriages, though these were often extended to eleven or twelve during peak holiday periods. In addition to these named trains, there were also regular Pullman services to other resorts, including Eastbourne and Bognor.

The line from Nine Elms to Southampton, via Basingstoke and Winchester, was completed in May 1840 and proved to be a popular and prestigious route. Wealthy travellers bound for America or the Far East usually journeyed by train from London to Southampton Docks. The line itself was a real engineering achievement. Gradients were deliberately kept to a minimum, while severe curves were avoided by short tunnels, making for fast and smooth running. Sir William Tite, architect of the Royal Exchange, was commissioned to design the buildings at Nine Elms and Southampton. The latter's Terminus Station, consisting of a central three-storey block with an open balustrade and dentil cornice, flanked by lower, rusticated wings, is a fine classical structure. Unfortunately, air travel has captured most of the liners' business and Terminus was closed to passengers in 1966. However, the building has remained as a communications centre, though of a more ethereal kind: it is now used by B.B.C. local radio. Consequently trains run only to the new Central Station and no longer terminate in the town, but continue to Bournemouth or Weymouth. There is also a regular service to Portsmouth, which, as well as being an important naval base, has developed as the main gateway to the Isle of Wight, being closest to the east-coast resorts. Hampshire play county cricket here, and it is possible to get a free but fleeting view of play from the train as it skirts the ground.

Eastleigh is a railway creation, as in 1891 the L.S.W.R.'s carriage shops, and in 1909 their locomotive works, moved from Nine Elms to these flat lands on the banks of the River Itchen. Built to house the railway workers, brick terraces flank the northern side of the main line. Eastleigh was once an important junction controlling the lines north-west to Salisbury and south-west to Portsmouth. The station's former rising fortunes can be judged by its various additions and the progressive

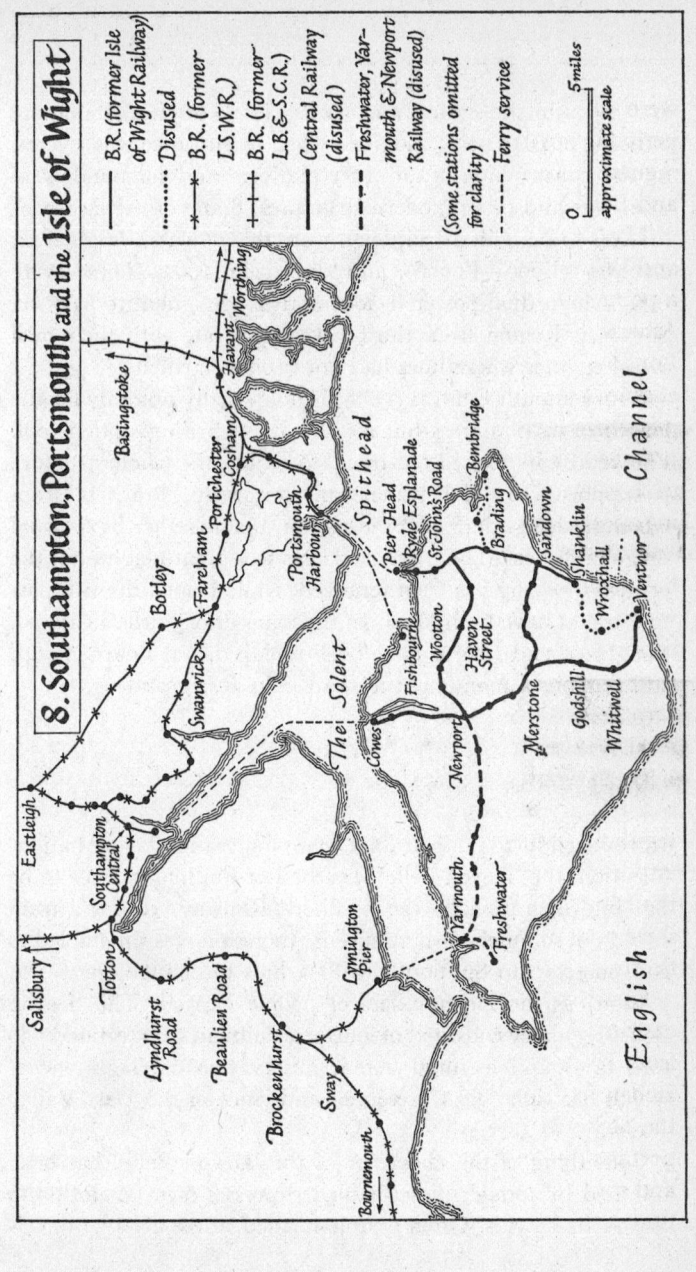

extensions to the sidings and yards, Tite's original Italianate building of 1841 being modified when its entrance was severed by the construction of an outer platform and surrounded by inter-war and more modern structures. Some of the last locomotives to be built at Eastleigh were the 73 class's original six electrics (E6001–E6006), introduced in 1962. These were B.R.'s first dual-powered locomotives designed to run on Southern Region from third-rail supply but with their own diesel engines where lines had not been electrified.

Bournemouth Central (1885) is noteworthy not only for the length of its platforms but also for its surprising station roof. Flanked by buttressed red-brick side walls, the whole structure is supported by rather inelegant decorative brackets, from which lattice girders span the station, tied together by unusual diagonal braces. The train-shed rises to a great height, but the central covering has been removed, while below, the two passing tracks have been lifted. In the manner of Carlisle Citadel, the glazed end screens have been replaced, but Bournemouth still remains a monument to the L.S.W.R.'s grandeur.

WATERLOO TO EXETER

Introduced in 1947, their final year of operation before nationalization, the 'Devon Belle' was the last Pullman service to be put into operation by the Southern Railway. It was a train noted not so much for high speeds (though it was timetabled to run non-stop to Sidmouth, with a halt to change engines at Wilton) as for the numbers of people carried. The 'Devon Belle' regularly consisted of fourteen Pullman cars (around 550 tons tare) and featured a rear observation carriage, one of which has since been preserved and runs on the Dart Valley Railway.

Something of the character of the 'Devon Belle' has been retained by today's diesel-hauled expresses from Waterloo to Exeter St Davids. Often double-headed, these class 33 diesel-electrics offer a pleasant contrast to the electric stock which form the bulk of Waterloo's services, though they cannot compare with the Merchant Navy Pacifics which formerly worked these crowded holiday expresses. The train swings south-west on the broad brick viaduct which channels the lines to Vauxhall, Clapham Junction and on to suburban Surbiton in commuter territory. Beyond Esher Station the railway runs along one side of Sandown Park racecourse, while the section between Weybridge and Byfleet offers a similar view of the derelict Brooklands racetrack and the more modern airfield. Woking, being the terminus for the slower suburban trains, is the first stop. Basingstoke follows and is the limit of electrification, which continues southwards on the main line to Winchester, Southampton and Bournemouth.

The journey from Basingstoke to Exeter, through unspoilt countryside between market towns and villages, is particularly attractive. Rolling grassland devoted to dairy cattle, tree-lined hedges and much original railway architecture present a varied and quintessentially English panorama. Salisbury is a junction (of reduced importance) with spacious island and side platforms, still painted in Southern green and cream and featuring original iron columns and decorative valancing. The disused trackbed which runs parallel to the main line for the first few miles west of Salisbury is the end of the former G.W. line to Westbury via Warminster. The route is operated by B.R. but joins the Waterloo line much further to the west, avoiding the duplication caused by company rivalry.

Tisbury, Gillingham and Sherborne are now the only stations open on the Salisbury–Yeovil Junction section, Wilton, Dinton, Semley, Templecombe and Milborne Port having been closed. Yeovil, where the L.S.W.R. and G.W.R. met, was the key railway junction in Somerset. Today it is a much reduced station, though the twin island platforms with their generous umbrella awnings bear witness to its former importance. Yeovil's situation, well away from the town itself, underlines its function as a junction. Yeovil Pen Mill Station is on the former

G.W. line from Castle Cary to Dorchester, though it no longer connects with the Waterloo service.

Long sections of this main line from Basingstoke are in fact single track with passing points, and this is especially true of the last part from Yeovil to Exeter. Crewkerne is a most unusual station. Constructed from darkened grey-ochre ashlar in a restrained Tudor manner, it consists of a central block with projecting gables at each end, one towering high above the other, with a sharply pitched slate roof and elegant stone chimneys. Crewkerne was designed by Sir William Tite and completed in 1860. It is also thought that he was responsible for Sherborne (1860) and Gillingham (1859).

The train calls at Axminster and Honiton (rebuilt by B.R.) before running into Exeter Central. Originally called Queen Street, the station was rebuilt in 1933, when a parade of shops was incorporated in the plan. Constructed from dull-red brick simply adorned with white stone dressings, it is a typical example of thirties' architecture. The platforms below the station building are set in a broad cutting which also accommodates a goods yard. Exeter Central is a terminus for the d.m.u. service south to Exmouth, via Topsham and Lympstone. A short journey by tunnel through St David's Hill takes the train parallel to the River Exe and on to its destination at Exeter St David's (see p. 104).

The Merchant Navy class Pacifics, which formerly hauled West Country holiday trains, were designed by O. V. Bulleid, the Southern Railway's distinguished chief mechanical engineer. He had worked as an assistant to Gresley for fourteen years, learning a great deal about express locomotive design, but was invited by Sir Herbert Walker to join the Southern as their chief mechanical engineer and accepted the challenge.

After four years' work his new 4–6–2, the Merchant Navy class, emerged. The engine featured a considerable number of mechanical innovations – a welded-steel firebox, a valve motion entirely enclosed in an oil bath in an attempt to reduce regular maintenance and perforated-disc driving wheels. The last, designed to reduce their weight, gave these locomotives a slightly American appearance. Having learnt from Gresley's streamlining experiments, Bulleid designed a modified form of engine casing which he described as 'air-smoothed'. The straight polished lines created by the casing and the tender gave these engines a sleek look. In fact, Bulleid's mechanical innovations meant that they belied their appearance and until modified, the Merchant Navy class were prone to breakdown, needing frequent overhauls. Later in their B.R. careers, the casing was removed to facilitate maintenance. Also their coal consumption was very high. But despite their mechanical drawbacks, crews appreciated the all-round enclosed cabs which provided excellent protection against the elements. To assist the fireman swinging a loaded shovel, Bulleid had provided a foot pedal to open the firebox door.

In order to reduce running costs and eliminate the mechanical troubles, Bulleid designed a lighter, less powerful but more reliable variant, the West Country class. The first of these were introduced in 1945 and were immediately distinguished by their distinctive livery – malachite green with three horizontal yellow lines running the length of the engine and tender, with the word 'Southern' painted along the latter. They were all named and often displayed their town's coats-of-arms as well. The names adopted for the class point to the destinations and landmarks of the Southern's territory: *Exeter, Bude, Ilfracombe, Dartmoor, Westward Ho, Crediton* and *Yes Tor* for example. Some of these also had their casing removed in B.R. days, though smoke deflectors, a feature of the Southern, were fitted. One of the most famous of this class was No. 34051, *Winston Churchill*, the engine used to haul Sir Winston's funeral train in 1965.

In the late 1950s, a group from this class – those named after R.A.F. squadrons, leaders and aerodromes – were withdrawn for further modification. Their casings were removed to give the engines a more conventional appearance, though some drivers argued that this had no effect on their running. In addition, Walschaerts valve gearing was fitted – much to the annoyance of Bulleid. Apart from various Squadron numbers the 'Battle of Britain' class had other distinctive names, including *Fighter Pilot, Lord Dowding, Biggin Hill, Spitfire, Anti-Aircraft Command* and *Manston*.

Suburban Services

Suburban Britain and the railway systems which connect these areas with their central city districts are a relatively modern phenomenon. The suburbs are younger than the railways themselves, for, until the coming of the steam train, towns generally consisted of a genuine mixture of dwellings. Artisans' homes, shops, public buildings and luxurious residences rubbed shoulders with one another, and were often pressed together by medieval walls. The Industrial Revolution started to break up this pattern by creating new manufacturing districts with tenement housing, and even created towns in their entirety, such as Crewe and Wolverton. The railways allowed people to live a fair distance from their workplaces, while the pollution and crowding associated with industrialization encouraged this movement.

Although factory hands, miners and workers generally could not afford this luxury, the ever-expanding and increasingly prosperous middle classes were able to move away from the city centres to the pleasant suburbs. Here they built their villas, spacious terraces and later semi-detached houses. The railways both encouraged and profited by this development. Consequently, a complex network of suburban lines was constructed in the latter part of the nineteenth century. Radiating from Victoria, Charing Cross, Waterloo, Cannon Street, London Bridge, Holborn Viaduct and Blackfriars Stations, a comprehensive service was established by what was later to become the Southern Railway. Commuter trains operated as far west as Reading, Basingstoke and Portsmouth, south to Brighton, Eastbourne and Worthing, and east to Sheerness, Hastings,

Dover and Margate. Important junctions and depots were established at Clapham, Nine Elms, Ashford and Norwood.

The basis of the suburban system was constructed piecemeal through the efforts of small railway companies building local lines. It was not the work of a few large organizations following a grand plan. There was little co-ordination of the system's development, and this led to some unnecessary duplication. Some of these early companies, subsequently swallowed up in the formation of larger units, included: the West End & Crystal Palace, the Kent Coast, the Tooting, Merton & Wimbledon, the Epsom & Leatherhead, the Wimbledon & Dorking, the Banstead & Epsom Downs, and the Wimbledon & Epsom Railways. The very repetition of these names illustrates the rather haphazard development of the system.

However, the 1860s and 1870s witnessed a series of amalgamations, the result of which was the formation of three major companies, the London & South Western, the London, Brighton & South Coast and the South East & Chatham Railway. These three then set about modifying routes and removing inconsistencies. As the numbers of commuters using the service grew, so they were responsible, in the early years of the twentieth century, for initiating a programme of electrification.

In fact, electric trains had become well established before they were adopted in the south-west. London Transport's tube framework, laid down between 1898 and 1907, was an electric system. Three companies in the north of England (the Mersey in 1903, the North Eastern between Newcastle and Tynemouth, and the Lancashire & Yorkshire between Liverpool and Southport, both in 1904) had already begun electric working. At the time the L.S.W.R. was handling the heaviest suburban traffic in London and Sir Herbert Walker, then its General Manager, perceiving the success of these early schemes, advocated electrification. The first section of their line to be electrified was between Waterloo and Wimbledon, via Wandsworth and East Putney, in 1915. In the following year the service was extended to Strawberry Hill, Barnes and Clapham Junction. Despite the disruptions caused by the First World War, the numbers of passengers using these suburban routes increased steadily. In 1913 there had been 25 million suburban passengers using the South Western, but by 1918 there were 40 million, an increase of 74 per cent. The post-war decade witnessed a gradual extension in the number of lines operated by electric trains. A 1930 map of the Southern shows that almost all the network within twenty miles of the capital had been electrified.

With only a few exceptions, electrification had justified the heavy capital expenditure it demanded. However, its development had been pursued in a rather haphazard fashion. For the first fifteen companies which adopted electric traction, there were at least eight separate technical systems in operation. With the exception of the London Underground, no train of any one company could run on another's tracks. The current was transmitted through overhead wires on the Midland, Brighton and Shildon–Newport lines, by a single electric rail on the L.S.W.R., and by two on most of the remainder. In addition, the Metropolitan and District Railways quarelled over the merits of alternating and direct current for their electric stock.

One feature of the new electric trains on the L.S.W.R. was the provision of just two classes of carriage. As on the Midland, the second class was omitted. This innovation proved to be an indication of future practice and today many electric suburban trains, especially those operating over short distances, have no first-class carriages at all.

As would be expected, certain London termini serving the Southern developed as commuter stations, in contrast to stations such as Paddington and Euston, which largely handled long-distance travellers. London Bridge, Holborn Viaduct, Cannon Street and Charing Cross all fall into this category of suburban termini.

CHARING CROSS

Over 70 per cent of Charing Cross's passengers are commuters. Situated off Trafalgar Square, it is one of the few really central London stations. It was originally opened in 1864 as the west end terminus of the South Eastern Railway's extension from London Bridge. The building was engineered by Sir John Hawkshaw (also responsible for Cannon Street) and featured a single-arched train-shed, which backed on to a new bridge over the Thames.

Because the station dealt with a prestigious Continental traffic, the directors decided that it would benefit from the addition of an impressive hotel. A symmetrical, twin-towered, ornate design was produced by E. M. Barry, who had just completed the Royal Opera House at Covent Garden. It is still of course a fully operational hotel under the management of British Rail. Neither as large nor as ornate as St Pancras, Charing Cross nevertheless presents a distinguished and dignified façade, though it is unfortunate that the top two storeys have been modified and that the two towers which helped to balance the composition have been removed. The hotel is said to have been one of the first English buildings for which artificial stone was extensively used in the exterior. The splendid main restaurant, originally named after Simon de Montfort – because of Parliament's proximity – has recently been rechristened after Sir John Betjeman. At the renaming he recounted how he and his friends used to meet regularly at the hotel, in a smoking room, where it was possible to 'walk on to a balcony, drink in hand, to survey the crowds and trains of the station below'.

LONDON BRIDGE AND
THE LONDON TO GREENWICH LINE

The capital's oldest railway is the London & Greenwich, completed in stages between 1836 and 1838. It ran from the site of the present London Bridge terminus to Greenwich, via Spa

Road, Southwark Park and Deptford, though the first two stations were closed in 1915. The entire line was supported by an arched, brick viaduct, and it was the company's plan that the spaces below should be let out as homes or workshops. The scheme was not quite the success they had envisaged, as people did not take to living under a railway. A print entitled 'Over London by Rail', sketched by Gustave Doré in the 1870s, captures the unpleasant reality of this mix of squalid terrace housing and high-level travel. The viaduct, at $3\frac{3}{4}$ miles, remains the longest in the world. The South Eastern finally completed the route to Dartford in 1878, when the gap between Greenwich and Charlton was closed. Cannon Street terminus was opened in 1866 and the line extended into the City itself.

There is a regular service along this route to Dartford, with electric suburban trains leaving from Cannon Street. Unfortunately this station was heavily bombed during the Second World War, and has recently been rebuilt. The concourse has been modernized and the old City Terminus Hotel, also designed by E. M. Barry, has been replaced by an extensive office block. All that remains of the former Cannon Street are Barry's massively sublime side walls executed in stock brick, their twin towers, cupolas and spires still dominating the skyline, Hawkshaw's train-shed having been removed after bombing.

Bridge and viaduct soon carry the line past Courage's Anchor brewery to the high-level platforms of London Bridge. Though extensive modernization and rebuilding have obscured the distinction, the station was formerly in two parts. The L.B. & S.C.R. and the S.E. & C.R. shared the site, but kept their platforms and buildings entirely separate. Externally all that remains of the old station are the solid arcaded walls supporting the whole structure. The concourse, shops and ticket offices have all been modernized, while the departure boards are operated by computer. The former L.B. & S.C.R. train-shed survives intact (Platforms 10 to 16) and consists of decorative cast-iron columns and delicate, scroll brackets supporting a central barrel vault with flat-roofed side aisles.

The line from London Bridge continues along the original 1836 viaduct, though it has been much widened, first in 1850 and latterly in 1904. Deptford is now the first stop. Greenwich Station follows, and the train descends to ground level. The restrained Italianate buildings, opened in 1840, were reconstructed in 1878, when the station was moved to its present site. Greenwich is a two-storey brick structure with stone dressings, stately windows and a central porch flanked by Ionic columns. In a different setting it would serve as a modest country house. From here the connection with the armed forces is well established. Maze Hill is the nearest stop for the National Maritime Museum. Westcombe Park is pleasant enough, though its sleepy, suburban atmosphere is disturbed by the near-by motorway. Charlton follows and the football ground is clearly visible close to the railway.

Woolwich Dockyard, in Frances Road, is an interesting Victorian station. It lies parallel to the Royal Naval establishment and has become something of a curiosity, for all around the old terraced houses have recently been replaced by tower blocks and council estates. The station is set in a deep-sided cutting marked off by a curved brick wall. Although its surface buildings are limited, the traveller has only to descend into its depths to return to a Dickensian atmosphere. High sootblackened walls, stygian tunnel entrances at each end of the platforms, foliated iron columns supporting original valancing, together with green and cream signboards, evoke a former age.

The line continues along brick-lined tunnels and cuttings to the near-by Woolwich Arsenal. This is a similar station, with more extensive buildings, serving the Artillery barracks and the Royal Arsenal near by in Plumstead Road. There was a railway which ran around the munition works and connected with the main line at Plumstead. The strong naval association is upheld by trains to Gillingham, which call at Chatham, another dockyard. Other important stops include the cathedral town of Rochester, and Gravesend for the ferry to Tilbury.

To return to London Bridge (but this time to the L.B. &

S.C.R. side), there is a half-hourly service to Victoria, via the suburbs of south London, which takes in some fine views of the capital and its rail network. The line starts on the same viaduct as the Greenwich line, running south-east to South Bermondsey, but soon swings westwards to Queens Road. This area (and indeed the continuation to Peckham Rye) is particularly anachronistic. Blocks of flats and housing estates dating from the 1930s to the 1970s rub shoulders with the nineteenth-century terraces, warehouses and factories. Victorian pubs and schools stand out like islands in their desolated or more modern surroundings.

Then the railway descends from the vantage point provided by the viaduct and runs on to Denmark Hill, which possessed one of the finest stations in the whole region. Splendid and extensive beyond its recent function, it was constructed on a road bridge over the tracks. The central entrance hall was flanked by symmetrical wings, with low mansard roofs, while three sets of covered staircases led down to the platforms. This ornate building was demolished in 1980.

The train then passes over the complex junction at Brixton, running close to a curious Gothic clock tower erected in the centre of this confusion of lines. The section between Clapham, Battersea Park and Victoria presents a rare treat to the railway traveller. The route divides at Factory Junction and swings over the main lines from Waterloo and Clapham Junction. It is a magnificent panorama of rising and falling viaducts, intersections, broad acres of tracks, signal boxes and engine sheds, surrounded by warehouses and terraces with their never-ending rows of chimney pots. Battersea power station and the near-by gasometers provide the final backdrop. From here the line crosses the Thames and winds its way into the wide terminus of Victoria.

North Dulwich, on the London Bridge–Sutton line, is a station of distinction. When the younger Charles Barry built Dulwich College, he also designed a Tudor-style station for the L.B. & S.C.R. at North Dulwich in 1868. The main buildings, constructed over the railway in Red Post Hill, have a splendid three-arched entrance supported by coupled columns with a fretted parapet above, while tall clusters of chimneys decorate the roof-line. The platforms are built at the base of the cutting walls, which in contrast to the entrance are a triumph of the sublime, consisting of a succession of recessed brick arches alternating with solid buttresses.

HOLBORN AND BLACKFRIARS

The smallest of London's termini, serving stations to Sutton, West Croydon and Sevenoaks, are Holborn Viaduct and Blackfriars. Both have sadly altered buildings. Holborn Viaduct and its hotel have been replaced by a modern office block and concourse. From here the line runs along the original brick viaduct to cross Ludgate Hill. The railway bridge, incongruously sandwiched between Victorian premises over this busy City junction, has been the subject of several pictures. Jacques-Émile Blanche painted the scene (*Ludgate Hill*, Tate Gallery) in the 1880s, capturing the bustle, smoke and varied skyline dominated by distant St Paul's.

Between Holborn and Blackfriars (where Apothecary Street passes under the viaduct) are the remains of the L.C. & D.R.'s Ludgate Hill Station. The twin towers which supported the curved train-shed stand out. Executed in Italianate style and constructed from London stock brick decorated with white stone, they offer a memorial to this once splendid station.

Blackfriars (originally called St Paul's Terminus) was damaged during the blitz. This was particularly unfortunate as the District Railway had sited London's only Turkish-style station here. It was a highly decorated three-storey building with twin minarets, but only the first floor has survived the bombing; its white Portland stone and grey-ochre brick are visible around the entrance to the Underground station. Three groups of moorish windows with ornate borders, and two ironwork balconies, are all that remain. The former L.C. & D.R. station around the corner in Queen Victoria Street has been completely rebuilt. The original structure was in Italianate style. The quoins between its windows were carved with the company's more distant connections – St Petersburg, Vienna, Constantinople, Brindisi and Cannes were mentioned. Fortunately, these have been preserved and grouped together to form a diverting part of the concourse walls. However, Blackfriars no longer offers services to the Channel ports and the modern office block which houses the booking hall and platforms has no unusual exterior features. The L.C. & D.R. bridge over the Thames is quite distinctive. Its lattice-work cage is supported by thick columns, topped with decorative abutments containing the company's coat-of-arms and Victoria's initial with the date 1864.

NINE ELMS AND CLAPHAM JUNCTION

Because of its very complexity and the piecemeal means of construction, the Southern Region has produced a number of important junctions and depots – Nine Elms, Clapham and Ashford. Nine Elms was to develop as the great locomotive workshops for the L.S.W.R. Originally it was chosen as the terminus for the London & Southampton Railway before the construction of an extension to Waterloo in 1848. Before the railways moved in, the area had been described as 'a low swampy district, occasionally outflowed by the Thames'. When the line was extended north into the capital the station lost much of its importance, except as a local passenger halt. From then on its significance, like that of Swindon and Crewe, lay in its role as a locomotive depot. The Beatties, Adams and Drummond all had their design offices here, and their engines were produced from its workshops.

One of the best-known junctions on the Southern system is at Clapham. It is the meeting point of the lines from Victoria and Waterloo, with a branch running to Kensington Olympia. Because of the growing number of trains passing through the station, it was progressively enlarged, while its marshalling yards extended their area and grew to be the world's busiest railway station. Today Clapham Junction is still a busy and complex station. The entire network of lines and their buildings are supported by a broad brick viaduct, with tunnels providing vital connections for passengers. The oldest and most atmospheric buildings are those on Platforms 9 and 10. Constructed from blackened stock brick with borders in red, there are Gothic arches with original iron columns and brackets, while the remainder are more recent reconstructions. Clapham was the site of the first railway museum, but it has subsequently moved to York, leaving the London exhibits, previously displayed at Syon Park, at Covent Garden.

PRESERVED STEAM RAILWAYS

The Bluebell Railway

Because of the continued use made of the commuter system and the enduring popularity of the south-coast resorts, the Southern has probably survived the recent policy of closures more successfully than any other region. Nevertheless, there are several lines which have been re-opened for steam running, one of the best known of which is the Bluebell Railway.

The Bluebell Railway has the distinction of being the first standard-gauge line to re-open, on 7 August 1960, after closure by British Railways in the pre-Beeching era. The route is five miles long and runs from Sheffield Park to Horsted Keynes, and is single-track. Originally the line was part of the Lewes & East Grinstead Railway, completed in 1883. It was not a financially successful enterprise, having to rely on such local business as this rural area produced, while the timetables were poorly organized, with passengers often having to let freight trains take precedence.

Faced with this situation, British Railways finally closed the line in March 1958. In the following year the Bluebell Railway Preservation Society was formed. However, in 1963 the branch line from Haywards Heath to East Grinstead, via Horsted Keynes was closed and in 1964 the tracks were lifted, leaving the railway isolated. This presented considerable problems, as new items of stock had to be transported by road to the railway. Being a junction, Horsted Keynes is a spacious station with five platforms. It has been restored to its Southern Railway livery, while Sheffield Park has been repainted in the older L.B. & S.C.R. colours.

Probably the best-known locomotives on the line are the Terrier class tank engines. Designed by William Stroudley for the L.B. & S.C.R. and named after the characteristic 'bark' of their exhaust, they were a compact, hard-working and reliable 0–6–0T locomotive and are among the oldest steam engines working today. No. 72, *Fenchurch*, was built in 1872 and No. 55, *Stepney*, three years later. One of the most striking locomotives is No. 21C123, *Blackmore Vale*, a West Country class engine, the streamlined casing repainted in the Southern's malachite green with bright yellow lining. There is also a so-called 'Dukedog' class, No. 3217, *Earl of Berkeley*, from the G.W.R. Turned out from the Swindon works in 1938, No. 3217 is a reconstruction from the frames of a Bulldog class locomotive No. 3425 and a Duke of Cornwall class engine, No. 3258.

There are two other interesting vintage locomotives, an L.B. & S.C.R. 0–6–2T, No. 473, *Birch Grove*, built at Brighton in 1898, which may be distinguished by the company's umber livery; and an Adams L.S.W.R. 4–4–2T, No. 488, built in 1885 and now restored to its attractive medium-green livery with black and white lining. In addition, there are steam locomotives from other companies and periods of varying type. The Bluebell Railway also possesses a broad range of rolling stock with carriages from pre-grouping, Southern and B.R. days.

The Kent & East Sussex Railway

The Kent & East Sussex Railway was originally called the Rother Valley Light Railway and ran between Headcorn and Robertsbridge, both on the S.E. & C.R. This private standard-gauge steam line had been pioneered by Colonel H. F. Stephens and, renamed the Kent & East Sussex Light Railway, escaped grouping, remaining independent until nationalization in 1948. The railway was closed in 1961 having run a goods only service since 1954.

Enthusiasts succeeded in getting the line re-opened in 1974 and at present trains are run over a three-mile stretch from Tenterden to Wittersham Road, with a planned extension to Bodiam. True to its tradition the railway maintains a variety of engines and rolling stock. There are two Terrier tanks, No. 10, *Sutton*, and No. 3, *Bodiam*, which was one of the engines purchased by Colonel Stephens in 1901. It had been built at the L.B. & S.C.R.'s Brighton works in 1872 and named *Poplar*. These engines were named after the suburban districts through which they operated, and serve as an evocative reminder of their early tasks. There is also an S.E. & C.R. P class 0-6-0T, which has since been christened *Pride of Sussex*. One of the most unusual engines on the railway is a Norwegian State Railways Mogul, No. 19, built in 1919.

The rolling stock is just as varied. There are two Pullman cars, Maunsell coaches, S.E. & C.R. 'birdcages' and an L.S.W.R. bogie carriage, together with a four-wheel brake from the L.N.W.R. There are a number of goods vehicles, including a 'Shell' oil wagon.

The Romney, Hythe & Dymchurch Railway

One of the most successful steam railways in the Southern region is, of course, the Romney, Hythe & Dymchurch Railway. It has been an entirely independent organization from its inception in 1927. It operates a fifteen-inch-gauge line over the fourteen miles between Hythe and Dungeness. The railway was conceived and constructed by two racing car drivers, Captain J. E. P. Howey and Count Zbrowski. The Count was killed in a crash at Monza and the task was left to Howey to complete, the first section of the line, from Hythe to New Romney, being opened in 1927 and extended to Dungeness over the next two years. The Southern Railway had encouraged the work as it provided a valuable link between two of their ailing seaside stations, Hythe and New Romney.

As his engineer, Captain Howey appointed Henry Greenly who was responsible for the design and construction of the railway's Pacific locomotives. He selected Gresley's A-1 class engines and scaled their gauge down to approximately one quarter, while the superstructure was reduced to one third. A total of ten engines were built between 1925 and 1931, of which eight were Pacifics and the remainder 4-8-2s.

The line flourished each summer till the outbreak of war in 1939. With the fall of France in 1940, the railway found itself on a coastline threatened by invasion. For the remainder of the hostilities, it was given over to war work, and it took almost two years to repair and restore the system for passenger running.

Four of the original Pacifics still operate on the line. These are numbered 1, 2, 7 and 8 and are named respectively *Green Goddess*, *Northern Chief*, *Typhoon* and *Hurricane*. Nos. 5 and 6 are the two 4-8-2s and have been christened *Hercules* and *Samson*. A later addition to the railway are the scale Canadian Pacific engines, Nos. 9 and 10. They are quite distinctive, with their cow catchers, bells mounted on the buffer beam, and black livery, lined out in white.

The Isle of Wight Steam Railway

Being a popular Victorian holiday resort, the Isle of Wight encouraged the growth of a railway network. Several companies built lines running north-south and east-west across the island, while the Isle of Wight Railway constructed a branch linking up the resorts of the east coast, from Ryde Esplanade to Ventnor, via Sandown and Shanklin. Today this is the only line in regular operation, and has since been electrified, the Shanklin to Ventnor section having been closed. From 1967 it has been operated by London Underground trains (repainted in B.R.'s blue livery with yellow cabs and grey doors), which present a rather incongruous sight as they travel across the rural parts of the island. The other branches have been closed down and much of the track has been lifted, as on the Freshwater, Yarmouth & Newport Railway. The gravel bed which once carried busy holiday trains is now overgrown but in places makes an ideal footpath. Preservation is however under way, but further to the east, based on Haven Street Station. The line has been restored for two miles north-west to Wootton, where a new station has been built. Trains use a variety of pre-grouping carriages painted in S.R. green. There are two vintage locomotives: No. 11, *Newport*, a Terrier (originally No. 40, *Brighton*, but renamed when sold to the I.W.C.R. in 1902) restored to the livery of the Isle of Wight Central Railway, black with red and white lining; and an L.S.W.R. class 02 0-4-4T, No. 24, *Calbourne*, built in 1891, which has been repainted in Southern Railway livery. While these two were being preserved, trains were hauled by the Hawthorn Leslie 0-4-0ST, No. 37, *Invincible*, first built for the Woolwich Arsenal during the First World War.

The Mid-Hants 'Watercress' Railway

The Mid-Hants Railway operates over the $2\frac{3}{4}$-mile section between Alresford and Ropley on the former Alton, Alresford & Winchester Railway. In 1884 it was taken over by the L.S.W.R. and when the Southern electrified the Woking to Alton line in 1937 through services to Winchester were withdrawn. British Rail finally closed the line in 1973 and Alton became the terminus for their operations to London. However, the track between Alresford and Ropley was saved and there are long-term plans to re-lay the $7\frac{1}{4}$ miles back to Alton.

The railway has an interesting collection of former Southern stock, including an N class 2-6-0, No. 31874, now named *Anzar Line* (built from parts machined at the Woolwich Arsenal to relieve post First World War unemployment, and assembled at Ashford). There are, in addition, a Urie-designed 4-6-0, No. 30506, a U class 2-6-0, No. 31806, and a number of industrial saddle tanks.

6 The Railways of Eastern England

With the exclusion of the former Great Northern line from King's Cross to Doncaster, the railways of East Anglia, the Fens and Lincolnshire are self-contained. Routes tend to radiate from London to the coast, with connecting links in between. In this region railways were not built to supply manufacturing centres but ran through farmland to fishing ports and to holiday, ecclesiastical and university towns. In a sense, the railways themselves were then the only industrial element in this large area of England.

Engineers were not presented with any tough problems. The land is flat and in most places firm, only the residual marshes of the Fens presenting any obstacles to track laying. Before 1865 (and afterwards by the Great Eastern) East Anglia was dominated by the Eastern Counties Railway, the Fens were shared with the Great Northern, while Lincolnshire was the preserve of the G.N.R. and the Great Central. The somewhat relaxed nature of local services meant that these companies often became butts for humour. Priestley, in his *English Journey* (1934), travelled through the region by railway, recording that from Lincoln to Boston it 'is no great distance, but the train makes a leisurely journey of it, lounging along by the side of the river, the Witham, like an angler'. This characteristic, by no means an unpleasant one, has endured in some parts of the system.

In areas of Essex and Hertfordshire, town and country merge together imperceptibly. The commuter services from Liverpool Street, King's Cross and now Moorgate have helped to push

London's limits into agricultural lands. Though probably more akin to the capital than their still rural counties, these outer suburbs are examined here within this regional and company grouping. Finally, a word will be said on the preservation societies which have expanded so swiftly in the last decade.

LIVERPOOL STREET

Formerly the London terminus of the Great Eastern Railway, Liverpool Street was designed by Edward Wilson and opened in 1874.

The main component of the G.E.R. was the Eastern Counties Railway, whose station was at Shoreditch (later named Bishopsgate; after being used as a goods depot, it was destroyed by fire in 1964). Bishopsgate was clearly too small and, being to the north of Spitalfields, was slightly too distant to cater effectively for the growing volume of commuter traffic. The plan to build a larger terminus closer to the City was one of the earliest decisions taken by the new company under the chairmanship of Lord Salisbury. Considered to have been Britain's finest Foreign Secretary, he was also a businessman of great acumen and it was unfortunate that pressing political commitments should have forced him to resign his chairmanship in 1871.

Like the Midland at St Pancras, the Great Eastern chose the Gothic style for their terminus. Their original station consisted of the present Platforms 1 to 10, the remainder having been added in 1891. Although Liverpool Street may be considered grand even now, it was far grander then, the blitz and subsequent standardization having taken their toll. The buildings are constructed from yellow-ochre East Anglian bricks, with cream stone dressings. The roofs and gables (as at Broad Street) were topped with ornate ironwork, while the clock tower had a decorative tiled spire. The ironwork has gone, and the spire, damaged during the war, left in its unhappy truncated state.

Today the interior, presenting a superb vista of tall iron columns, fan-shaped brackets and interlocking beams, is far more impressive than the exterior, and successive writers have spoken of Liverpool Street's cathedral-like appearance. The train-shed is divided into two main vaults supported by double columns and flanked by aisles, while the side walls are pierced with rows of lancet windows. The capitals were originally decorated with ironwork leaves, but these were removed after the war. The best way to see the train-shed and the more recent addition is to take the high-walk which twists its way from one side of the station to the other. When shafts of sunlight filter through the dusty atmosphere, blotting out modern signs with indefinite shadows, it is not difficult to drift back a century to the days when steam engines filled the station with their sounds and exhaust fumes. This footway also leads to the Edwardian buffet in the older train-shed. It is built in Jacobean style, with bay windows overlooking the concourse and in these there survives a little *art nouveau* stained glass. A similar building opposite is the station master's office.

Liverpool Street is one of the few major London termini to retain a number of pre-nationalization departure boards. Each features an individual clock-face, the train's destination and below in double columns a list of stopping points, or 'calling ats'. The whole is surmounted by the platform number on an oval disc, mounted in a simple pediment. They are informative, easy to operate and understand, while their careful proportions and layout make them interesting to study. Although they may require more man-minutes to manipulate than a computer-controlled device, they are certainly cheaper, more reliable – and no doubt soon to be taken down in the cause of efficiency.

The Great Eastern Hotel, constructed in red brick and white stone, is a later addition. The first hotel, designed by E. M. and C. E. Barry and opened in 1884, survives in Liverpool Street but it is dominated by the much larger extension which fronts Bishopgate. Designed by Colonel Robert Edis in French Renaissance manner, it was completed in 1901. The company's initials can be distinguished beneath the short, central spire above the main entrance. The interiors were splendid, some of the rooms being executed in Louis Seize style and others in Elizabethan. Its Abercorn Rooms were used for concert rehearsals by the company's Staff Musical Society, which gained a sound reputation. Today the building is coated with a century of City grime, though the traveller who wishes to see its cleaned state should look at the rear of the hotel, which connects with Platforms 9 and 10, where the brick is revealed in its fresh, deep red.

COLCHESTER TO NORWICH

The Eastern Counties Railway was responsible for the line to Colchester. In July 1836 their Bill to lay a railway to Norwich and Yarmouth received the Royal Assent. Work began from their Stratford terminus and the first section to Romford was opened in June 1839, being extended to Colchester in March 1843. However, the company's terminus was placed well away from the town centre to avoid steep gradients and to take advantage of cheaper land. Its isolated situation tempted Samuel Morton Peto to erect the large and expensive Victoria Station Hotel. Designed by Lewis Cubitt, it cost £15,000. Insufficient traffic doomed it to failure and in 1850 the building was converted into an asylum, while today it serves as a hospital and is visible from the rebuilt Colchester Station.

The railway between Colchester and Clacton was electrified in 1959 as a testing ground for the conversion of the main line from Euston to Manchester. The line branches east and runs around the campus of Essex University, parallel with the River Colne. This must be one of the few places in England where it is possible to look across flat sedges to see electric trains rushing past ocean-going ships, as they work their way into dock between Wivenhoe and Colchester. Clacton is both a holiday resort and a commuter town, owing its rise and prosperity to the railways. Ninety-minute Pullman excursions on summer Sundays began in July 1922 and proved successful, their name being changed to the 'Eastern Belle' in 1929.

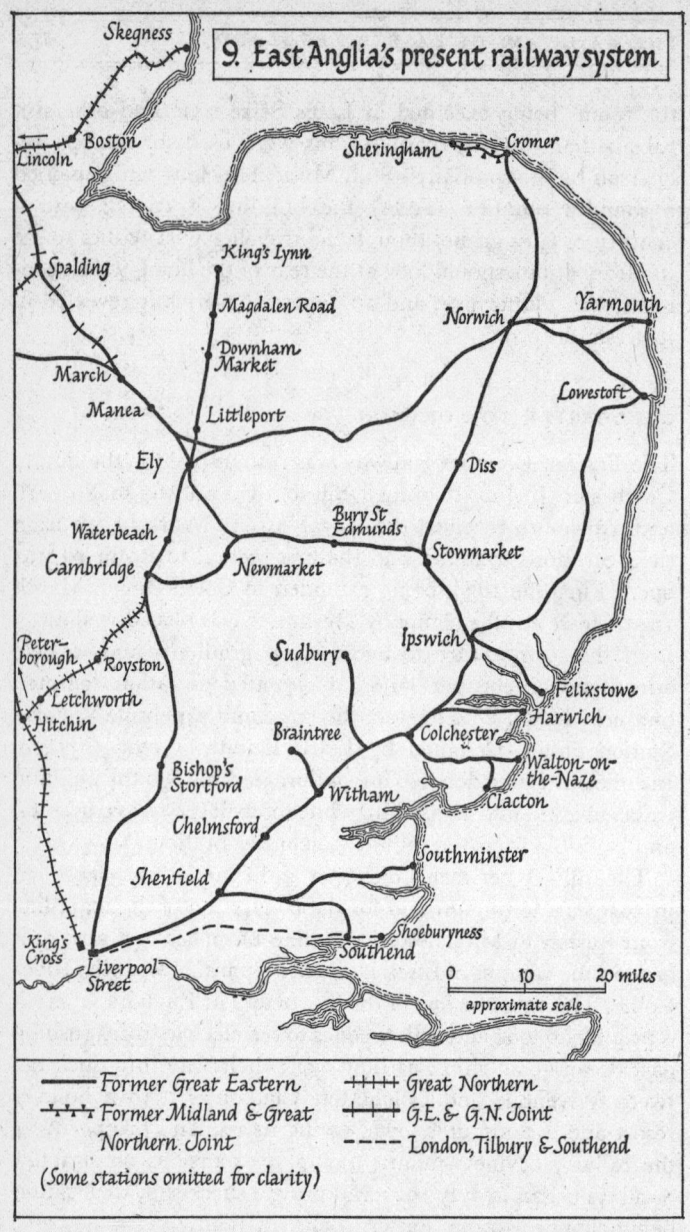

The line from Colchester to Ipswich was constructed by the Eastern Union Railway when the E.C.R. found itself financially unable to continue with its plans, and was opened in June 1846. The major difficulty was the crossing of the two broad arms of the River Stour (still an impressive part of the journey) a problem solved by the construction of two timber pile viaducts. The company was also responsible for laying the rail link to Harwich, completed in August 1854. Harwich and Felixstowe are busy passenger ports, with services to the Hook of Holland, Hamburg, Bremerhaven, Gothenburg, Esbjerg and Kristiansand. However, things were not always so prosperous and it was not until the formation of the Great Eastern in 1863 that shipping services were carefully planned to connect with railway timetables. Sailings to Rotterdam and Antwerp, originally in chartered steamers, helped to establish Harwich as an important Channel port.

Ipswich itself was a lively port with a number of agricultural processing industries in the early part of the nineteenth century, the completion of a rail link with London being all that was needed to establish its prosperity. The E.U.R. originally terminated its line at a temporary station, just south of Stoke Hill, subsequently the site of the engine-sheds. Meanwhile, another company (the Ipswich & Bury Railway) had been formed to connect the port with Bury St Edmunds, via Stowmarket. Parliamentary sanction, granted in July 1845, also contained provision for a branch from Haughley to Norwich – today's main line. Construction proceeded with extraordinary speed and the route to Bury St Edmunds was opened to passenger traffic in December 1846.

The Ipswich & Bury was noted for some fine examples of railway architecture. Their station at Stowmarket, designed by the Ipswich architect Frederick Barnes, is a pleasing Jacobean structure, where flowing Dutch gables, stone dressings and twin octagonal towers contribute to a balanced and original composition. Bury St Edmunds, also designed by Barnes, is his finest station. The two platforms, set high on an embankment, are dominated by a pair of domed towers, treated in free Renaissance style, forming, as at Cannon Street, an elegant gateway for passing trains. Ogee gables and mullioned oriel windows make for an interesting and unusual façade.

The E.U.R. purchased the proposed Norwich extension from the I. & B. Railway and work started in February 1847. Track was laid from both directions and the final section from Burston was completed in November 1849. The line terminated at the now closed Victoria Station and it was not until grouping that a connecting spur was constructed to Norwich Thorpe. This was originally the terminus for the joint Midland & Great Northern Joint Railway from Nottingham or Leicester, via King's Lynn and Melton Constable. Norwich Thorpe is one of the few palatial stations in the region. It was designed by John Wilson (assisted by W. N. Ashby) in free Renaissance style, and completed in 1886. The central structure has a fine convex roof with a pedimented clock and decorative urns. This is fronted by a handsome *porte cochère* and flanked by two symmetrical wings. The windows are decorated with alternate curved and angled pediments, the whole executed throughout in red brick with Bath stone dressings.

From Norwich there are three branches to the coast. To the north is the railway to Cromer and Sheringham, while to the east run lines to Yarmouth and Lowestoft. Like Skegness on the Lincolnshire coast, these towns grew up as holiday resorts based around older fishing villages. A great boon to Yarmouth's tourist trade was the completion of the Eastern & Midland (later the Midland & Great Northern Joint) line, bringing holidaymakers from the north. Both Cromer and Yarmouth had Beach Stations, offering a hint of their function. The site of Cromer High can still be seen, but its placing is a monument to the G.E.R.'s inability to get down the escarpment.

Lowestoft was, in addition, an important trawler harbour and *entrepôt*, similar to Grimsby. Their rise was directly connected with the completion of national rail links. For example, Barking on the Thames was London's major fish supplier in the eighteenth and early nineteenth centuries. As soon as Grimsby and Lowestoft were provided with railway connections, they concentrated the industry, relying on fast fish trains to distribute their catches throughout the country. Smaller ports sited closer to large cities, like Barking, declined as land transportation became more efficient.

CAMBRIDGE, ELY AND KING'S LYNN

The other major trunk route through East Anglia runs from Liverpool Street to Cambridge and Ely to terminate at King's Lynn. The first part of this journey, to Broxbourne, is described in the suburban section (see p. 161). From this junction the line continues north-east in the Stort valley to the historic market town of Bishop's Stortford. The station here has largely been rebuilt and has received praise (p. 350).

The route to Cambridge is not entirely over flat land, for Audley End heads a section of cuttings and embankments which lead to an impressive tunnel. The south portal is decorated with the arms of Lord Braybrooke – the railway was forced underground so that it should not spoil the rural calm of his estates. Audley End Station, first called Wendon, was probably designed by Francis Thompson in 1845. It is a classical building executed in light-ochre brick, and has been recently restored by B.R.

Cambridge Station, with its extensive sidings and marshalling yards, betrays nothing of the town's scholastic history. Unlike those at Oxford, the colleges are very distant and not visible from the railway line. Although Cambridge Station has been modernized, Thompson's original Italianate structure dating from 1847 has been preserved, retaining its fifteen-bay loggia decorated in the spandrels with the arms of the university colleges. The track layout is rather unusual, as both arrivals and departures use the same lengthy platform, though there are shorter bays let in to each end to accommodate local services. It is unfortunate, and most inconvenient for those without cars, that the former L.N.W.R. line between Oxford and Cambridge was closed in the 1960s, as it saved a double train journey into and across London. This cross-country route called at Bletchley and Bedford and provided a direct rail link between these rival scholarly and sporting towns.

The countryside certainly becomes flatter and damper after Cambridge, as the train works deeper into fenland. Large arable fields are drained by a network of straight geometrical channels. Indeed, Ely Station, completed in 1845, cost the E.C.R. £81,500 to build, because it was sited on an area of marshy swamp. Today Ely is distinguished more by its situation than its station buildings. As the train leaves en route for King's Lynn, the majesty of the many-towered Ely cathedral is high to the left and its proximity has been the subject of several pictures. There are also services from Ely direct to the cathedral towns of Norwich and Peterborough.

Similar flat scenery stays with the railway to King's Lynn. The line was extended to here in 1847 to encourage the growth of the town's harbour on the River Ouse. At its peak King's Lynn had railways running to all four points of the compass, while today the single route from Ely is all that remains. The northern extension to Hunstanton is closed, as is the Harbour branch and the former Midland & Great Northern Joint line calling at South Lynn. The course of this once-important east–west connection (to Spalding and Melton Constable) can still be seen just south of Harbour Junction signal box, where a grass-covered embankment, running at right angles to the main line, stops short at brick bridge supports. The viaduct has been removed and the trackbed supports wild life rather than trains.

The architecture of King's Lynn terminus has been criticized. The station was rebuilt in 1871 in French Renaissance style with an interesting roof. Most is in slate, but the central section, over the entrance, is glazed, decorated on each side with stone finials and topped with intricate ironwork. The timber buffet, dating from Great Eastern days, features a pleasant bow window, some interesting decoration and an empty clock pediment. Opposite is the 'East Anglia Hotel and Posting Establishment' and from the width of the double doors it looks as if it could have accommodated horse-drawn travellers as well as railway passengers.

The rural stations between King's Lynn and Ely all appear to be Great Eastern. Though by no means substantial, they survive as examples of a distinctive regional style, mostly being constructed from timber; Magdalen Road and Littleport are decorative reminders of the carpenter's craft. Downham, completed in 1847, is most unusual in that it is constructed from carefully matched stone chips, with ogee gables, and features original lozenge-latticed windows.

KING'S CROSS

Today the distinction between civil engineer and architect is clear, though their close co-operation is both necessary and desirable if new exciting buildings are to be erected. In the nineteenth century this distinction was blurred, Brunel being station designer, bridge builder and route surveyor. King's Cross, constructed to the plans of Lewis Cubitt, a member of the famous family firm of builders, is a functional, engineering achievement which has received praise in recent years as popular taste has turned full circle. The terminus's unadorned twin-arched exterior executed in drab yellow London brick could almost have been constructed in the last twenty years.

The obvious comparison to be drawn is with its neighbour, St Pancras. It is hard to believe that a mere fifteen years separates them, though it ought to be remembered that St Pancras is largely hotel and King's Cross simply train-shed. Nevertheless, there is a fundamental difference in treatment. For example, St Pancras's clock tower bears a clear resemblance to the ornate, Gothic edifice which houses Big Ben, while King's Cross possesses a square, restrained tower. It sits centrally between the two arches and only hints at an Italianate roof. The clock tower on St Pancras is not symmetrically placed, nor does it balance a twin.

King's Cross, the London terminus for the Great Northern, was opened in 1852. It consists of two round-arched train-sheds, originally one for arrivals, the other for departures. Even the brackets and columns supporting the roof are restrained for the period. King's Cross's beauty lies in this very simplicity, where brick and iron are pushed to their engineering limits and stand on their own merits without help from classical antiquity or medieval romanticism.

Despite this simplicity King's Cross was not a practical building in terms of railway operation. This mainly resulted from the narrowness of the two tunnels leading under the Regent's Canal and Caledonian Road. British Rail has recently reorganized the track layout to permit a freer flow of traffic. In addition, the diversion of the 'Great Northern' suburban service to Moorgate and the closure of York Road Station (situated at the north-eastern corner of the present terminus with an entrance in York Way) has relieved much of the pressure.

The entrance and concourse have been modernized by B.R. The station hotel was not constructed across the end of the train-shed, as it is in most termini, but was placed independently at the side. The Great Northern Hotel, also designed by Lewis Cubitt, is another restrained building, though the Italianate styling has been allowed to come through more freely. It too is built from London stock brick, with stucco quoins and decorated pilasters.

KING'S CROSS TO DONCASTER

The Great Northern's line from London to York, sanctioned in 1846, was then the largest railway scheme authorized by Parliament. It was opened in 1852 with the completion of the section between Peterborough and Retford. After various amalgamations and agreements, it was to become the southern half of the famous East Coast Route to Edinburgh. This was always a busy line, but it became noted for particularly fast running. In 1873 there were around twenty main-line services daily, in both directions, and this was doubled by 1893. By 1867 express timings had been reduced to 97 minutes to Peterborough, falling to 86 by 1895, while on a trial run the 'Silver Jubilee' completed the journey in a mere 55 minutes in September 1935. Today the High Speed Trains are scheduled to run non-stop to Peterborough in 49 minutes.

Peterborough, besides being a distinguished cathedral town, is also an interesting railway centre. It is a junction for several cross-country lines, to Spalding, Ely, Norwich, and to Leicester in the west, via Oakham and Stamford. The former G.N. hotel is still operated by British Rail and connects directly with the platforms. The London Brick Company's works are sited close to the main-line approach to the town, and their extensive clay pits, rows of kilns and stock piles of baked red Fletton bricks indicate that they are still a flourishing industry. The company presumably took its name not from its present situation, but from the location of its customers or original site. Railways were an ideal means of transporting bulky low-value goods cheaply and efficiently to the towns where they were needed.

Grantham follows, with connections for Boston and Skegness in the east and Nottingham in the west. Retford and Newark stations have both been modernized. Newark offers branches to Lincoln, Market Rasen and Grimsby, while Retford has services to Gainsborough and Sheffield. Doncaster, where the main line has branches to Hull, Wakefield and Leeds, is an important stop before York. Doncaster is both a railway and a racing town, being the site of the former Great Northern locomotive works. There are still extensive workshops to the south and west of the station, where diesels are maintained and stored. Much of the Great Northern station survives. It is not, however, a particularly distinguished building, though in keeping with the company's practice the broad platforms are covered with generous awnings. Constructed in red brick, patterned with cream, most of the original brackets and valancing have been replaced, except on Platform 8.

The most spectacular engineering achievement on the line is the Welwyn or Digswell viaduct, designed by Lewis Cubitt's brother William and opened in 1850. Situated to the north of Hatfield, it is 519 yards long and carried by forty massive arches. Its sheer size cannot be fully appreciated from the train, as its solid parapet and straight course tend to conceal its height and length. Being only wide enough for two tracks, the viaduct is something of a bottleneck, but the expense of widening such a vast structure has proved prohibitive.

Lincolnshire's present railway network was dominated in the south by the Great Northern and in the north by the Great Central. Although most of the major lines across the county had been authorized by 1846, a shortage of capital occasioned by the Mania delayed their construction. In March 1848 the G.N. first ran trains from Louth (now closed) to Grimsby and New Holland. 1848 proved to be a fruitful period in England for railway completion, as Peterborough was linked to Boston and Lincoln in October, while Lincoln and Market Rasen were connected in December.

It is not surprising that Lincoln should have developed as an important railway junction. Commanding a gap through the Lincolnshire Edge on the River Witham, it was a communications centre from medieval times. Though a large number of the county's cross-country routes have been closed, Lincoln still retains its two stations: Central (on the former G.N.R. but used by the G.C.R. and G.E.R.) and St Marks (former Midland to the south, and Great Central to the north). Curiously their roles have been reversed by the exigencies of today's reduced network. Central, built from ochre brick in confident, manorial style, with eight platforms, by the Great Northern, is the larger. It is now the terminus for local services, while St Marks, a smaller, restrained classical structure commissioned by the Midland, is the main-line station. St Marks was originally a terminus, but the end buildings were demolished in 1846 to allow a connection with the Manchester, Sheffield & Lincolnshire Railway.

Spalding, though once a busy railway junction, with lines radiating to all points of the compass, now serves one passenger line, the former G.N. & G.E. Joint route from Ely to Sleaford, with a branch to Peterborough. However, the many and extensive platforms, the broad goods yards and the substantial brick station still reflect its former importance.

Suburban Services

THE GREAT EASTERN:
LIVERPOOL STREET TO HERTFORD EAST

Liverpool Street is the terminus for a large number of local services running through north-east London. One of the oldest is the former Northern & Eastern's (leased to the Eastern Counties Railway in 1844) route to Hertford and Bishops Stortford. The first section, under the direction of Robert Stephenson, was completed between Stratford and Broxbourne in September 1840, and the line was then extended to Bishops Stortford in 1842 and Hertford East in the following year. The railway was originally laid with the five-foot gauge track used by the E.C.R. However, both companies realized that they could soon be isolated, and in September 1844, with Stephenson's guidance, the line was converted to standard gauge.

As with most City termini, the exit from Liverpool Street is by smoke-darkened cuttings and still blacker tunnels. The North London line on its high brick viaduct forms a barrier to the left. Soon, however, the train emerges into daylight, while the surprised and blinking passenger finds himself set high above the surrounding streets. It is a typical London panorama. Nineteenth-century factories and warehouses are mixed with modern flats, and derelict open squares marked off by corrugated iron sheets. Hackney Downs, a Victorian structure with generous sweeps of valancing, is the first stop. Two sets of

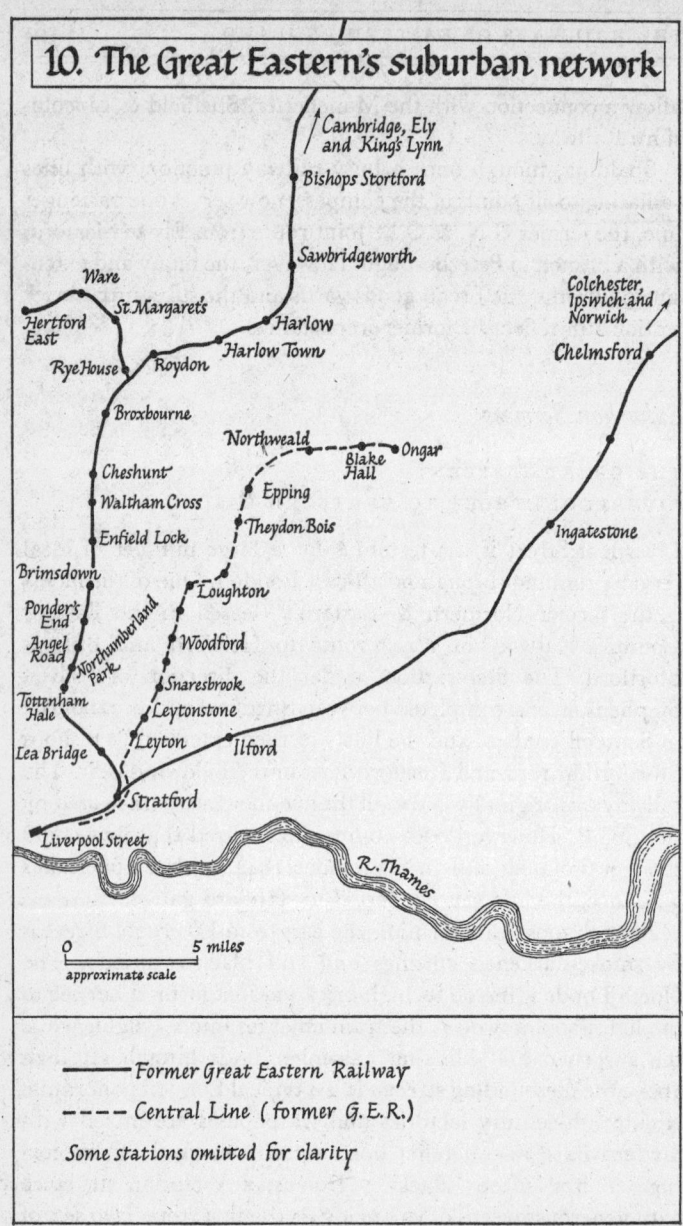

broad platforms bear sad witness to an age when railway travel was more popular. Clapton, though undistinguished architecturally, is a station rich in atmosphere. Set in a shadowy cutting, its soot-blackened brick walls, iron columns supporting gloomy awnings, make for a dark, satanic scene. Another feature of these stations are the sharp, pointed arches over windows and doors, unusual when executed in brick.

Not for the first time the line then crosses the Lea Navigation, and turns northwards to run up its gentle valley to Hertford. The land is characterized by poor marsh grasses. Reservoirs and lakes cover its floor till Broxbourne. Light industry, small gasholders, rows of terraced houses (semi-detached after Brimsdown) and modern estates back on to the railway. Most of the stations between Tottenham Hale and Rye House have been completely rebuilt, but there are a few Great Eastern benches, and in places the initials of the L.N.E.R. may be detected on the 'chairs' supporting the rails. Another survival are the rows of small bells suspended above minor roads or tracks crossing the line, which were rung from the nearest signal box to warn of an oncoming train. This is a route of level crossings – which are cheaper to build than bridges.

This area was famous in the eighteenth and early nineteenth centuries for its market gardens, which supplied London with vegetables and flowers. The coming of the railways, with their ability to shift goods cheaply and quickly, meant that gardens could be sited further from their customers, and this function declined in the Lea valley. There are still a number of nurseries, though broken, disused glasshouses seem in the majority. Near Broxbourne open fields become general and the scenery is rural rather than suburban. Here the line divides, with one branch continuing to Bishops Stortford and Cambridge, while the other turns westwards for Hertford.

The last three stations have been left virtually untouched since G.E.R. days. St Margaret's and Ware are both brick buildings with original columns and valancing, though the last has been trimmed. Ware is a single-track station but it does possess an old engine-shed. Maltings, an indication of the town's former principal business, back on to the line, and overgrown trackbeds reveal that they used the railways to ship their malt to London brewers.

The line becomes double-track again and runs along the green valley of the Lea to Hertford. The terminus, though in need of restoration, is a delightful building. It is constructed in Jacobean style from clear red brick and cream stone. There are three mansard roofs (all with sky-lights) covering the concourse behind the booking office, which has an original plaster ceiling featuring moulded arabesque ornaments and a fine egg and dart border, with a frieze below. There are two *portes cochère*, one lacking a roof. The detailing is of a high standard: window and door lintels, chimney stacks and strapwork pilasters are all carved with intricate designs, while the iron columns lining the platforms are highly decorated with arabesque motifs and fluted shafts. Unfortunately the valancing has been trimmed, removing the patterned ends.

Opposite is The Dolphin public house. Constructed in similar red brick though in a freer Renaissance style, it is contemporaneous, and was no doubt erected to serve the station. The present terminus (completed in 1888) was not the first. The site of the original station may be seen further down Railway Street, opposite the Great Eastern Tavern, which from its date looks as if it might have been constructed for the same reasons as The Dolphin. All that remains is the trackbed and the rebuilt brick foundations for the buffer stops.

In addition, there was a single-track line from Hertford East to Hertford North, which then continued to Welwyn and Luton. It left the present railway to run north of the terminus, traversing Mill Road by a level crossing. The white gates with their split red circle are still in place and the rails firmly embedded in the tarmac. Not since 1966, when the railway was finally closed, have trains passed over these metals. Elsewhere the track has been lifted, though its course can be traced from various landmarks in the town. There is a road bridge in Port Hill, with an L.N.E.R. sign, which crosses the disused line. The trackbed is overgrown, but there appears to have been a coal yard here with a short platform for unloading. The spur and embankment at Hertford North are also clearly visible from the station itself.

THE CENTRAL LINE: STRATFORD TO ONGAR

The Central Line from Stratford to Ongar runs over Great Eastern tracks and calls at many of the former company's stations, though some, like Loughton (designed by Murray Easton in 1940) and Leytonstone, have been rebuilt to characteristic L.T. designs. Woodford still has a number of benches with G.E.R. initials worked into their supports and retains the original valancing and iron columns with their unusual Jacobean strapwork motifs on the shaft – as at Hertford East. Epping, surrounded by woods and open grassland, is a typical G.E.R. station, constructed in red brick and featuring emphasized quoins and window frames.

The railway was progressively converted to electric traction by London Transport after the Second World War. Central Line trains ran to Leytonstone from May 1947, to Loughton in November 1948 and reached Epping in September 1949 while the single-track service from here to Ongar was steam-hauled till November 1957. The original watertower survives at the eastern end of Epping Station and the operating chain and level indicator are intact, though the rubber hose has gone.

It is rather unnerving to travel in modern Underground stock surrounded by metropolitan advertisements, through woods, across ploughed fields high on an embankment, and call at rural stations. Blake Hall remains unaltered from Great Eastern days and only its L.T. signs are new. Ongar is a pleasant terminus, doubling as a station master's house. There is a disused engine-shed backing on to a coal yard, but the tracks leading from the line have been lifted, and the signal

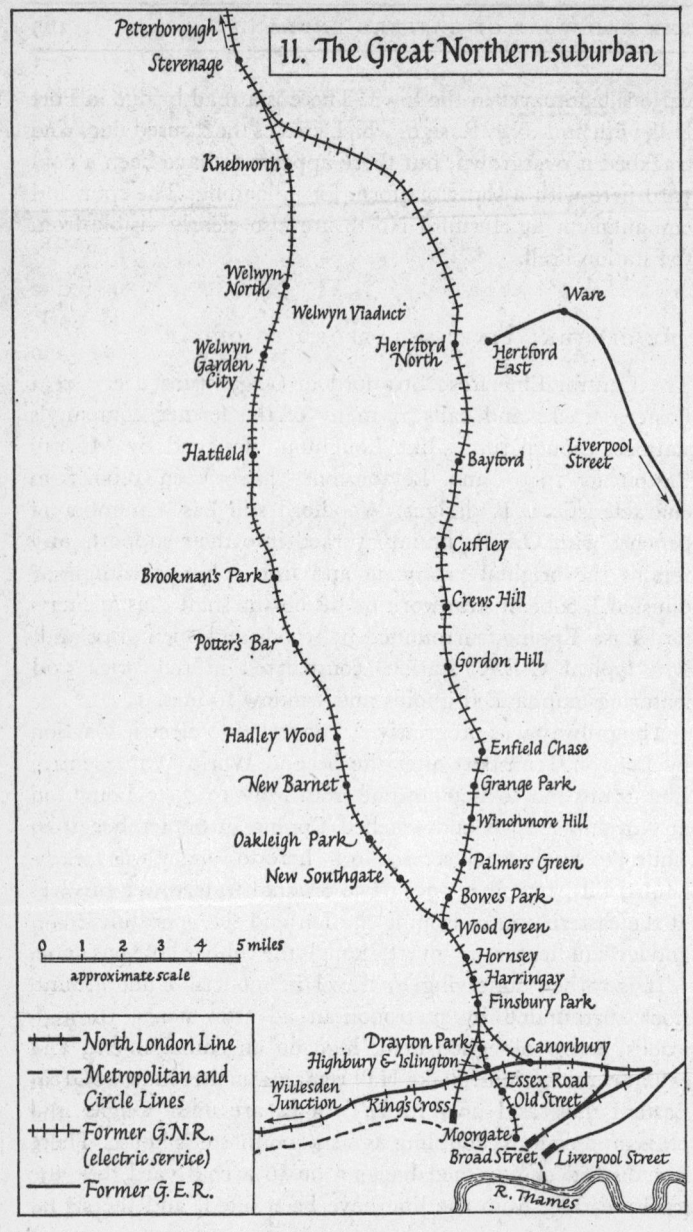

box controlling these sidings is somewhat dilapidated. All the buildings are constructed from red brick and the quoins and frames emphasized in darkened grey-ochre bricks.

THE GREAT NORTHERN: KING'S CROSS TO STEVENAGE

By an Act of June 1846 the Great Northern was empowered to build a railway from King's Cross to Doncaster and York. With its completion, the company not only possessed an excellent route to Yorkshire, but it had the makings of a suburban service for North London. However, early requests by residents for stops were treated with disdain by the G.N.'s directors, who focused their attention on prestigious expresses and the coal trade, regarding such local business as being beneath their dignity. Eventually they conceded and in July 1861 a station was opened at Seven Sisters Road – renamed Finsbury Park in 1869.

As London's population grew, so the number of season tickets multiplied. In 1867 there were 2,500 sold annually by the G.N.; rising to 6,500 in 1873. The company increased the number of trains, with the result that the section between King's Cross and Finsbury Park became seriously congested. This dramatic and largely uncontrolled development led contemporaries to remark that the system had been visited by an incubus. As a result Finsbury Park was rebuilt and made the grand junction for the growing suburban network. A connecting line was laid to Canonbury for Broad Street, though this section was closed to passenger traffic in 1976 when Moorgate became the new terminus.

By 1870 London had spread beyond Finsbury Park. Hornsey and Wood Green grew rapidly in the 1880s and 1890s. The railway was extended from Wood Green to Enfield Chase in April 1871 and to Hertford North, with a loop back to the main line at Stevenage, in March 1918. New Barnet, on the Hatfield branch, was particularly prized in the Edwardian era, being an area of high ground where spacious villas could be

constructed offering a fine view. Galsworthy depicted that
middle-class obsession with property in his Forsyte novels.
Soames, a wealthy solicitor, commissioned a fashionable
architect to build a large house in its own grounds, part of the
attraction being its privacy, setting and lovely panorama. It
was connected to the City by train, the station being but a
short dog-cart journey from the house.

Given that this was a difficult network to operate, B.R.
decided to reorganize and electrify the suburban service from
King's Cross. This would have the added advantage of freeing
main-line trains from persistent delays. The opportunity was
also taken to simplify the track layout from King's Cross
through Gas Works and Copenhagen tunnels, the complexity
of the G.N.R.'s arrangement having earned it the nickname
'The Throat'. Electrification using overhead cables involved
much engineering work and seven bridges were demolished,
a further twenty-nine being completely rebuilt. The Moorgate
terminus has been thoroughly modernized, while there are
new stations at Hatfield, Cuffley, Stevenage and Royston.

Electric multiple units began running to Welwyn Garden
City and Hertford North in November 1976. They are a new
and original design bearing greater resemblance to Underground surface stock than to their B.R. suburban predecessors.
Fitted with semi-automatic double doors, with their benches
arranged to face one another, leaving a broad gangway, they
have lots of standing space. They are, however, capable of
running at 75 mph and receive their current through a pantograph. With the electrification of the suburban service from
St Pancras to Bedford and plans to extend this system, these
trains clearly represent the shape of things to come.

FENCHURCH STREET TO SOUTHEND

An important excursion and commuter route was the London,
Tilbury & Southend Railway from Fenchurch Street (see
p. 81) to the resorts of the Thames Estuary. Though a number

of stations have been rebuilt (Chalkwell, Upminster) or closed (Dagenham, Hornchurch), the line survives virtually intact. The company was authorized to lay a railway to Tilbury in 1852, and Southend via Upminster in 1856. It proved to be a convenient and popular resort for Londoners. An esplanade and mammoth pier were constructed, while the Palace, a hotel which formerly rivalled Scarborough's Grand in ostentation and scale, still survives, though without most of its decoration. Only the iron galleries with their balconies, columns and awnings remain. The 'ozone', the amusements and the pier, with the railways, guaranteed Southend's prosperity.

The L.T. & S.R. built stations at Westcliff-on-Sea and Southend Central. The first is a simple yellow-brick structure, distinguished by the survival of its ornate iron brackets incorporating the company's intricate monogram. Southend (1884) is a larger affair with several sets of platforms and more substantial red-brick buildings. The pilasters are decorated with floriated caps and egg and dart borders. There are two entrances, the northern one featuring an impressive cast-iron *porte cochère* over a cobbled drive. The Great Eastern's Victoria Terminus (1889) is further from the beaches in the town centre. It too has many platforms and is executed in red brick, but with cream stone dressings. The *porte cochère* is timbered and has unusual spandrels which exhibit an oriental flavour. There are named G.E.R. seats here, while L.T. & S.R. benches survive at Benfleet Station.

The whole of the L.T. & S.R. network (including the loop from Barking south to Tilbury and Pitsea) has been electrified by B.R. In fact the Midland Railway's great coup of 1912, when they acquired the company from under the noses of the G.E.R., was supposed to have been accompanied by an undertaking to convert the network to electric traction. From Stepney East to Upminster the B.R. tracks run parallel to the District Line. Indeed these Underground stations were only recently handed over to London Transport and as a reminder of their former ownership most have L.T. & S.R. benches, while East Ham retains the company's ornate monogram brackets.

PRESERVED STEAM RAILWAYS

The Bressingham Live Steam Museum

This museum is located at Bressingham Hall, Diss, in Norfolk. There is a wide range of locomotives encompassing a number of narrow-gauge types. For standard-gauge engines, there are 500 yards of demonstration track which are used by No. 70013, *Oliver Cromwell*, a Britannia class express locomotive. Probably the most interesting exhibit is No. 80, *Thundersley* (1909), from the London, Tilbury & Southend Railway, a 4–4–2T which has been overhauled and repainted in their original green livery. Amongst the other steam locomotives stored here are the class A–1x Terrier No. 662, *Martello*, No. 6100, *Royal Scot* (the first of the famous 4–6–0 class), and No. 6233, *Duchess of Sutherland*, the last two from the L.M.S. In addition, there are a number of European and small industrial engines.

The North Norfolk Railway

This consists of three miles of standard-gauge line from Sheringham (now also a terminus for British Rail services from Norwich and Cromer) to Weybourne, on the former Midland & Great Northern Joint Railway to Melton Constable. The line was closed in February 1959. However, a preservation society was formed and in April 1976, after the granting of a Light Railway Order, the three-mile section was re-opened for passenger running. In the meantime, much work had been completed on track and station maintenance, while a number of industrial tank locomotives had been acquired. More interesting is No. 65462 (originally G.E.R. No. 564), an 0–6–0 tender locomotive. These were general-purpose engines, all 189 of which were built at Stratford between 1883 and 1913, the last surviving in service until 1962. For express operation, there is the Great Eastern designed B12 class 4–6–0, No. 8572

(1928). To complete the picture, the railway has acquired an ex-G.E.R. bogie coach and a 'quad' set of Gresley's articulated coaches – four carriages on five rather than eight bogies. The railway occupies the M. & G.N.J.R.'s original station at Sheringham following B.R.'s move to a new terminus east of the former level crossing.

The Peterborough and Nene Valley Railway

This is a five-mile standard-gauge line operating between Wansford and Orton. The Society possesses a large number of saddle-tank locomotives and four European steam engines, together with a collection of Continental rolling stock. The enterprise began with the purchase of the class 5MT 4-6-0, No. 73050, now named *City of Peterborough*. Under restoration is the Bulleid 'Battle of Britain' class, No. 34081, *92 Squadron*. The railway is situated to the south-west of Peterborough on the former L.N.W.R. line which ran due west to Seaton and Market Harborough and connected with the G.N.'s East Coast Route. British Rail still operates the connection with the main line, which has facilitated stock movements.

The Stour Valley Railway

With the progressive closure of the Stour Valley branch, it was decided to try to preserve a section of the line for steam operation. In December 1970 the Stour Valley Railway Society moved into Chappel and Wakes Colne Station. Most of the locomotives here are saddle-tank engines, though there are two interesting exceptions, which include No. 80151, a B.R. 2-6-4T (awaiting restoration), and the last Great Eastern locomotive to be built at Stratford works, 0-6-2T, No. 999. There are a number of unusual carriages here, including a vintage M.S. & L.R. six-wheel coach built in 1899, a composite first/third built in 1924 for the 'Flying Scotsman', a Post Office tender No. E70268, and a S.R. Pullman motor-brake third-class coach (1931). The society's steam centre runs parallel to B.R.'s branch line from Colchester to Sudbury and has been able to use Chappel and Wakes Colne Station for steam specials.

The Colne Valley Railway

The Society purchased a mile of trackbed at Castle Hedingham in 1973 and proceeded to relay the line. Sible and Castle Hedingham Station was acquired and re-constructed on the present site. There are now five locomotives here, including the finely restored Avonside 0–4–0ST, *Barrington*, painted in L.M.S. maroon, and No. 190, an Austerity 0–6–0ST. There is a B.R. second-class open saloon, an ex-L.M.S. brake van and a signal-post wagon dating from 1911.

7 The Midlands

The Midland triangle is usually taken to mean the area bounded by Crewe, Gloucester and Nottingham, with extensions beyond, and is aligned towards the south-west. However, London's powerful influence on communications has meant that in railway terms the Midland triangle, as it is considered in this chapter, has been orientated to the south-east, ignoring Gloucestershire, while including Bedford and Luton in its apex.

The Midlands were dominated by three major railway companies: the London & North Western, the Midland, and latterly the Great Central. Euston, St Pancras and Marylebone respectively were their London termini. Because these were companies with much wider connections (the L.N.W.R. to Cheshire and North Wales, the Midland to Lancashire and Scotland, and the Great Central Railway to Lincoln and Yorkshire), the Midland triangle was for many passengers simply an area of transition, to be passed through as quickly as possible. Of course it is also a region of industry in its own right. The Potteries, Birmingham ('the workshop of the world'), Nottingham and Leicester, with their textiles, and Crewe and Derby, with their railway yards, all produced a highly developed transport network.

There has been much change since nationalization. The main line from Euston has been electrified and most of its major stations rebuilt. The Great Central has been closed, Marylebone retains only local services to Banbury and

Aylesbury, while St Pancras has a much reduced timetable, and is at present being converted to electric traction. Nevertheless, there is still a wealth of history and interest in this Midland triangle. The region has also produced a number of railway societies: Tyseley Museum and the Main Line Steam Trust at Loughborough have become two of the leading steam preservation centres in the country.

EUSTON

The London & Birmingham was the world's first trunk railway. The last section was laid between Rugby and Birmingham Curzon Street under the direction of Robert Stephenson in February 1838. A regular passenger schedule was initiated on 9 April and extended to London in June. However, part of this journey ran over single tracks, and it was not until the following September that a full service was operating.

Much has been written about the new Euston terminus, and a great deal of it has been fired with passion. The Doric Triumphal Arch (the Propylaeum) and the original booking hall, designed respectively by Philip and P. C. Hardwick, father and son, were remarkable architectural features. The massive Triumphal Arch was a triumph of the sublime. Many have puzzled over the contrast between the exuberance and ostentation of the latter's booking hall with its lofty, coffered ceiling and ornate balcony (modified by Lutyens in 1916) and the restraint and simplicity of the Propylaeum. Philip Hardwick was fully aware of the importance of the railway and therefore decided that this gateway should be executed in the loftiest rhetoric. In the 1830s that was Greek Doric, then the Victorian's highest form of praise. There is a model of the Triumphal Arch and its four pavilions (the outer two were added in 1869–70 by Stansby) in the Museum of London at the Barbican. There seems little doubt therefore that British Railways were wrong to demolish the Propylaeum, and that their public image has suffered as a result. However, as slight compensation the pedimented clock which stood in the Great Hall has been preserved and is on show at York.

Indeed, the modern station, opened in 1968, replacing Euston's first terminus, does not do very much to rectify the blame for its demolition. It is a highly functional building with a concourse which is warm, spacious and well provided with facilities. The interior is clean and light. But from a purely architectural standpoint it does not measure up to its predecessor in style, variety and atmosphere, while the construction of an office block along the façade has destroyed any aesthetic pretensions it offered. All that remains of the steam age are the two L.N.W.R. pavilions on Euston Road. Their quoins are carved with the names of towns served by the company, though they are not those which stood either side of the Triumphal Arch.

EUSTON TO BIRMINGHAM

The line between Euston and Willesden Junction survives as a sublime working memorial to Victorian England. The construction of its tunnels and broad brick-lined cuttings fascinated Dickens, who portrayed the scene in *Dombey and Son* (1848). He perceived the great impact which the railways were having on England, not simply benefiting the economy but moulding the very landscape as well. This is his description of the works in the Camden area:

> The first shock of a great earthquake had, just at that period, rent the whole neighbourhood to its centre. Traces of its course were visible on every side. Houses were knocked down; streets broken through and stopped; deep pits and trenches dug in the ground . . . and fragments of unfinished walls and arches, and piles of scaffolding and wildernesses of bricks, and giant forms of cranes . . . In short, the yet unfinished and unopened Railroad was in progress; and from the very core of all this dire disorder trailed smoothly away, upon its mighty course of civilization and improvement.

Though the cuttings have been widened, the general impression is the same. The original south portal of Primrose Hill tunnel still exists, and may be seen from the junction of King Henry's and Primrose Hill Roads. Both arches are flanked by Italianate towers built on rusticated stone foundations. The cream stone and ochre stock brick forming the side walls is coated with thick black soot, but even this grime cannot hide the majesty of building on this scale.

The L.N.W.R.'s Camden Goods Station (in Chalk Farm Road) was an exceptionally busy depot even in the 1860s, as the following newspaper description shows:

> In the grey mists of the morning, in an atmosphere of a hundred conflicting smells, and by the light of faintly burning gas, we see a large portion of the supply of the great London markets rapidly disgorged by these night trains: fish, flesh and food, Aylesbury butter and dairy-fed pork, apples, cabbages and cucumbers . . . then at ten minutes' interval arrive other trains with Manchester packs and bales, American provisions . . . crates of pottery from N. Staffordshire . . . At a later hour in the morning these are followed by other trains with the heaviest class of traffic: stones, bricks, iron girders, ale, coal . . .

Depots like Camden serve as a reminder that the railways were originally conceived with goods traffic in mind, while passengers and later commuters were an aspect that many planners had failed to appreciate. Today much of the depot survives but no longer serves the railway, having been let out as warehouses for the sale of antiques.

South Hampstead is the first station on the line and its two platforms are set in the cutting. There was originally a second island platform for main-line trains but this is now disused and the extra staircase has gone. The surface buildings which lie across the tracks in Loudoun Road have been rebuilt, and the brackets and valancing removed from the platforms below. Nevertheless, the high walls and bridge supports in blue-black bricks, coated with a film of purple-brown rust, create a rich atmosphere. The cutting wall to the south, consisting of round arches supported by thick buttresses of soot-blackened ochre brick, is older. Suburban trains from Marylebone to Aylesbury and High Wycombe emerge from their tunnel to cross the line at right angles at the eastern end of the station.

From here the railway continues to Kilburn High Road and Queen's Park, a large four-platformed station with a light, lateral train-shed. Kensal Green, with its modern half-timbered brick booking hall which recently replaced the original dilapidated structure, follows, and then the line sweeps past the main locomotive depot, passes under the North London line, and runs into Willesden Junction.

Willesden is not the great junction of the past. The four L.N.W.R. platforms have been reduced to two, and it no longer handles main-line trains, which all by-pass to the south. Together with the high-level station and its service to Broad Street and Richmond, Willesden Junction is a complicated collection of lines set in a hollow surrounded by roads and bridges. At peak hours Underground trains from Baker Street call on their way to Watford. Indeed, Watford, Euston, Broad Street and Richmond are now its only destinations. It is surprising to think that Willesden once served places as far distant as Birmingham, Stafford and Crewe. James Tissot used it as the scene for his painting *Waiting for the Train* (Dunedin Art Gallery, New Zealand), depicting an attractive lady standing apprehensively at the platform edge surrounded by her luggage, while a N.L.R. train departs from the high-level platforms behind.

Rugby is the first major stop on the present main-line service from Euston. It retains its massive wrought-iron train-shed which spans the central concourse and buildings. There are three sections which lie laterally across the broad island platform, and extend over the through lines. Constructed in the L.N.W.R.'s typical red brick and Italianate style, Rugby Station has become somewhat dilapidated. It is so large that either demolition or restoration would be expensive undertakings. The large cantilever bridge crossing the main line immediately to the south of Rugby Station is the former Great Central Railway to London. Similar now purposeless bridges occur with sad frequency on the journey north. Coventry Station (1959-62), designed by W. R. Headley, soon follows. Ironically the L.N.W.R.'s station survived the extensive bombing of 1940, only to be demolished by B.R. Today's modern grey-brick and concrete building has kept its clean appearance as a result of electrification. Birmingham International is one of the few major stations to have been constructed since the war. It is an integral part of the new exhibition centre, which is sensibly sited outside the town alongside the main line, with ample parking facilities.

BIRMINGHAM

Birmingham New Street might shock the traveller who has not visited the city for a decade. The L.N.W.R.'s Grand Central Station was opened in 1854 and featured a massive, crescent train-shed (designed by E. A. Cowper and 211 feet across) supported by decorative brick side walls. To help passengers cross to their platforms, there was a memorable lattice-work high-walk. Though the Midland Railway had previously been permitted to use the station, in April 1897 the L.N.W.R. agreed to their joint ownership. Today it is more than a station. The old train-shed has been demolished and the cost of rebuilding was such that the upper floors were designed as a large shopping centre, while the concourse and offices situated below span the platforms. Escalators take passengers from the concourse to their trains. The walls are covered with white mosaics, and the pillars with white tiles. It is a sepulchral scene by night when illuminated by white neon – a modern, efficient, ice-box of a station.

The New Street site has turned out to be an exceptionally judicious choice. It is very central, lying in a natural bowl or amphitheatre, which has meant that its lines can enter and exit by tunnels without disturbing the town above. When New Street was enlarged in the 1880s, it came closer to the concept of a grand central station than any other in Britain, and the closure of Snow Hill (see below) made that a reality.

Naturally Birmingham, as a large, prosperous manufacturing town, created a complex network of railways and stations. Although the essential framework remains, there has been a great deal of pruning and modification. The London & Birmingham originally terminated at Curzon Street until the growth in the volume of traffic necessitated the construction of a bigger and more central station. Since then Curzon Street has acted as a goods and carriage depot. Fortunately, the original buildings survive and are visible from the London train lying to the north of the new sheds on the approach to New Street, though their scale and majesty is best appreciated from New Canal Street.

Also designed by Philip Hardwick, Curzon Street was meant to match the Euston Arch in style and dignity. Completed in 1838, it consisted of a classical three-storey stone block with a frieze and oblong pediment supported by four massive Greek Ionic columns. The grand entrance, surmounted by the arms of the two cities, is constructed in a restrained manner, the only obvious forms of ornament being the balustrades and trusses of the first-floor windows. Recently cleaned, Curzon Street terminus still has a breathtaking aspect and with the loss of the Euston Propylaeum must be Britain's finest memorial to the pioneering stage of railway history.

Snow Hill, which belonged to the Great Western Railway, was Birmingham's other major station. It too has been closed, and alas has been demolished, the site in Colmore Row having been converted into a car park. However, the tunnel entrances at each end survive, as do the surrounding walls. An entrance remains intact in Livery Street constructed from glazed sienna bricks (as is the G.W.R.'s former terminus in Moor Street) and a lighter-coloured terra-cotta, with the company's coat-of-

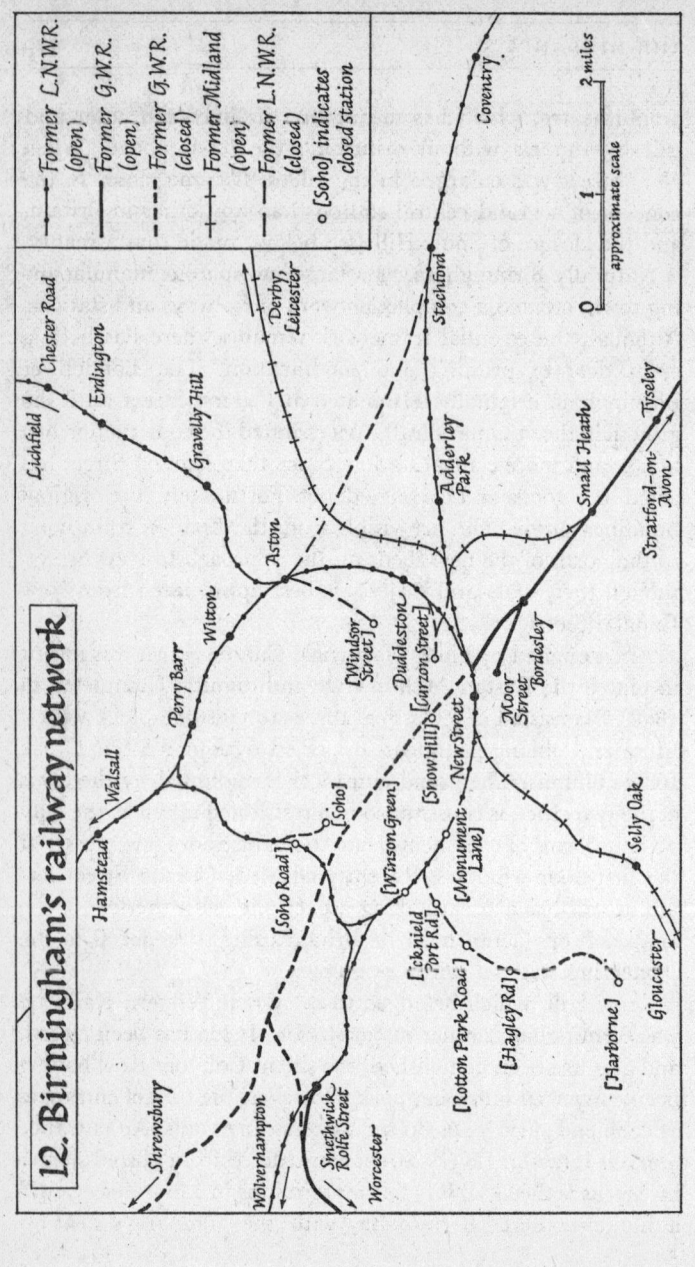

12. Birmingham's railway network

1. 222 Marylebone Road, British Rail's headquarters, formerly the Great Central Hotel, designed by Colonel R. W. Edis and completed in 1899.

2. The replica *Rocket* with an original L. & M.R. third-class carriage running on a temporary track in Kensington Gardens.

3. No. 60022, *Mallard*, now preserved at York and still holder of the fastest steam train record, 126 m.p.h.

4. No. 71000, *Duke of Gloucester*, Britain's most advanced steam locomotive, built by B.R. at Crewe in 1954 but never fully developed. Note the innovative and complex valve gearing.

5. No. 92220, *Evening Star*, a Standard 9 class locomotive and the last steam engine built by British Railways, being turned out from Swindon in March 1960.

6. A City & South London Railway electric train photographed in 1922.

7. A class 87 electric, the Midland Region's all-purpose locomotive.

8. The Advanced Passenger Train, with aerodynamically shaped cab and original livery.

9. (*top*) A 47 class diesel-electric locomotive hauling coke to Didcot power station; B.R.'s most common diesel-electric, used mostly for passenger services.

10. (*above*) Two High Speed Trains at the new Bradford Exchange terminus. The original station, which had a splendid train-shed, was further to the right.

11. (*left*) A dining saloon and attendants on the L.N.W.R. and Caledonian Railway's West Coast Route, *c.* 1912.

12. (*right*) A L.N.E.R. semaphore signal gantry, situated to the north of Hatfield on the East Coast Route.

13. (*below*) Birmingham New Street's computerized signal box looking more like a satellite tracking station.

14. A Metropolitan Line train from Amersham hauled by No. 12, *Sarah Siddons*.

15. District Line R stock heading for Hounslow. Note the push-buttons to operate the doors.

16. Interior of R stock. High-quality design for the period, working the L.T.'s bull's eye symbol into moquette seat designs.

17. The Bakerloo Railway's prototype all-steel motor car in 1906. They were designed and built in America, assembled in Manchester.

18. Gloucester Road Station as it was in 1916. The Piccadilly Railway's station is just visible to the left.

19. Acton Central Station on the North London Line, designed by E. H. Horne and completed in 1873, as restored by British Rail.

20. Notting Hill Gate Station in 1863, looking north. It is not much altered today, the train-shed and arcaded side walls having survived unscathed.

21. Chiswick Park Station, as rebuilt by London Transport in 1932, following the basic design pioneered at Arnos Grove.

22. A 1930's interior of a Metropolitan Railway Pullman car as operated along the Aylesbury line. Such standards of luxury and finish are unmatched today.

23. A Circle Line train composed of C69 stock, first introduced on the Metropolitan Line in 1970.

24. Victoria Line stock, showing the varied use of curved glass for wider visibility, introduced in 1967.

25. A King class locomotive hauling the 'Cornish Riviera' at Teignmouth in 1937. There are ten Ocean Saloons, the G.W.R.'s spacious carriages introduced in 1935.

26. (*top*) A Merchant Navy class, No. 35012, *United States Lines*, hauls the 'Devon Belle' near Basingstoke in 1950.

27. (*above*) A Great Northern suburban electrical multiple unit, a novel design for B.R. now operating on Eastern Midland, Scottish and Southern Regions.

28. (*right*) King's Cross Station, designed by Lewis Cubitt for the Great Northern Railway and completed in 1852.

29. The G.W.R.'s Cambrian Coast express at Abermule headed by a Duke class locomotive.

30. A Great Western 28xx class freight 2-8-0 locomotive hauling a coal train in Wales.

31. The Irish Mail bound for Holyhead emerges from the western portal of Robert Stephenson's Conway railway bridge (1848); here hauled by Royal Scot class No. 46164, *The Rifle Brigade*.

32. St Pancras Station, showing the former Midland Grand Hotel before cleaning. The hotel was completed in 1874 at a cost of almost a million pounds.

33. No. 506, *Butler-Henderson*, a 4-4-0 Director class locomotive built in 1919, the only surviving passenger engine from the G.C.R.

34. An Edwardian photograph of the opulent Midland Hotel, Manchester, designed by Charles Trubshaw in 1898.

35. No. 46236, *City of Bradford*, running south through Cumbria on the West Coast Route in 1948. The first carriage is a dynometer car used to test the locomotive's performance.

36. Robert Stephenson's Royal Border Bridge at Berwick-on-Tweed, designed in 1849. Here a class 47 diesel-electric hauls an Inter-City express bound for Edinburgh.

37. York Station, showing William Peachy's and Thomas Prosser's magnificent curved train-shed, seen here in 1943 with temporary shelters to protect passengers against falling glass caused by bombing.

38. Newcastle Station, designed by John Dobson and opened in 1850, shown here in an early photograph dating *c.* 1860. The four-storey building nearest the camera is the station hotel.

39. (*top*) The first 4–6–0 class, designed in 1894 by David Jones for the Highland Railway's freight trains. No. 103 has been preserved at Glasgow Museum of Transport.

40. (*above*) A three-car d.m.u. from Dundee crossing the Forth Bridge.

41. (*left*) A 1920s print of the Caledonian Railway's Princes Street Station Hotel; station entrance to the right and hotel to the left.

arms and its monogram above the doorway. Otherwise there is little to distinguish the once extensive Snow Hill Station. The adjacent Grand Hotel was presumably opened here to capture passengers as they emerged. Certainly the Midland Hotel was built for that reason to face New Street. It is a large red and grey brick building constructed, like their Manchester counterpart, around a square and offering a certain external resemblance.

The Great Western's terminus at Moor Street (1909) has remained open. Because their main station at Snow Hill was constructed in a confined space (the tunnel entrances constricted the London end), there was a need for a terminus to handle local services to the south, a need which has persisted despite the dimension of services to New Street. Moor Street is a typically Edwardian building, with its broad, gentle arches and free use of glazed sienna bricks giving the concourse an atmosphere akin to a swimming bath. Today there are trains to Stratford-upon-Avon and Leamington Spa, both via Tyseley.

WOLVERHAMPTON, STOKE, STAFFORD AND CREWE

The main line from Birmingham to Crewe calls at Wolverhampton and Stafford, the whole journey being over former L.N.W.R. metals. The connection to Stoke, and indeed the section of the route from Euston to Manchester running between Rugely and Macclesfield, is through the former North Staffordshire Railway's territory.

Wolverhampton and Stafford's stations have both been rebuilt to conform with the modernity of Euston and New Street. Wolverhampton, dominated by the L.N.W.R. and the Great Western, with a Midland connection, was formerly a considerable railway junction. The rivalry between these two railways dated back to their constituent companies. The Shrewsbury & Birmingham (G.W.R.) constructed a low-level station, while the L.N.W.R. (originally the Birmingham, Wolverhampton & Dudley) owned the high-level station.

Fighting actually broke out in July 1850 when navvies from each company met, police and troops being required to restore order. Electrification and rationalization has unfortunately meant that Wolverhampton's status as a railway town has declined. However, the original booking office (1849) survives on the corner of Railway Street and Horseley Fields. Like most early stations, it is a symmetrical Italianate building, executed in grey brick, with Doric columns and two square turrets. Disused, it awaits restoration.

Although Crewe has suffered from closures and modification, it has retained its importance as a junction and railway manufacturing centre. The huge train-shed and complex network of lines are largely intact and few can have travelled the English network without a pause at Crewe. There are three broad island platforms each with solid cream brick buildings, decorated with red and dark blue brick dressings. These feature a number of unusual bay windows comprising three groups of double curved lights, with ornamental Greek heads in the keystones. The whole is covered by a lateral train-shed supported on either side by buttressed brick walls, while glazed side-screens were also fitted to protect passengers from cross winds, as at Colwyn Bay and Rugby.

Dickens depicted the bustle and business of a railway junction in his *Lazy Tour* (1857); although not specified, it is thought that the description could have been based on Crewe.

> All manner of cross-lines of rails came zigzagging into it, like a congress of iron vipers; and, a little way out of it, a pointsman in an elevated signal-box was constantly going through the motions of drawing immense quantities of beer at a public-house bar. In one direction, confused perspectives of embankments and arches were to be seen from the platform ... Sidings were there, in which empty luggage-vans and cattle-boxes often butted against each other as if they couldn't agree; and warehouses were there ... Goods Train! Shimmering, whistling, trembling, rumbling, thun-

dering. Trains on the whole confusion of intersecting rails, crossing one another, hissing one another ... people frantic. Exiles seeking restoration to their native carriages.

Crewe grew naturally as an important junction in the L.N.W.R.'s network (routes from London and Birmingham divided here for North Wales, Chester, Manchester, Liverpool and Shrewsbury), while the siting of their goods depot and locomotive works added to its business and scope. The continued growth of traffic throughout the nineteenth century necessitated further rebuilding and expansion in the 1900s. Goods lines were tunnelled under the station to keep freight trains clear of the platforms and a long spider bridge carried staff across the complex maze of tracks. Much of this development was the inspiration and policy of Francis Webb, Locomotive Superintendent to the L.N.W.R. from 1871 to 1903. In 1851 there were a mere 840 houses in Crewe and 649 men employed in the company's workshops, but by 1903 there were 8,771 and 10,146 respectively.

Crewe is said to have been the first British station to possess an independent railway hotel, the Crewe Arms, opened in 1837. In 1864, it was leased by the L.N.W.R., who enlarged the building, retaining its original Jacobean manner, in keeping with the first station. The building survives.

The Potteries were one of the most specialized and self-contained areas in Britain. It is not surprising to discover, therefore, that they retained their own fiercely independent railway company, the North Staffordshire, until grouping in 1923. Stoke, centre of the district and the railway's headquarters, retains its magnificent Jacobean-style station and hotel, designed by H. A. Hunt and completed in 1850. The whole was carefully planned and might serve as an example to architects who believe that 'station complexes' are something new. The station itself forms one side of Winton Square, opposing the complementary North Stafford Hotel (no longer under British Rail ownership, and formerly much cleaner than the station), while the other two sides were filled with appropriately matched railway houses. All are executed in red brick with cream stone dressings and tiled roofs. The station, now grimy with soot, features dormer gables, a classically arched portico and high brick chimneys. Unfortunately the mullioned windows have been replaced and the portico modified. The company's shield, contained within a strapwork pediment, surmounts the entrance to both hotel and station.

One of the best-known features of the N.S.R.'s network was the Potteries' Loop. This was an inner-circle railway which branched from the main line at Kidsgrove to link Hanley, Burslem, Tunstall and Stoke. The Loop was authorized in 1865 but was not actually completed until November 1875 and was an immediate success. Arnold Bennett in his novels about the Five Towns often used the railway as a means of bringing his characters together. Hilda Lessways uses the Loop line on her way to London:

> On the following afternoon Hilda travelled alone by the local train from Bleakridge [presumably Cobridge] to Knype [Stoke], the central station where all voyagers for London, Birmingham and Manchester had to forgather... It was a custom of Five Towns hospitality that a departing guest should be accompanied as far as Knype and stowed with personal attentions into the big train.

Bennett illustrated the independent spirit of the N.S.R. by an incident in which the station staff at a Loop line stop could not produce a Bradshaw – they were oblivious to, or uninterested in, railways other than their own.

Unfortunately, the Loop line has long been closed, though of course the main-line section from Kidsgrove (originally called Harecastle) to Stoke via Longport and Etruria is still open. Only Longport has a substantial building, executed like Stoke, in Jacobean style with gables and patterned red brick. The northern part of the Loop to Golden Hill was used for colliery traffic until recently, but now the former railway is

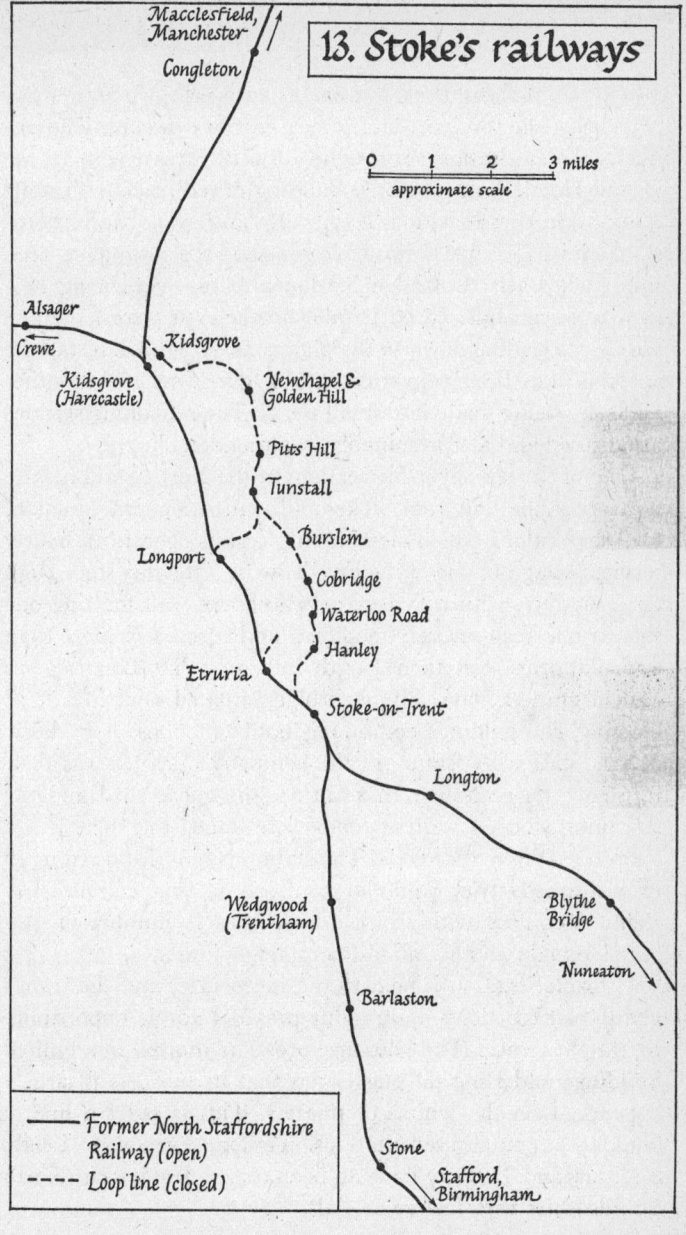

clearly visible from the main line as an overgrown and empty trackbed. The southern half is even less in evidence. The disused Hanley Station survives in Trinity Street, next to the Grand Hotel. A single-storey building of red brick with stone quoins and dressings, it is a typically austere north Staffordshire edifice. The platforms have gone and the cutting has been infilled in parts. Cobridge Station also survives, being of a similar design but placed parallel to the A50, across the line with steps leading down to the platforms. Around Tunstall the trackbed has been converted into a 'greenway', while other areas are being made into small parks. The remaining stations are disused and are presumably awaiting demolition.

One of the few surviving sections of the North Staffordshire network is the line from Stoke-on-Trent to Stenson Junction, for Derby, along which diesel multiple units operate an hourly service. Longton, one of the Five Towns, is the first stop. High on a viaduct, with a factory or warehouse wall forming one side, it has been severely modified, and is scarcely more than two platforms, but their length indicates that Longton has known grander days. Blythe Bridge, situated next to a level crossing, its buildings combining both functions, is a classic N.S.R. station. A feature of the company's designs was their insistence on economy. In addition, the goods shed and the adjoining wooden waiting room were linked together with a lean-to roof to reduce costs. The station is built from red brick in restrained style, while in contrast its iron columns are richly decorated with strapwork designs. A number of gas-lamps remain and are almost completely intact.

Uttoxeter Station is next to the racecourse, and the train's gentle passage along its straights provides ample opportunity to watch a race. The station's broad platforms but limited buildings underline the suggestion that its business is largely dependent on the whims of punters. This is sadly a line of demolished or disused stations. Fenton, Cresswell, Leigh, Sudbury and Tutbury have all been closed, leaving the North Staffordshire with few memorials.

Despite the fact that the North Staffordshire Company had a large locomotive works in Stoke (the Pennsylvania works, employing 900 men at its peak) producing their own engines, only one has survived. No. 2, an 0–6–2T(1923), designed by J. H. Adams in 1903, has been restored to its N.S.R. livery and is on display in the County Museum at Shugborough House near Stafford.

ST PANCRAS

St Pancras Station, fronted by the former Midland Grand Hotel, must be one of the finest nineteenth-century buildings in London and stands as a distinguished and fitting memorial to the Midland Railway and Victorian England. It is unfortunate that although the station is still a main-line terminus, the hotel no longer performs its original function, though it is a Grade One preserved building and under British Rail's auspices is undergoing extensive restoration.

The Midland did not always have a London terminus. In 1858 they had concluded an agreement with the Great Northern Railway to use King's Cross. Yet it soon became clear that traffic from the Midlands and beyond was increasing at such a pace that one terminus could not cope, and a crisis occurred in 1862 when the International Exhibition produced such a flood of passengers that the G.N. cut back the Midland's schedules. Consequently, plans were assembled for an extension of their lines to a proposed new station adjacent to King's Cross and William Barlow, the company's engineer, was made responsible for the construction of the train-shed. It was a massive 243 feet across, and when completed was the widest single-span building in the world. The wrought-iron ribs, supporting the roof, were supplied by the Butterley Company of Derby and their name may still be seen at platform level, along with the date of the ribs' erection. The station was not opened until 1867 and was then in an incomplete form.

Because the lines had to cross the Regent's Canal to the

north, St Pancras had to be built well above ground level. Indeed, the platforms are about sixteen feet higher than Euston Road and the tracks slope gently down to the buffers. Occasionally, inexperienced drivers have approached the station too quickly and because of the gradient have been unable to stop in time. When a collision has resulted, the whole hotel has shaken with the impact. Barlow made sensible use of the space below the station, constructing extensive cellars, which were used for storing beer barrels sent by the Midland from Burton-on-Trent. Today the cellars are still used for this purpose, though most of the drinks are canned. There is a printing works in the basement, which was originally employed to produce menus for the hotel and restaurant carriages.

An interesting feature of the station booking hall are the corbels along the north wall. In true Romantic tradition, an engine driver, a guard, an engineer and a signal boy are treated in the way that masons, prelates and artists were carved in medieval cathedrals. The actual ticket office, slightly modified from Scott's days, is still visible as a fine panelled construction. Unfortunately, the high vaulted ceiling was lowered and covered over in 1957.

The Midland Railway, anxious to enhance their prestige and outshine their rivals at King's Cross, decided that no expense should be spared on the construction of a mammoth hotel. Sir George Gilbert Scott won the competition to design the building, and eventually almost a million pounds was raised to pay for its completion. Scott had been compelled by Palmerston to adopt the Italianate manner in his designs for the new Foreign Office and was now presented with an opportunity to apply the Gothic manner, which he favoured, to an important public building.

The directors of the Midland wanted a hotel which would display their style, status and progress. Accordingly, it was constructed from Grippe's patent Nottingham bricks, with polished grey and red Peterhead granite columns and Ancaster stone dressings. The Midlands really had come to London.

Gables, pinnacles, casements, ornate oriel windows and turrets abound. Scott had made a thorough study of French and Italian Gothic details which allowed him to adorn the façade with authenticity and great variety. From a distance in the half-light, the hotel looks like a magnificent medieval castle, dominating the metropolis with all the romance of King Arthur's Round Table. Such was Scott's intention, for the interior is decorated with wall paintings of knights in armour, mythical beasts, carvings of saints and Christian figures. Off the grand staircase there survives an alcove painting by T. W. Hay depicting a garden scene from the *Roman de la Rose*.

The hotel was huge, having 400 beds and lavish public rooms. Around the curved west wing were magnificent dining and coffee rooms. Contemporary photographs reveal highly decorated pillars, capitals, beams and friezes. The walls were partly painted with medieval scenes, intricate iron and brass work abounded, while carpets, curtains and furniture were all of the highest quality. Attention to detail was exact and even the chimneys were fitted with their respective room numbers on the stacks to facilitate speedy cleaning. Indeed, parts of this most elaborate skyline were adorned even though they could never be seen by the passer-by below, while the ironwork along the staircases, balconies and roof-tops is of great intricacy and variety. Baedeker described the building in his 1896 *Guide* as being 'one of the best of the large terminal hotels' in London.

Though the Midland Grand was opened in 1873, it was not fully completed until 1877, some ten years after the station. It remained a hotel until 1935, when a lack of modern facilities and size compelled its closure. The building is now used as offices by British Transport Hotels, though it is hoped that the result of the massive restoration plan will be that parts of this incredible edifice are re-opened to the public. Certainly its powerful curving main staircase, lit by massive windows breaking up the west side of the building, is an awe-inspiring sight.

ST PANCRAS TO LEICESTER, NOTTINGHAM, SHEFFIELD AND DERBY

The main line from St Pancras to Bedford is dealt with in the suburban section of this chapter. Wellingborough follows Bedford as the next major town. On the evening of 2 September 1898, it was the scene of the only serious accident involving an express train on this route. A parcels truck had rolled across the platform and fallen on to the line. The 6.45 pm from London was late and racing to make up five minutes – had the train been on time the accident would not have happened, as the truck would have fallen after it had passed. Two station staff tried to remove the truck but the force of its impact had wedged it firmly between the rails. The express smashed into the obstacle, causing the engine to leap off the track and crash with a hissing roar into the embankment beyond the station. The wooden carriages telescoped into one another and a fire broke out. Six people were killed and sixty injured.

Kettering Station, designed by C. H. Driver and completed in 1857, is on a viaduct and some of the buildings are weatherboarded, which is unusual for this region. There are original iron columns, brackets and glazed awnings. The Midland Railway's careful attention to building materials has already been noted at St Pancras. For stations along the main line, the company used local materials, as illustrated by the disused but extant station at Glendon & Rushton (visible to the west past Kettering), which is executed in clean, cream limestone – an exceptionally attractive building, with lozenge-paned windows, ornate bargeboards and a varied skyline. The next stop, Desborough & Rothwell (also closed), is constructed in golden ironstone, while Kibworth, after Market Harborough, was built from local red brick.

Market Harborough is an unusual triangular station, with the main buildings between the junction of the lines. There were L.N.W.R. routes to Rugby and Northampton but these have been closed to passenger traffic, though the railway to

Northampton is still used for freight and parcels. The Queen Anne frontage in red brick with stone pilasters and dressings is not in keeping with the traditions of the railway companies, but assumes something of the town's Georgian vernacular.

There were originally two termini in Leicester serving local lines – Belgrave Road (G.N. & L.N.W.R. Joint) and West Bridge (Midland), both of which are now closed. In addition, there were two main-line stations. The first, London Road on the Midland, is now Leicester's only station, while Central on the former G.C.R. is closed and passes its time as a car park. Leicester's first railway was the Leicester & Swannington, built by George Stephenson to carry granite, coal and lime. The line was opened on 17 July 1832 and operated a passenger service as well, a side of its business which was scorned by the directors as people contributed a mere 5 per cent of receipts. Leicester's connections to Derby and Nottingham followed in May 1840, while rail links with Rugby, Hull and Leeds followed eight weeks later on 30 June. The development of the town's communication network broadened the market for its products and encouraged the mechanization of its hosiery and footwear industries.

Leicester was the home of Thomas Cook, the ardent temperance campaigner. To increase the effectiveness of their meetings he decided to hire a whole train to take supporters from Leicester to near-by Loughborough. From this excursion, on 5 July 1841, developed his travel business and the concept of the travel agent. Cook's main offices remained in Leicester until 1879, and there is a plaque at London Road Station to commemorate his first enterprise.

London Road is an impressive building. Designed by Charles Trubshaw and completed in 1892, it consists of a long *porte cochère* with massive arches, surmounted at the northern end by an angled, hexagonal clock tower. The exterior has been recently cleaned, revealing its red brick and light sienna terracotta. The departure and arrival entrances are denoted by porcelain signs featuring the Midland's red dragon symbol.

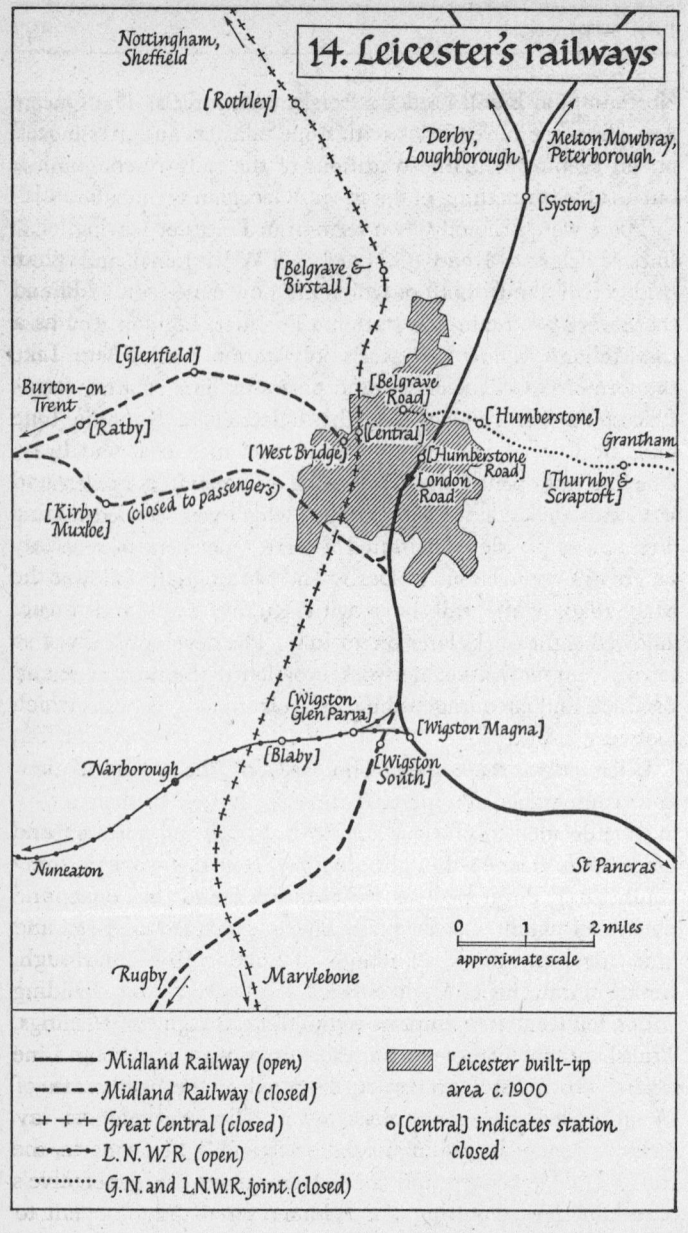

Unfortunately all the original platform buildings have been demolished (those on Platforms 1 and 2 consisted of a glazed cream and brown brick arcaded structure decorated with a terra-cotta frieze) and replaced by functional red-brick buildings lit by white plastic awnings.

Leicester Central, opened in 1899, is situated off Vaughan Way in Great Central Street, some distance from the Midland station. Today the platforms and the trackbed are used as a car park, while the main buildings serve as a warehouse. Like London Road it was constructed from red brick and terra-cotta – the popular materials of the Edwardian period. One of its entrances still proclaims: 'Great Central Railway, Parcels Office'. Although it features a baroque clock tower and a parapet with niches, urns and pediments, as a building Central is not as inspiring as its Midland rival, and probably the Great Central's most impressive feature in Leicester was the mile-long viaduct which the company was forced to construct to lift their railway into the central part of the town. Even so they had to demolish 300 houses, involving further expense and disruption. Central Station is actually on the viaduct, which was broadened to accommodate a large island platform, but this has now been demolished, as have other parts of their viaduct.

Loughborough is the mid-way point between Leicester and Nottingham. This was where the Great Central's more direct route to Nottingham crossed the Midland main line and continued in a north-easterly direction. The embankment and bridge are clearly visible from the end of Loughborough, Derby Road Station. It is a light, grey-ochre brick building with original fluted columns and decorative, glazed awnings, while Central Station is now the headquarters of the Main Line Steam Trust. The four miles of level track to the north of Loughborough were an ideal site for the Midland to lay water-troughs. These were longitudinal tanks placed in the centre of the tracks. A scoop was lowered from the locomotive's tender and the motion of the speeding train was sufficient to force fresh water up into its tanks, eliminating the necessity of stopping to refill from a watertower.

Between Loughborough and Nottingham, just before Trent Junction (and the line to Derby), are the Red Hill tunnels. They are best seen on the journey to London, as their northern portals have been castellated. Constructed from stone, each entrance has battlements, turrets, arrow loops and lancet windows completing the medieval image. They are short tunnels, only 154 yards long, and derive their name from the red marl through which they are cut. The story is told how the local landowner counted passing trains from a turret and then charged the Midland accordingly.

Nottingham, once a town with three main-line stations and a host of local stops, has since been heavily pruned. London Road Low Level (G.N.R.) is now a goods depot; Victoria (G.C.R.) has been demolished, leaving Midland, with its peculiarly awkward approach, as the sole survivor. The first line to reach Nottingham was the Midland Counties Railway from Derby which opened on 30 May 1839. Although it received this early connection, main-line routes did not follow so swiftly. Indeed, it was not until 1880 that the loop from Kettering was completed and 1899 when the arrival of the Great Central gave the town a direct link with London.

The approach from Loughborough is through extensive goods yards dominated to the north by the castle on its rocky heights, the line finally being channelled into Nottingham Midland (1900) by warehouses and sheds. The station bears a close resemblance to Leicester London Road, since both are constructed from red brick and sienna terra-cotta, featuring large *portes cochère* dominated by an ornate clock tower. The arches are decorated with swags of fruit and display the initials M.R. The southern end retains the original *art nouveau* gates and railings with their characteristic flowing designs. The concourse, as at Leicester, is on a grand scale with a high mansard roof. The two platform buffets still have their original interiors: the 'Lacemaker' is tiled in cream and sienna with rose motifs and an egg-and-dart frieze, the other being panelled with fluted pilasters and having a fireplace supported by Ionic columns.

The Great Northern's London Road Low Level Station, built in 1865 further to the east on the same tracks, is now the town's goods terminal. Seen from the junction of Station and London Roads, it fits into a varied industrial landscape. The Nottingham Canal flows beneath the railway, while the disused high-level line, which connected with the Great Central, lies derelict to the north. London Road Station is a curious red-brick building in a mixture of styles. Jacobean is used in the *porte cochère* and parapets and seems to dominate, although there are French gables and Venetian windows.

Nottingham's Victoria Station has been overwhelmed and almost completely absorbed by the new shopping centre. Only its giant red-brick clock tower, with its Darley Dale dressings and turquoise copper cupola, has been preserved, and it might be argued that it is the only element of architectural interest in the complex. The Great Central's adjacent Victoria Hotel, constructed from the same materials and featuring broad dormer gables and Jacobean windows, survives.

As at Leicester, the Great Central was forced to carry its main line across the town on a number of dark blue brick viaducts and their cantilever bridge over the Midland Station remained until 1980, though the viaduct to the Victoria tunnel (393 yards) survives. A small park has been laid out at its entrance and affords a good view of the overgrown trackbed, a garden of weeds winding across the town.

By virtue of its timing the Great Central was really doomed before it began. It arose from the Manchester, Sheffield & Lincolnshire Railway which in 1893 was authorized to build a line from Annesley in Nottinghamshire to a junction with the Metropolitan Railway at Quainton Road. Changing its name to Great Central in 1897 it then decided to build its own terminus at Marylebone (see p. 82), rather than use Baker Street. The line was formally opened on 9 March 1899;

important agreements had been concluded with the G.W.R. permitting an extension from Rugby to Banbury and the use of their tracks to High Wycombe and Princes Risborough. Unfortunately, the cost of construction far exceeded expectations and the company never paid a dividend on its ordinary shares. The grand plan to double Marylebone's capacity (today only half of the broad concourse is used) never materialized. The problem was that there was insufficient business for an additional main-line company, or at least that traffic did not continue to grow as it had done in the nineteenth century. The First World War, the depression and finally the development of the motor car conspired to defeat the Great Central.

This was a pity, as their line was exceptionally well engineered. Between Leicester and Quainton Road gradients barely exceed 1 in 176, with carefully controlled curves all in contrast to the parallel Midland route. The Great Central also built up a sound reputation for fast and reliable running, while their carriages were amongst the most comfortable and well served in Britain.

In Sheffield (see p. 295), the Great Central extended their earlier station (constructed by the M.S. & L.R.), building a new frontage in 1908. Their simple red-brick clock tower survives, and though Sheffield Victoria is now closed to passengers, the adjacent Royal Victoria Hotel still flourishes. The present building was opened in September 1862. It is a restrained edifice constructed from red brick and Pennine stone. The hotel is approached by a magnificent stone-sided driveway, which formerly served the station as well, and there is a grand Jacobean-style ballroom, originally the restaurant, with a minstrels' gallery and much strapwork ornamentation on the columns and plaster ceiling. The lounge has an iron firegrate decorated with the shields of the Great Central, while the grandfather clock comes from the former Midland Hotel in Bradford. One room has been dedicated to the Great Central Railway. Its wallpaper bears the company's armorial device

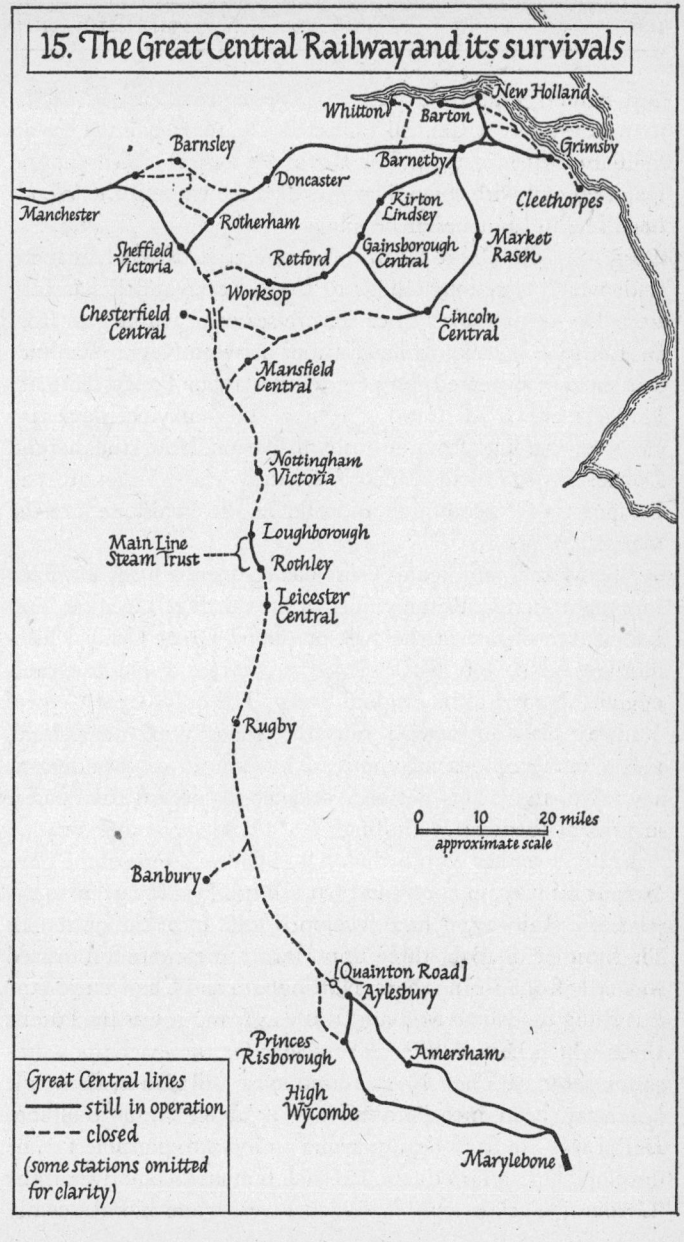

and contains a portrait of Alexander, Lord Faringdon, Chairman of the Great Central from 1899 to 1923, painted by Sir William Orpen in 1924. The Royal Victoria is a pleasant and historic hotel with splendid views of the town and the Woodhead line to Manchester behind.

In 1923 the Great Central became part of the L.N.E.R., with western sections falling to the L.M.S., and it has continued to decline ever since. Expresses were withdrawn from Marylebone in 1960, while all trains between Rugby, Banbury and Aylesbury ceased on 3 September 1966. Today there are few former Great Central routes still carrying passenger services. The lines from Grimsby to Barton, New Holland and Doncaster, south to Lincoln Central via Market Rasen, Retford via Gainsborough and Sheffield to Penistone, are the main survivors.

The Main Line Steam Trust has re-opened a section from Loughborough to Rothley, just to the north of Leicester, and has charge of one of the two preserved Great Central locomotives – No. 506, *Butler-Henderson* (1919), a 4–4–0 express engine, restored to its original livery. The only Great Central Railway class to survive into the 1960s were the 'O–4s', 2–8–0 tender goods locomotives, introduced as long ago as 1911. No. 102 (1911) has been selected for preservation and is at present shedded at Dinting.

Derby, together with Swindon and Crewe, is one of the most famous railway junctions and workshops. Headquarters of the Midland Railway, it had developed lines from the outset. In the summer of 1836, three important routes were authorized to Derby from Birmingham, Nottingham and Chesterfield (the last being the North Midland Railway), and it was the latter's sheds which became the real nucleus for the extensive workshops of today. Their No. 1 roundhouse still stands, though it has since been incorporated into a much larger building. Derby was Stanier's headquarters and was responsible for the development and production of such famous locomotives as the 'Coronation' class and the Black Fives, while more recently the High Speed Train and the Advanced Passenger Train were designed here.

Derby Station, opposite the railway works on the edge of the town centre, is a curious mixture of Victorian and post-war architecture. The main buildings are in red brick with grey stone quoins and dressings. It is a symmetrical design flanked with pavilions, each featuring a typanum and small cupola. In the centre a clock pediment is supported by the winged dragons of the Midland Railway. As at Leicester, the entrance hall has original glazed tiles and frieze. The platforms have been re-modelled and their buildings, awnings and footbridges are simply constructed in concrete. They are dilapidated, dull and something of an eyesore which is all the more annoying when it is recalled that the original Tri-junct train-shed (1839-41), designed by Francis Thompson and Robert Stephenson, was a distinguished engineering achievement, its triple sheds, supported by fluted columns and decorative cross girders, spanning 150 feet, the largest being 56 feet wide. However, Thompson's Midland Hotel (1840) does survive and remains the oldest station hotel in existence. It is a restrained Italianate structure whose stone façade would much benefit from cleaning.

A number of Midland Railway locomotives, built at the company's works in Butterley, have been preserved and stored there. They include No. 158A, a 2-4-0 tender engine (1866), No. 1418 (now No. 1708) and an 0-6-0T (1880). No. 1000, an exceptionally handsome 4-4-0 (1902) of the famous 'Compound' class, has been fully restored and is usually on display at York Railway Museum.

The former Midland main line from Derby to Manchester has been severed at Matlock and the section north-west to Chinley Junction (on the Hope Valley line; see p. 298) has been lifted. However, the Peak Railway Society has plans to re-lay the line from Matlock to Buxton (M.R.), as British Rail operate a service from Manchester Piccadilly to the former Buxton L.N.W.R. terminus. It is an ambitious project which would culminate in the re-opening of a historic and exceptionally picturesque route. Matlock Station, an Italianate stone building designed by Joseph Paxton, has been leased by the Society as a shop and office. At present B.R. operate a weekday pay train schedule from Derby, via Belper to Matlock, over a route which has largely been reduced to single track (an economy measure designed to save staff whereby passengers buy their tickets from the guard rather than at station booking offices). Parts of the original Matlock Bath Station (completed in the 1880s) survive. To accord with the Derwent Valley's romantic atmosphere and function as a spa, Swiss chalets were built to shelter passengers on the platforms. The alpine building is distinguished by its overhanging eaves, herringbone pattern brickwork and lozenge lattice windows.

Suburban Services

ST PANCRAS TO LUTON AND BEDFORD

St Pancras is not particularly noted for its suburban services. Indeed, it is the only London terminus which has a single line with no branches, the sections from Harpenden to Hemel Hempstead and the link from Cricklewood to Willesden Junction both having been closed. Neither were ever particularly important. One of the reasons for St Pancras's failure to develop a broad commuter network was the constricted approach to the station, caused by the need to cross the Regent's Canal. The bridge over Pancras Road is narrow and accommodates only six tracks. In days when the Midland operated important expresses to Scotland and west-coast towns, as well as south Yorkshire and the Midlands, there was precious little time or space for local trains.

Today there are suburban services to Luton and Bedford. At present they are hauled by diesel multiple units, but electrification is under way and when completed will involve the introduction of trains such as are used on the 'Great

Northern' suburban from Moorgate. The erection of overhead cables has altered the character of the line. Coloured light signals replaced semaphore arms, bridges were raised or demolished and tunnels modified. The broad expanse of St Pancras's train-shed has been broken up and confused by short pylons and lengths of cable.

Leaving St Pancras the railway passes a cluster of Victorian gasholders, a disused watertower and a small turntable (diesels do not need to be turned about) and plunges into a series of deep brick-lined cuttings to Kentish Town. West Hampstead, out in the open, follows. There are extensive yards and sidings at Cricklewood, where carriages and engines alike are stored – the Midland's equivalent of Old Oak Common on the Great Western. The freightliners and bright containers waiting to be lifted on to their trucks are a sign of developments in goods transportation. The line then continues north and runs parallel to the M1, semi-detached houses become more intermittent and London is left behind.

A number of stations are being rebuilt as a part of the policy of electrification. Elstree & Borehamwood has retained its Victorian red-brick structure, but Radlett in semi-rural Hertfordshire has been modernized. St Albans had already been re-modelled and Harpenden was rebuilt in the inter-war period. The approaches to Luton are characterized by sidings filled with goods vehicles, while the railway is carried through the town by a series of embankments and bridges. The football ground with its terraces and floodlights is clearly visible over the slate roof-tops of red-brick terraces. The station itself was rebuilt between 1937 and 1940 and is rather dreary as a result

Good rail connections helped to make Luton an attractive town for expanding engineering and chemical industries. The first major works were established in 1871, followed by Vauxhall Motors in 1905 and Commercial Cars in 1906, bringing increased employment and extra freight traffic. Consequently the schedules to Luton Midland were improved. Slip coaches were provided, and as many as twenty-nine express trains called each way in the 1930s. Today there are usually three trains every hour, one of which is a semi-fast, together with an hourly Inter-City service.

Leagrave, Harlington and Flitwick are all small, late-Victorian stations built from brick with stone dressings. They are soundly constructed, providing accommodation for the station master, while Harlington features a number of ornate cast-iron gaslamp standards and name board holders. Just before Bedford the skyline to the west is dominated by row upon row of slender chimneys belonging to the London Brick Company, and huge pits with mechanical shovels balanced precariously on their edges indicate their previous output. The kilns were established near the railways to supply the demands of a greedy capital and its suburbia.

Bedford urgently needed a railway in the nineteenth century, having to rely on barge traffic along the River Ouse for its heaviest goods. George Stephenson visited the town in 1844 and his discussions resulted in the rail connection to Bletchley, completed in November 1846. This later became part of the well-liked, but now closed, Oxford to Cambridge route, though this section, via Millbrook and Woburn Sands, still operates. The Midland reached Bedford from Leicester en route to Hitchin (closed to passengers in 1962) in October 1858 and gave the town direct access to King's Cross, though their London Road Station was not opened in Bedford until February 1859. With the decision to build a terminus at St Pancras and stop using King's Cross, the Midland laid their own line to London, via Luton and St Albans, this being completed in 1868. As Bedford is the terminus for the electric suburban service, a modern tinted-glass station has been constructed and the platforms re-aligned to allow the erection of sheds to store the new trains.

An important part of the general electrification project has been the construction of the Midland City Line: the underground extension from Dock Junction (slightly to the north of

St Pancras) westwards to King's Cross, Farringdon, Barbican and Moorgate. In the days of steam, B.R. operated a service from Moorgate parallel to the Metropolitan Line as far as the old King's Cross Underground station (still evident from the arcaded brick side walls) where it tunnelled to York Way Station and joined the main commuter flow northwards. With the completion of the Finsbury Park–Moorgate electrification (see p. 168), the original service via Farringdon was reduced and in May 1979 the limited peak-hour d.m.u. trains were finally withdrawn to allow modernization to proceed. Although the Midland City Line mostly runs through existing cuttings and tunnels, the introduction of overhead cables has necessitated the lowering of the trackbed where there is insufficient headroom. As on parts of the suburban line to Bedford slab track has been laid (continuous welded rail embedded in two layers of concrete requiring a small construction depth and little maintenance, but allowing precise and permanent positioning), the remainder having been re-ballasted. Platforms have been lengthened at Moorgate terminus and rebuilt at Barbican and Farringdon, while an interchange station has been constructed at King's Cross. St Pancras has suffered in the past from limited suburban traffic; the Midland City Line will not only help to solve this problem but will also ensure the continued use of a historic and atmospheric stretch of London's railways.

EUSTON TO NORTHAMPTON

Most of Euston's suburban service is operated over parts of the main line to Birmingham. The southern sections were the first to be constructed, the railway between London and Boxmoor (for Hemel Hempstead) having been completed in June 1837. It was extended to Denbigh Hall (Bletchley) in April 1838 and reached Rugby in September of the same year. It was certainly no simple engineering operation. There were deep cuttings at Tring and Blisworth, a one and a half mile viaduct and embankment across the Ouse valley at Wolverton, and long tunnels at Watford, Primrose Hill and Kilsby.

The first section of the route as far as Willesden Junction has already been described (p. 175). From here to Watford, the railway cuts through the various rings of London's suburban growth. The Victorian terraces and villas of Harlesden give way to 1930s semi-detached estates at Wembley. Harrow, being an older residential district, breaks up the sequence, but subsequently the trend is towards modernity.

Watford has developed as an important commuter centre. Before the coming of the railways it was a declining market town with a number of craft industries. The construction of the London & Birmingham Railway produced an about-turn in Watford's fortunes and it developed rapidly as a residential area for the City's wealthier workers. By 1861 Watford's population had reached 6,546, and it exceeded 10,000 by 1881. The L.N.W.R. encouraged this migration by offering a free twenty-one-year season ticket to buyers of substantial houses, the pass being attached to the property, not the occupant. This growth continued in the inter-war period with the completion of the Bakerloo Line to Watford in 1917. Inter-City trains to the industrial north call at Watford to save passengers the extra journey into Euston. The Manchester Pullman, for example, which leaves London at 8.00, is essentially a businessman's train, calling only at Watford and Stockport, a town with a similar commuter tradition.

For a large part of its course between Watford and Rugby, the railway runs alongside the Grand Union Canal. Completed in 1805, this waterway was designed as a direct freight link between London and Birmingham. It is no coincidence that the railway sticks so close to its route. Both forms of transport are sensitive to slope and took the line of least geographical resistance, landowners permitting. Often railway companies purchased canals in their area – the Great Western bought out the ailing Kennet & Avon Canal – and used their lands for additional lines or sidings. Certainly it was the railways' superior ability to carry goods cheaply and quickly which resulted in the waterway's decline. The Grand Union has little commercial traffic today, performing merely a recreational role.

Wolverton, to the north of Bletchley, is one of the lesser known railway towns. In 1831 there were a mere 417 inhabitants. As Wolverton lay mid-way between London and Birmingham, the London & Birmingham Railway chose it as the site for their new railway works. The sheds and workshops were opened in 1838. The company also constructed houses, schools and a church for its employees, and even took responsibility in a *laissez faire* age for providing gas and water. With the steady growth in railway business, so the town expanded and in the 1850s there was further housing development at Bradwell. By 1901 greater Wolverton had 9,200 inhabitants, rising to 15,000 in 1951. At their peak the locomotive works employed over 5,000 men and covered thirty-five acres, while today there are around 2,000 workers spread over an area of twenty-four acres.

Wolverton's function has also changed with this gradual reduction in the workforce. Until 1861 it was the L.N.W.R.'s chief repair depot for the southern half of their network, when all locomotive work was concentrated at Crewe. Subsequently it was responsible for carriage and wagon construction and maintenance, though since 1962 it has dealt with coach repair alone. The Midland Railway six-wheel composite carriage (1885) on display at York Museum was restored to its original livery and condition in its shops. Before the introduction of dining and buffet cars, Wolverton was a refreshment stop. However, a new station was constructed in 1881 when the main line was re-aligned to the east of the growing workshops, which had spread on both sides of the original route.

At first it seems surprising that an important and historic town such as Northampton should not be situated on the main line to Birmingham. It has been suggested that the town's conservative inhabitants scorned this modern development and resisted its intrusion, but this is less than fair. In fact, the

London & Birmingham Railway avoided Northampton because of its unfavourable geographical situation. The town grew up on the north bank of the River Nene at the confluence of its two tributaries, with hills surrounding the town on three sides. The only easy approach is towards the east from Wellingborough and Peterborough. This was finally the route selected by the town's first railway, a branch of the London & Birmingham from Blisworth, opened in May 1845. However, the line proved prone to flooding and was closed to passengers in 1964 in favour of the more direct route from Roade (now closed) to the old Northampton Castle Station. This railway was laid by the L.N.W.R. in February 1859 and continued on to Market Harborough, where it joined the Midland main line from St Pancras. The northern section is now reserved for freight only, and passenger trains rejoin the Birmingham route at Rugby, via Long Buckby.

The Northampton Loop was electrified in 1966 along with the West Coast line as far as Manchester. This was accompanied by the construction of a new station, and the introduction of hourly trains to Euston, Rugby and Coventry. Even today it has proved impossible, because of the concentration of freight in the area, to run an Inter-City service through Northampton.

MARYLEBONE TO BANBURY AND AYLESBURY

The route from Marylebone to Aylesbury is duplicated as far as Amersham by fast Metropolitan Line trains from Baker Street. It might seem curious that British Rail should allow the Underground to use this part of its network but in fact the Metropolitan Railway constructed the line originally, reaching Aylesbury in September 1892 and obtaining permission to share the Great Western's station two years later. When the Great Central were planning their trunk railway from Sheffield, it was agreed that they should join the Metropolitan at Quainton Road and use Baker Street as their London terminus. In the event, they built their own station at Marylebone (see p. 82), though the cost of laying a new line into the capital forced them to use Metropolitan metals from Aylesbury to Finchley. With the doubling of these tracks, it became a common sight to see a Metropolitan electric locomotive battling with a Great Central steam engine as they hauled their respective trains to Rickmansworth – until 1958 the limit of electrification.

In April 1906 the Great Central concluded an alliance with the G.W.R. to allow them to operate over their line from Northolt Junction, via High Wycombe and Princes Risborough (with its branch to Aylesbury), to Grendon Junction. This gave them an alternative route to Marylebone and a wider commuter network.

On leaving Marylebone, trains pass through three lengthy tunnels (the first and second being separated by a short viaduct over the Euston main line) to Finchley, where the railway runs parallel with the Metropolitan and Jubilee Lines. The two diverge after Neasden, and Wembley Complex (formerly Hill) follows. The section between Neasden and Northolt Junction, calling at Sudbury & Harrow Road, Sudbury Hill Harrow (formerly South Harrow) and Northolt Park, was constructed by the Great Central to complete the connection with the Great Western's route from Paddington to Birmingham, via Banbury. Hence there is a clear change in station architecture beginning with Northolt, though South Ruislip has been modernized.

The G.W. buildings at West Ruislip set the pattern for the larger stations at Denham, Gerrards Cross, Beaconsfield, Princes Risborough, High Wycombe and Bicester. They are constructed from clean red brick with honey-coloured dressings and though lightly adorned exhibit a real charm and character. Ladbroke Grove on the Metropolitan Line is of an identical pattern, the explanation being that the Great Western ran trains there from Paddington. Although the Marylebone to Princes Risborough service was G.W. & G.C. Joint, it was actually constructed by the former, the latter simply purchasing running rights.

The journey from West Ruislip is through rolling grassland dotted with clumps of woodland. It is surprisingly unspoilt and retains much of the flavour of a rural branch line. The impression created in MacDonnell's *England Their England* (1942) has hardly changed from when the Great Central passed 'through lovely, magical rural England ... It goes', he observed, 'to places that do not need a railway, that never use a railway, that probably do not yet know that they have got a railway ... It glides past the great pile of willow branches that are maturing to make England's cricket bats. It is a dreamer among railways, a poet, kindly and absurd and lovely.'

High Wycombe is the terminus for most local trains and is unusual in that its platforms are staggered, dominated by a high blue-brick cutting wall opposite the main platforms and entrance hall. In the past it was a busy station, with a branch to Loudwater, Marlow and Taplow; the disused trackbed is visible to the south on the approach to the station. In addition, there were extensive goods yards, while the station was a passing point for through trains – hence the staggered platforms and four tracks.

The line from High Wycombe to Banbury is particularly attractive. The railway is carried above unspoilt countryside on embankments and brick bridges to Princes Risborough and Bicester, both characteristic G.W. stations. Further north the line swings over the top of the Oxford–Birmingham main line and then descends to join it just before King's Sutton.

Banbury Station was rebuilt in 1958 and was praised at the time for its architectural qualities and practical good sense. It is a period piece, constructed from concrete and yellow-ochre brick, with generous windows, particularly in the foot-bridge, while the platform awnings and their side walls are simply constructed without adornment – a functional contrast to any Victorian design. With four through lines and several bay platforms it is certainly better able to accommodate Inter-City, local and freight trains than its predecessor.

Something of a bottleneck was created when in 1900 the Great Central built their line to Banbury and the already inadequate Great Western station was forced to cope with the extra traffic. The extensive sidings to the north of the present building indicate the scale of its earlier business. The Great Central's line has been lifted, but the embankments and bridges remain. There was another station in Banbury, Merton Street, the L.N.W.R.'s terminus for the line from Bletchley, opened in May 1850. But with the general decline in receipts the railway was closed to passengers in January 1961, and freight in September 1964.

PRESERVED STEAM RAILWAYS

The Birmingham Railway Museum, Tyseley

Tyseley is very much a working museum. Fully operational steam engines are shedded here between runs and locomotives rescued from the scrapyard are restored and maintained. The museum is situated on a spacious site behind the existing British Rail depot. There are two large sheds containing lathes, milling and grinding machines which enable its volunteers to carry out comprehensive repair work on the largest locomotives.

There is a broad range of locomotives from a variety of companies on display here. From the Great Western stable there are No. 7029, *Clun Castle* (which was one of the few of its class to be fitted with multiple jet blast pipes and a double chimney in an effort to increase performance), No. 7027, *Thornbury Castle*, and No. 4983, *Albert Hall*. Equally impressive in its L.M.S. maroon livery is the Jubilee class No. 45593, *Kolhapur*. Two of the oldest locomotives to have been restored at Tyseley, but since moved, were the former L.S.W.R. class T9, 4–4–0, No. 120 (Dugald Drummond's most successful express engines, of which sixty-six were built, No. 120 being among the first to be turned out from Nine Elms in 1899) and

No. 1008, a 2-4-2T from the Lancashire & Yorkshire Railway. This engine was completed in 1889, being the first to be built in the new works at Horwich. Under the L.M.S. No. 1008 (then 10621) was briefly sent to Kentish Town to haul suburban trains from Euston. No. 1008 has, however, been restored to its original livery. There are also two G.W.R. (ex-London Transport) 57 xx class pannier tanks at Tyseley, No. 7760 (L90) (1930) and No. 7752 (L94) (1930).

The Main Line Steam Trust, Loughborough Central Station

The Main Line Steam Trust is unusual in that it was formed not to preserve a branch line or a depot, but to re-open a section of the former Great Central main line. The disused Central Station at Loughborough was chosen as the headquarters. Single-line track has been preserved for five and a half miles, south to Rothley, via Quorndon and Woodhouse, and the station buildings restored. Steam-hauled trains are operated regularly along this stretch throughout the year. It is a particularly picturesque area, with magnificent views from the Swithland viaduct.

The Trust has the facilities to maintain and overhaul locomotives in its Loughborough sheds. As a result it has attracted a number of interesting engines, including the Great Central's No. 506, *Butler-Henderson* (1919), and No. 71000, *Duke of Gloucester*. This engine was the prototype for a new class of express locomotives, designed by R. A. Riddles and built in 1954. However, the decision was taken to abandon steam working and no further examples were constructed, leaving No. 71000 as unique. It was claimed that its three cylinders and advanced valve gearing offered great potential, but these possibilities were never fully explored.

Restored to L.M.S. livery is one of the ubiquitous 'Black Fives', No. 5231. Representing the Southern Railway is No. 34039, *Boscastle*, a rebuilt West Country class. From the L.N.E.R. is a 4-6-0 general purpose locomotive, No. 1264. These B1 class engines were designed by E. Thompson and introduced from 1942 onwards. There are in fact over twenty engines in various states of preservation, including several European examples, while the passenger stock is mostly early B.R. with two L.N.E.R. catering vehicles.

The Quainton Railway Society

Quainton Road is a former station on the G.C. & Metropolitan Joint line north of the present terminus at Aylesbury, though the track between them is still used by B.R. Quainton was the point where the Great Central and the Metropolitan met and many of the locomotives and some of the rolling stock reflects this fact. Representing the latter is No. 1 (L44), an 0–4–4T built in 1898; there is an ex-G.W. pannier tank L99 bought from London Transport and now numbered 7715, while the Society's oldest engine is No. 0314, a 2–4–0 well tank built by Beyer, Peacock in 1874 for the L.S.W.R.

There is a splendid collection of vintage carriages, mostly from the London region, including a four-wheeler from the N.L.R., a G.N.R. six-wheeled third-class brake coach (1895), G.C.R. six-wheelers and a L.N.W.R. first-class kitchen/dining car No. 77 built in 1901. On open days there has been a d.m.u. service from Aylesbury to Quainton Road, via Waddesdon Manor, the station opened for Lord Rothschild's convenience.

The Midland Railway Centre, Butterley Station

Situated on the former Midland Railway near Ripley in Derbyshire, this centre has an engine-shed, sidings, a length of single track, and an impressive array of carriages and locomotives. Among the latter are four 'Jinty' 0–6–0Ts, including 16440 restored to its original maroon livery, the Pacific No. 6203, *Princess Margaret Rose*, a class 5 with Caprotti valve-gear, No. 73129, and an elegant Midland 'Single' 4–2–2, No. 673 (1897), designed by S. W. Johnson.

8 Railways in Wales and the Borders

Unfortunately Wales and her railways have been prone to neglect over the years. First, the country was ignored by the companies themselves, who laid down a comprehensive network throughout England and parts of Scotland with hardly a consideration for their western neighbour. Even by 1850, after some twenty-five years of construction, Wales possessed only two main-line routes and both were coastal. In the north, the Chester & Holyhead Railway ran via Flint, Colwyn Bay, Bangor and Holyhead to take passengers for packets to Ireland, while in the south a line had been laid from Gloucester along the coastal margin to Cardiff, Swansea and Carmarthen – areas which later were dominated respectively by the L.N.W.R. and G.W.R. companies. In addition, there were many valley railways designed to carry coal from the pits down to the ports, the Taff Vale being among the earliest and most successful of these schemes.

It was not until the third quarter of the nineteenth century that projectors turned their full attention to the Welsh hinterland. Standard-gauge and narrow-gauge lines were set into the uplands, both north and south, while the west coast was dotted with a series of stations and halts. Of course, it was this second phase of railway building which suffered in the 1960s as a result of the Beeching axe. Many mountain lines, constructed to serve a pre-car population, had now lost their passengers, who had either moved from the hills or purchased other means of transport. Today there are just half a dozen routes which cut and wind their way through the central uplands, between the coast and the Welsh Borders. It is perhaps fitting that Barry, a port built by a railway company to facilitate the shipment of coal in the 1880s, should now be the resting place and ultimate graveyard for so many steam engines.

However, Wales has remained a country of narrow-gauge railways. There are a large number, including the Talyllyn, Festiniog, Welshpool & Llanfair, and the Snowdon Mountain Railway. British Rail still operates steam engines on the Vale of Rheidol line between Aberystwyth and Devil's Bridge.

Wales has more recently been neglected by the historian and to a lesser extent by the preservationist. There are few works documenting the delayed evolution of the country's network. However, the Great Western Society has established a South Wales branch, while at Caerphilly and Llangollen there are thriving railway centres. Otherwise Wales is rather short in the field of restoration. There is no national museum to compare with York and Glasgow. The former, together with the National Museum of Wales, has taken on this role for the present. Perhaps the railway interest here will rise up, spurred on by the tragic vision of Barry, to rectify this historical neglect.

It is probably easiest to divide Welsh railways into five groups: the main-line routes constructed along the coastal plains; the upland railways; the Border lines from Chester, south to Shrewsbury, Hereford and Gloucester; the narrow-, gauge railways; and the preservation societies.

COASTAL MAIN LINES

In May 1848 the Chester & Holyhead Railway opened its first section, the fifty-eight miles from Saltney Junction to Bangor. The remainder to Holyhead was completed in March 1850 with the construction of Robert Stephenson's Britannia Bridge over the Menai Straits. Up to this time passengers were conveyed by road from Llanfair over Thomas Telford's suspension bridge to Anglesey. Stephenson's structure was a real engineering achievement. The wrought-iron tubes (constructed from plates riveted together) which supported the line were then the longest in use, each having a span of 460 feet. Originally trains were completely enclosed in a cast-iron casing as at Conway, but the bridge was vandalized in 1970 and B.R. was forced to rebuild it, permitting the traveller a magnificent view of the Straits and Telford's structure to the east. The C. & H.R. was worked by the L.N.W.R. from 1856, and incorporated two years later.

The main line from Chester to Holyhead performed a number of functions and connected a variety of towns. North Wales is, of course, a land of castles. The most prolific of the castle-building English kings was Edward I, who constructed six major fortresses here: Harlech, Beaumaris, Caernarvon, Flint, Rhuddlan and Conway. It is not entirely a coincidence that the last three were all touched by the Chester & Holyhead Railway, with a fourth, Caernarvon, only a short distance down the line from Bangor, while Harlech is situated on the former Cambrian coast railway. These castles were built on the coast beside rivers and roads to control communications through the northern uplands. Railways were usually constructed along the line of least geographical resistance and as a result medieval garrison towns often became railway towns in the nineteenth century – Lancaster, Chester, Colchester and York are similar examples.

Conway is the classic case of an ancient fortress being confronted by a Victorian railway. Because of the town's location and the course of the River Conway, the engineers had no alternative but to run their tracks around the south face of the castle walls, at which point they built an embankment and a bridge. In order to blend with this medieval backcloth, but more important because the Gothic image and ethic was then popular, the whole was constructed in stone and decorated with false turrets and battlements.

The distinguished railway architect Francis Thompson was responsible for a large number of stations on the L.N.W.R.'s

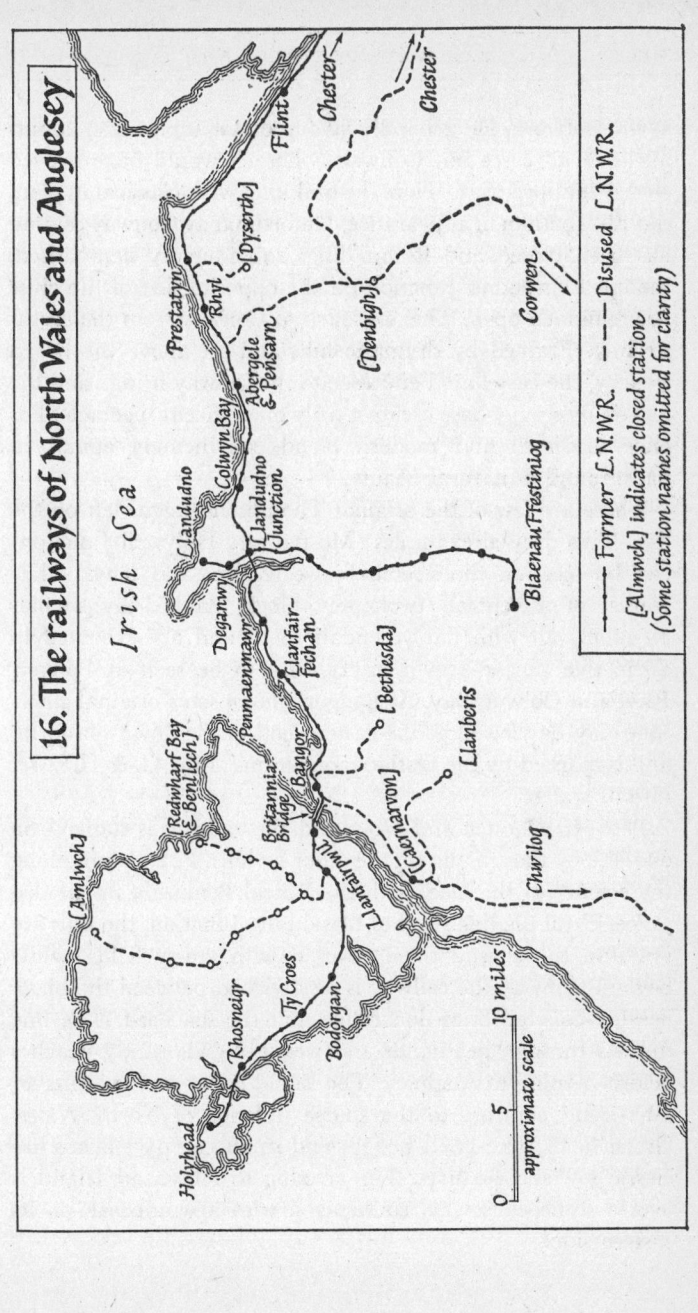

Welsh network. He generally favoured Italianate style, adopting it in all cases but Conway, where it would have proved clearly inappropriate. Here the buildings were classical in plan, but Elizabethan in appearance. Unfortunately Conway Station has been closed and its buildings subsequently demolished, though Llandudno Junction on the opposite side of the river has remained open. The approach to Conway from the east is striking. Framed by dramatic hills and set above the broad estuary, the castellated entrance to the railway bridge and the fort on its craggy base create a truly magnificent spectacle. For once medieval and modern blend convincingly against a background of natural beauty.

There are few of the original Thompson designs left on the line. Two disused examples (Mostyn and Holywell Junction) can be seen on the stretch between Flint and Rhyl. They consist of a central, two-storey block, flanked by smaller pavilions, all with flat verendah roofs, and are executed in distinctive purple-brown bricks, also to be seen at Bangor, Rhyl and Colwyn Bay. At Bangor Thompson's original structure may be viewed at the eastern end of the down platform, and is marked by the Gothic monograms of the C. & H.R. set into its walls.

Between Chester and Holyhead the railway is flanked on one side by the sea and on the other by hills. First it runs along the estuary of the Dee, with the Wirral Peninsula in the distance. Until the line reaches Llandudno Junction, the hills are low and the coastal plain covered with grassy fields, while beyond Conway the railway is sandwiched between the bleak heather-covered Snowdon range and the sea itself. The line tunnels through headlands and weaves beside sandy beaches before crossing to Anglesey. The island is flat and presents an interesting contrast to the sparse uplands of North Wales. Green fields, tree-lined hedges and small compact farms are classic lowland features. The crossing to Holyhead Island is over a stone causeway, constructed with a windbreak on its eastern side.

Holyhead itself has an interesting terminus, clean, bracing and full of fresh sea air. The buildings have been much altered. Originally a large Station Hotel dominated the space between the two train-sheds. Completed in June 1880, it was demolished in 1978, having fallen into disuse. Only one train-shed survives (Platform 2), an elegant, curving structure featuring a clerestory roof and delicate fern-leaf brackets. The buildings were all executed in bright red brick, patterned with purple-brown and cream bricks, while the central driveway is supported by a rough stone viaduct, and still exhibits its ornate gaslamp holders.

The Chester & Holyhead Railway performed an important function as a route for the 'Irish Mail'. Until its completion passengers and parcels were forced to go further north to Liverpool. The government and Admiralty Commissioners had reported favourably on the Holyhead route to Ireland as early as 1839 and it was with some state assistance that the project was promoted – an unusual occurrence in the history of railway construction. The 'Irish Mail' still runs from Euston, leaving at 9.30 pm on weekdays and reaching its destination in just under five hours.

The North Wales coast also developed as a holiday resort for the industrial population of Cheshire and Lancashire. Naturally towns and villages with beaches by the sea and a regular railway timetable expanded as tourist sites. Llandudno, with a branch to the bay, Bangor, Penmaenmawr, Rhyl and Colwyn Bay all grew as trippers took advantage of excursions and specials. The very size of their many platforms bears witness to the past popularity of these resorts. In 1923 the L.N.W.R. became part of the new London Midland & Scottish Railway. In the thirties the L.M.S. were advertising 'weekly run-about tickets' valid at any of these resorts for seven days, the cost being ten shillings and six pence, third class.

The other major coastal line has a very different character from the historical and holiday atmosphere of the north. At first the L.N.W.R. did not have any influence in South Wales. It is an area of coal, iron and steel, dominated by the Great Western, no small user of Welsh minerals. The first trunk railway to penetrate the area was authorized in August 1845 and was aptly called the South Wales Railway, being designed to run from Gloucester to Fishguard and Pembroke. At 194½ miles it was then the longest line projected and passed by Parliament. Clearly the S.W.R. was to be of great significance in that it would link the major towns and ports in the region, Newport, Cardiff, Neath, Swansea and Carmarthen, while a branch from Newport to Monmouth was also planned. The first section, the seventy-five miles between Chepstow and Swansea, was opened in June 1850. Merthyr was reached in 1853, the final section from Haverfordwest to Neyland Pier following in April 1856. Though the line had not yet been acquired by the Great Western their influence was apparent: the track had been laid with a seven-foot gauge throughout and in 1863 the S.W.R. passed into G.W. hands.

The laying of this main line along the coastlands of South Wales was to prove of fundamental importance in allowing the continued exploitation of the valley mines and the expansion of the iron and steel industries. Hitherto, there had been a number of private colliery railways running the length of the largest valleys to carry coals to the coast for shipment by sea. However, there were no direct communications, except the roads, and the workings were limited in size by their ability to get coals away for export or home consumption. It was the completion of this coastal railway, linking the valley heads with the big ports and foundry towns of Cardiff, Newport, Neath and Swansea, which permitted the great Victorian boom in South Wales' economy. Other towns which grew up en route as a result of this fresh activity included Port Talbot, Llanelli and Bridgend.

By the 1880s the volume of traffic had grown to such a size that again the major problem was one of transportation, as existing ports could no longer handle the volume of coals

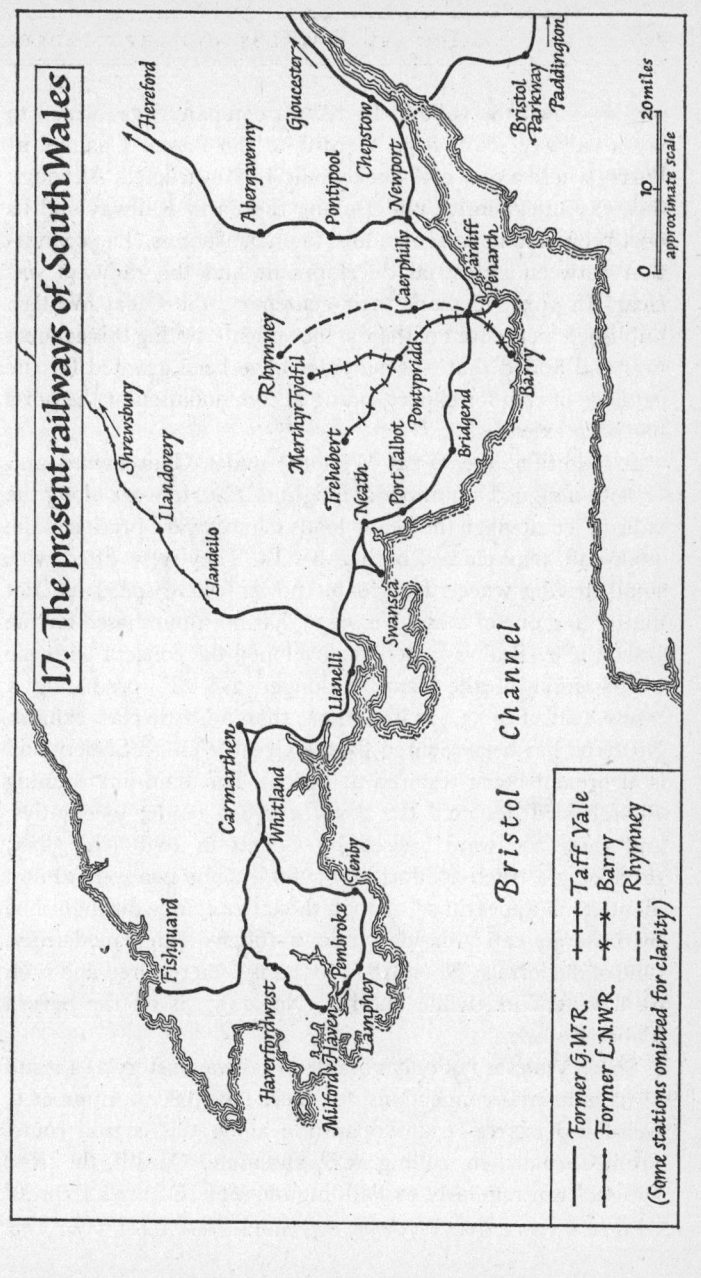

coming down the valleys. In 1884 a company was formed to lay a railway south from Cardiff to the Bristol Channel at Barry, where a new coal dock would be constructed. Although this was an expensive undertaking the Barry Railway and its port proved to be a tremendous financial success. The connection between industrial development and the railways was clear. In 1935, to mark their centenary, the Great Western published an account of their achievements, noting this connection and added that 'special rates have been granted for the carriage of coal for export, siding accommodation at the ports has been extended . . .'[1]

In addition, the Great Western, under Churchward and Collett, designed a number of freight engines to work along the valleys. To manage the heavy loads Churchward produced the 42xx and 52xx classes, both 2-8-0Ts. They were fitted with small driving wheels for greater power where speed did not matter and one of these, No. 5239, has been purchased for the Dart Valley Railway. Collett developed the concept with the introduction of the 72xx, a longer 2-8-2T, producing a tractive effort of 33,170 lb. – more than a Castle class express. No. 7202 has been secured by the Great Western Society and is at present being restored at Didcot. For main-line running Churchward designed the 28xx, a 2-8-0 tender locomotive, and these too were revised by Collett in 1938 (the 38xx) producing a tractive effort of 35,380 lb. The two were almost identical in appearance, though the latter can be distinguished by the larger cab with side windows – often a sign of modernity. One of the former, No. 2818 (1905) has been restored and is on display at York, while another, No. 2857, is on the Severn Valley Railway.

South Wales is not only notable in railway history as a result of its industrial connections, for there have been a number of well-loved express trains operating along this coastal route. From Carmarthen, calling at Swansea and Cardiff, the 'Red Dragon' ran regularly to Paddington. The 'Capitals Express'

---

[1] *Great Western Progress 1835–1935*, reprinted Newton Abbot, 1972, p. 70.

linked Cardiff with London, while the South Wales Pullman provided a luxury service to Swansea. Though British Rail runs numerous rugby specials when there are internationals at Twickenham or Cardiff Arms Park, Western Region no longer has any named trains running to Wales, which is a pity and a rejection of a rich and varied history of express services. Nowadays the route to Swansea is worked by High Speed Trains which have dramatically reduced travelling times. The quickest journey to Newport takes a mere eighty-eight minutes, while the trip to Swansea can be completed in two and three quarter hours.

One enduring feature of British railway history is its station architecture and, though British Rail may cover up details or close buildings, in most cases the essential structures have survived. Unfortunately, South Wales has been blessed with few stations of distinction. Originally the heavy industrial nature of the region discouraged companies from spending large sums on elegant buildings. Accordingly the Great Western rebuilt Cardiff Central, Swansea and Newport in the 1920s, the first two being constructed in a restrained, classical style from Portland stone, and the latter in dull red brick. None are distinguished. Cardiff Queen Street, the former headquarters of the Taff Vale Company, had an intricate Gothic station with pinnacles, gables and mullioned windows. Sadly, cost caused B.R. to pull it down and its modern successor is functional, but little else.

The terminus at Bute Road, Cardiff, built in 1841, is thought to have been the work of I. K. Brunel, and one of his stone viaducts remains in use on the line to Merthyr Tydfil. Also constructed in 1841, it spans the Afon Taf at Quaker's Yard in a fine sweeping curve of six arches.

Cardiff's Central Hotel backs on to the main line, with its entrance in Penarth Road. Opposite, in Saunders Road, is the Great Western Hotel, both hotels being sited near to Cardiff Central Station to serve its passengers. The first was built in Italianate style with brick pilasters and Corinthian capitals, while its competitor was constructed from local stone in the rival Gothic manner, with ornate lancet windows and a central clock tower.

The major interest in South Wales lies with the industrial scenery bordering on an upland setting, rather than the railway architecture. At Newport, Port Talbot and Neath, the main line passes enormous steel works, all supplied by train. Their furnaces, rolling mills, gas holders and rows of slender chimneys emitting steam and flames may not be pleasant to live with, but they do present a spectacular sight for the traveller. The route winds its way along the coastal strip to link up these industrial centres and the approach to Swansea, though not beautiful, is certainly awe-inspiring. The line crosses the River Tawe on a high embankment and viaduct. The steep, sparse slopes are covered with rising rows of terraced houses, while chapels and workshops break up the flowing rhythm. The valley floor is littered with derelict foundries and disused trackbeds. It is an incongruous mixture of desolate uplands and dreary housing with modern shops, offices and estates.

Most of Swansea's local and industrial railways have been pruned or lifted. Truncated stone viaducts, isolated bridge piers and remote sections of rail embedded in the dockside survive as memorials to a once extensive network. Unfortunately the Mumbles Railway (which ran from Rutland Street in the town centre south-west round the coast to Mumbles Pier) was closed in 1960. Constructed in 1807, it was the world's oldest fare-paying passenger railway. Horse-drawn until 1877, when steam engines took over, the latter were in turn replaced by double-decker electric railcars in 1929. Its course, now a footpath and indicated in places by disused bridges and embankments, is easily traced, while the town's museum has a collection of historic photographs illustrating its operation.

Fortunately much of the Cambrian Railways (plural because it comprised so many discontinuous sections) has survived the sixties' closures. The company was formed on 25 July 1864 from five enterprises, two based at Oswestry and three at Newtown. Consequently the former was selected as their headquarters. However, one of the largest of the five was the Aberystwyth & Welsh Coast Railway, destined to become the route for the famous Cambrian Coast Express. It had been authorized by Parliament in the summer of 1861 and opened in sections throughout the remainder of the decade. The line between the terminus, Pwllheli and Barmouth was completed in October 1867.

This west-coast railway still runs from Pwllheli in the north down to Aberdovey and Dovey Junction, where the route divides to pass due east to Newtown and Welshpool, and from there to Shrewsbury. The remainder continues south along the coast to Aberystwyth, to connect with the Vale of Rheidol Railway. Although the Cambrian was the largest of the independent Welsh companies and proud of its origins, the directors had established their headquarters in the most suitable place, over the border at Oswestry in Shropshire. Curiously the town is no longer part of the national network and the station has been closed. Grouping in 1923 meant that the Cambrian was placed under the auspices of the G.W.R., and today is part of Western Region.

Because the Cambrian coast line crosses some particularly rugged terrain, it required engines which could tackle steep gradients without exceeding the weight restrictions imposed by the less substantial bridges. After the route fell into Great Western hands, Collett, their engineer, realizing the necessity of producing a new locomotive, designed the 'Manor' class, introduced in 1938. A 4–6–0, they were fitted with smaller driving wheels than the Hall class for maximum effort at low speeds. They were considerably lighter and provided with a smaller tender to reduce their weight still further. A number of these attractive locomotives have been preserved, including No. 7808, *Cookham Manor* (Didcot); No. 7820, *Dinmore Manor* (Minehead); No. 7827, *Lydham Manor* (Kingswear); No. 7812,

Erlestoke Manor; and No. 7819, *Hinton Manor* (both on the Severn Valley line). The Cambrian Railways Society, based at Oswestry, have purchased No. 7822, *Foxcote Manor*.

INTERNAL UPLAND RAILWAYS

Many of these tortuous lines cut along valley sides, over and through hills, were part of the Cambrian Railways' network. However, the general pattern of ownership follows that for the coastal lines and the railways which cut in from the northern coast (the only survivor is to Blaenau Ffestiniog) were part of the L.N.W.R. Mid-Wales was dominated by the Cambrian, while routes from the south into the Brecon Beacons and central massif were mostly Great Western, with the Taff Vale being an important exception.

British railways were generally much more expensive to build than their American or European counterparts, averaging £40,000 per mile, three to four times higher than elsewhere. This was partly the result of heavy compensation payments to property owners in a small island (in the United States lines were laid across the open prairies, where the land was often free of charge) and the cost of getting Bills through Parliament. However, in the Welsh uplands the nature of the terrain added greatly to the cost. Engineers normally insisted on well-bedded tracks (the standard was far higher than in other countries), built fine stone viaducts across depressions and bored through hills, often lining their tunnels with brick and designing ornate entrance portals. Expense was one reason, therefore, why these upland railways were among the last lines to be laid down in Britain, and indeed, why they were often the first to be closed.

The only remaining standard-gauge mountain railway in North Wales is the line from Llandudno to Blaenau Ffestiniog. It was opened in June 1863 but then only ran as far as Llanrwst, ten and a half miles into the Snowdon range. The branch was taken over by the L.N.W.R. in 1867, who extended it to

Betws-y-Coed in the following April, and Blaenau Ffestiniog in July 1879. Further to the west the L.N.W.R. operated two lines running from the coast to the hills: one from Bangor to Bethesda and the other from Caernarvon to Llanberis, the terminus of the Snowdon Mountain Railway. Both have been closed by B.R. and the same fate has befallen the former Bangor & Caernarvon Company, an extension from the Chester & Holyhead line at Menai Bridge. It ran across the Lleyn Peninsula, via Penygroes, to join the Cambrian coast line at Afon Wen.

The only standard-gauge line still operated by B.R. in mid-Wales is not strictly an upland railway. Though it runs east–west through the centre of the country from Aberystwyth, it takes advantage of the Dyn and Severn valleys, winding its way through Machynlleth, Caersws and Newtown to Welshpool, an exceptionally picturesque route. To the north, there were a number of real mountain lines, which eventually came under the control of the G.W.R. The Bala & Festiniog Railway received its royal assent in July 1873 and was completed in 1883. Meantime the Ffestiniog & Blaenau Railway had been converted from its original 1 foot $11\frac{1}{2}$ inch to standard gauge; the two were merged and vested in the Great Western in 1910. The Bala line was one of the most remote and impressive in Britain, making its closure in 1960 a sad event.

In the southern half of the country, there are a number of upland routes within the B.R. network. Four branches run northwards from the Plain of Gwent: the line from Cardiff to Treherbert divides at Pontypridd, one branch continuing to Merthyr, the line to Caerphilly runs as far as Rhymney and the Newport–Hereford line calls at Pontypool and Abergavenny.

In June 1836 the Taff Vale Company had been authorized to lay a railway from Cardiff to Pontypridd. It was completed four years later and the first passenger train took thirty-one minutes to cover the twelve miles. The Dinas branch, up the Rhondda valley, was opened in 1841 and by 1856 the T.V.R.

ran locomotives as far as Treherbert. By 1923 the company had collected twenty-three branches serving the colliery districts of Glamorgan.

Further to the east, a line was constructed from Newport along the Usk valley, via Pontypool and Abergavenny to Hereford. It was completed in October 1855 with the co-operation of the Monmouth Railway. There is still one major route through the central massif, from Llanelli along the Towy valley to Shrewsbury, via Llandovery, Builth and Broome. Most of it belonged to the L.N.W.R., though the last portion, from Llandeilo south, was Great Western. In addition, there was formerly a more mountainous route running almost parallel from Swansea to Brecon via Hay to Hereford, but this has been closed. Eventually both fell entirely into the hands of the Great Western. A number of lines ran from the south-west coast north to Cardigan Bay. The Whitland & Cardigan Railway, an extension of the line to Crymmych Arms, was projected in 1877 and completed in 1886, but this too was taken over by the G.W.R. in 1910.

A number of photographs survive from the turn of the century which convey something of the atmosphere of these Welsh branch lines. Many stations, whether situated high in the hills or nestling in the grassy valleys of mid-Wales, were often a focus of activity. Photographs show sun-washed platforms, littered with barrows of luggage and large wicker baskets. Groups of travellers from all classes are depicted waiting for the arrival of a tank engine with several coaches and a single goods wagon. Iron footbridges, decorated awnings, brick chimneys, colourful noticeboards, station signs, time-tables, gaslamps and distant signals are all memorable features of these evocative scenes.

THE WELSH BORDERS

In the Middle Ages, the Borders were an area of continual strife, when English kings gave their fiercest barons lands in this area to stem these advances and to keep law and order. In a sense, this region became a battlefield once more during the nineteenth century as various railway companies fought for supremacy along the frontier. The L.N.W.R. disputed with the Midland in Cheshire; Shropshire was divided between the Cambrian and the Shrewsbury & Hereford; while the south gradually succumbed to the might of the Great Western. The old garrison towns, Chester, Gloucester, and Shrewsbury, became important railway centres. Their medieval walls and gateways were matched in splendour by fine station buildings, each constructed as an outward sign of a company's prosperity and prestige. Chester, for example, is quite palatial in its size and style.

It is said that Crewe was entirely the creation of the L.N.W.R., a railway town with few other means of support. A line which had helped to establish its ascendancy was the Chester & Crewe Railway, opened in October 1840. The way was then prepared for the coastal route to Holyhead, and Chester was firmly established as a communications centre, having rail connections with Wrexham to the south, and linked to the Wirral by the Birkenhead Railway. Much of this service operates today, though the coastal section from West Kirby to Neston has been closed. The Cheshire Lines Committee (the Midland, Great Northern and Great Central Joint) set down their southern terminus at Chester, though their title was deceptive. The Company's most important network was based in industrial Lancashire, between Liverpool and Manchester – the former C.L.C. line from Chester Central to Altrincham, via Cuddington and Northwich, is still in use.

Chester General is a fine example of an early station design on a large scale, and is possibly Francis Thompson's best. Built in his favourite Italianate style, it consists of a central two-storey block, flanked by arcaded wings, each having angle turrets of a distinctly Roman appearance, while Venetian windows and balconies complete the Mediterranean image. The whole is constructed in greyish red-coloured brick with stone dressings. Completed in 1848, Chester, owned jointly by the L.N.W.R. and G.W.R., was one of the many shared stations in the region. Wrexham is the next stop on the line south to Wolverhampton, Birmingham and ultimately Euston. There are still three stations here, though neither Exchange nor Central on the former Great Central are particularly distinguished buildings. Wrexham General, owned by the G.W.R., was constructed from local stone, and a fine clerestory roof was built. Despite this seeming abundance, the railways had come comparatively late to Wrexham. In 1839 Chester businessmen had commissioned George Stephenson to lay a line here, but nothing materialized and it was not until 1844, with the projection of the North Wales Mineral Railway, that work got under way. The only route for coal traffic had been from the Pontcysyllte Wharf on the Welsh branch of the Shropshire Union to Chester, a railway being needed to facilitate the transportation of coal, limestone and steel.

The next important stop on B.R.'s main line along the border is at Shrewsbury. This was a town of real railway rivalry, where the L.N.W.R., G.W.R., Cambrian and Shrewsbury & Hereford Companies all had stations. Whether it was as a result of this competition or mere coincidence, Shrewsbury gained a truly distinguished station. Designed by T. K. Penson and completed in 1848, it consists of a long two-storey castellated façade in grey stone. There is a clock tower with battlements, four corner finials and a central oriel window, while the chimneys are of moulded brickwork in authentic Tudor style. This Gothic design could be forgivably mistaken for an Oxford college or ancient public school. Unfortunately, the building was modified in 1903–8 to allow a third floor to be inserted. Bristol Temple Meads and Stoke-on-Trent are station buildings of a comparable kind.

The fourth major Border town is Hereford (see p. 100, which is easily reached from Shrewsbury by the service between Crewe, Newport and Cardiff. Hereford too has an interesting Gothic station, designed by Johnson of Birkenhead and com-

RAILWAYS IN WALES AND THE BORDERS

pleted in 1855. In plan it almost forms a Tudor 'E', though the central gable is not developed and consists only of a dormer window, extended from the steep slate roof. Built in light red brick with stone dressings and finials, it has lancet windows and narrow perpendicular doorways. The buffet features some inter-war floral stained-glass designs.

Before the opening of the Severn tunnel in 1886, Gloucester commanded the approaches to South Wales. Expresses were forced to travel north-west from Swindon, via Stroud, to cross the River Severn, and then swing southwards through Lydney and Chepstow for Newport. It was clear that the journey would be greatly shortened if the Severn could be traversed further west, nearer to Bristol. A plan had been projected as early as 1865 by Charles Richardson but it was not taken up by the Great Western till 1872. Richardson, in conjunction with Sir John Hawkshaw, constructed the longest tunnel in Britain (4 miles 606 yards), at a cost of £1½ million. Banking locomotives were provided to help the heaviest passenger and freight trains ascend the slopes at each end, while warning wires were laid along its length so that signalmen could be alerted should an engine fail in its depths. It was a determined feat of engineering, and has proved a sound and safe short-cut to Wales.

The completion of the Severn tunnel reduced Gloucester's importance as a railway junction. However, the Midland Railway had constructed a line here from Birmingham and completed their Eastern Station in 1896. The Great Western's Central Station was rebuilt several times, the last being in 1889 by Lancaster Owen. Both have been demolished and B.R. has recently opened a new, functional station, which like Cambridge consists of a single long platform.

NARROW-GAUGE RAILWAYS

North Wales is the most important area in the British Isles for narrow-gauge lines. As upland railways are expensive to build, an obvious way to reduce costs was to reduce the width of the trackbed, embankments and viaducts. Few of these lines have resorted to diesel traction, having been preserved much as they were when first constructed. Most are now geared to the tourist trade, and their steam locomotives are an essential part of this attraction.

The Festiniog Railway

The Festiniog Railway was originally designed to link the slate quarries around Blaenau Ffestiniog with the harbour at Porthmadog, on the Cambrian coast. Its tortuous thirteen-mile route was opened in 1836, though its first steam locomotives were not introduced till 1863, passenger traffic following two years later. The gauge is 1 foot $11\frac{1}{2}$ inch. With the decline of the slate industry, the line was closed in 1946, a preservation society was formed in 1951 and a trust established in 1964. The track was restored in stages, the first mile being completed in 1955, and work is still under way, though most has been done.

There are three types of engine operating on the railway. *Princess*, *Prince* and *Welsh Pony* are all 0–4–0STs (with tenders), as are *Linda* and *Blanche*. The first three were built by George England & Co. in 1863 and are originals, though they have been substantially rebuilt. The last two were constructed by the Hunslet Engine Co. in 1893 for the Penrhyn Quarry Railway and have recently been modified and fitted with forward trailing wheels. Most unusual are the two 0–4–4–0 double Fairlies, *Earl of Merioneth* and *Merddin Emrys*.

The Talyllyn Railway

The Talyllyn Railway is a slightly broader gauge, 2 feet 3 inches, and runs from Tywyn Wharf (also on the Cambrian coast) to Nant Gwernol, some seven miles. It too was built as a slate quarry railway and as the trade declined so the line was closed in 1950. A preservation society was formed and started operating passenger services the following year. Traffic has increased, the schedules doubled, stations rebuilt and the line extended beyond Abergynolwyn to Nant Gwernol.

No. 1, *Talyllyn* (0–4–2ST), and No. 2, *Dolgoch* (0–4–0WT), are both original locomotives. *Sir Haydn* and *Edward Thomas*, 0–4–2STs, were purchased from British Rail when the Corris Railway closed, while a sixth engine, *Douglas* (0–4–0WT), was presented to the line in 1953.

The Vale of Rheidol Railway

The Vale of Rheidol Railway is the only regular steam service still operated by B.R. It is a 1 foot 11½ inch gauge line from Aberystwyth to Devil's Bridge, a distance of 11¾ miles. Built to carry lead ore, the railway also performed an important passenger and tourist function. The independent company was first taken over by the Cambrian Railways in 1913, becoming part of the G.W.R. in 1923 and the Western Region in 1948.

Towards the end of the 1960s the line became very dilapidated. Enthusiasts negotiated with B.R. for its purchase, but the proposed sale was cancelled when British Rail decided instead to develop the line themselves. Tracks were laid into the main station to terminate at the former 'Carmarthen Bay' platform. Locomotives and coaches were repainted in standard blue livery and their nameplates were replaced. There are three steam locomotives at work. They are all 2–6–2Ts: No. 7, *Llywelyn*, No. 8, *Owain Glyndwr*, and No. 9, *Prince of Wales*. The last, introduced in 1902, is the oldest; the others were built by the G.W.R. at Swindon in 1923.

The Welshpool & Llanfair Railway

The Welshpool & Llanfair is a 2 foot 6 inch gauge railway from Llanfair Caereinion to Sylfaen, a journey of 5½ miles. Although constructed and owned by an independent company, the line was operated by the Cambrian from the start. Passenger services ceased in 1931, while freight traffic continued until November 1956. A preservation society, formed within the same month, was not able to lease the railway from B.R. till

1962 but has since purchased the railway outright. At present, there are two locomotives, both 0–6–0Ts built by Beyer, Peacock in 1902, working trains: No. 1, *The Earl*, and No. 2, *The Countess*.

Some of the rolling stock is original, though much was unfortunately scrapped. Some carriages have been purchased from the Zillertalbahn, a railway in the Austrian Tyrol. The Society has since acquired four other locomotives, *Monarch*, *Sir Drefaldwyn*, *Joan* and the unnamed No. 85, formerly of the Sierra Leone Government Railway.

The Snowdon Mountain Railway

The Snowdon Mountain Railway was built in the 1890s as a tourist attraction running from Llanberis to the summit. It is a 2 foot 7 inch gauge line with a rack and pinion system, based on Swiss designs, to aid ascent and slow descent. The opening in 1896 was marred by an engine leaving the rails and crashing into a ravine. Fortunately the driver and fireman had jumped clear. For safety the coaches had not been coupled and were stopped by their own brakes, but not before one passenger had been killed. As a result guard rails were fitted, and no further accident has occurred. It was thought that extreme frost had distorted the track.

The seven steam engines operating on the railway were all built by the Swiss locomotive works at Winterthur. Nos. 2 to 5 were constructed in 1895–6, and Nos. 6 to 8 between 1922 and 1923. All have specially inclined boilers so that they lie almost level when the loco is climbing the mountainside.

The Fairbourne Railway

The Fairbourne Railway is a 15 inch gauge, two-mile line from Fairbourne Station to Penrhyn Point on the Mawddach Estuary. Unlike the other companies mentioned here it is operated by miniature locomotives – scale models of standard-gauge counterparts. The railway passed through a variety of hands, until its present owners purchased the line in 1946.

Since then more engines and improved coaches have been acquired. Most impressive are the two 2–4–2 tender engines, *Siân* and *Katie*, built in 1950, and bought in 1965. There are two others, both scaled designs, a 4–4–2, *Count Louis* (1925), and the 4–6–2, *Ernest W. Twining* (1949).

The Llanberis Lake Railway

The Llanberis Lake Railway, opened in 1971, is one of the modern Welsh narrow-gauge lines, though it was constructed on the trackbed of the former four-foot-gauge Padarn Railway. It is 1 foot 11½ inch gauge, and runs two miles between Llanberis and Penllyn. Locomotives were adapted from the near-by Dinorwic Quarry, while two 0–4–0Ts were imported from Germany. There are both passenger and freight trains operated along the line.

The Bala Lake Railway

The Bala Lake Railway is also a 1 foot 11½ inch line and runs from Llanwchyllyn to Bala, a distance of 4½ miles. It was opened in August 1972, having been laid on part of the trackbed of the former Great Western Railway between Barmouth Junction and Ruabon. One of the few narrow-gauge railways to use diesel power, it features a Bo-Bo, *Meirionydd*, built in 1973. However, steam was introduced in 1975 with the arrival of the Hunslet 0–4–0ST, *Maid Marian* (1903). Her sister engine, *Holy War*, is also on loan to the line. The Bala Lake Railway is an extremely pleasant route which runs for most of its course along the lakeside, and offers an alternative means of seeing the older, upland branch lines.

The Severn Valley Railway

The Severn Valley Railway was originally part of a line designed to link the towns of Worcester and Shrewsbury. It was promoted by the Oxford, Worcester & Wolverhampton Company in 1853, but work was postponed for five years, while earth slips delayed its completion till the autumn of 1861. The official opening ceremony was performed in January 1862 when the Mayor of Bridgnorth provided a champagne civic banquet. By this time the railway had become part of the West Midland Company, which in 1863 joined the Great Western empire, though it did not relinquish its title until 1872.

Today steam is only operated over part of the original Severn Valley line. It was closed in 1963 as a result of the Beeching recommendations. Preservationists gathered together and were able to raise £25,000 to purchase the trackbed between Bridgnorth and Hampton Loade in 1966, and this four and a half mile section was thoroughly restored and re-opened for steam running in the summer of 1970. Since then the Severn Valley Railway Company has succeeded in acquiring the further ten miles south to Bewdley and Foley Park and services now operate between Bewdley and Bridgnorth. The line between Bewdley, Foley Park and Kidderminster on the main line from Birmingham to Worcester, via Droitwich Spa and Stourbridge, remains, over which B.R. operate open day specials.

Being situated on former Great Western territory the Company has preserved a number of its engines. One of the most attractive designs is the Collett 0–6–0 tender locomotive, No. 3205. These were produced for medium freight or light passenger trains and are a direct successor of the ubiquitous Victorian goods locomotive. No. 3205 was built at Swindon in 1946. Originally shedded at Gloucester, 3205 was transferred to Worcester in 1956 and actually worked on the Severn Valley line until withdrawal in 1965.

In addition, the railway has purchased one of the famous G.W.R. pannier tanks. A number had been acquired by London Transport and continued to be operated long after steam running had ended on British Rail. When L.T. eventually decided to replace them, they were readily bought up by preservation societies. No. 5764 (formerly L95) was acquired for the Severn Valley. Though there is an obvious family resemblance, the railway's other pannier tank engine, a 15xx class No. 1501, is a much rarer sight. Designed by Hawksworth and introduced after nationalization in 1949, they are indeed a hybrid locomotive. The general shape of the boiler, side water tanks and cab are all classically Great Western, while the outside cylinders, the Walschaerts valve gearing and the absence of a footplate give them a British Rail appearance.

The railway has assembled an impressive array of locomotives from the L.M.S., including No. 45110, *R.A.F. Biggin Hill*. These engines, called 'Black Fives' after their livery and class number, were among the most versatile and efficient locomotives ever produced and have built up a considerable following amongst enthusiasts. No. 45110 was completed in 1935, shedded at Holyhead and used to haul fast passenger and freight trains to Chester, Birmingham, Manchester, Liverpool and London. Another ex-L.M.S. locomotive shedded here is No. 8233, a 2-8-0 class 8F, produced for heavy freight. More recent is the Ivatt 2-6-0, No. 46443, completed in 1951, though the first of these class 4 locomotives introduced before nationalization came out in L.M.S. livery.

Possibly the best known of the Severn Valley's locomotives is No. 70000, *Britannia*, the first of the twelve standard designs introduced by British Rail from 1951. Intended to be produced in large numbers, they were of course curtailed by the adoption of diesel and electric power. *Britannia*, completed at Crewe, represented the new breed of express locomotives and continued to run till the end of steam in 1968.

The Llangollen Railway Society

This famous Eisteddfod town, tucked into the narrow valley of the River Dee, has developed into a living centre of transport history. Besides being the picturesque dock for the Welsh branch of the Shropshire Union Canal, it was an important stop on the G.W.R.'s Bala Lake Railway from Ruabon and Wrexham. When the line was closed in 1965, the station was boarded up and the track lifted. A preservation society was founded in 1972 to re-open Llangollen Station and re-lay the line to Corwen, about ten miles to the west through Carrog, Glyndyfrdwy and Berwyn. The station and yards were acquired in July 1975 and the track re-laid for half a mile along the route to Corwen. Llangollen Station (1846-8), an attractive collection of stone buildings in Tudor style with a footbridge and signal box, has been restored to its former glory.

A number of saddle-tank engines have been secured, including a Kitson 0-6-0ST (1932), named *Austin I* because it had formerly been employed in the British Leyland works at Longbridge, Birmingham. There are two carriages, a G.W.R. brake third, No. 5539 (1938), and a B.R. non-corridor passenger coach, No. E43182 (1954). An unusual locomotive is the Sentinel shunting engine, No. 9596, built in 1955 to the original L.N.E.R. design.

The Caerphilly Railway Society

It is pleasing that the Rhymney Railway's former locomotive works at Caerphilly have been taken over as a centre for preservation. Among the engines undergoing restoration, it is apt that the Society should have No. 28 *Taff Vale* (1897), an 0-6-2T, built at the company's works in Cardiff. *Taff Vale* was then sold to the G.W.R. and renumbered 450. Withdrawn in 1960, it was presented to the National Museum of Wales, who in turn sent it here for a complete overhaul and repainting. In addition, the Society has No. 41312, an L.M.S.-designed 2-6-2T, completed in 1952, and a number of saddle-tank locomotives.

The Gwili Railway

Based at Bronwydd Arms Station on the former G.W.R. Carmarthen–Aberystwyth line, it runs for a mile north to Cwmdwyfran. Services are operated by a Peckett 0-4-0ST *Myrddin/Merlin* and other industrial tank engines. It is hoped to acquire a few locomotives of G.W.R. origin.

9   The North-West

To anybody interested in railways, the north-west offers a rich panorama, since it possesses some of the country's earliest historical remains and finest engineering achievements. This diverse network encompasses long, fast stretches between Crewe and Carlisle on the Scotland run, hard climbs up the Pennines, tortuous, scenic Lakeland branch lines, together with all the interest of an intricate system centred on Manchester. Indeed, the Liverpool & Manchester Railway, opened in 1830, though not the world's first, may be said to have been the earliest line regularly carrying passengers. There were steam-hauled trains operating along double tracks, recognizable stations and a regular public schedule.

From this early experiment a whole network spread throughout industrial Lancashire. The county was connected to most major towns in Britain and express services were run to London by the Midland and L.N.W.R. By 1878 the M.R. had successfully reduced travelling times to $4\frac{3}{4}$ hours for the journey from St Pancras to Manchester. Timings were cut by a further half an hour in 1884, while their rivals the L.N.W.R. operated trains to Euston in only $3\frac{3}{4}$ hours by 1902. Even as late as 1966, the Midland Pullman took three hours and ten minutes. Electrification that year produced a dramatic reduction in travelling times, and today the Manchester Pullman makes the journey in two hours and thirty-five minutes, at an average of over 70 mph. Liverpool, with its Lime Street terminus, the remains of the Overhead Railway and the new underground link line, is a city of continuing developments. Besides these industrial and mercantile areas, there are the dramatic Lakes and Pennines with their narrow-gauge or upland railways. As elsewhere, Lancashire and the north-west have produced a number of preserved steam societies and museums, which help keep alive this important aspect of the island's history.

THE LIVERPOOL & MANCHESTER RAILWAY

As the Industrial Revolution advanced increasing numbers of people moved into the new manufacturing districts. Liverpool, as an important port, experienced terrifyingly rapid population growth in the first four decades of the nineteenth century. Manchester and its satellite towns developed manufacturing and cotton-based industries. This growth was such that the canals, linking the port with the inland mills, could no longer cope with the increasing demands put on them. Merchants in Liverpool and businessmen in Manchester, frustrated by the waterways' inability to cope with the rising volume of trade, by their monopolistic position and consequent over-charging, determined to construct a tram-road between the two towns.

Because of his recent success with the Stockton & Darlington Railway, George Stephenson was selected to survey the line. Although there was much opposition to the Bill, both from landowners and canal investors who feared financial losses, the Act was eventually passed in 1826 after one abortive attempt. Stephenson's principal engineering achievement was to cross Chat Moss, a huge area of marshland extending five miles west of Manchester and blocking the railway's path. It was felt that the weight of railway tracks, subjected to the additional pressure of a locomotive and loaded carriages, would be beyond any engineering solution. Stephenson adopted a novel approach by laying a foundation of branches and reeds to a depth of twenty-five feet, hoping that this would support trains by floatation; that is by distributing their weight over a much greater area. His idea worked and it is said that the lineside still shudders as trains pass over Chat Moss. This springing sensation can best be felt around the old station at Astley, where fast expresses cause a compression wave which depresses and then lifts the trackbed.

The other notable engineering feature of the line was the arched stone and brick viaduct over Sankey Brook. This was Britain's first canalized river, completed in 1757 and heralding the Canal Age itself. It is a curious coincidence that the world's first passenger railway should have crossed the country's earliest artificial waterway.

Originally it was agreed that trains should be pulled by stationary engines located at the lineside. However, a prize of £500 was then offered to the designer of a locomotive which could haul a load of twenty tons forty times over a stretch of line 1¾ miles long (equal to the distance between Liverpool and Manchester and back) at a minimum speed of ten miles per hour. Rainhill was chosen as the site for the contest and a plaque on the station platform marks the event. Stephenson's *Rocket* was the only locomotive which succeeded in fulfilling all these conditions. *Rocket*, now missing many parts, and *Sans Pareil*, an unsuccessful entrant, can both be seen in the Science Museum, South Kensington.

After several trial runs, the Liverpool & Manchester Railway was opened on 15 September 1830. An inaugural special was assembled and the Duke of Wellington invited to perform the actual ceremony. Unfortunately, it was not to be an entirely happy day. Eight of the company's locomotives, *Northumbrian, Phoenix, North Star, Rocket, Dart, Comet, Arrow* and *Meteor*, were used on the run from Liverpool to Manchester. On arriving at Parkside, William Huskisson, a former President of the Board of Trade and M.P. for Liverpool, alighted to speak to the Duke. Afterwards, while climbing back into his carriage, he slipped and fell into the path of the oncoming *Rocket*, which severed his left leg. Though he was rushed to hospital by *Northumbrian* he subsequently died and a memorial tablet was erected to record this first railway fatality, on the south side of the line between Newton-le-Willows and Earlestown.

The railway proved not only a great novelty but also a business success. People flocked to travel by this new means of transport and such was the demand that freight trains, for which the line had originally been constructed, were delayed or cancelled to make way for additional passenger services. Other companies were soon formed once the financial durability and engineering abilities of the railway had been demonstrated.

Fortunately much of the original railway survives, and parts are being preserved. In Manchester, the Liverpool Road terminus has been restored, the tracks relayed and converted into a steam museum, the opening coinciding with the 150th anniversary of the L. & M.R. The façade is somewhat simple, resembling a row of spacious terraced houses. The main doors, flanked by plain pilasters, let into an entrance hall, from where a broad flight of stairs took passengers up to the departure platform. The original second-class booking window survives, as does a frame where a clock was fitted, surmounted by a mantle for a gas light, while simple iron columns support the timbered roof. Further down the line and over a bridge is the arrival platform.

Opposite the main buildings, which also served as the station master's house, are a number of brick warehouses. It was in the upper storey of one of these that Wellington ate his cold collation after his journey from Liverpool. With the construction of the Victoria and Exchange Stations, Liverpool Road closed to passengers and became a goods depot for the L.N.W.R., but as freight services were streamlined, it fell into disuse in the 1970s. Nevertheless, with its elegant brick warehouses, cranes, sidings and massive iron Doric columns supporting defunct viaducts, it has a powerful atmosphere. In the distance is the magnificent lattice-work viaduct constructed by the Cheshire Lines Committee to sweep their expresses into their Central Station. Each pillar is decorated with arrow loops and battlements resembling medieval turrets. It is sad to think that trains no longer pass its length into the mighty arched Central terminus, which has been defeated by the motor age and converted into a car park (see p. 245).

The journey from Manchester to Liverpool is still a fascinating one. Nowadays diesel multiple units operate from Victoria station, running through the empty Exchange buildings, over viaducts, across intersections, and join the original route just after the line divides for Salford. The Liverpool Road goods depot lies away to the south. Beyond Eccles the train cuts across Chat Moss, which with its peaty soils, short trees and stunted bushes still looks menacing and marshy. At Newton-le-Willows there is a pleasant station built from brick and stone in Jacobean style – even the doors are decorated with linenfold panels. The railway then passes through St Helens, Rainhill, Huyton and on to historic Edge Hill (1836), where the station buildings have been restored and used as a temporary museum. The last few miles of the run into Liverpool's Lime Street terminus are truly inspiring. The line is taken through deep soot-blackened sandstone cuttings. Sharp vertical sides cut out much of the light, while water seeps down the sides, encouraging the growth of clear green moss and ferns. Originally most of this section was through tunnels, but the gradual expansion of Lime Street's business led the L.N.W.R. to broaden the cuttings and open up many of the tunnels to accommodate extra lines. Before entering the curved trainshed, the carriages are plunged into darkness, suddenly to emerge at their destination.

MANCHESTER

In many ways Manchester stands as one of England's finest memorials to the Industrial Revolution. Here King Cotton set down his throne and built his capital. Mills and manufacturing made the city prosperous in the late eighteenth and nineteenth centuries. The solid, confident town hall, designed by Alfred

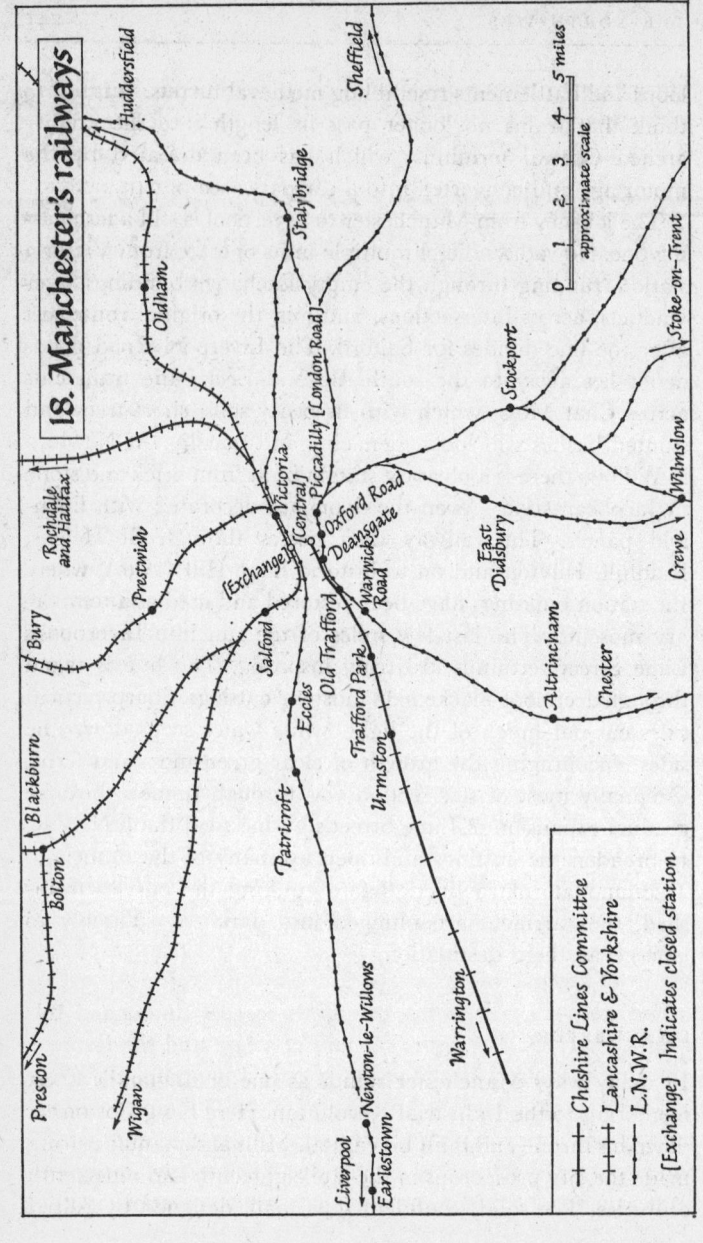

Waterhouse in 1868, reflects the wealth, ideals and aspirations of Mancunians. Theirs was a conurbation which relied on trade and as a result the city developed a detailed and complex railway network to provide transport facilities for its people and industries. Because the railways were owned and operated by independent companies a number of stations were constructed which, as obvious signs of their railway's status and quality, were built in a variety of styles with various attractions. There were four major termini: London Road (now Piccadilly), Exchange, Central and Victoria. Now only two exist, one in a changed form. Since the city has yet to build an underground railway, much of the suburban system has survived in its original state.

The L.N.W.R.'s main terminus for trains arriving from the capital was called London Road. However, the buildings fronting the train-shed were pulled down by British Railways in 1959 to make way for a new ten-storey office block containing passenger facilities on the ground floor. The old station, constructed from stone, had been substantially rebuilt in 1865, when a broad symmetrical frontage was erected, designed in a restrained Italianate style. Two rows of windows surmounted the canopy and an ornately pedimented clock was set on the roof, suggesting a Louis XVI clock on a mantelpiece. Today the station, renamed Piccadilly, is very different. It was the first terminus to have been rebuilt since the last war and conforms with British Rail's policy of expanding their business activities to include the rental of shops and offices. Piccadilly was opened in 1966 to coincide with the electrification of the line from Euston.

The train-shed itself has remained largely untouched by these alterations. However, the end of steam and the limited use of diesels has meant that the interior has retained a light and airy atmosphere, where rows of Corinthian columns support an intricate lattice roof. Gone is the soot and grime which obscured structural details and gave many stations a mysterious and cavernous quality. One innovation is the computerized departure board, operated from the main signal box. It has the clean lines and clear finish of the post-war world. These machines offer an interesting comparison with the more homely but less efficient boards which serve local services out of London's Liverpool Street, or Manchester Victoria.

The Lancashire & Yorkshire Railway built their station between Corporation and Victoria Streets, hence its name. In contrast to Piccadilly, Victoria is one of the least altered stations in the city. The ashlar frontage was erected by William Dawes in 1909 and is noted for the richness and variety of ornament. The stone had been blackened by generations of smoke fires but has since been cleaned. The canopy, stretching the length of the building, features glass panels proclaiming the railway's destinations – Blackpool, Scarborough, Goole, Scotland, Ireland and curiously enough Belgium are all mentioned. Inside, the station preserves the atmosphere of melancholy. There is a huge brick map in the entrance entitled 'Lancashire and Yorkshire Railway'. Reproduced in glazed black and white tiles are the company's lines, while rival railways are deliberately omitted. Passengers who did not possess Bradshaw's comprehensive timetable could have been led into taking lengthy and unnecessary journeys. The concourse features a panelled ticket office and an ornate refreshment room with a decorative glass-domed ceiling. Even the bookshop has its name displayed in a mixture of green, yellow and white mosaic squares. Platforms 12 to 17 are now disused and overgrown, a legacy of bombing in September 1940.

Until 1880 the Lancashire & Yorkshire Railway allowed the L.N.W.R. to use their Victoria Station, but with the railway's increasing popularity the facilities became overcrowded. Consequently, the L.N.W.R. decided to build a new station across the River Irwell, adjacent to Victoria, and along the same lines. One result of this combination was to create Britain's longest platform, which began as Platform 3 in Exchange and continued, over the Irwell, as Platform 11 at

Victoria, the total length being 2,194 feet. Unfortunately, Exchange Station was bombed and the entrance hall and main buildings were destroyed in 1940. Although trains regularly pass through Exchange, they no longer stop to let off passengers and the entrance bridge, concourse, platforms and some of the trackbeds are now used as a car park.

There are two other major stations in Manchester: Oxford Road and Central. The first has been modernized and thrives as part of the busy suburban service from Altrincham to Wilmslow. Central Station, in Windmill Street behind the Midland Hotel, has been closed and serves as another car park. It is a magnificent single-arched construction 210 feet across, and like St Pancras train-shed was built from powerful unsupported ribs with extensive cellars below. Opened in 1880, Central was designed by Sir John Fowler for the Cheshire Lines Committee – a joint enterprise formed in 1865 by the Midland, Great Northern and Manchester, Sheffield & Lincolnshire Railway (after 1897 the Great Central; see p. 195). Central Station became their terminus for services to Liverpool via Warrington Central, offering competition to the L.N.W.R. line from Exchange along the former Liverpool & Manchester Railway. In addition, Central also rivalled London Road's services to the capital and it must have been an exciting experience to have travelled from St Pancras by the Midland to Manchester Central, staying at the company's hotels at each end. The final approaches, winding into central Manchester from the south-west, along the superb lattice-work viaduct into the majestic train-shed, were a fitting finale to a historic and varied route.

The Midland Hotel was designed by Charles Trubshaw in 1898 and completed in 1903. Built from polished granite and glazed sienna bricks, the Midland, with its turrets, towers and decorative façade, has been described architecturally as the 'final apotheosis of the Victorian hotel'.[1] It was built around a quadrangle with the best suites facing outwards. In order to

[1] R. Dixon and S. Muthesius, *Victorian Architecture*, London, 1978, p. 84.

keep the inner rooms as light and pleasant as possible, the inside walls were faced with creamy white, glazed bricks. Its magnificence extended to the interior. There was a large theatre, a number of luxurious suites, a famous French restaurant, a billiard room, Russian and Turkish baths, a hairdressers, banqueting and ball rooms, and, as a contemporary report noted, 'the whole structure has its central point marked by a beautiful garden ... with about fifty flower beds of green faience ... and arranged to contain hundreds of creepers, flowering plants, ferns &c.' When first opened a fine breakfast of 'porridge and cream, and grilled chops, steak or two cutlets' could be taken for two shillings and sixpence, while a single room cost from four shillings.

As Manchester's premier hotel it has attracted many distinguished visitors. Messrs Rolls and Royce first met here to discuss the notion of car manufacture, while Edgar Wallace once locked himself in his rooms and, living on a diet of tea and toast, wrote a complete thriller. Mario Lanza and Sarah Bernhardt both stayed in the Midland with their retinues. It is sad that this flourishing railway hotel is now devoid of the terminus for which it was constructed.

Manchester, like London but on a smaller scale, has built up an intricate network of suburban services radiating from the central termini. One of the most popular lines, with strong sporting connections, is from Wilmslow in the south to Piccadilly, Oxford Road and west to Altrincham. It passes close to Manchester United's ground at Old Trafford and most years its trains are featured on Test Match broadcasts as they curve around the cricket ground. Indeed, both the station and one bowling end have been named after Warwick Road.

The high-level section from Piccadilly to Old Trafford is one of the most interesting in the city. The brick viaduct carrying the tracks winds its way past cotton warehouses, mills, office blocks and dilapidated workshops, while periodically stepping over the Bridgewater Canal, set in a dark channel formed by manufactures and high walls. To the north the docks shimmer in the distance, with their saluting cranes and ocean-going vessels. But coal yards and mills give way to terraced houses as the line returns to ground level at Old Trafford.

There are a number of other local railways. Several lines run from Piccadilly to Hadfield, Glossop, Buxton, Stockport and New Mills. Victoria has the largest number of local services, with lines operating to Bury, Salford, Bolton, Rochdale, Preston, Wigan and Blackburn, and east to Stalybridge and Huddersfield on the main line to Leeds. There is an additional service from Oxford Road (formerly from Central) to Liverpool via Warrington Central.

Because the railway system was constructed by a host of independent companies, working without a master plan, Manchester has been left with a group of large stations set some distance apart, and over the years various schemes have been suggested to link them up. As early as 1912 an underground railway was proposed, while in 1945 it was suggested that a new station, called Trinity, should be constructed between Exchange and Salford Stations. It would have taken over their business, together with Victoria's, and have had connections to Piccadilly and Oxford Road. In the event Central and Exchange were both closed and an underground railway was planned to link the remaining two termini, though this scheme has foundered owing to a lack of cash. A circular tube service running through central Manchester is clearly the best answer; but it is also the most expensive. To ease the problem slightly, British Rail has constructed a link at Castlefield joining the lines to Salford and Deansgate, facilitating travel between these two areas.

Manchester's railway map is as complicated as a spider's web. Even in the mid nineteenth century the distances which separated Manchester from the specialized manufacturing villages and towns which surrounded it were not too short for the operation of an effective and profitable railway service, nor were they so great that linkage became awkward and expensive. Two circles drawn from the centre, one with a

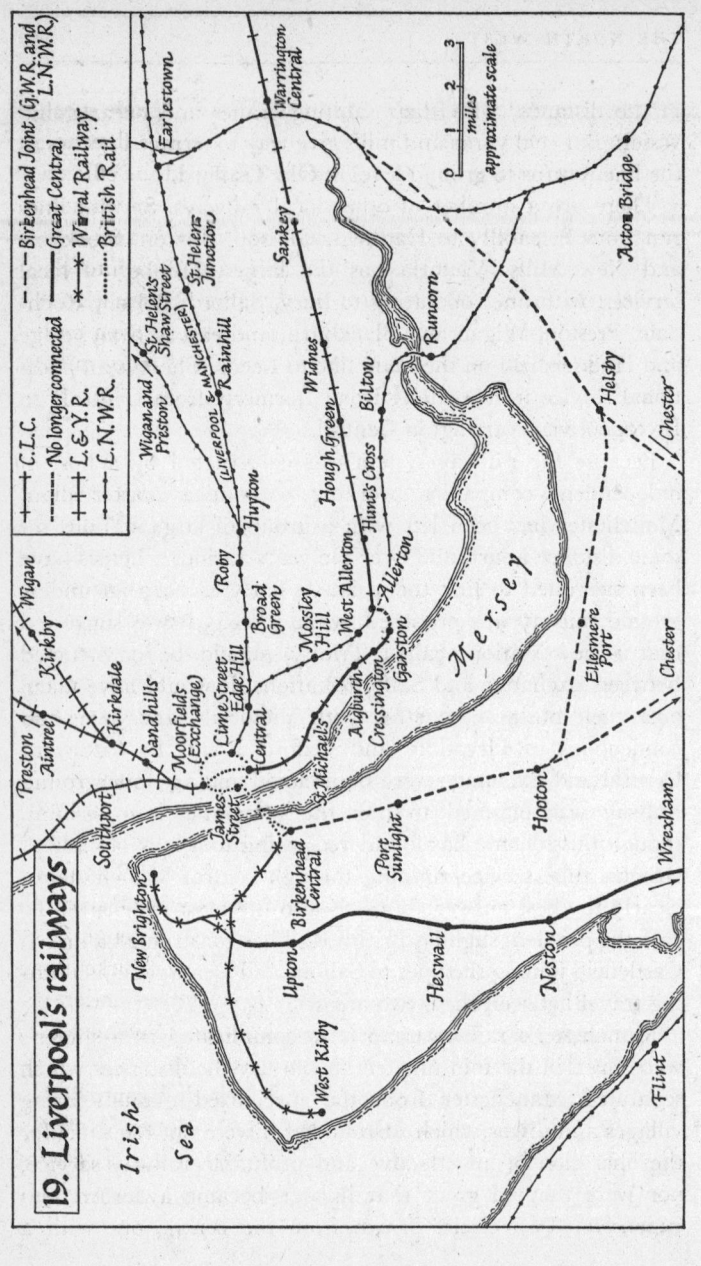

19. Liverpool's railways

radius of ten miles and the other thirty, would include most of the satellite manufacturing and processing centres dependent upon Manchester. The *Preston Chronicle* described the efficiency of their new railway to the city in 1839. Brokers, it noted, despatched cotton yarn from Manchester at 3 am, which arrived at Preston just after 9 am, was converted into cloth within two and a half hours and was returned on the 4.20 pm train, arriving at 7 pm ready to go on sale the following morning. This was all the result of the advent of the 'very millennium of railway velocity'.[1]

LIVERPOOL

Liverpool was once the leading port in Britain. With the expansion in commerce to the Americas and the West Indies throughout the late eighteenth and nineteenth centuries, the town experienced one of the fastest population growths in the country. By 1841 there were 299,000 people living in the conurbation and only London was larger. Trade was the spring which gave Liverpool life. Consequently, the town's early railways were principally designed to transport cargoes from the docks to the rising manufacturing districts of Lancashire and beyond. Originally Liverpool possessed few factories or processing industries, relying for its importance and prosperity on its function as an *entrepôt*. Lime Street, Central, Exchange and the goods stations at Crown Street and Bankfield were all termini constructed to serve the port and its passengers. At first, lines were constructed from Merseyside and Birkenhead without any connecting branches, either over or under the river, being built for freight rather than the convenience of local inhabitants.

It was not until the latter part of the nineteenth century that specific suburban railways, such as the Mersey Railway (opened in 1886), were laid down. The Overhead Railway,

[1] J. R. Kellett, *The Impact of Railways on Victorian Cities*, London, 1969, p. 172.

inspired by American example, was not completed until 1896. Indeed, the last few years have witnessed the construction of an underground loop line and the re-opening of a local service to Hunts Cross, via Cressington and Garston. These modern schemes are a direct response to the earlier inadequacies. Although many docks have been shut down, the Overhead Railway demolished and Exchange Station closed, Liverpool still has an interesting and lively railway system, while its history is being carefully recorded.

The Liverpool & Manchester was of course the first railway to reach the town, and its history has already been outlined (see p. 238). The success of this scheme encouraged the projection of other lines to the Midlands and the south, including the Grand Junction Railway to Birmingham and London, one of the most ambitious enterprises. The popularity of the railways and the construction of new lines soon rendered the small terminus at Crown Street inadequate. In 1832 the L. & M. was authorized to build a tunnel from Edge Hill to Lime Street and a new station was opened here in 1836 in time for the inaugural service to Birmingham. In 1846 both the L. & M. and the Grand Junction amalgamated and became part of the L.N.W.R.

Edge Hill continued to expand as a goods depot with extensive coal yards and sidings. The area had also been selected as the site for the Grand Junction locomotive works, taking on additional importance as a marshalling yard. For until 1870 the gradients were so steep on the final section to Lime Street that trains were worked into the terminus on cables powered by stationary engines. Locomotives were detached at Edge Hill, replaced by 'tunnel brakes' and the carriages then hauled into the station. Coaches were also fitted with oil lamps at this stage to light them through the last mile of darkness. In addition, Edge Hill rapidly developed as a focal point for freight trains, its traffic increasing so much that extensions to the sidings were required where the various lines converged. The original red sandstone station buildings, probably designed by John

Cunningham, were restored to coincide with the Liverpool & Manchester's 150th anniversary in 1980.

Lime Street has been enlarged several times since its opening in 1836. Substantial development was hampered by the highly restricted entry imposed by the narrow tunnels and it was not until 1885 that much of the tunnelling from Edge Hill was finally opened up. The cuttings were widened to permit the quadrupling of lines and the construction of an additional train-shed. A larger train-shed with a span of 153 feet, designed by Richard Turner and Joseph Locke, had been erected in 1849–50. It was a single-arched construction assembled from girders cast in Turner's Dublin works. However, this was replaced in 1879 by William Barlow's present double-arched train-shed, each half having a span of 200 feet and the whole costing half a million pounds. The end screens slope backwards, resembling the stern of a Napoleonic man-of-war, and are decorated by a circular clock rather than a ship's coat-of-arms. The L.N.W.R.'s Gothic hotel (Lime Street Chambers), designed by Alfred Waterhouse and erected in 1871, fronting the station and facing St George's Hall, has been cleaned and restored. Although it ceased to serve travellers in the 1930s, it retains some fine public rooms. The former restaurant has a magnificent plastered ceiling which it is hoped will be uncovered and repainted.

Alas, the opening of the Merseyside loop line has involved the closure of Exchange Station and the destruction of Central, the former being the terminus for the East Lancashire and the Lancashire & Yorkshire Railways. Both lines made their exit through the north of Liverpool, via Sandhills, where the line divides between Preston and Wigan. Because of its joint ownership Exchange had dual booking offices, waiting rooms and even two buffets. The terminus was designed by Sir John Hawkshaw in an Italianate style, opened in 1850 and enlarged in 1884–8. It now stands empty and disused.

Central Station, since replaced by a smaller, underground version, housed Liverpool's first connecting service. Initially it was designed as the terminus for the Cheshire Lines Committee. When planned in 1862 it caused a considerable stir, as its construction involved the demolition of a large number of houses and shops, and there was much wrangling over the course which the line was to take to Ranelagh Street, delaying completion until 1874. The fine arched roof was its main feature, offering an interesting parallel with Manchester's Central Station, opened six years later. Unfortunately the similarity goes further. In 1966 passenger trains were diverted to Lime Street, using a connecting curve at Allerton to reach the former L.N.W.R. line and until 1972 the station continued to be used only in a limited form.

Central Station was also the terminus for the Mersey Railway. There was clearly a need for an efficient railway system to carry people across the River Mersey, while its width and tidal nature encouraged the construction of an underground line. Plans were drafted as early as 1866 but insufficient funds delayed completion of a tunnel until 1885. The Mersey Railway, opened in January 1886, was steam-operated and ran from James Street, under the river to Hamilton Square and then south to Green Lane in Birkenhead. Short extensions to both north and south were finished over the next five years, including a section from James Street to Central Station, completed in 1892. It was not an easy railway to operate as there were steep gradients on each side of the river which steam engines had difficulty in mastering. So great were the clouds of smoke emitted by the toiling locomotives that the company was forced to install huge steam-powered fans which, it was said, 'not only expelled the fumes but absorbed the profits of the undertaking'. The railway was electrified in 1903 – the first steam railway in England to be converted to electric traction. Today the line has been thoroughly modernized and incorporated into the loop system.

Because much of its equipment had been supplied by the American company Westinghouse, Liverpool's underground assumed a transatlantic appearance, but not as much as the

Overhead Railway did. The need for a passenger railway following the north–south line of the docks was recognized as early as 1852. The Harbour Board promoted a Bill in 1878 which was passed in 1882, having been amended by the Board of Trade to ensure that the line should be double-track throughout. It was later decided that the railway should be electric, as steam engines always presented a fire risk, particularly in areas where large quantities of timber were stored. The first section, between Herculaneum and Alexandra, was opened in March 1893 – not only Liverpool's first electrified railway, but the first elevated electric line in the world. The metals were then extended northwards to Seaforth Sands and south to Dingle by 1896, making its total length 6½ miles.

It is a great pity that the Overhead Railway has been demolished – it was a curiosity which would have attracted many visitors to Liverpool. Because of the shelter which its arches offered, it had been nicknamed the 'dockers' umbrella'. The rolling stock, purchased from the United States, consisted of square-sided timber carriages built for lightness. Their width, shortness, slatted seats and general appearance were characteristically American. Since Liverpool was an important port for transatlantic liners, these trains must have provided visiting Americans with a familiar welcome and offered departing Europeans a taste of what was to come. One motor car, No. 3, has been preserved and is at present in the transport section of the County Museum. This coach suggests an unusual comparison with the other exhibits, a Mersey Dock saddle tank engine, and *Lion*, a vintage L. & M. locomotive with its replica carriages. Unfortunately, the Overhead Railway's popularity fell in the post-war period. When it was announced in 1956 that major and expensive repairs were required, the company decided that the service should be terminated and the line demolished, though it was still financially viable and carrying a good number of passengers.

There is one other flourishing monument to Britain's railways in Liverpool, the Adelphi Hotel. The present building was constructed for the Midland Railway in 1914. The company had commissioned Frank Atkinson to design a magnificent new hotel which would have, as their publicity pamphlet noted, 'all the modern innovations of New York . . . solid British comfort, and that subtle air of refinement characteristic of a Parisian salon'. The constant passage of rich American tourists and wealthy Europeans meant that the Adelphi could rely on a large number of important guests. The building was appointed on a luxurious scale and included an indoor swimming pool as well as a Turkish bath, squash and tennis courts, shooting galleries and a billiards room. As at Manchester there was a splendid French restaurant. An innovation stressed by the publicity was the provision of 'telephones with direct communication throughout England and Europe generally'.

The key to Liverpool and its railway system is the port itself. The docks and their goods were the driving force behind the construction of its rail network, and for a long time freight traffic was considered by railway directors to be of greater importance than passengers. Hence, Liverpool produced just three termini (the first was initially small and had to be progressively enlarged) and a suburban system which was late to develop. Many of the inadequacies have only recently been rectified by the new link and loop lines.

BLACKPOOL

The connection between seaside resorts and railways is a strong one. Though spa towns had developed in the eighteenth century, producing splendid buildings at Brighton, Scarborough and inland at Bath, they remained the preserves of the well-to-do. It was not until the coming of the railways that seaside towns were used by the mass of the population – at first largely by day trippers. Contemporary newspapers show that special trains were provided for visits from the industrial conurbations to Redcar, Saltburn, Whitby, Blackpool, Windermere and Harrogate (an old spa) in the 1860s. As the nineteenth century passed, workers were granted longer holidays and earned more money. The resorts developed as places where people could stay for several days or a week, and long lines of hotels were erected along seafronts. Magnificent iron piers were constructed to allow visitors to sample the invigorating 'ozone', and theatres and mechanical amusements followed. Railway stations multiplied and services were doubled and trebled during the summer season. Blackpool, with its tower, its famous illuminations, its many boarding houses and, not least, its landladies is a thriving holiday haunt, retaining two stations, named North and South (Central has been closed).

In 1801, at the time of the first national census, Blackpool was a mere village, with a population of under 500. Its first railway, from Poulton, was completed in 1846 and visitors were attracted to the beaches from the start. An important 'coast line' from Lytham was opened to Central Station in 1863 providing access to Preston. By 1861 Blackpool had become so popular that its resident population had risen to over 4,000 and it became the first sizable town in Britain wholly devoted to holidays and excursions. The town's pleasant prospect, railway links and its proximity to an important and expanding industrial district were the main reasons for its success.

The railway companies were not the only bodies which arranged special seaside excursions to Blackpool. Works outings, Sunday school treats and trade union 'galas' all took advantage of the steam engines' speed and cheapness. Even the Burnley, Blackburn and Rochdale Guardians organized a regular trip to Blackpool for the children living in their workhouses. In 1895 the first Club carriage was operated between Blackpool and Manchester. There was an annual fee and membership was limited to those holding first-class season tickets. The scheme was well patronized and in years to come exceptionally luxurious carriages were constructed. However, these were commuter trains for rich businessmen who preferred to reside in the healthier suburban districts of Blackpool and travel into Manchester daily.

Blackpool experienced its most rapid growth in the last quarter of the nineteenth century. Its first pier had been built in 1863. This was extended in 1870 and the famous tower was opened in 1894. The town's popularity in 1919 was such that the Lancashire & Yorkshire Railway could no longer cope with the numbers wishing to travel to the resort. They were forced to introduce a form of limitation described by the press as the 'rationing of travel'. In fact, they simply initiated a system of advance booking for the busiest holiday periods, and almost a million passengers travelled to Blackpool from Manchester in that year under this scheme.

As the town itself increased in size and as the numbers of holidaymakers staying in Blackpool mushroomed, so the railway companies built new larger stations or redeveloped the existing termini. Central Station, rebuilt by the L. & Y.R. in 1900, had fourteen platforms. It was an interesting design executed in Accrington brick and featuring twin corner turrets and a central clock gable. The largest terminus was at Talbot Road, now renamed North Station, which had fifteen platforms. The first station was demolished in the 1880s when it could no longer cope with the increasing traffic, and the older stone structure, finished in a classical style, was replaced by a less distinguished brick building with a low clock tower. The interior was more impressive than Central's, the broad platforms being enclosed by a double-span roof instead of individual umbrella awnings over each platform.

Today Blackpool has two termini. North Station is now used by trains to Euston which formerly travelled along the southern route via St Annes and Lytham. With the closure of Central in 1964, South Station (called Waterloo Road until 1932), the next stop on the former Preston & Wyre Railway, became the other terminus. With its illuminations, 'golden mile', political conferences and continuing popularity as a resort, Blackpool looks certain to maintain the traditional association between seaside holidays and railway excursions.

LANCASTER AND THE ROUTE TO CARLISLE

Situated on the main West Coast Route between Preston and Carlisle, Lancaster was an important railway town. It is also an ancient route centre with a splendid castle. In the eighteenth century Lancaster was a spinning town which developed a number of associated industries, including linoleum and oil cloth production. The completion of a railway to Morecambe in 1848 gave Lancaster an additional port and potential seaside resort. The railways themselves made a contribution to employment with the establishment of the Lancaster Wagon Works, noted for the construction of L.N.W.R. and Great Central rolling stock.

Today it is easy to believe that the British railway system was laid down according to a grand plan. The smooth run north from Crewe to Carlisle is very misleading, as this stretch was actually completed by a number of separate companies acting independently. The first railway to reach Lancaster was from Preston and had been opened in 1840 – the Lancaster & Preston Junction Railway. It was logical to continue the line northwards to Carlisle. Although an East Coast Route to Edinburgh from London had already been completed, there was still a need to bring Westmorland and Cumberland into the circle of railway communication. Accordingly the Lancaster & Carlisle Railway went ahead, the line being finished in September 1846. The question now arose whether trains setting out from Carlisle would be allowed to continue their journey south over the metals of the adjoining company. It was ridiculous for passengers to have to keep changing trains along a through route simply because they had entered another company's jurisdiction. At first, the L. & C.R. exercised their right to use the southern section. However, a serious accident occurred in 1848 when a Euston to Glasgow express crashed into a local train at Bay Horse, reinforcing the need for a proper settlement governing line operation. The L. & C.R., in fact, remained an independent company until 1859, when the

L.N.W.R. succeeded in taking out a lease on its section, and it was formally absorbed in 1879.

The short railway between Lancaster and Morecambe was projected by the North Western Company. However, a few weeks after receiving the royal assent for its Bill, the railway was taken over by the L.N.W.R. Curiously the first title had taken a deep root, and when the line was completed two years later it continued to be called the 'Little' North Western to distinguish it from its powerful, parent company. The railway operates today with a single stop at Bare Lane. It had been electrified in 1908 (between Lancaster Castle Station and Green Ayre). An overhead system was adopted, which remained in operation until 1951 when steam engines were reintroduced until a new electric service could be installed.

Morecambe itself owed its rise as an important resort largely to the efforts of the N.W.R., supported by the Midland. With its impressive bay and views of the Lake District it had the natural qualifications for a holiday haunt. It simply required capital investment. The railway company not only provided an efficient transport link, it also built a hotel, and the Furness Company operated a packet steamer from Piel Pier. The harbour facilities were extended when boats from Northern Ireland began calling at Morecambe. The N.W.R. and Midland jointly established a steamer service to Belfast in 1853 when they bought two small boats, named *Laurel* and *Arbutus*, in the following year.

It is unfortunate that the old Promenade Station in Northumberland Street was closed in 1907, when a new, more convenient building was opened in its place. The earlier station, as old photographs reveal, had an exceptionally fine roof structure. Although no engineering achievement, its height, combined with the interlocking iron ribs supported by slim Corinthian columns, produced an elegant effect. The town's other terminus at Euston Road was finally closed in 1962 and the service via Bare Lane diverted to the new Promenade Station.

CARLISLE

Situated in the Border lands at the head of the English section of the West Coast Route, Carlisle developed as one of the country's most important railway junctions. It was also the terminus for local services operating through the Pennines, due east to Newcastle and around the coast to the Lake District. It was not surprising, therefore, that the town's traditional role as a strategic garrison was superseded in the nineteenth century, when it became a railway centre. Six major railway companies used Citadel Station: the L.N.W.R., Midland, North British, North Eastern, Caledonian and Furness.

The major route to Carlisle and beyond was the L.N.W.R.'s line from Lancaster. The company had concluded an agreement with the Caledonian Railway to allow trains to pass on to Glasgow or Edinburgh. However, the North British were anxious to infiltrate this territory, and as early as the 1840s they had assembled plans to capture the area described by the triangle between Berwick, Edinburgh and Carlisle. However, it was not until 1862 that they succeeded in extending their line south from Hawick to Carlisle – the 'Waverley route', named after Sir Walter Scott's novels. This development angered the L.N.W.R. and their Caledonian allies. Any through traffic arriving at Carlisle from the south was deliberately sent along Caledonian metals to limit the North British's business. Even the N.B.'s locomotive parts, purchased from the Midland at Derby, were sent to Edinburgh labelled 'via the Caledonian'.

The main station at Carlisle was the L.N.W.R.'s Citadel, designed by Sir William Tite, a distinguished railway architect. He constructed an asymmetrical two-storey building in Tudor style, with a clock tower, much buttressing and sturdy chimney stacks. A number of lozenge lattice windows survive, while the *porte cochère* is carved with the arms of the Lancaster & Carlisle and the Caledonian Railways. Perhaps most interesting is Tite's original refreshment room, also in the Tudor manner. Large many-paned windows, wooden panelling and screens, a high, timbered, octagonal patterned ceiling and a stone fireplace all remain. Even the door handles are decorated in a fitting style.

The station was named after the near-by Citadel law courts and was designed to blend with them and the city walls. The train-shed, enlarged in 1881, is an unusual lateral construction supported by rows of wrought-iron rings. Both ends were fitted with glazed Gothic screens, manufactured according to 'Rendel's Patent Indestructible System'. Unfortunately it has not lived up to its name, or at least B.R. has been supplied with the secret of its vulnerability. However, the stone side walls with their recessed perpendicular arches remain.

Possibly the finest of British Rail's upland routes is between Settle and Carlisle, via Appleby. This expensive and engineeringly demanding line was constructed late by the Midland Railway and opened to passengers on 1 May 1876, having cost £3½ million. It is a magnificent journey. The railway winds its way along valley sides, cuts across others by high viaducts (the longest being the Ribblehead Viaduct, 1,200 feet long, 156 feet high, supported by twenty-four arches) and tunnels through the unyielding outcrops. Rolling grasslands give way to open moors, exposed grey rocks and slopes newly planted with pine trees as the train climbs steadily northwards. The flattest areas are covered with a network of stone walls, while the only other signs of human activity are occasional quarries and clusters of farm buildings.

Most of the stations en route have been closed. It is unusual, but understandable, that they should all be of the same pattern. Almost all are built from local stone – limestone from Ribblesdale in the south, gritstones from Dent and Garsdale and sandstones from the Eden valley in the north – and feature twin, linked pavilions, with a central canopy supported by decorative iron columns and brackets. They are a pleasing contribution to such an empty landscape.

BARROW AND THE FURNESS RAILWAY

Barrow-in-Furness, along with Swindon and Crewe, is one of the towns which historians mention when they are discussing railway-induced settlement. The line was originally opened in 1846 to convey coal from the Dalton and Kirkby mines to Barrow for shipment along the coast, being extended to Broughton in 1848. With the ready availability of coal and iron ore, it was not surprising that the Furness Company selected Barrow as the site for their locomotive works. The manufacture of engines and iron goods became the town's most important source of jobs in the second half of the nineteenth century.

The second Barrow Central station, completed in 1863, was constructed from local brick in Italianate style. The town's growing population, based on the continued expansion of its industries, encouraged the building of a new station. This much enlarged edifice, painted in contrasting colours to give a rustic effect, was typical of the Furness Company's distinctive timber-framed structures. It was apt that the railway, with its foundries in Barrow, should have produced some of the finest ironwork for station fittings. Their roof brackets, containing the F.R. monogram, consisted of an intricate arrangement of delicate leaves. These were fitted at Dalton and Ulverston, while Grange and Whitehaven featured other floral designs. The company's station benches were among the most decorative ever produced. The ends featured squirrels, bunches of grapes and a network of branches and leaves. A few survive on the system and there is a restored version at York.

Ulverston (1873), a former F.R. station, is a superb Italianate building executed in dark red ashlar. Its asymmetrical plan and two-storey booking office is dominated by a square clock tower, decorated with urn finials and ornate ironwork. The entrance and the two broad platforms are covered by delicate glazed ridge-and-furrow awnings. The platforms are unusual in that they are separated by only a single track, with their canopies extending over trains on each side. It is a station of real elegance and style which decay has not impaired.

B.R.'s coastal line from Barrow to Carlisle is a route of contrasts. The southern part between Barrow and Whitehaven over former F.R. metals is largely through pleasant farmland, while the central section from Whitehaven to Maryport (once L.N.W.R. territory) assumes a bleaker industrial character. Workington developed as an important steel town and is still dominated by its furnaces and rolling mills. There were formerly three stations (Central and Workington Bridge having been closed), leaving Workington with its extensive sidings to serve industry. Unfortunately the Gothic station at Maryport has been demolished and nothing remains of the former southern headquarters of the Maryport & Carlisle Railway. The final section is inland via Aspatria, Wigton and Dalston. Again the railway generally passes through flat grazing land, the peaks of the Skiddaw range lying well to the south. Only between Foxfield and Bootle, in the southern part, do the uplands encroach on the railway, forcing it to cling to the narrow coastal margins. Foxfield was the junction for the branch line to Coniston Water (see p. 263), while Ravenglass to the north has a connection with the narrow-gauge railway along the Esk valley (see p. 267).

Among the Furness Company's directors in the late nineteenth century were a group of landed peers, including the Duke of Devonshire as its chairman, Lord Cavendish, M.P., and the Duke of Buccleuch. This involvement by the aristocracy in railway enterprises was not unusual. These families had realized that Britain's economic future lay with her manufacturing industries and that if they wished to remain influential, they had to invest in such schemes. Often they owned estates which were traversed by new lines and so had an additional interest in their operation.

THE LAKE DISTRICT

Although the Lakes have remained an immensely popular holiday area, most of their internal railways have been closed. Apart from the Furness coastal route, only the former L.N.W.R. line from Oxenholme to Windermere terminus is still part of B.R.'s network. Once double-track, a set of rails has been lifted and the formerly busy Windermere train-shed now accommodates a single line. This is a pleasant stone station with an elegant *porte cochère*, supported by slender fluted Corinthian columns. Oxenholme has retained its original stone side walls, but has been modernized and reduced in scale to reflect its diminished importance. Kendal, Burneside and Staveley are the intermediate stops, none having been closed.

The Furness Railway's line from Foxfield north to Woodland, Torver and Coniston Lake has been closed and the track lifted. However, the most picturesque and spectacular of these routes was from Penrith due west to Workington, via Braithwaite and Keswick. The last section, from Cockermouth to Workington, was over L.N.W.R. metals, while the main part was owned by the Cockermouth, Keswick & Penrith Railway. This was a truly upland line, winding its way through the valleys of the Skiddaw slates. The railway to Windermere, by contrast, is a lowland line that conveyed visitors to the foothills of the volcanic core. Most of the stations on the C.K. & P.R. were typical 'cottage' structures, but at Keswick (the largest settlement in the central Lakes) and Cockermouth important exceptions were made. For the former, a two-storey building was constructed, connected to the company's hotel by a short glazed passage way which bore the portraits of famous artists in coloured glass. The hotel is still a thriving concern (though seasonal), while the dilapidated station buildings house a model railway. It is rewarding to trace the line's former course through the northern part of the town. Cockermouth was almost as large, with an elaborate glazed timber waiting area on the platform. Unfortunately nothing now remains of the station, which today serves as a lorry park, though the trackbed and bridges survive. Penrith, on the West Coast Route, is still open. The original buildings, designed by Sir William Tite and executed in local light red sandstone in a Tudor manner, survive, while its mullioned windows overlook the ruins of Penrith castle.

THE ISLE OF MAN'S RAILWAYS

For such a small area, the Isle of Man has a remarkably diverse and historic railway system, featuring a number of vintage narrow-gauge steam engines. There is also an electrified section some eighteen miles long between Douglas and Ramsey, while the Snaefell Mountain Railway from Laxey provides holidaymakers with a fine view of the island's varied scenery. There are two museums, one for the steam railway at Port Erin and another on the west coast at Kirk Michael.

The three-foot gauge railway was originally constructed to provide an efficient transport service around the south-eastern coast of the Isle of Man. The first section was completed between the terminus at Port Erin and Ballasalla in 1874. For sheer grandiose scale, the railway's early buildings did much to rival many standard-gauge stations. Douglas, completed around 1890, had a French-style tower, Dutch gables, and a palatial entrance arch with turrets, pinnacles and a central pedimented clock. Port Saint Mary was served by a Tudor-style building executed in yellow brick, with much decorative timbering, while Castletown, completed in 1874, and Port Erin, 1903, were both twin pavilion structures. The first was built from grey stone and the latter in brick and terra-cotta. This variety was continued in the northern sections of the railway, Ramsey being pebble-dashed and Peel (now disused) a half-timbered station.

However, the steam locomotives are the most interesting feature of the line. They are all 2–4–0 tank engines and were built between 1874 and 1926 by Beyer, Peacock and Co. of

Gorton, Manchester. They are exceptionally attractive in their mid-green livery lined out in black and white, with fine polished domes and brass numbers on the chimneys. Every engine is named, and they include *Loch* (1874), *G. H. Wood* (1905), *Maitland* (1905), *Hutchinson* (1908) and *Kissack* (1910), while the other nine are in store. The coaches, brightly painted in red and cream, are all original stock and date from 1926.

Originally there was a total of forty-seven miles of track, sixteen working locomotives, seventy-five carriages and over a hundred goods wagons. There were nearly a hundred passenger trains a day during the summer season. Since then the northern half of the railway has been electrified and the lines from Douglas to Peel, St Johns to Foxdale, and Ramsey to Kirk Michael have all been closed. The Museum at Port Erin has done much to preserve this history. The railway's first locomotive, *Sutherland*, built in 1873, is preserved here, as is the last, *Mannin* (1926). There is a royal carriage, together with a host of other memorabilia, including tickets, photographs, signs and signals.

Not all the island's railways are steam powered. In fact since 1893 the eighteen miles from Douglas to Ramsey have been operated by the Manx Electric Railway. It is Britain's only electrically worked light railway, each train usually consisting of a motor car and trailer. The M.E.R. connects at Laxey with the mountain railway to Snaefell, a 3 feet 6 inch gauge electric line.

PRESERVED STEAM RAILWAYS

The Lakeside & Haverthwaite Railway

The Lakeside and Plumpton branch of the Furness Railway was opened in June 1869. From the outset it was a holiday line, taking tourists from Ulverston into the centre of the Lake District, with special excursions from London, Blackpool and Leeds. However, the gradual loss of its regular passengers led Dr Beeching to recommend closure, though it did continue to run freight trains until 1967. Immediately a preservation society was formed with the idea of reopening the whole line, but this proved too ambitious a task and work was concentrated on the three-mile section between Lakeside and Haverthwaite, via Newby Halt.

In 1970 British Rail granted the new company permission to begin restoring the permanent way. Locomotives and rolling stock were purchased and on 2 May 1973 the single-track railway was reopened. Haverthwaite has been selected as the Society's headquarters, having a pleasant yellow brick station, a good number of sidings and road access.

There are four 0-6-0 tank engines and one 0-4-0T, *Caliban*, which perform most of the railway's passenger duties. In addition, there is an 0-6-0ST Hunslet tank, named *Cumbria*, built in 1953 for the army to replace similar wartime engines. Larger and more powerful are the two 4MT class 2-6-4 tank engines, designed by Charles Fairburn for the L.M.S. in 1944 and intended for light passenger and goods duties. No. 2073 was built in 1950 and No. 2085 in 1951. Though a modification of an earlier Stanier engine produced for the Midland, wartime disruptions meant that they were actually constructed in Brighton for use on the Southern. No. 2073 required little maintenance, while 2085 needed extensive restoration and complete retubing. The first has been painted in the L.N.W.R.'s blackberry black livery and the second in the mid-blue of the Caledonian Railway.

The railway possesses ten carriages, most of which are standard British Railway designs. However, two are older, a former L.N.E.R. parcels van built at York in 1936 (one of the first to have been finished in metal rather than teak) and a riding van and brake, completed at Derby in 1913 for the Midland – originally a clerestory-roofed compartment carriage.

One of the numerous guides produced in the late nineteenth century for holidaymakers and visitors to England was devoted to the Lake District. As well as pointing out places of interest, hotels and short walks, it also gave suggestions for travel arrangements. 'For 12 shillings,' it noted, 'you may "go as you please" wherever the Furness Railway, as well as its steamers on Windermere and Coniston Lakes, can take you,' for a week. The same company also offered a selection of tours throughout the Lakes. It is a pity that many of their branches fell into disuse as motor cars became more popular, though the Lakeside Railway has at least kept one line operating.

The Ravenglass & Eskdale Railway

There is one other steam railway operating in the Lake District. This, however, is a narrow-gauge line and runs from Ravenglass on the coast (part of British Rail's local service) to Muncaster Mill, Irton Road, Eskdale Green, Beckfoot and Dalegarth. The railway was opened in 1876 as a three-foot-gauge line to serve a group of iron mines in Eskdale but was abandoned in 1912 when the last pit closed.

From 1915 to 1958, as a passenger service with a slightly broader gauge, the line passed through various hands. Then freight carriage was included to increase its revenue and in 1948 the Keswick Granite Company took it over, but decided to sell it ten years later. The Ravenglass and Eskdale Preservation Society then bought the line, ended freight traffic and converted it to a fifteen-inch gauge.

There are four steam engines working on the railway. *River Esk*, the first 2–8–2 locomotive built in England, was completed in 1923 and is painted in blackberry black livery with red and white lining. *River Irt*, a rebuild of Sir Arthur Heywood's *Muriel* (1894), is the world's oldest fifteen-inch gauge engine in service. In 1967 these two were joined by *River Mite*, built by Clarkson of York from the steam tender chassis originally used behind *River Esk*. In the railway's centenary year another engine, *Northern Rock*, designed and built at Ravenglass, was added to the stock. Each locomotive has an individual livery and this engine has been painted in a yellowish-green called 'muscat' and lined out in red and black. There are also several diesels operating on the railway, and one, *Shelagh of Eskdale*, resembles a Western class diesel-hydraulic, but is painted in royal blue.

A recent innovation was the adoption of radios to control running. Since much of the route is single-track, there are loops to enable trains running in opposite directions to pass one another. Each engine is fitted with a receiver and reports its position on approaching one of these sections, when directions are given from Ravenglass to govern the right of way. On a railway of this kind a radio system clearly has many advantages over the traditional telegraph signal, which cannot tell the operator precisely where each train is along the line.

Steamtown, Carnforth

Steamtown Railway Museum is at Carnforth, Lancashire (adjacent to the B.R. station and the main line), about six miles north of both Lancaster and Morecambe. It is on the site of a former marshalling yard and locomotive depot and comprises three miles of track spread over an area of twenty-three acres. Besides the sheds and sidings for storing and running the engines and rolling stock, there are facilities for their restoration. The junction at Carnforth was historically significant, being the meeting place for three railway companies – the L.N.W.R., the Midland and the Furness. Today the pleasant stone station is simply a stop on the Lancaster to Barrow local service and one can only watch expresses as they race past on the West Coast Route.

A variety of locomotives have been preserved here, not simply from the north-west. There are engines from the Great Western, the Southern and L.N.E.R., the L.M.S. being prominent among the engines without names, while the depot's signal box was removed from the Midland's line between Settle and Carlisle. Since British Rail lifted the ban on steam working over their lines in 1972, Steamtown has repeatedly supplied locomotives for special excursions. Their usual route has been from Sellafield, through Barrow, Carnforth, Skipton, Leeds, Harrogate and York to Scarborough.

Probably the most famous engine housed at Steamtown is No. 4472, *Flying Scotsman*, completed in 1923 and designed for fast running up the East Coast Route to Edinburgh. In 1928 No. 4472 achieved fame by hauling the first non-stop train from King's Cross to Waverley Station and on a trial run in 1934 it became the first steam engine to secure an officially recorded 100 mph run. It was fully restored in 1963.

Among the other L.N.E.R. exhibits at Steamtown is *Mayflower*, an Edward Thompson locomotive and one of the survivors of the once numerous B–1 class. *Mayflower* has also been restored to the L.N.E.R.'s apple-green livery. The other express locomotive from the Gresley stable is the A–4 streamlined Pacific, No. 4498, named *Sir Nigel Gresley*; with its sleek moulded casing, this locomotive suggests speed itself.

From the G.W.R., No. 6960, *Raveningham Hall*, was rescued from Barry scrapyard and restored at Carnforth. *Lord Nelson*, No. 850, from the Southern Railway, is distinguished by the characteristic smoke deflectors, the shape of the boiler and the short cut-away tender, the marks of a Maunsell engine. These 4–6–0s were designed as a more powerful successor to the King Arthur class, and were used on expresses, boat trains and holiday excursions to the south coast. Equally well-known, but not so glamorous, are the two 'Black Fives', Nos. 44871 and 44932, which have been restored to their original Midland livery, black with red lining. They were both built in 1945, the first at Crewe and the second at Horwich. Another locomotive from the L.M.S. is the Ivatt-designed 2MT class 2–6–0, No. 6441 (1950), which has been painted in L.M.S. maroon and lined out in yellow and black. The museum has a number of tank and suburban engines, the oldest being No. 1122, an 0–6–0 tender locomotive built for the Lancashire & Yorkshire Railway in 1891. There are also a number of French and German engines preserved at Steamtown, including the French express No. 231K22, which had formerly been used on the 'Flèche d'Or' service between Calais and Paris.

Steamtown possesses a fine collection of carriages to supplement their many and varied locomotives. They have a good collection of 'official' coaches – saloons fitted with observation sections, dining facilities and lounges so that senior company officials and engineers could inspect their systems in comparative comfort. The North Eastern Director's Saloon, No. 305, has now been restored to its original bright maroon. It has a clerestory roof, original carpets, fittings and furniture, and is a fine example of Edwardian coach building. Other carriages include the Great Western saloon, 'Stapleford Park', No. 9004, and a Great Eastern Chairman's coach complete with balcony, diner and shower.

Dinting Railway Centre

Dinting Railway Centre is based at a former Great Central engine-shed on the line from Manchester Piccadilly to Hadfield or Glossop. Dinting Station has a 'V' plan, the northern arm being the line to Hadfield (and on to Woodhead, Penistone and Sheffield), with the Glossop line opposite. Accordingly there are four sets of buildings, executed in red brick with stone dressings and decorated with attractive bargeboards. The platforms and the depot are linked together by a series of lattice footbridges. The centre's first acquisition was a Jubilee class, No. 5596, *Bahamas*, followed by No. 46115, *Scots Guardsman*, a Royal Scot class locomotive. It is apposite in view of the shed's history that No. 102, a Great Central 2–8–0 (built in 1911 for heavy freight), should have been loaned to the centre for restoration. Dinting, in the Pennine foothills, has a delightful setting high on the valley side with views along its grass green length to Glossop in the east and the railway viaduct in the west.

Steamport, The Southport Locomotive and Transport Museum Society

Southport on the Lancashire coast was once an important railway junction, being the terminus for the C.L.C.'s line south from Liverpool, via Aintree, Lydiate and Woodvale, while a number of the Lancashire & Yorkshire's routes (from Liverpool, Wigan and Preston) also met here. Today the railway to Preston has been closed, though the L. & Y.'s line to Wigan and their coastal route to Liverpool have both remained open. Steamport's depot and sidings are equipped for the restoration of locomotives. A 'Black Five', No. 44806, built in 1944 and now named *Magpie*, and a Riddles' 2–6–0, No. 76079 (4MT class), are shedded here. There are also a number of saddle-tank engines together with a selection of goods and passenger rolling stock.

10 The North-East

The north-east is an area of great variety and interest for the railway traveller. It has a more open and less testing terrain than Lancashire and the Lakes. The North York Moors and the Yorkshire Wolds are neither so extensive nor so mountainous as the uplands of Cumberland and Westmorland, and did not, therefore, present a serious barrier against railway construction to Scotland. Only the Cheviot Hills, north-west of Newcastle, caused the main line to be diverted. Rivers rather than uplands occupied railway engineers. A number of rivers flowing from the Pennines and emptying into the North Sea by the Humber, together with the Tyne, Tees and Wear, formed an east–west obstacle. Hence, bridges and viaducts, rather than tunnels, steep embankments and deep cuttings, are the recurring features of the north-east network.

The railway towns of the north-east may be divided into a number of groups. There are the coastal ports, Hull, Grimsby, Hartlepool, Middlesbrough, Sunderland and Newcastle, with seaside resorts at Scarborough, Cleethorpes, Whitby and Bridlington. The great rivalry between the L.M.S. and the L.N.E.R., fought out in the 1930s for supremacy over the route to Scotland, was conducted inland along the line between Doncaster and Berwick. Intermediate stations at York, Darlington and Newcastle witnessed to the flying expresses battling for ever quicker times. York, once a centre for the York & North Midland Railway, is now well known for its fine curving train-shed, the Royal Station Hotel and the National

Railway Museum. Darlington was a station on Stephenson's first public steam railway from Stockton, opened in 1825. Newcastle, like Liverpool on the west coast, possesses its own complex network of local lines, and is particularly remembered by through passengers for the famous diamond cross-over.

Further inland, situated at the base of the Pennines and in its deepest valleys, are a group of manufacturing towns. Concerned with woollens and the production of iron and steel goods, they demanded an efficient transportation system. When the canals could no longer cope with their growing orders, the railways were constructed. Leeds, Bradford, Halifax, Huddersfield, Wakefield, and to the south Sheffield, developed a number of stations, complex junctions and goods yards.

THE 'RACE TO THE NORTH'

The mergers of 1923 produced two railway companies which competed for passenger traffic between London and Scotland. The West Coast Route, between Euston and Glasgow via Carlisle, was operated by the L.M.S., largely making use of former L.N.W.R. tracks. The East Coast Route, originally the preserve of the Great Northern, the North Eastern and the North British Railway Companies, ran from King's Cross to Edinburgh. These three were now incorporated into the L.N.E.R. The rivalry increasingly concerned itself with speed rather than punctuality or the range of facilities offered by the train. Faster and ever faster runs became the goal, the competition culminating in the production of Gresley's streamlined A–4 Pacifics, and *Mallard*'s record-breaking steam run.

Racing had not been confined to the 1930s. There had been an earlier outbreak of speed competition in the latter part of the nineteenth century when improved locomotive design permitted a jump forward in operating times. Journeys were timetabled at nine and ten hours for the East and West Coast Routes respectively. In 1888, after some fast running, they were both reduced by sixty minutes, finally agreeing on eight

and half hours as a new compromise time. There was a further
spell of racing in 1895, with the completion of the railway
bridge across the Firth of Forth, giving the East Coast rivals
a direct link to Aberdeen. The two lines met at Kinnaber
Junction and, of course, the first to arrive had priority and
took the glory of winning the race from London. However, a
nasty mishap at Preston in 1896 frightened companies from
further competitions and they agreed to work within safe
schedules.

The battle was revived by the L.M.S. in 1927. Although the
amalgamations had taken place in 1923, actual combat was
delayed by subsequent re-organization and the General Strike
of 1926. With the impending introduction of the 'Royal Scot'
class in August, plans had been made to revise the timetable.
The faster train was named after the engines. But the new
locomotives (4-6-0s) were not really powerful enough for such
an arduous and sustained run and the non-stop schedule was
dropped after a single winter. Meanwhile, Gresley's A-3
Pacifics (introduced in 1923) hauling the new 'Flying Scotsman'
service were notching up faster times over the flatter
terrain of the East Coast Route.

Pressure was put on William Stanier, who had left the
G.W.R. to become Chief Mechanical Engineer to the L.M.S.,
to produce a powerful express locomotive. In 1932 he had been
ordered to design six types of engine to cover all aspects of
railway working, priority being given to the prestigious West
Coast Route. The first two Pacifics, built at Crewe, were ready
by the summer of 1933, and No. 6200, *Princess Royal*, gave its
name to the class. They were large engines and a daunting
prospect for firemen accustomed to the smaller Royal Scots.
Their long tapering boiler, the shape of the firebox and their
elegant lines betray something of Stanier's G.W. origins. Once
modified, they proved to be a fast, reliable and smooth locomotive.
Heavier trains were provided, timings reduced and
the 402 miles from Euston to Glasgow covered in seven and a
half hours.

The L.M.S. was not to have the last word. Although the Princesses succeeded in getting their times down to under six hours in 1936, Gresley's streamlined A-4 locomotives were able to match their speeds. In September 1935 he had introduced his first streamlined Pacific, No. 2509, *Silver Link*. The metal casing, running the length of the engine and curving down over the buffer beam, was not very dissimilar in shape from the front of today's High Speed Train.

On the inaugural run *Silver Link* broke the world speed record, reaching 112 mph on two occasions. The commercial success of the 'Silver Jubilee' service encouraged the L.N.E.R. to introduce another streamlined express, the 'Coronation', which ran between King's Cross and Edinburgh in six hours. The L.M.S. rose to the challenge and began their own streamlined service, 'The Coronation Scot' which, on its trial trip the train, headed by a streamlined Coronation class engine, is claimed to have set up a new record of 114 mph, though it almost ended in disaster as the brakes were applied late on the approach to Crewe. Engine and carriages rocketed over the junction smashing crockery and jolting passengers off their feet.

The L.N.E.R., anxious to regain the title, closed this chapter of speed rivalry. In July 1938 it was proposed to run brake tests on No. 4468, *Mallard*, and the opportunity was taken to log a fast run. *Mallard* raced down Stoke Bank and reached an incredible 126 mph – a steam speed never bettered. Gresley had by this time been knighted and the hundredth of his Pacifics had been named after him. By this time the L.M.S. had given up the fight, while the outbreak of war in September 1939 put an end to these activities.

The major railway towns on the East Coast Route are here examined from York to Berwick, via Darlington, Durham and Newcastle, as if travelling northwards along this historic line.

YORK

With the opening of the National Railway Museum at York in September 1975, the city's connection with railways was reinforced. The station and its hotel, completed in 1877 and 1878 respectively, are among the finest monuments to the Victorian era. Trains had come early to York. George Hudson used it as the headquarters for his York & North Midland Company. The first meeting, held on 10 August 1836, saw him elected as chairman and a line was projected to run from York south-west to join the Leeds & Selby Railway at Milford, which was completed in May 1839. Hudson, later nicknamed the 'Railway King' for his skill in capturing companies, leased the Leeds & Selby Railway in 1840 and began building up a network of lines around York. In 1845 a branch was projected from Church Fenton to Harrogate, via Tadcaster and Wetherby, involving the construction of a magnificent viaduct across the Crimple valley. Eventually the Y. & N.M.R. came to control a number of lines radiating from the city; in 1849 there were branches to Whitby, Scarborough, Bridlington and Hull.

It might be appropriate here to consider the career of the former York draper George Hudson. His name is readily associated with financial trickery and share mania. Although this cannot be denied, to fail to mention Hudson's achievements would be to ignore the way in which Britain's railway network was assembled. The system was not constructed according to a grand plan with arterial lines laid down between London and the major cities. For example, the East Coast Route was made possible only when three major companies – the North British, North Eastern and Great Northern – agreed to allow each other's trains to use their tracks without hindrance. The first two had originally been composed of a number of much smaller companies. Hudson's genius was to perceive the possibilities of amalgamation, to create through routes between distant towns, eradicating irregularities and working towards a truly national system.

Hudson was not an engineer and knew little about the workings of a railway, being first and foremost a financial manager. His master stroke established the Midland Railway Company in 1844 out of a host of smaller but adjacent enterprises. As a result similar combinations followed. The Grand Junction, the London & Birmingham and the Manchester & Birmingham merged to form the L.N.W.R., while five companies, producing a single line between Manchester and Grimsby, amalgamated under the title Manchester, Sheffield & Lincolnshire Railway. Hudson's financial empire based on the Midland Railway was eventually toppled by the completion of the Great Northern's route from London to York, thirty miles shorter than his route via Derby.

Hudson's original terminus at York was actually constructed within the city walls near Tanner Row, and the grassy banks decorated with flower beds opposite the present buildings were formerly the station's carriage sidings. The site is now used by British Rail as the headquarters for its Eastern Region. Mounting business and the restrictions imposed by the medieval walls prompted the N.E.R. to build a new and larger complex in 1865. It proved to be a daunting task and the station with its hotel was not completed until 1878.

The station was in fact the work of three successive architects to the N.E.R. The plans were draughted by Thomas Prosser. When he retired in 1874 Benjamin Burleigh took over but died two years later to be succeeded by William Peachy. Prosser had drawn on Dobson's designs for Newcastle's curved trainshed. The frontage, plainly constructed in yellow Scarborough brick, belies the power of the interior, where Prosser had concentrated his energies. The effect of the curved roof beams swinging round the bend of the tracks is a magnificent trick of perspective. Massive Corinthian columns support the roof, while the bracket spandrels are decorated with the Yorkshire rose and the triple shields of the North Eastern. The two sets of signal lights are attached to ornate brackets featuring the company's initials. The grandeur of the ironwork is offset by the simplicity of the brick side walls, which are simply adorned with a succession of round arches and an upper row of circular lights.

The station also features a glazed tile map of the North Eastern Railway's system set in the concourse wall, with the larger towns' individual networks magnified around the border. William Bell's Edwardian tea rooms, a timbered structure with a symmetrical pavilion with cupolas on each side and a central entrance, best viewed from the rear entrance to the Royal Station Hotel, also survive. The finest feature is probably the *art nouveau* stained glass, with its characteristic flowing leaf design. No longer a tea room, the building is now used by British Rail as a souvenir shop.

Many commentators have remarked that both the station and its hotel have uninspired exteriors, while the interiors are surprisingly striking. Certainly the façade of the Royal Station Hotel does not match the palatial qualities of St Pancras, the opulence of Manchester's Midland or the elegance of the Grosvenor and Charing Cross. It is constructed from yellow Scarborough brick, with cream Tadcaster stone dressings and rows of light red tiles in a controlled Italianate manner.

The interior certainly belies the restrained exterior, featuring a splendid, ornate staircase which swings up four flights from the lounge. The bar, decorated with railway signs, plans, models and lamps, is an outstanding piece of late-nineteenth-century exuberance. Tiled throughout in cream, raw sienna and light green, even the fireplace and breastwork are ornately constructed from glazed earthenware. The restaurant is more simply designed, with four central Corinthian columns supporting a lightly decorated ceiling. Through the lounge runs the 100-yards-long corridor, which extends along the full length of the hotel, and tradition claims that trainers staying in the hotel ordered their jockeys to run back and forwards along it to lose weight before a race. The first station hotel, completed in 1852, is now used as offices by British Rail and can be found within the city walls, near Tanner Row.

The National Railway Museum was opened at York on 27 September 1975. There had always been a smaller transport collection at York, founded by the L.N.E.R. after the centenary celebrations for the Stockton & Darlington Railway in 1925. An old engine-shed in Queen Street next to the station was used to house exhibits. After nationalization in 1948 the British Transport Commission set up a museum in Clapham to display both road and railway relics. The trams and buses held there have since been handed over to London Transport, first at Syon Park and now at Covent Garden. Under the 1968 Transport Act, Clapham and York became the responsibility of the Science Museum and B.R. was directed to find a single home for the two collections. York was selected as a well-connected site with a suitable historical railway background. A large hall was constructed from the former North Loco Shed. There are two turntables, exhibition galleries, a library and a lecture theatre, while direct access to the main line has enabled engines to be taken from display and steamed. The museum is an overwhelming success and the move from London has proved a sensible one, allowing people from the north a chance of making the journey, but keeping it within range of visitors from the south.

DARLINGTON

Darlington, described as the birthplace of English railways, has been the site for two major celebrations – one in 1925 organized by the L.N.E.R., the other in 1975, when the branch to Shildon was used to commemorate the Stockton & Darlington's completion and 150 years of railway operation. Today's large station maintains its historical associations, though the two vintage engines, *Locomotion* and *Derwent*, which were on display there have been moved to a new station museum at Darlington North Road.

The Stockton & Darlington, the world's first steam-hauled railway, had its origins in a plan formulated in 1818 to lay a

tramway between these two towns for the carriage of coal. The
scheme received Royal Assent in 1821 after one abortive
attempt, when a branch was also authorized to run from
Darlington west to the Durham coal pits at Shildon. George
Stephenson, assisted by his son Robert, was asked to survey the
line and after presenting his report, was appointed resident
engineer. An important revision occurred in 1823 when the
Act was amended to permit the running of 'loco-motive or
moveable engines... for the purpose of facilitating the
transport, conveyance and carriage of goods, merchandise and
... passengers'. Robert Stephenson took overall responsibility
for the design and construction of the first engine on the line,
Locomotion No. 1.

An inaugural service ran from Shildon via Darlington to
Stockton on 27 September 1825, when a mixed train of trucks
loaded with coals and passengers plus the company coach,
aptly named 'Experiment', travelled the first journey. It was
estimated that between 550 and 600 people were carried. The
scene was memorized by John Dobbin, who re-created the
crossing of Skerne Bridge in a sepia wash sketch depicting a
long and crowded train hauled by *Locomotion*, watched by a
large and attentive crowd.

Although passengers were carried on the inaugural run, the
directors of the Stockton & Darlington did not perceive their
commercial potential. The line had been designed for the
conveyance of coal alone and it was not until 1833, after the
success of the Liverpool & Manchester Railway, that they
considered operating a regular passenger service. Until then
people had been conveyed in horsedrawn vehicles. Today
the reverse is true and railways are seen primarily as a means
of transporting travellers, while freight has been relegated to
a subsidiary function.

It is still possible to travel over parts of the Stockton &
Darlington Railway. A weekday pay train from Darlington to
Bishop Auckland, via Shildon, runs over Stephenson's line.
The eastern half of the route has been considerably modified

since 1825. Nevertheless, there is a service from Darlington to Stockton via Dinsdale and Allen's West, though the only original section is between Oak Tree Junction and Eaglescliffe Station. Tees-side Airport is, of course, a new stop on the line – different forms of transport are not always in conflict.

Darlington Bank Top, designed by William Bell, is a good example of a multi-purpose station. Situated on a fast main line, but as the central terminus of a local system, it had to perform a number of conflicting roles. Like Leicester Central and Rugby Midland, it was constructed with a very broad island platform. Let into this at each end were shorter bays for suburban trains. Platforms on each side of the train-shed serve longer expresses. For the prestigious non-stop trains to Newcastle and Edinburgh, lines were laid around the building, by-passing the station altogether.

Darlington Bank Top is a typical N.E.R. structure. Bell, who favoured high arched roofs, constructed a majestic double span train-shed at Bank Top in 1887. The bracket spandrels, as at York, are decorated with the triple arms of the company. The main buildings were in red brick, while the offices on the central concourse are timbered. Formerly *Locomotion* and *Derwent* were on display here. *Derwent*, constructed by Kitching and Co. of Darlington in 1845, was sold to Pease & Partners for work on their colliery lines after being withdrawn from the S. & D. in 1869. Presented to the N.E.R. for preservation in 1898, it joined *Locomotion* at North Road Station after restoration.

Durham City Station, situated high on the side of the Wear valley, must occupy one of the finest urban sites in the country. The town slopes away from the railway, and on the opposite bank, rising up in the distance in all its medieval magnificence, is Durham cathedral. The railway crosses part of the city on an arched stone viaduct. On a misty winter's day, looking from this viaduct at the roof-tops with their rows of brick chimney stacks disgorging pit smoke, it requires no great imagination to slip back a century. Durham is a quiet ecclesiastical centre where it appears that the railway is the only modern influence.

The station, designed by George Andrews, is a pleasant building, constructed from dark stone in Jacobean style. Panelled doors, Gothic windows and the unusual canopy over the northbound platform distinguish the City Station. The iron columns and wooden roof structure have been painted in brown, beige and dark red, making a pleasant change from the usual B.R. colours.

NEWCASTLE

John Dobson, the architect of Newcastle Central, argued that stations, as public buildings, 'structures seen by thousands of people', might do much 'towards improving the taste of the public'. His imposing station is classically simple, being fronted by a massive *porte cochère*. Composed of a series of broad arches with clocks on all three sides, it is constructed in sombre grey-ochre stone. Dobson's greatest achievement lay with the interior and the construction of the three semi-elliptical train-sheds, built on a sharp curve. One of the railway's engineering accomplishments was the arched iron roof, improved structures allowing wider spaces to be covered. The techniques these engineers developed were re-applied in market halls, shopping arcades and factories. In fact Dobson had a number of precedents to draw upon – Paxton's greenhouse at Chatsworth and Decimus Burton's Palm House at Kew both offered botanical examples, though neither of these were constructed on a curving line. Dobson's train-shed was finished in 1849 and the main buildings followed a year later, though the station as a whole was not completed until 1865.

Newcastle Central was once the most important station on the North Eastern, handling nearly 1,200 arrivals and departures daily at its peak. Accordingly, the refreshment rooms were constructed on a grand scale, though only a little of their majesty can be guessed at today. There is still a high, ornate ceiling, with decorative Corinthian columns and sienna tiled walls. The buffet has, of course, been 'modernized' and is now an unhappy mixture of bright seventies' simplicity and faded Victorian exuberance.

The train makes an impressive entrance to Newcastle Central, crossing the Tyne high up on the King Edward bridge. To the west there is a road bridge and to the east a new bridge for the Metro system, while beyond that is B.R.'s High Level Bridge used by south-bound trains leaving Newcastle Central from the eastern exit. In fact the track layout is based on a square, with the two bridges on opposite sides and the station and engine-sheds forming the northern and southern sides respectively. It is a fascinating though rather circuitous network to travel round, with diamond cross-overs at the intersections, best seen from the castle next to the station. Sets of signal boxes controlled these complex junctions, but these have since been replaced by a single electric box at Tyne Yard.

The present Newcastle network can be divided into two sections. First, there are the main lines, which include the north–south route to Scotland from London and the east–west routes from Carlisle to the coastal ports of Sunderland and Hartlepool. Secondly, there is the Metro, including the circular suburban service to Whitley Bay and Monkseaton, returning to Central Station by Gosforth and Jesmond, together with the line south of the Tyne, via Jarrow, terminating at South Shields. Long sections of the original N.E.R. network have been retained, the finest stations being restored. Although the new electrical multiple units bear little resemblance to any earlier rolling stock, something of the system's former character has been preserved, not least in its architecture.

The loop line had its origins in the Blythe & Tyne Railway which in 1864 had completed two lines from their Newcastle station (New Bridge Street), one north-east to Monkseaton via Backworth and the other due east to Tynemouth. Although

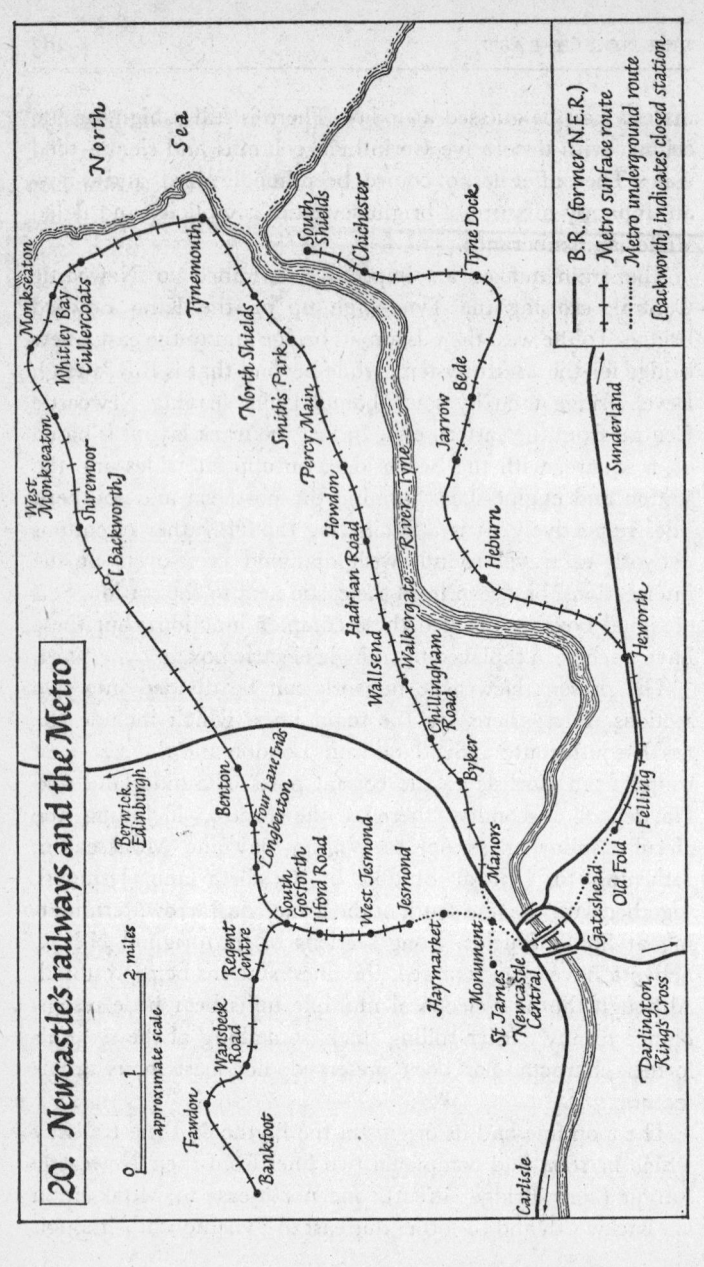

a coastal railway linking these two termini was authorized in 1872, work did not begin until 1874, when the company had been taken over by the North Eastern, who completed the loop in July 1882. B R. inherited the service from the L.N.E.R., and when steam was phased out diesel multiple units were introduced.

The service departs from Platforms 1 to 3 at the eastern end of Central Station. The buffer stops are still wooden blocks covered with iron plates, while ornate railings decorate the platform ends. The train pulls out over the diamond crossover, cutting through Newcastle on a high viaduct. It is a short run to the rebuilt Manors and the new Byker viaduct is soon visible – a simple white concrete structure, presenting a sharp contrast to the adjacent brick road bridge. The line passes on to Chillingham Road (formerly Heaton), where the first station was a typical wooden bridge building supported on iron pillars, running at right angles to the railway itself with steps leading down to the platforms. Most of the time the Tyne with its cranes, docks and ships is close at hand. Factories and offices give way to suburbs, Walkergate and Wallsend, with their brick terraces, inter-war semi-detacheds and 1950s estates.

Howdon-on-Tyne has an old station house, a lattice-work iron foot bridge and a level crossing, though two large gasometers dominate the scene. Percy Main and North Shields follow, where the carriage lights are switched on and the train plunges into a tunnel, to emerge into a long stone-lined cutting with ferns and greenery hanging down from the skyline. Suddenly the lights go off and the train swings around a curve into Tynemouth. It is a huge station but shows all the signs of being rarely used. Rusting rails, boarded-up windows and a walled-up concourse testify to a former grandeur. There are six platforms protected by an elegant canopy. A number of semaphore signals with a disused weatherboarded box complete the decaying atmosphere.

The train has now reached the coast and Newcastle's riverside docklands have been exchanged for the North Sea, the pier ball room, tennis courts, parks and more spacious housing. Cullercoats, also in a dilapidated condition, is followed by Whitley Bay, a station which was formerly busy with holiday-makers. William Bell spent much time and money on its construction, designing a tall clock tower adorned with fashionable festoons of terra-cotta fruit and flowers, topped with an ogee-shaped dome. Railings still divide the concourse from the platforms. They are fitted with broad sliding gates and ornate overhead brackets for departure boards. Monkseaton, another Bell station, with its solid red brick and stone buildings, is also spacious and elegantly Edwardian. On the north side of the line at West Monkseaton, corn fields stretch to the distance, while housing estates dominate to the south.

Because British Rail knew that the Metro system was on the way, they spent little on the line. Consequently the old lozenge red and cream signs were everywhere to be seen, while stations retained early B.R. colours. The Metro has taken over the whole of this circular route and a number of stations have been rebuilt (Wallsend, Howdon, Smith's Park), though the most interesting ones at Whitley Bay, Tynemouth and Walkergate have been retained. The line to South Shields has been incorporated, involving the construction of another railway bridge over the Tyne. The electrified system is operated by overhead cables. Trains travel under the city centre, so that Manors, Haymarket, Monument, Central, St James and Jesmond are all beneath ground. The electrical multiple units are similar to but shorter than those working on the 'Great Northern' suburban system, with semi-automatic doors, ample standing room and a single class.

Like the hotel at York, the Royal Station Hotel, Newcastle, is an integral part of the station. There had been an earlier building, the present hotel dating from 1893. Designed by William Bell, it was appointed in grand style and is still a magnificent structure, though much of the original panelling and faïence work has been removed or painted over. The main staircase is reminiscent of York, with a central well, ornate balustrading and a fine mansard ceiling. The restaurant has original panelling and a decorative fireplace, while the Stephenson Room is highly ornate, with decorative columns, panelled walls and more faïence work. *The British Architect*, reviewing the building in November 1893, noted the all-round improvement and added that 'the long classic frontage of the station is now extended by the addition of a lofty hotel building with projecting bays, an entrance porch, and a tower'. The article recorded the various sub-contractors who had worked on the building, including 'Messrs Diespecker & Co., London, Roman mosaic work; Messrs G. Izant & Sons, London, electric bells; Mr G. Siemens, London, electric light'.

NEWCASTLE TO BERWICK AND CARLISLE

Though Newcastle is a regular stop for the 'Flying Scotsman' and other east-coast expresses, it by no means represents the limits of the North Eastern's network. There are some fifty miles to the Scottish border, and the line to Berwick still has a local service. The railway skirts the Cheviot Hills and runs along the coastal plain through arable farmland, calling at the 'cottage' stations en route, Cramlington having been completely rebuilt and Alnmouth partially modernized. Acklington and Widdrington are both pleasant original Newcastle & Berwick Railway structures. In fact the company's stations were characterized by this individuality, very few being alike. For example, the former is constructed from brownish-yellow stone with a platform canopy and a lightly decorated, asymmetrical plan, while Widdrington offers no definable style, but features patterned bargeboards. The stations were all designed by Benjamin Green, a popular railway architect in the region.

Berwick, approached from the south by an impressive round-arched stone viaduct (the Royal Border Bridge, designed by Robert Stephenson in 1849) across the River Tweed, is a more substantial structure. The station is built on the site of Berwick castle. Medieval walls and turrets still stand on its western flank and run down to the river bank. It is a two-storey red sandstone building, symmetrical with decorative pilasters surmounted by a central clock pediment. The entrance canopy is supported by iron brackets displaying the monogram of the N.E.R. A model of No. 717, *Border Lass*, a 4-6-2 express locomotive in L.N.E.R. livery, is aptly on display in the booking hall. The station has been modified so that only the island platform is now used, but it has a group of elegant Edwardian timber waiting rooms and offices. Being a border town, Berwick was the point where the North Eastern and North British companies met. In addition, a number of branch lines converged here, joining at Tweedmouth in the south (the overgrown trackbed and junction is visible) and Reston to the north-west. Both of these stations have since been closed.

Newcastle has railways radiating to all points of the compass. One of the most attractive routes is due west to Carlisle along the Tyne valley between the Cheviots and the Pennines. Today the service is a local one and operated solely by diesel multiple units which, although they might accurately be described by the historical term 'rattlers', do provide an excellent view of the scenery and the railway itself.

This is a particularly historic line, being the first to be laid across England. Constructed by the Newcastle & Carlisle Railway, it was planned as early as 1824 but the first section, between Hexham and Blaydon, was not opened until March 1835, and the remainder not until June 1838. It was latterly operated by the N.E.R. from Newcastle Central, by agreement trains terminating at Carlisle Citadel. Leaving Newcastle, the broad valley of the Tyne has an industrial flavour, with factories and warehouses channelling the line to Blaydon. As with most of the surviving stations, Blaydon has been modified to accord with its diminished importance. Nevertheless, it retains a pleasant iron footbridge and a disused red brick watertower. Wylam, the next stop, has a light-ochre stone building with gables and a pleasant view of lush fields. It too was designed by Benjamin Green and has a Tudor look to its windows and chimneys. Green was responsible for most, if not all, of the stations on the line.

Hexham is the most important stop on the railway. It was formerly a junction, offering a connection with the North British network across the Southern Uplands and more specifically to Redesmouth, Hawick and St Boswells. The signal box is sited on a massive iron gantry built across the tracks at the eastern end of the station, and has an impressive array of arms. The station itself is constructed from ashlar in a restrained Tudor manner, though the booking office has two tiny lancet windows for the sale of tickets, completing the Gothic image. Leaving Hexham the railway continues its gentle climb up the valley to the Tyne Gap. Bardon Mill is unusual in that its platforms are not situated opposite one another, but are staggered. Haltwhistle is distinguished by a splendid watertower. Supported on arcaded red-brick foundations, the grey tank has a decorative oval plaque which records 'Peter Tate, Engineer, 1861'.

From here on the scenery loses something of its rich quality and takes on an increasing upland character. Sheep and woodland become more common. Between Haltwhistle and Brampton the railway enters the Irthing valley and begins its gentle descent to Carlisle. This is a fascinating line to travel along, offering a sharp contrast to the modernity of the East Coast Route. Short lengths of rail supported on timber sleepers combine to produce that historic railway rhythm, in contrast to the unbroken singing of the main line's continuous welded track. Semaphore signals are controlled by a succession of traditional signal boxes, often with level crossings as well, while the stations are all original. The solid, rattling carriages still convey local people on their daily trips; it is not a businessman's or a holidaymaker's railway.

LEEDS AND SOUTH-WEST YORKSHIRE

The West Riding has traditionally been a woollen area. Leeds, Bradford, Wakefield, Huddersfield and Halifax developed as textile centres in the seventeenth century, while the Industrial Revolution led to mechanization and the construction of large steam-powered mills. It also resulted in the exploitation of the Yorkshire coalfield. As a concomitant of mining, manufacturing and engineering trades developed in these major towns and most particularly in Sheffield. This range of industrial enterprise produced one of the most complex rail networks in Britain, and a host of companies laid down their metals in an attempt to capture passenger and freight receipts. At one time Leeds had no less than three termini and two additional goods depots, plus a considerable number of local stations. While it was not unusual for a city to have three companies competing for business, Leeds had as many as seven (with an eighth on the fringe).

It is fitting to start with Leeds, not merely because of its size, but because it was the first to develop railway connections, later becoming a major junction. The Leeds & Selby, promoted in 1829 and opened in 1834, was the first passenger railway constructed in the West Riding. As was often the case (and a reason why reformers backed the railways), the Leeds terminus was constructed in the dirtiest quarter of the town and resulted in a certain amount of slum demolition.

The most notable feature of the line was the 700-yard tunnel at Richmond Hill. Passengers were still very wary of railways and were dubious about travelling through a confined and darkened space beneath ground. As this was the first tunnel on a public railway, the L. &. S.R. had the walls whitewashed and polished copper sheets placed under the ventilation shafts to reflect daylight about the sides. Indeed, it was said that a newspaper could comfortably be read in the tunnel. Early excursions were operated along the line in 1835, when trippers were taken to Selby, coaches taking them on to York for the Festival.

Once the L. & S.R. was established, other railway companies were formed with the idea of linking Leeds with other important towns. A number of trunk routes opened, including connections to York in 1839, Manchester in 1841 (the M. & L.R.) and Bradford in 1844. Slowly but surely Leeds was linked with Lancashire and the other Riding towns, and by a similar process of construction and amalgamation reached London itself.

By 1900 a passenger could travel to Leeds from the capital by one of four major routes. He could take the Midland from St Pancras, the L.N.W.R. from Euston, the Great Northern from King's Cross or the Great Central from Marylebone to Sheffield and then take a local train. While this abundance of choice might lend great variety to travelling, it also resulted in a waste of resources and passengers did not always get the most efficient service. Changes were often necessary and delays resulted from a lack of co-operation between rival companies.

As might be expected Leeds developed a number of termini. Central Station, initially the busiest, was jointly operated by the G.N., L. & Y., L.N.W.R. and N.E. railways, though the first two were most prominent. There was much bickering between the various companies and a bitter dispute actually halted construction work. Wellington Station was the terminus for the powerful Midland Railway. However, Wellington goods depot was the preserve of the G.N. and N.E. companies. New, owned by the L.N.W.R. and N.E. railways and destined to become the major station in Leeds, was the third main-line station.

New Station's importance had more to do with the logic of track layouts than with the beauty or facilities of particular stations. It was a mean structure with no frontage at all, the architect, Thomas Prosser, having concentrated all his energies on producing a splendidly shaped and decorated train-shed. However, in 1938, after much negotiation, Wellington and New were linked together and unofficially named

City North and South. When British Rail decided to simplify the network further, they selected these two for development. North was to be a parcels and goods depot, while South was enlarged for passengers. Work started in 1959 on an ambitious plan, but funds became scarce and rebuilding was halted in 1961. The contractors resumed in 1963 with revised plans and the modifications were completed four years later.

The line from Leeds City to Long Preston (on the route to Settle and Carlisle; see p. 260) affords an interesting view of industrial valleys as they run into the Pennine foothills. Leeds is a high-level station entered by embankments and viaducts. The railway crosses the Leeds & Liverpool Canal and swings westwards for Shipley. Even though there are still a large number of lines radiating from the city, empty bridges and broad widths of disused trackbed indicate that the region's railways have experienced a decline. Shipley is a rare triangular station with platforms on all three sides. It was the junction for the Great Northern and Midland lines from Leeds and Bradford. Here long mills, tall chimneys, saw-toothed roofs and rows of terraced houses present an intriguing pattern of industrial horizontals and verticals.

Just before Bingley and the famous 'Five Rise' (a group of five locks on the Leeds & Liverpool Canal visible on the north side of the railway) is Saltaire. This industrial complex is sandwiched between the railway and the River Aire, both being used for shipments. The massive mill with its dominating chimney was completed in 1853 and is constructed in the Italianate style from clean ochre stone. The owner, Sir Titus Salt, a Congregationalist, also built a complete town with chapels, schools and clubs for his workforce, believing that manufacturers had obligations beyond paying wages. Keighley Station is divided between railway preservationists (see p. 306) and B.R., the two being distinguished by their distinctive liveries.

Bradford once possessed one of the region's finest train-sheds – the first Exchange terminus. It was almost exclusively a textile town involved with the spinning and weaving of woollens and worsteds. As we have seen, the first railway to Bradford, completed in 1844, was from Leeds. With the opening of the Halifax to Low Moor line in 1850, the wool capital was put in more direct contact with Manchester and this improved transportation resulted in the further expansion of the town's textile businesses, creating in turn the need for additional railway links.

At the peak there were three termini in Bradford, Market Street (renamed Forster Square in 1924) for the Midland Railway, Exchange, owned by the Lancashire & Yorkshire, and Adolphus Street, the terminus for the Great Northern. The last has since been closed down and the second rebuilt. Forster Square has been run down and is primarily used for goods, though it does retain two platforms for the local service to Keighley and Ilkley. The Midland Hotel, which forms part of the terminus buildings, is shut and stands unused at its side. The original Exchange was closed in 1973 and a partially completed (the architecturally-minded might say inferior) substitute was opened, retaining the same name. Although Exchange's frontage was meagre to say the least, the double-arched train-shed, completed in 1888, was quite splendid. It was distinguished by its fan-like end screens, formed by radiating glazing bars, and the delicate upright brackets with their decorative whorls and curves, supported by Corinthian columns.

The site of the first Exchange terminus, to the north of the present station, now serves as a car park, only the surrounding stone foundations and cast-iron railings having survived. However, the Victoria Hotel which fronted the building flourishes. The massive side walls of Adolphus Street remain in the cleared wastes between Wakefield Road and Dryden Street.

Huddersfield has one of the most talked-about stations in England. Sir John Betjeman has described it as having 'the most splendid station façade in England ... like an enormous classical country house'. It was designed by J. P. Pritchett Senior of York and consists of an elegantly balanced Corinthian portico fronting the central office building. Symmetrical colonnades lead out to terminal pavilions, featuring coats-of-arms of the L. & Y. Railway and the Huddersfield & Manchester Railway & Canal Company. They had been bitter rivals who had settled their differences and decided to show Yorkshire what, when combined, they were capable of producing. Few could quarrel with their argument.

The present line from Leeds City to Manchester Victoria via Huddersfield (formerly L.N.W.R.), is an important east–west communication across the Pennines. The first section from Leeds to Huddersfield is dominated by disused stone mills and weaving sheds. The railway threads its way along the Wear and Holme valleys, no longer discoloured by smoke from their many and varied chimneys. Batley Station, set high on an embankment, presents a splendid industrial panorama. Huddersfield itself is approached along a stone viaduct which leads to an atmospheric train-shed.

The second half of the journey to Manchester Victoria has a series of lengthy tunnels as the railway crosses the Pennine hills. The longest is Standedge (3 miles 64 yards), just past Marsden. Rough stone-sided cuttings and viaducts work the train south-west to Mossley, Stalybridge and Ashton-under-Lyne. The contrast between Lancashire and Yorkshire is here apparent: red brick (from Accrington) dominates where light-ochre Millstone Grit had widely been used for construction, while the mills tend to be larger and the manufacturing more varied as Greater Manchester approaches. Miles Platting Station, constructed from brown and cream glazed bricks, makes an unusual change in the railway architecture.

The Huddersfield & Sheffield Junction Railway, completed in 1850, is a fine example of a line built against the grain of the country. Pennine valleys tend to lie on an east–west axis. The difficulties associated with the construction of a route running diagonally south are apparent. The railway had to cross the valleys of the Rivers Colne, Dearne and Don, while tunnels were needed to take it through the intervening hills. The longest bore, almost a mile, was at Thurstonland (1,631 yards), while Cumberworth tunnel was 906 yards long. The Lockwood viaduct over the River Holme is one of the largest in Britain, being 136 feet high, and the Penistone viaduct is one of the longest, 330 yards. The whole line is an example of how determined and skilful railway engineers could be in the mid nineteenth century. Their achievement seems all the more remarkable when it is recalled that there were no settlements along the line, its sole purpose being to shorten the distance between Sheffield and Huddersfield. It succeeded and the journey was reduced from forty-four to twenty-seven miles.

SHEFFIELD

Sheffield is, or was, world famous for the manufacture of steel goods, and most particularly cutlery (see p. 196). The importance of the town's railway system may be gauged from the rapid growth in its manufacturing trades, which produced a quadrupling of the population between 1840 and 1890.

In fact, Sheffield has connections with the very earliest railways. From the eighteenth century there were wooden tramways here to carry coal from local pits. The town's first steam railway arose as a result of Hudson's proposed line between Derby and Leeds. The inhabitants were annoyed that George Stephenson, who had been contracted to survey the line, preferred to by-pass Sheffield in favour of a more lenient terrain. Following this outcry a connecting branch from Rotherham to Sheffield was projected and it was opened in 1838. Two years later the Y. & N.M.'s railway was completed from Derby to Rotherham, completing the link between Sheffield and London, via Hampton, a journey which took around $9\frac{1}{2}$ hours.

The new railways encouraged the growth of the ferrous industry and by 1845 five major companies had transferred

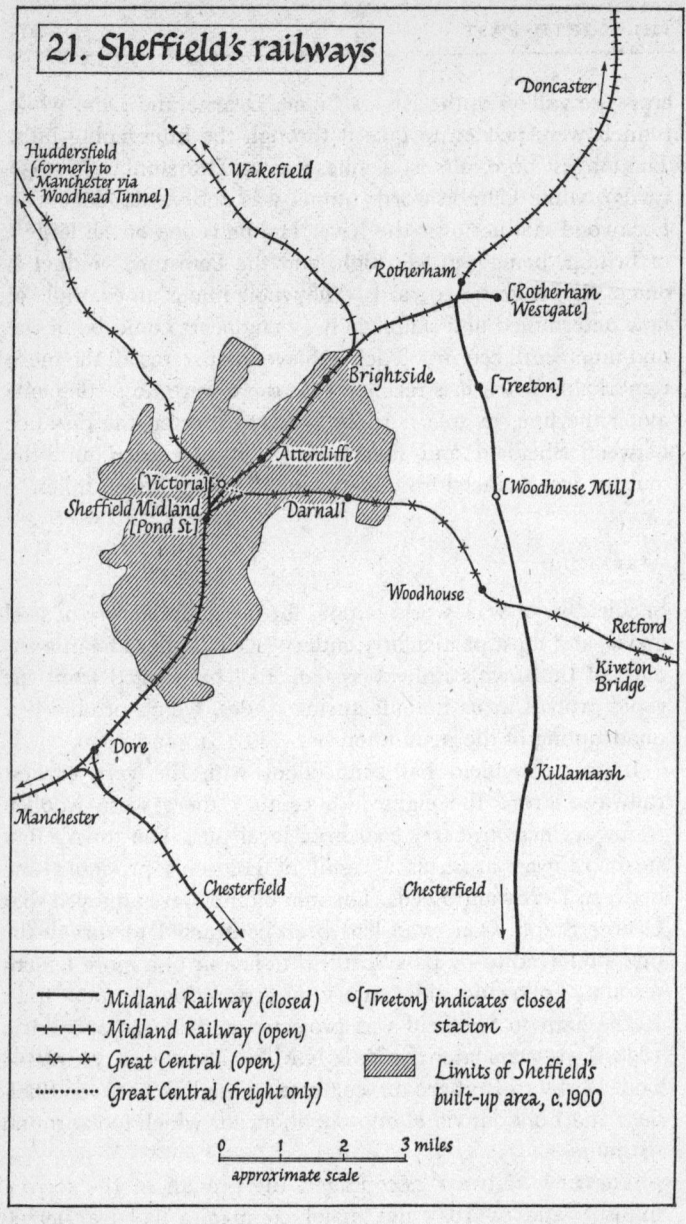

THE NORTH-EAST

their works to sites along the line. John Brown's vast iron and steel business (he was later chairman of the Sheffield, Chesterfield & Staffordshire Railway) was largely based on his invention and development of the conical spring for buffers in 1848. The town soon became a major producer of rails, metal tyres and axles, exporting them throughout the world.

In December 1845 the Sheffield, Ashton-under-Lyne & Manchester Railway was completed. This involved the construction of the Woodhead tunnel, which, at three miles twenty-two yards, was then the longest in the country. A second bore was made a year later when it was realized that it could not cope with the traffic demands being made. This was more carefully constructed and was opened in February 1852. Sheffield's first link to the east came with the incorporation in 1846 of the extension of the S.A. & M. to Gainsborough and Lincoln, while the Great Grimsby & Sheffield Junction Railway (extending the line from Gainsborough) had been finished in the previous year. In addition, Great Northern wanted to extend its network to Sheffield but was prevented from constructing its own line and forced to rent the Manchester, Sheffield & Lincolnshire's Victoria terminus.

By the late nineteenth century Sheffield had developed a number of termini. Wicker Station in the north and Pond Street in the south both served the Midland Railway, the Great Central used Victoria and Park Station for goods, while the Great Northern used City depot for their freight service. Although there had been a certain amount of pre-nationalization pruning, in 1961 B.R. embarked on an extensive programme of reconstruction to simplify Sheffield's spider's web of lines. It resulted in the creation of the gigantic marshalling yards at Tinsley and the selection of Pond Street (now called Sheffield Midland) as the town's principal station. In 1970 Victoria closed after almost 120 years of operation and the historic Woodhead line to Manchester was closed to regular passenger traffic.

In 1936 the L.N.E.R. had decided to electrify the Woodhead

route between Sheffield Victoria and Manchester London Road (now Piccadilly). The erection of overhead cables was well under way when war broke out and the scheme was temporarily halted. A new tunnel which had to be constructed at Woodhead to accommodate the wires took six years to complete, being opened in 1954. Until recently goods trains have continued to use the line but it now seems destined for closure (see p. 53).

Passenger trains to Manchester have been diverted along the former Midland line through the Hope valley. This route via Edale and Chinley is certainly picturesque. It traverses the Peak District, offering the passenger a panorama of unspoilt rolling grasslands and moors, in contrast to the industry and bustle of Sheffield and Manchester at each end of the journey.

HULL AND THE HUMBER

Although there are several fast trains from King's Cross to Hull, most services involve a change at Doncaster. The journey from here is not in a streamlined H.S.T., but in creaking, slightly cramped and ageing diesel multiple units. However, these trains, with their generous windows and sedate speed, do offer a better view of the countryside and call at many more stations than the direct expresses. There is a regular local service from Hull's Paragon terminus along this line to Manchester and Sheffield, with a branch at Gilberdyke to Selby and Leeds.

Leaving Doncaster for Hull the line curves away from the main East Coast Route, swings towards the North Sea, passes through Stainforth and Thorne, crosses the Humber and runs on to Goole. Here it turns due east, following the north bank of the broadening estuary through Broomfleet, Brough, Ferriby and Hessle to Hull. Part of the journey from Doncaster to Paragon terminus runs along a section of the first railway to Hull. The last miles from Gilberdyke to the city itself were formerly part of the Hull & Selby Railway, promoted in 1834 and completed in 1840. From Selby there existed a connection to Leeds, opened in 1839 as a branch of George Hudson's growing York & North Midland Railway empire. Indeed, the Hull & Selby Railway was later taken over by the Y. & N.M.R., which in turn became an element in the North Eastern.

The first half of the line from Doncaster had originally been constructed as a branch terminating at Thorne. The final connection was only made possible by the construction of a short link with the former M.S. & L. line to Barnetby. Passengers had previously to travel due west to Selby and change there for a train due south. The gradual laying-down of a railway network by independent companies encouraged enterprise and cost-cutting competition, but as this example shows it did not always produce efficient routes.

The former Great Central station buildings at Stainforth (completed in 1913) are quite distinctive. They are single-storey structures constructed from grey-cream bricks decorated with black, the striped gables being considered *avant garde*. Their long, low appearance is punctuated by the sharp 'V'-shaped arches over their doors and windows. There are also a number of rustic station seats dating from N.E.R. days, which, though manufactured from iron, have been cast to resemble trimmed branches (p. 261).

Goole has a delightful red-brick station, though there were originally two separate buildings in the town. The Lancashire & Yorkshire Railway built a station in 1848 in the dock area, while the N.E.R. constructed the present structure in 1869, a half a mile to the north. Much original ironwork and a double-faced station clock survive on the down side, giving a real Victorian flavour. There is even a 'serpent seat', where the cast-iron ends of a bench have been designed to form a snake coiled to support the back and base boards – a simple but effective device, not without a trace of humour.

Throughout the line semaphore signals are in operation. From a distance, a gantry crowded with arms, silhouetted beside a signal box, presents a fine sight. There is also an example of a pair of truncated signals, where the arms have been placed at the driver's level of vision, a practice which was adopted when a low bridge or a sharp curve might obscure a distant signal placed at the normal height.

The last section of the journey into Hull is along the north bank of the River Humber. When the sun is shining low over the broad estuary it can be an inspiring journey. The railway passes by the new road suspension bridge, whose steel sections were stored at the lineside ready to be lifted over the railway and locked into position. There was formerly a paddle-steamer service operating between Hull and New Holland, started in 1845 by the Great Grimsby & Sheffield Junction Railway, who had purchased a local ferry company. One of these paddle steamers, the *Tattershall Castle*, has recently been moored on the Thames Embankment below Charing Cross and is now used as an art gallery. In 1872 the Hull, South & West Junction Railway proposed building a tunnel under the Humber. They estimated the cost at almost a million pounds and though the scheme was well supported by local residents, the House of Lords rejected the Bill on engineering grounds.

Hull's Paragon terminus, incorporating the Royal Station Hotel, is a complicated, rather dilapidated set of buildings. It was originally designed as a one-sided terminus with the entrance hall and offices running parallel to the tracks. However, the need to increase the number of platforms to accommodate the growing number of trains meant that this was inconvenient for passengers. Consequently, when Paragon was rebuilt in 1904 it was planned as the more common 'head' terminus, with the concourse and booking hall at right angles to the buffers.

Fortunately, this has meant that the first station buildings (1846–8) have survived. George Townsend Andrews, a distinguished railway architect consistently employed by George Hudson, was responsible for their design. He had been commissioned to undertake the stations at Whitby Town and Scarborough, though Hull was probably his most successful enterprise. Using grey-gold ashlar, he designed a classical but asymmetrical building. The central block has a balustraded first-floor terrace supported by coupled Doric columns enhanced by corner pilasters, while the elegant upper windows are decorated alternately with curved and angled pediments. On each side there were office blocks, one of three and the other of two storeys. Nowadays the buildings, in need of repair, serve as a parcels depot, but they can be viewed from behind the station hotel.

When the train-shed was extended in 1904, the task of designing a new frontage was offered to William Bell. In true Edwardian style he produced an exuberant, lofty booking hall. Its wide, curving windows, set high up, echo Green's designs for London's Underground stations. The walls were tiled in green, cream and raw sienna, while the mosaic floor still boasts the initials N.E.R. The teak booking offices were elegantly panelled. Bell was also responsible for the *art nouveau* wooden offices and refreshment rooms built on the concourse behind the buffers, which still feature gentle bay windows, some with their original stained glass. He developed this theme further in his designs for the tea rooms at York Station, finished in 1906 (see p. 278).

Today only three of the five arches of the train-shed actually cover working tracks, the last two having been converted into a car park, always an ironic development. There were once as many as fourteen platforms: 1 to 9 were for regular services, 10 was a short platform used in the 1930s for fish trains hauled by Sentinel railcars, while the remainder, 11 to 14, were reserved for excursions and specials.

George Andrews was also the first architect to incorporate a hotel within station buildings – at York in 1838. Hull followed in 1851, when he constructed the Royal Station Hotel across his terminus buildings. Designed in the same classical style as the terminus, it features a series of decorative columns in the main façade, while a number of rose motifs remind the traveller that he is now in Yorkshire. Although Hull was heavily bombed during the war, Paragon terminus fortunately escaped serious damage.

Hull, like the other major ports, has its own railway network. A number of lines radiated from Paragon to distant towns which had suburban stops on their innermost sections. On the railway north to Scarborough, there is a station at Cottingham; Sutton-on-Hull and Marfleet stations (now closed) were similarly placed on the routes to Hornsea and Withernsea respectively. In addition, there was a central loop line. The York & North Midland Company realized the growing importance of Hull's docks and in 1852 proposed the construction of a semi-circular freight railway from Victoria Dock to the main line which was opened to traffic in the following year. A passenger service charged 3d. first class and 2d. second class, for any distance. The scheme was not a success and passenger trains were withdrawn in November 1854, though after various modifications the service started again ten years later, with stations at Botanic Gardens, Stepney, Wilmington and Southcoats, and a terminus at Drypool, Victoria Dock. The line has now been closed, but some of the buildings remain.

The subsequent expansion of Hull beyond the semi-circular railway link caused local traffic problems, as level crossings had been constructed where the line encountered an existing road. The institution of a regular service on the main suburban routes in 1929 accentuated the inconvenience to road users. Consequently, Hull developed a reputation for level crossings. Some have been replaced by bridges, as on the Hessle and Anlaby Roads, while line closure has done most to solve the problem.

At the mouth of the Humber Estuary, and on the south bank, is the port of Grimsby. There are two stations, Town and Docks, both on the former Great Central line from Barnetby to Cleethorpes. In addition, a short branch runs from Habrough north to New Holland Pier on the Humber, opposite Hull.

SCARBOROUGH

Known as 'the queen of watering places', Scarborough may lay claim to be the finest Victorian seaside resort. Its popularity was based on a mineral spring, a magnificent prospect and fine beaches – and the railways. George Hudson saw the potential for extending his Y. & N.M. system to the coast. The line was completed in 1845 and G. T. Andrews was commissioned to build Central Station, though his restrained classical design consisting of three linked pavilions has on several occasions been modified.

Scarborough rapidly developed as Yorkshire's holiday resort, with the N.E.R. regularly running excursions from their industrial towns. Boarding houses multiplied, promenades were laid down, amusements appeared, travelling entertainers called, while the new Grand Hotel at South Sands, set high on the cliff, dominated the proceedings. Designed by Cuthbert Broderick, it was completed in 1867 on a monumental scale in château style, with a prominent mansard roof and four corner cupolas. If Scarborough is the queen of resorts, then the Grand must surely be her palace.

Because of the town's growing popularity and rising status, the N.E.R. felt that their Central terminus ought to be improved and an ornate clock tower was added in 1884. Though designed in a classical style, it looks top-heavy and rather incongruous on its earlier simpler base. The Corporation had agreed to pay for the gas required to illuminate the clock, if the N.E.R. provided an impressive face. The station had nine platforms to accommodate holidaymakers, the last being built outside the original train-shed. By the turn of the century Central had become incapable of handling the hordes of visitors descending on Scarborough and another station, named Excursion, was completed in 1908. Latterly called Londesborough Road, it had a single-bay platform with a wide concourse where trippers could be assembled.

Today Scarborough is still a popular resort, though the

railway is no longer so important. Nevertheless, British Rail has operated steam specials from Leeds to Central station, which have been so successful that the turntable at Scarborough has been rebuilt, so that locomotives can be turned around for the return journey. Diesels, of course, have not needed this facility.

MIDDLESBROUGH

Middlesbrough is a truly industrial town. Until the Stockton & Darlington extended their line here in 1830, it was a mere village with a handful of inhabitants. By 1901 there were 91,300 people living here. The construction of the railway was critical, encouraging the town's development as a port for the shipment of coal from the Durham pits to London and the south. As it grew in size iron smelting also developed. In fact the coal trade steadily declined from 1850 onwards as the railway network, which had initially sparked it off, became more unified. It was then more profitable for merchants to send their coal south directly by rail than by sea from Middlesbrough.

In the latter half of the nineteenth century, Middlesbrough's prosperity was based on the manufacture of pig iron. Ore, coal and the finished product were handled by trains and as a result Middlesbrough's settlement patterns were increasingly dictated by the railways. After 1850 the area between the railway and Grange Road was built up. From 1860 the Newport district developed as a factory area featuring long rows of terraced houses and a railway system of its own. By 1870 the main shopping centre had formed on either side of Middlesbrough Station and a gridiron pattern of streets was taking shape. Today Middlesbrough is once again an important port and Cargo Fleet Station is playing a significant role in this function.

SUNDERLAND

Sunderland on the Wear, like Newcastle on the Tyne, lies astride a major river and its railway network has been influenced accordingly. Both towns had lines running along each bank with important routes crossing the river at right angles. Sunderland's main station (Central) lies on the coastal route from Hartlepool to Newcastle and is situated south of the Wear. The town's first line was constructed by the Durham & Sunderland Railway primarily for coal traffic and opened in August 1836. However, it was worked by stationary engines and ropes, not being converted to locomotive traction till the late 1850s. After the N.E.R. had gained control of the town's railways, William Peachy was instructed to design a new Central Station, which was completed in 1879. A Venetian Gothic structure with a turreted clock tower, it bore a resemblance to St Pancras. Then William Bell (who followed Peachy as the N.E.R.'s architect) constructed a superb single-span train-shed over the cutting in which the station was set. Unfortunately, Central was badly bombed during the war and in 1965 rebuilt, using only one island platform for passengers.

Monkwearmouth, formerly the terminus of the Brandling Junction Railway, was once one of the leading stations in Sunderland. When the line extended southwards into the town centre, it declined and was eventually closed by B.R. It has since been converted into a local transport museum and there are a number of restored goods vehicles on display in the sidings adjoining the station. Monkwearmouth Terminus, designed by Thomas Moore of Bishopwearmouth and completed in 1848, is a splendid classical structure dominated by a striking Ionic portico.

PRESERVED STEAM RAILWAYS

The North Yorkshire Moors Railway

The North Yorkshire Moors Railway is not only one of the longest preserved lines in the country, but also operates over an exceptionally historic section of track. Originally part of the Whitby & Pickering Company formed in 1833, the line was planned by George Stephenson and opened in 1836. However, its first trains were pulled by horses, while the carriages were really road coaches with special wheels. Steam engines were not introduced for a further ten years. In 1845 George Hudson bought the W. & P.R., merging it with the York & North Midland Railway, which had just laid a line to Scarborough with a branch to Pickering. Today eighteen miles of the railway between Grosmont and Pickering has been re-opened. The first section between Grosmont and Goathland is steam-hauled, while the remainder to Pickering is operated by diesel.

There is a broad range of locomotives preserved on the N.Y.M.R., though most once worked in the north-east. Among the medium-power N.E.R. engines here are No. 2238, a T–2 class built in 1918, and No. 2392, a P–3 class, completed in 1923. Although No. 2005, a K–1 class 2–6–0, had been designed before nationalization, it was actually built by British Railways in 1949. Three locomotives are being restored from other regions, including a 2–8–0 from the Somerset & Dorset Railway, an ex-G.W. 0–6–2 tank engine and a B.R. Standard class 4, 2–6–4. The oldest engine operating on the line is an 0–6–0ST, built for the Great Northern in 1891.

No. 4767, an ex-L.M.S. 'Black Five', was named *George Stephenson* after the engineer of the W. & P.R. at the Shildon 150th anniversary celebrations. The name is particularly apt as this was the only locomotive from a class of 842 which was fitted with Stephenson's link-motion valve gear. The other 'Black Five' on the railway, No. 5428, has been named *Eric Treacy* after the former Bishop of Wakefield.

The Keighley & Worth Valley Light Railway

The Keighley & Worth Valley Light Railway runs through the Aire Gap between the North and South Pennines. Keighley station is situated on the former Midland main line between Leeds and Carlisle. In 1861 John McLandsborough, a civil engineer, had drawn up plans for a railway to run from Keighley down the Worth valley to Oxenhope. He persuaded the directors of the Midland to operate the line in return for half the receipts. An Act was passed in the following year and the railway was completed in 1867. In 1883 Keighley Station was rebuilt on a new site to accommodate the G.N.R.'s double-track line from Halifax. Grouping in 1923 resulted in the railway's absorption into the L.M.S., while under British Railways the number of passengers and the volume of freight using the Worth Valley line declined and it was decided to close the railway in 1961. Shortly afterwards a preservation society was formed to re-open the branch.

The railway has one of the largest collections of locomotives in the country, over thirty. The two oldest engines on the line both originate from the Lancashire & Yorkshire Railway. They were both 0-6-0 tender engines, but the elder, No. 752 (1881), was rebuilt fifteen years later as a saddle tank. The other, No. 957, was not completed until 1887 and survives in its original form as British Railways No. 52044. There is a 4-F class goods engine from the Midland Railway, No. 3942, built at Derby in 1920. There are also two former Great Western engines, the first being a tank engine, originally No. 85 on the Taff Vale Railway and later No. 426 on the G.W.R., and the second a pannier tank, L89. It was built at Swindon in 1929 but was purchased by London Transport in 1963 to work engineers' trains and has been repainted in their maroon livery.

There is a group of three L.M.S. engines, including a 'Black Five' class, No. 45212, and a heavy freight class 8-F 2-8-0 locomotive. In addition, there are a number of 'Austerity' locomotives built during the Second World War for service overseas, including two built in America: *Vulcan*, an 0-6-0T, and Tr 203.474, a 2-8-0, which had worked throughout Eastern Europe. The largest locomotive preserved on the railway is the 4-6-2, No. 34092, *City of Wells*, a West Country class engine built in B.R. days. A variety of industrial locomotives, a broad selection of carriages and other rolling stock may also be seen on the railway.

The K.W.V.L.R. is unusual among preserved lines in that it runs for most of its length through an industrial landscape. Parts are across fields and open moor, but mostly it is flanked by mills, terraced houses, machine shops, warehouses and tall chimneys. Keighley Station is constructed on a 'V' plan. The western side belonging to the K.W.V.L.R. has been restored to its Midland livery, while B.R.'s half is in more subdued tones. It has a pleasant stone façade with cast-iron brackets featuring the Midland dragon. Some platforms have retained their glazed ridge and furrow awnings.

The Yorkshire Dales Railway

This preserved railway runs from Embsay towards Holwell Bridge. It is not far from the Worth Valley line, as the Embsay terminus is about 1½ miles from Skipton station, which is situated on the main line to Carlisle from Leeds. This branch was originally part of the Midland network and continued to Ilkley with connections to Leeds and Harrogate It was closed in 1965 under the Beeching Plan, and at present the tracks are gradually being re-laid towards Bolton Abbey, some five miles east of Embsay.

The Yorkshire Dales Railway is largely worked by a number of 0–6–0 industrial tank engines. There is, however, an 8–F class heavy freight engine, No 48151, which is at present under restoration. Two of the tank engines in the collection are unusual in that they have side tanks rather than saddle tanks. They were built by Hudswell-Clarke for the Coal Board and are numbered S100 and S140. In addition, there are some interesting carriages on the railway, including a six-wheel personal saloon once belonging to Sir Vincent Raven, Locomotive Superintendant of the N.E.R., which was built in 1896. Two coaches constructed in 1931 for the electric railway (to

Altrincham) are also stored on the railway together with a Pullman car and a standard B.R. coach.

The Middleton Railway

The Middleton Railway, re-opened for steam working in 1960, was the first preserved standard-gauge railway to run a passenger service, beating the Bluebell by two months. Sited in the Hunslet district of Leeds, it originally consisted of a wooden tramway designed to carry coal, while from 1812 steam engines operating on rack rails were introduced. Having been replaced by horse traction in 1834, steam reappeared in 1866 and the track was altered from 4 feet 1 inch to standard gauge in 1881. When the coal mines were nationalized in 1948, the railway fell into the hands of the National Coal Board. In June 1958 a special bicentenary passenger train was run, though closure loomed large.

A preservation society was founded and the mile-long line between Tunstall Road and Middleton Park Gate was re-opened in 1960. Most of the trains are worked by industrial tank engines and include a Peckett, No. 2003, a Hudswell-Clarke, No. 1309 (*Henry de Lacy II*), and a Bagnall, No. 2702, named *Matthew Murray* after the line's first locomotive builder. There are also two former L.N.E.R. engines, a Sentinel No. 59 (B.R. No. 68153) and No. 1310, an 0-4-0 tank engine built for the N.E.R. in 1891.

11 Scotland

Scotland is customarily divided into three regions, the Highlands, the Central Lowlands and the Southern Uplands, each with distinct geographical characteristics, which have exercised a powerful influence on settlement patterns and hence the railway networks. Briefly, the Central Lowlands has the richest farmlands and possesses extensive coalfields. As a result, the mass of Scotland's population has been concentrated here. Its industrial and commercial centres encouraged the construction of a comprehensive railway system, based on Glasgow in the west and Edinburgh in the east.

The Southern Uplands and the Cheviot Hills over the border have presented something of a communications barrier with England. The oldest trunk roads and the main-line railways have been forced to use the coastal margins. The latter were constructed via Kilmarnock and Dumfries to Carlisle, and via Dunbar and Berwick to Newcastle. The North British Railway did subsequently lay a few branch lines through the Uplands, but these have all since been shut down. The railway which runs along the foothills of the Cheviots through the Tyne Gap has remained an important east–west route linking Carlisle and Newcastle, as closures have meant that there is no comparable route north of the border.

The Highland region was the last to experience the influence of the railways. With the completion of the English and Welsh trunk routes, promoters turned their attention to Scotland.

There are few easy routes through the Grampians and lines tend to hug the coastal plains wherever possible, while most Highland railways were single-track. Nevertheless, the latter half of the nineteenth century saw the spread of a network which reached as far afield as Thurso, Wick, Fraserburgh, Kyle of Lochalsh and Mallaig, and a small railway system was projected for Skye, though none of the islands has ever been served by trains.

The country has witnessed post-war closures and almost all of the Great North of Scotland's network has been closed, except the section from Keith Junction to Aberdeen. But because the Highland railways were built late and – in view of the expense – quite cautiously, they have suffered least. The Southern Uplands and the Central Lowlands have been pruned most heavily, having experienced the greatest growth at the outset. There is a measure of social justice here, as the railways in the north often serve remote areas where people cannot always afford cars.

A number of preservation societies have been formed. However, their task has not been made any the easier by the grouping arrangements of 1923. There was no separate Scottish Region then, and the country was divided solely between the L.M.S. and the L.N.E.R. Consequently, new locomotives and rolling stock tended to come from English workshops. It was asking a lot of the pre-grouping locomotives to continue work until the 1960s, and few succeeded. As a result, there are but a handful from these early companies, almost all preserved in the Glasgow Transport Museum. At one stage it looked as if the once mighty Glasgow & South Western Railway would go unrepresented but an 0–6–0T, No. 9, was rescued from a Welsh colliery and restored in its original livery.

THE SOUTHERN UPLANDS

There were once four major railway lines through the Southern Uplands. Three survive: from Carlisle to Glasgow Central via

Carstairs and Motherwell, from Carlisle to Glasgow via Dumfries and Kilmarnock, and in the east from Berwick via Dunbar to Edinburgh Waverley. They were among the first lines to be constructed in Scotland and were all completed by 1852. There was much controversy surrounding the closure of the fourth, the 'Waverley Route', in January 1965, which was over North British metals and ran from Carlisle to Riccarton Junction, Hawick, St Boswells, Heriot and on to Edinburgh via Portobello.

The East Coast Route is the shortest and least spectacular of the three survivors. It too was built by the N.B.R. and opened in June 1846. The railway clings to the coastal margins and runs through pleasant arable farmlands for most of its course. There was one tunnel, the Penmanshiel, between Berwick and Dunbar, bored through an outcrop of the Lammermuir Hills. Part collapsed unexpectedly in 1979, killing two workers, and the resulting fall blocked the tunnel so effectively that it has never been re-opened, the main line being re-routed to avoid this obstacle.

The single-track branch (the only survivor of a once extensive network) to North Berwick leaves from Drem. Longniddry and Prestonpans, small stations served by local trains, follow, while Portobello Station has been closed, though its yards are still used for carriages and there is a modern freightliner terminal here.

The two main lines from Carlisle offer more varied scenery as they cut through the Uplands themselves. The West Coast Route via Carstairs climbs into the hills by the Annan valley, reaching Beattock Summit and descending down the Clyde valley. The railway was originally surveyed by Joseph Locke for the Grand Junction Company in 1837, though the scheme was adopted by the Caledonian, who christened it the 'National Line'. Its completion in February 1848 allowed the C.R. to offer a service from Glasgow to London without a change of carriage. They took advantage of the popularity of the 1851 Great Exhibition, advertising reduced fares and running special trains for clubs and societies that wished to see the magic of the Crystal Palace.

Carstairs is the first stop on the north side of the Southern Uplands – an important junction with trains to Edinburgh and Lanark. In the past it controlled a spider's web of lines, which explains the extent of the station yards. From here northwards the scenery assumes an industrial cloak, steel smelters, tips of rusting scrap metal, rolling mills and railway sidings dominating the view to Motherwell and continuing into the outskirts of Glasgow itself.

The third route, via Kilmarnock, is not as hilly as this former G. & S.W.R. line and runs west from Carlisle along the coastal margin to Dumfries. Ascending the Nith valley through the Lowther Hills, it descends into Ayrshire and continues to Kilmarnock. The approach to Glasgow is from the west via Stewarton, Dunlop, Barrhead, Nitshill and Kennishead. Dumfries is among the most interesting stations in the south-west. Constructed from red sandstone with a succession of round-arched doors and windows, it retains the original columns and brackets. The glazed awnings are a feature of the G. & S.W.R.'s stations, while the tall, ornate platform lamps are unusual. Dumfries was an important junction and so merited special treatment.

The former Glasgow & South Western Railway's line to Challoch Junction has survived because of the Irish packet service from Stranraer to Larne. As well as serving the local population, this was an immensely popular holiday railway for Glaswegians. Troon, Prestwick and Ayr, situated on the coast, have stations close to the beaches and golf courses and were close enough for day trippers. As resorts they expanded dramatically with the completion of this rail link. The L.M.S. reported in 1938 that they were carrying between 40,000 and 50,000 passengers to these Ayrshire towns on Saturday afternoons throughout the summer. In the same year they carried 397,000 people to the coast in their 'evening breather' trains leaving Glasgow when the shops and factories closed;

fares were kept low: 1s. 3d. (6p.) return for these excursions.

Stranraer was originally a station on the Portpatrick & Wigtownshire Joint Railway, which was linked to the G. & S.W.R. from Dumfries at Castle Douglas, and from Ayr at Challoch Junction. Except for the short section from Challoch to Stranraer, the line has since been closed. It was the scene of Richard Hannay's pursuit in John Buchan's *The Thirty-Nine Steps* (1914). Running from German agents, Hannay took the train to Galloway to hide on the remote moors. 'The station,' he recalled, 'proved to be ideal for my purpose. The moor surged around it and left room for the single line, the slender siding, a waiting room, an office, the stationmaster's cottage and a tiny yard of gooseberries and sweet-william. There seemed no road from it anywhere...' The description also applies to a number of British Rail's halts on the West Highland line.

GLASGOW

Glasgow dominates the Scottish railway system in the way that London is at the hub of the English network. There were once four mighty termini in Glasgow: Central, High and Low Levels (Caledonian), Queen Street (North British), St Enoch (Glasgow & South Western) and Buchanan Street (Caledonian). Today only the first two survive. St Enoch and Buchanan Street have been demolished and their sites are now car parks. A model of the former, with its massive Gothic hotel (Scotland's largest when opened in 1876) and the mosaic from the foyer, are on display in the city's Museum of Transport. It had been constructed by the City of Glasgow Union Railway, supposedly to serve all companies; in fact St Enoch was dominated by the G. & S.W.R. and N.B.R. to exclude the Caledonian. In 1883 it fell into the hands of the Glasgow & South Western, but by agreement was used by the Midland Railway as the terminus for their route from St Pancras, via Settle and Carlisle. When

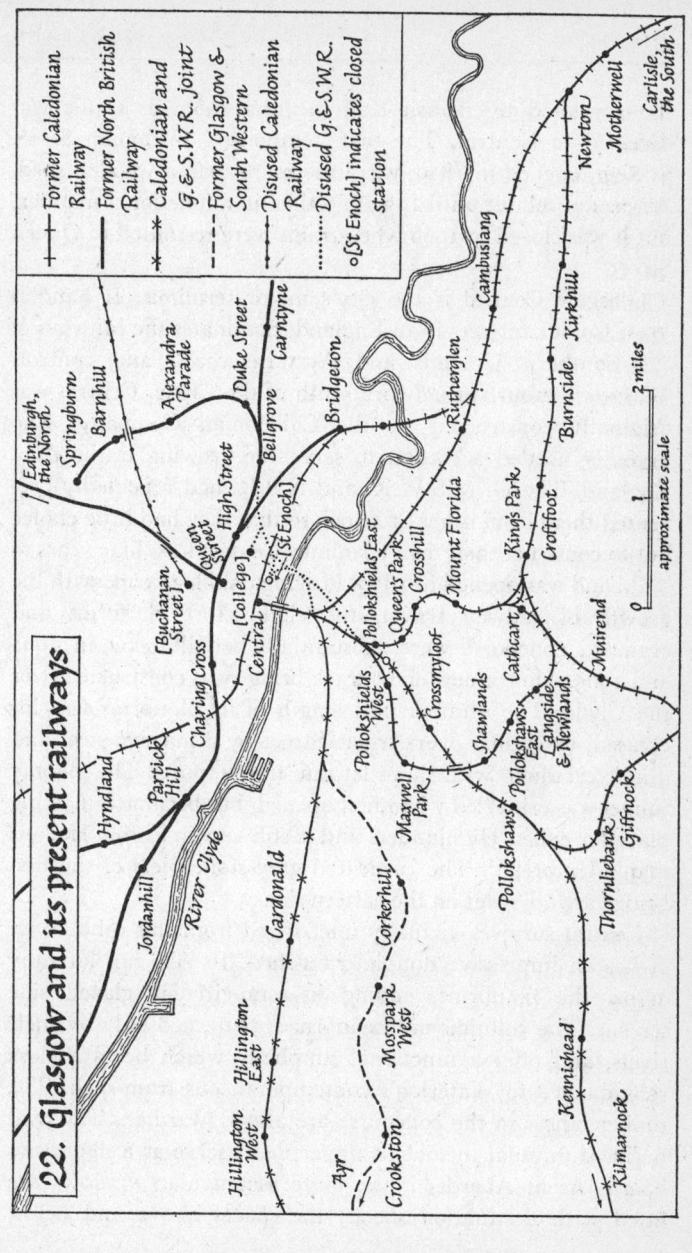

it was closed by British Rail in June 1966, its traffic was diverted to Central. The first 'temporary' Buchanan Street Station, opened in 1849, was little more than a wooden shed. It was not rebuilt until 1933 and then in a functional manner, but it was closed in 1966 when trains were re-routed to Queen Street.

Glasgow Central is the city's major terminus. It handles West Coast expresses from England, dominates the railways of the Southern Uplands and Ayrshire coast, and controls Glasgow's suburban network south of the Clyde. Central was originally constructed by the Caledonian Company, who urgently needed a station to serve the growing traffic from England. The G. & S.W.R. and N.B.R. had repeatedly prevented them from using St Enoch so that they had little choice but to construct their own terminus. Central took four years to build and was opened in 1879. Proving unable to cope with the growth of railway travel, the eight short platforms and cramped concourse were substantially rebuilt between 1901 and 1905, while a new eight-track bridge was constructed over the Clyde. The number and length of its platforms was increased, extending over Argyle Street by a massive steel and granite viaduct, with shops let into the supports. The gloomy tunnel was criticized when first opened, but became a meeting place for exiled Highlanders and is still known as the 'Heilanman's Umbrella'. The rusticated grey stone piers of the first bridge are adjacent on the eastern side.

Central survives virtually unchanged from this rebuilding. It has an impressive double train-shed. Its ribs run laterally across the platforms, ending in semi-circular glazed side screens. The columns are unadorned, patterned only by their rivets, and offer a functional simplicity which bears a close resemblance to Waterloo's contemporaneous train-shed. The timber offices in the concourse are also Edwardian. The oval buffet is unusual in that its upper floors serve as a departure board. As at Aberdeen, the large rectangular windows are fitted with destination sheets, the spaces above and below indicating platforms and departure times. The boards are of course put in their correct place by a team of highly skilled men. It is fascinating to watch them working in the rush hour, particularly if there are changes in the scheduled arrangements. They inspire a confidence which is lacking in the modern computer-controlled boards.

The train-shed is fronted by the magnificent Central Hotel, which pre-dates the re-building of the terminus, having been opened in June 1883. Central Hotel was designed by Sir Robert Rowand Anderson, a pupil of Sir George Scott. Solidly constructed from grey-brown stone, it is an 'L'-shaped structure with its entrance on the corner of Gordon and Hope Streets, beneath a massive 'Swedish' tower, topped by pedimented clock gables. The five storeys are freely treated, and round-arched Italianate windows decorate the lower floors, while a succession of angled pediments dominate the heavily gabled slate roof. The station entrance is protected by an elegant glazed *porte cochère*. Victorians were impressed by the scale and solidity of these huge hotels, the *Illustrated London News* for 14 July 1883 recording that '1,000 yards of Axminster have been used for the staircase and corridors, 800 yards of Wilton for the public and sitting rooms ... 12,000 electric bells communicate with 600 indicators ... and the wires in connection with the bells measure 29 miles and weigh $2\frac{1}{2}$ tons'. This information reassured potential guests fresh from the train, suggesting that it was a building on which substantial sums had been carefully expended and where a person 'of property' might rest without qualms. Central Hotel is a listed building and its interior preserves much of its original atmosphere. The Malmaison Restaurant (Scotland's second French restaurant – the Caledonian's hotel at Gleneagles had the first), opened in 1927, has retained the Empire decor copied from the Château Malmaison, home of Empress Josephine.

Glasgow Central also has a Low Level Station running at right angles to the main terminus. It would more appropriately be described as an underground station, and having been steam-operated was once a smoky and sulphurous cavern, where regular passengers used paper bags as gloves to open the soot-coated door handles. It has since been rebuilt and is an important interchange on the Argyle line, running from Helensburgh Central through northern Glasgow, crossing the Clyde to the southern suburbs and on to Motherwell. Previously, there had been no direct link between the railway system based on Queen Street and that south of the Clyde based on Central. The critical link is from Partick (formerly Partick Hill) to Central Low Level, involving the re-opening of stations at Finnieston and Anderston, then east to Bridgeton via Argyle Street, south to Dalmarnock and over the river to Rutherglen, making use of many abandoned tunnels formerly constructed for the Glasgow Central Railway. This underground line, authorized in 1888, was no easy project, and was not completed till 1896. It was a busy service and around 260 steam-hauled trains ran through Low Level every day at the turn of the century. Today the route has been electrified and new electrical multiple units operate along its length. They are the same type as those which run on the 'Great Northern' suburban, with semi-automatic sliding doors and generous standing space (see p. 36).

An important element in this improved railway system is the modernized Glasgow Underground or 'Subway'. Work began on this circular line in March 1891 and was not completed until the summer of 1896. There were several significant similarities with the London Underground, as it was also designed to link up the major railway termini and reduce traffic congestion in the city centre. There were stations at St Enoch, Buchanan Street, Bridge Street and Partick Cross to cater for rail passengers. In addition, it crossed the Clyde and took in the docks at Cessnock and Copland Road, while Hillhead served the Botanic Gardens and Kelvin Bridge the university.

At first the trains were hauled by cables which were driven from a powerhouse in Scotland Street, the drivers being known as 'gripmen' because they disconnected the clamp before a station, allowing the train to coast to a halt, and then gradually re-engaged it to draw the train forward again. In 1935 the system was electrified, and the original rolling stock, manufactured by Hurst Nelson & Company of Motherwell, was fitted with motors. Until the closure of the Subway in 1977 for modernization, there had been no replacement of rolling stock. The first plum and cream livery was replaced in 1935 by signal red and ivory on the platform side only (all stations had island platforms with trains running on each side in opposite directions, the inner and outer circles). In 1954 carriages were painted entirely in red. Unusually advertisements were pasted on the outside of the car roofs, because the trains were at all times beneath ground level.

The interiors altered little over their eighty years of life, though the longitudinal benches were replaced by leather seats and the lighting improved at the time of electrification. Entrance was by means of lattice gates and sliding wooden doors at each end of the cars. A special gallery in the city's Museum of Transport has been prepared to house a train and depict its operation.

The new stock built by Metropolitan-Cammell of Birmingham (also responsible for the London Underground) is of a similar design, though larger curved windows, automatic doors, slightly increased dimensions and improved technical apparatus distinguish them. In all, thirty-three coaches have been constructed to the original four-foot gauge. Because the system was entirely self-contained, trains had to be lifted out of the tunnels at a hoist pit in the locomotive works at Govan. Cars were hoisted out every ten days and usually replaced on the opposite circle to even out wear on their wheels.

Most of the Subway's stations have been substantially rebuilt, partly to accommodate the longer three-car trains (all were previously two-car sets), but also because the original buildings were dilapidated. They were the simplest of stations with a single island platform and steps leading up to street

level, which in the case of Buchanan Street numbered 139.
Escalators, automatic ticket machines, closed-circuit television
and new tunnel linings match the modern rolling stock.

The Subway's most impressive memorial, St Enoch Station,
has been incorporated within the new system. Although all has
changed beneath ground, its entrance building, a red stone
'castle', has been carefully preserved. It is certainly an unusual
edifice with baronial turrets on each corner, oriel windows,
decorative balconies, clock pediments and urn finials.

Before considering Queen Street Station, it ought to be
mentioned that southern Glasgow has a complex and historic
suburban network, which has been simplified by British Rail.
There is an interesting circular service operating from Glasgow
Central at half-hourly intervals, with trains alternating in their
direction. Travelling clockwise, the first stop over the Clyde is
Pollokshields East, a small modernized station beneath a road
bridge and next to the Museum of Transport. A narrow stone-
sided cutting channels the train from here to Maxwell Park.
Most of the ex-Caledonian stations, consisting of a single
island platform and a central wooden waiting room with
extended eaves for protection against the rain, are identical.
The cutting continues to Crosshill and Mount Florida, leaving
the passenger to speculate from the tiny gap between the
carriage side and the side wall what scenery surrounds the line.
At Cathcart the train emerges into the open. This is an
important junction, with routes to Neilston in the south and
Newton to the east. Here the railway swings south-west to
make the return journey through spacious stone villas and
inter-war semi-detached houses. Langside Station has been
rebuilt. The line is then carried on a viaduct to Pollokshaws
East, which provides a long view of tower blocks and their
older and much lower counterparts. Shawlands, Maxwell Park
and Pollokshields West are all typical stations, though the
latter is set in a pleasant grassy cutting. The line joins itself
again before Pollokshield's eastern neighbour and returns to
Central along a gently rising stone viaduct.

Queen Street, like Central, has both High Level (the mainline terminus) and Low Level (an underground east–west route) Stations. The train-shed (1878–80), designed by James Carswell, is an impressive single-arched structure supported on each side by massive cast-iron Corinthian columns. The ends are enclosed by glazed screens with radiating bars, having a certain resemblance to Liverpool Lime Street. The exterior and its few buildings have been modernized. Yet the real attraction of Queen Street lies in its situation. Set into a hill, its stone side walls continue beyond the train-shed to form a deep and blackened cutting, where its many tracks become two and disappear into the stygian blackness of the single tunnel entrance. From here trains climb the Cowlairs Incline, a 1-in-43 ascent, to daylight. The gloom of the tunnel is twice broken up by shafts of dusty white light, these openings having been constructed to provide a draught for the steam engines which formerly toiled along its metals. At Cowlairs are the remains of the N.B.R.'s locomotive sheds. Engines ceased to be built here in 1923 when the company was absorbed by the L.N.E.R. and today the yards are used for storage and maintenance.

The North British Hotel, adjacent to Queen Street Station, in contrast to Central, is a stuccoed classical building. This symmetrical and ordered structure, light on decoration, is topped by a short balustrade and central pediment containing the monogram of the N.B.R. The wings have fluted Corinthian pilasters, supported by a rusticated ground floor. The original twin porches have been sealed off so that admission is by a new entrance next to the station.

The journey from Queen Street to Edinburgh is one of the most historic in Scotland. This is the route taken by the country's first trunk railway, the Edinburgh & Glasgow, opened throughout on 21 February 1842. From Cowlairs it is one of the flattest stretches of track in Britain, the steepest section being a mere 1 in 600, while fifteen miles are dead level. This is not entirely due to the terrain, but resulted from the skill of the engineers Grainger and Miller, backed with substantial funds. Although this was not the first railway to be constructed in Scotland, those which had come before – the Monkland & Kirkintilloch, the Ballochney and the Slamannan Railways – were local lines primarily built to carry coal. The E. & G.R. was the Scottish equivalent of the Liverpool & Manchester in England. Just as the latter was absorbed into the L.N.W.R. in 1846, so the E. & G.R. became part of the North British in 1865.

The journey is through rolling arable country and grassland, and presents the traveller with a clear contrast to the spare uplands to north and south. Bishopbriggs, Lenzie and Falkirk High Stations have all been modernized, though the last does retain a number of ornate iron brackets. Though this is lowland country, cuttings are a feature of the line, and after Croy Station the railway enters a mile-long cutting hewn into solid rock. Its jagged vertical sides indicate that much effort went into its execution, while beyond Linlithgow there is another cutting, which seems endless, as it is nearly four miles long, demonstrating the emphasis laid on keeping the line level. It leads, however, to a finely proportioned stone viaduct over the River Almond, over a third of a mile in length, supported by thirty-six arches. From this part of the line it is possible to see the upper half of the mighty Forth Bridge away to the north.

The outskirts of Edinburgh follow. Murrayfield rugby ground is situated close to the line and it is possible to look down on the terraces into the field of play, but only for a fleeting moment. Haymarket, designed in 1840 by John Miller, is the last stop before Waverley. The railway originally terminated here, but was extended to Waverley in 1846 after much wrangling with the owners of Princes Street, who were concerned that their gardens should not be spoilt by an intrusive railway and insisted that it tunnel beneath. Haymarket Station is being modernized, so that one half consists of simplified white awning and the other retains the original decorative columns, brackets and intricate valancing, a comparison which does not bear thinking about too hard.

EDINBURGH

The present Waverley Station was not the first. As at Glasgow Central, with the continued growth of railway traffic, the original building soon became crowded and confused. Between 1892 and 1899 the directors of the North British were forced to undertake a major reconstruction programme costing £1½ million, a huge sum for those days. Waverley is similar to Birmingham New Street, being entirely below ground level. The booking hall and offices are placed centrally in the broad cutting. Through lines pass it on each side, while local services run from bay platforms situated at each end of the central concourse. The station is entered from road and footbridges running across the tracks, cars – and formerly carriages – being led down to the platforms by ramps. The side walls are executed in light yellow-brown stone and decorated with a row of recessed Italianate arches. The main buildings are based on a glazed rotunda decorated with cherubs and swags of fruit, an unusual choice for a station. The interior has been much altered (the original panelled booking offices have been removed) and much of its careful design is obscured by garish signs, making a strong case for re-thinking the 'modernization' of Waverley.

The superb North British Hotel is an integral part of the station. It was designed by William Hamilton Beattie and opened in October 1902. The lavish *Souvenir Guide* (1902), written by John Geddie, recorded that the architects had opted for 'a free rendering of the Renaissance period' and it certainly exhibits features from a variety of styles. Its square plan is dominated by a massive clock tower, decorated with corner turrets flanking four pedimented clock faces and surmounted by a lead corona. The lower floors have solid groups of round-arched windows, while the treatment is lighter and more ornate above. This light-umber stone building has become an important architectural landmark in Edinburgh. Princes Street is balanced by the North British and Caledonian Hotels at each end with the Scott Monument acting as an off-centre pivot.

There is a fine view of both station and hotel from the front of the National Gallery of Scotland. This classical building stands over the railway tunnels to the west, and from the surrounding pathway it is possible to look over Waverley's approach roads and into the train-shed itself. It is a busy station and the continual flow of traffic is controlled by the main signal box below. The eastern end of the station is spanned by the triple-arched North Bridge, a mighty road bridge of iron and stone, while the North British Hotel lies adjacent to Waverley and alongside this flying thoroughfare. In fact part of the hotel's foundations form the side wall of Waverley's train-shed, and there is an entrance in the central rotunda for hotel guests.

Although Edinburgh possesses this magnificent centrepiece, it may justifiably be described as Scotland's saddest railway city, having retained only two stations, Waverley and Haymarket. The story which follows, therefore, is one of progressive pruning and closure, until just the main lines to Berwick and Glasgow remain.

The city was dominated by just two major companies, the Caledonian and the North British, the latter having survived the closures most successfully, though its suburban services have entirely disappeared. There were N.B. lines to Granton, North and South Leith on the Firth of Forth. In addition, there was a circular route through the southern part of Edinburgh calling at Portobello, Joppa, Morningside Road, Craiglockhart, Gorgie and then back to Haymarket and Waverley, originally the Edinburgh Suburban & Southside Junction Railway, opened in December 1884. The service was discontinued in 1962 and the departure bays at Waverley have been filled in, but were on the site of the present G.P.O. offices at the eastern end of the central concourse.

Only the Caledonian Hotel survives in Edinburgh as an active reminder of that once formidable railway company. Their terminus, Princes Street (directly behind the Caledonian Hotel in Lothian Road), was closed in September 1965 and demolished, and the site has been turned into a car park, a new dual-carriageway (West Approach Road) running under its bridges and over the trackbed. There are still remains of red sandstone side walls and station entrances, while the old parcels office stands in Lothian Road, large gilded letters proclaiming its existence. Much of Lothian Road Goods Station survives, the earlier grey-ochre stone offices opposite fronting another car park.

Princes Street Station had a broad lateral train-shed and generous curved platforms. An ornate wooden clock tower dominated the concourse and it is a pity that it was not preserved. Princes Street had, of course, been the Edinburgh terminus for trains travelling up the West Coast Route from Euston – a journey which took nine hours in 1950. Their rivals were the Midland, running over the famous 'Waverley Route' from St Pancras via Carlisle to Waverley, which in that year was an hour and forty minutes slower. In addition, the Caledonian operated a suburban schedule from Princes Street. Their first branch line to Granton was completed in 1861 and extended to Leith in September 1864. The electrification of the city's trams and the introduction of buses in the inter-war years meant falling receipts. North British services to North Leith ended in 1947 and to Leith Central in 1952, the Caledonian being forced to follow suit in April 1962.

The Caledonian Hotel stands as a fine memorial to its company. Opened in 1903, it was designed by J. D. Peddie and executed in red sandstone. The hotel was in fact built on top of the original 1894 station, explaining the clear difference in styles between the ground and first floors; the hotel porch was formerly the station gateway. The left-hand arch was the terminus's carriage entrance, the centre (with the tympanum and company's arms) formed the pedestrian entrance, while the third led to the refreshment rooms. With the closure of Princes Street, the hotel was free to expand and an extra wing was added, while part of the station concourse was incorporated to form the Lothian Lounge. The door pediments are decorated with the Caledonian's shield and supporters carved in red sandstone.

PERTH AND DUNDEE TO ABERDEEN

The route from Glasgow to Perth runs via Stirling, Dunblane and Gleneagles. Stirling is an important railway town with routes to Falkirk, Edinburgh and south to Cumbernauld, Motherwell and Carstairs. Consequently, it is a large station with several island platforms, retaining the original timbered buildings, cast-iron columns and valancing. Dunblane is a much smaller Caledonian station with brick and stone buildings. Just outside is the disused line to Callander, with connections to Oban and Ballachulish, though it remains as an overgrown embankment.

Gleneagles is a well-known station with a fine hotel and near-by golf course. The broad island platforms with their timber and sandstone buildings show something of the station's past popularity. The pleasant rolling scenery is interspersed with conifer plantations and woods of silver birch trees. The Highlands themselves are but a distant blur, though the Ochil Hills lie as a foretaste to the south.

Perth is an unusual but attractive junction station, 'V'-shaped in plan. The northern arm is enclosed in a train-shed, while its southern counterpart has original columns and brackets with newer umbrella awnings. The oldest ochre stone buildings, designed by Sir William Tite in 1848, are among the most decorative in Scotland. The splendid Gothic interior enclosed by the train-shed features perpendicular arches with mouldings, oriel and bay windows, and an ornate double-sided clock.

The North British route from Edinburgh Waverley to Dundee takes in two of the finest railway attractions in Scotland, the Tay and Forth bridges. The train swings north from Haymarket and races through the city's suburbs, past the airport to the oil terminal at Dalmeny. The Forth Bridge swiftly follows. It consists of three cantilevered sections, each shaped like a graceful diamond, with their steel tubes and beams making up the many faces of these precious engineering stones. The scale of the bridge can only be fully appreciated by actually travelling its full length, as the distance diminishes its might. Designed by Sir John Fowler and Benjamin Baker, it was completed in 1890, and including the approaches is over one and a half miles long. In the past passengers customarily threw coins into the firth to make a wish or for good luck, a practice which has since died out. Today tankers may be seen taking on North Sea oil from the jetty in the estuary, while nuclear submarines are docked at the naval base of Rosyth on the northern shores, served by Inverkeithing Station.

The railway divides at Inverkeithing, the main line continuing along the coast to Kirkcaldy, while a loop takes in Dunfermline and Cardenden and rejoins at Markinch. Both are former North British routes, as the company had secured a complete monopoly over Fife and Kinross, while the Caledonian ran along the northern bank of the River Tay.

At Aberdour the railway runs close to the ruined castle made famous by the *Ballad of Sir Patrick Spens*. The view today is no longer dominated by medieval images but by breakers' yards and docks. The Forth Bridge is visible in the distance (and its road neighbour opened in September 1974), with its languidly relaxed spans holding hands across the estuary.

Kirkcaldy has a distinctive smell, which results from the linseed oil used in the manufacture of linoleum. The line itself runs past factories, refineries and mills, and the station has extensive sidings. Ladybank is a pleasant panelled station with

North British columns, brackets and valancing. Cupar has original stone buildings, while Leuchars has been rebuilt. There was a railway from here running around the coast, calling at St Andrews, Crail and Anstruther, rejoining the main line at Thornton Junction, but it has since been closed and there is a bus service to St Andrews. Religious landowners had been so strongly opposed to the construction of this branch (its intrusion was often regarded as a radical force) that the company was not allowed to run trains on Sundays, in an attempt to limit its pernicious influence, or at least encourage people to attend church by severing one means of escape.

The line soon reaches the Firth of Tay and crosses it, not by the first railway bridge, but by the second, designed by William Barlow and opened in 1887. The first, which was an insubstantial structure, was destroyed by a storm in 1879 only a year after its completion. It was particularly tragic that a train had been crossing the bridge when it collapsed. Something of its frailty may be guessed from the limited size of the brick and stone piers which runs along the east side of the present bridge. This is a much more solid construction, two miles and seventy-three yards in length. Its completion allowed the North British to challenge the L.N.W.R. and the Caledonian again in the 'Race to the North'.

The disused station to the east on the southern bank is Wormit, situated on the line to West and East Newport and Tayport, returning to Leuchars. Dundee formerly possessed three stations: East (Dundee & Aberdeen Joint Railway), West (Caledonian) and Tay Bridge (North British). The first two were termini and have been closed along with Esplanade (also N.B., situated at the northern end of the Tay Bridge), leaving Tay Bridge as the sole survivor, a functional building with a central platform and buildings. However, the exit to Aberdeen is particularly interesting, as the railway runs along the dockside past factories, old jute warehouses, timber yards and refineries. Rails are set in the cobbled harbour side for

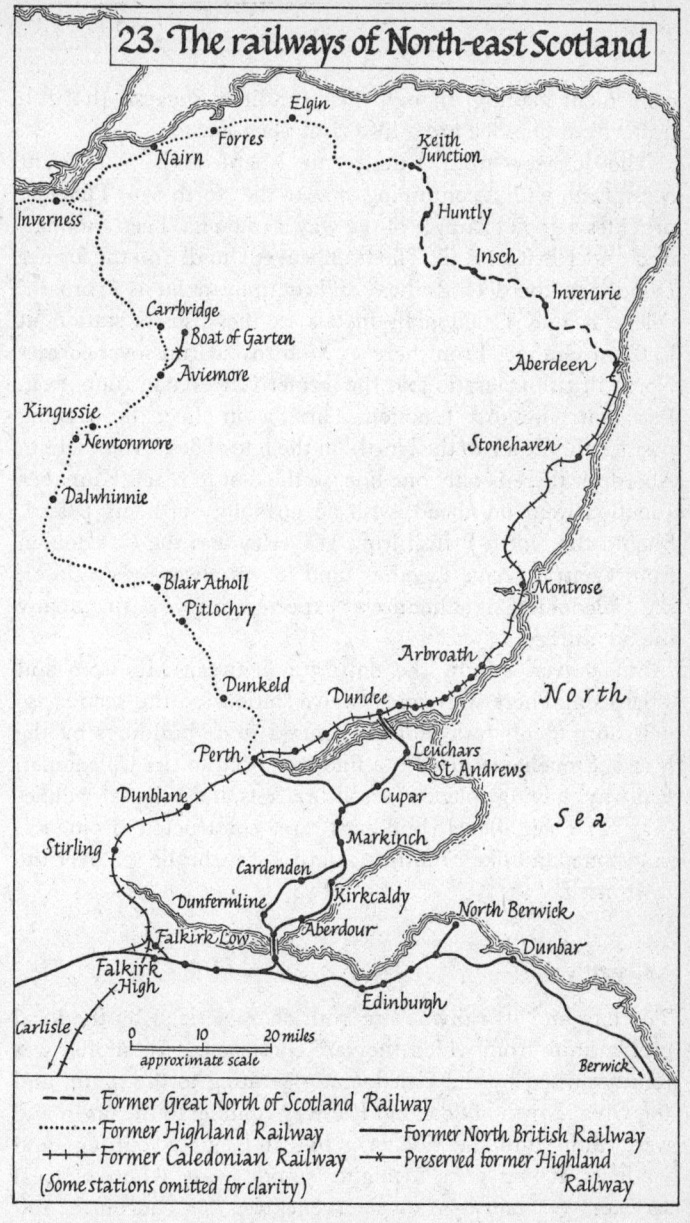

convenient loading, though their condition suggests that fish trains from Dundee are a historical phenomenon.

The journey from Dundee to Aberdeen is a pleasant coastal run with a continuing view of the North Sea. This line provides a good example of the way a route has been rationalized under British Rail. The train leaves Dundee on the former Dundee & Aberdeen Railway and continues as far as Arbroath, where it uses Caledonian metals to the disused station at Letham Grange. From here to Montrose it runs over former North British tracks to join the former Caledonian route from Forfar at Kinnaber Junction. This was in effect the winning post for the 'Race to the North' in the late 1880s. From here to Aberdeen there is only one line, so the first to reach Kinnaber Junction went on ahead, with no possibility of being passed. Should the North British from Waverley and the Caledonian from Central arrive together (and it was always very close), the Caledonian signalman was expected to give his company the advantage.

Stonehaven is now the only stop between Montrose and Aberdeen. There were once twelve stations on this section, so it is no difficult task spotting disused stone buildings by the tracks. Stonehaven itself is a fine memorial to the Caledonian Railway, having splendid scroll brackets and original valancing. The high-level buildings are constructed from red sandstone, and like Montrose afford a view of the sea over the town itself.

ABERDEEN

The city and its railway are both characterized by the local grey granite from which they are constructed. Its station was jointly owned by the Caledonian operating to the south, and the Great North of Scotland Railway running to the north and west. Built into the side of a hill and fed by cuttings and viaducts, it was once a mighty station with a host of local services. A central train-shed encloses the concourse and departures board, which, like that at Glasgow Central, is operated by men placing destination boards in large windows. Through lines lie behind, while for local trains, bays are let into each end, protected by individual umbrella awnings. There is a splendid signal gantry at the southern end, its many arms resembling a row of coloured flags stretched out in a sea breeze.

The Great North of Scotland's network has suffered from closures, only the section between Keith (for Inverness) and Aberdeen remaining open. Consequently the station's northern bays which served this region have fallen into disuse, the rails having been lifted and the platforms infilled for use as a car park. From being four tracks in the station, the line is soon confined into one. Gardens decorate the cutting side leading up to Union Terrace, where a turntable foundation is still intact, while small factories, paper mills and houses crowd close to the railway on the eastern side. The line is crossed by two solidly splendid granite bridges carrying Union Street and School Hill. Beneath the latter there is a disused station, as there were several suburban halts on this stretch (School Hill, Hutcheon Street, Kitty Brewster and Don Street) and their platforms still survive. Aberdeen is Scotland's third largest city, but its railway services, like Edinburgh's, have experienced a sharp decline.

The Station Hotel is adjacent to the main line and overlooks the disused suburban and goods yards. Constructed from grey granite, it has a rather austere façade dominated by twin pedimented gables and oriel windows. The re-modelled station exterior, featuring five broad semi-circular windows set above the entrance canopy, is similarly restrained. The bus station is situated opposite, while the Victoria Dock and Albert Basin lie behind these two, making for a veritable communications centre.

THE HIGHLANDS: WEST COAST

The former North British line from Glasgow to Mallaig, via Fort William, is one of the most picturesque upland journeys in the country. Trains leave from Queen Street and head for the north bank of the Firth of Clyde at Dumbarton. The railway continues along the valley side to Dalreoch where a branch runs due north to Balloch Pier (for steamer services across Loch Lomond). Docks with their cranes and warehouses line the edge of the Clyde here. The railway divides again at Craigendoran with an electrified branch to Helensburgh Central, terminus for the Argyle line. Helensburgh Upper, designed in a so-called 'Swiss' style, is the first of the typical Highland stations. It consists of a single island platform with single-storey timbered buildings which have brick foundations and extended eaves for protection and are decorated with wooden shingles imported specially from Switzerland. The West Highland line is, of course, single-track throughout and stations are used as passing points. However, the additional track at Helensburgh has been lifted and is now overgrown. A number of these island stations have small signal boxes on the platform to control the sidings and points at each end of the platform.

Between Helensburgh and Garelochhead, there are Royal Naval dockyards, where a few ships, many cranes and a number of submarines enliven the eastern edge of Gare Loch. From here the scenery becomes increasingly barren as the railway penetrates the heart of the north-west Highlands. One of the finest views is just before Tarbet, where the railway passes between the hills separating Loch Lomond and Loch Long. Ardlui Station is not the original, the first having been damaged by subsidence. At Crianlarich the line joins the former Caledonian route for Oban. Surprisingly the station has a small buffet, described by the ancient sign as 'Refreshment Rooms'. Although the North British did not complete their line to Fort William until 1894, the Caledonian had opened their railway to Tyndrum by 1876 and to Oban in 1880.

Passengers reached Crianlarich from Glasgow or Edinburgh by travelling to Stirling and Dunblane, where there was a direct north-eastern link via Callander and Balquhidder.

The Crianlarich to Oban line is an exciting journey. It is dominated by Ben Cruachan (3,689 feet), forcing the railway through the Pass of Brander, between Dalmally and Taynuilt Stations. The signals in the pass are worked independently of the normal block semaphores, being brought to danger should rocks fall on to a safety fence, so preventing the train from running into a barrier of boulders. Oban terminus is built on a pier forming one side of the harbour – local townsfolk were suspicious of the railway and forced the Caledonian away from the town centre. The station consists of a short lateral train-shed fronted by a curious half-timbered entrance and clock tower with a spire. Perhaps the architect was striving to capture the Swiss effect which is said to characterize these Highland railways. The Caledonian Hotel opposite is executed in stone in the traditional Scottish baronial manner.

The line to Fort William continues northwards from Crianlarich to Tyndrum Upper and Bridge of Orchy. It is difficult to describe the magnificence and drama of this Highland scenery, as the effect is partly achieved by its sublimity and remoteness. There are only subtle variations in shade and texture which emphasize this barren quality. Light sienna moors, outcrops of grey rock, darker patches of bracken or heather and black areas of peat are repeated for mile after mile. Smoothed 'U'-shaped valleys, craggy peaks and their scalloped corries, hanging valleys with cascading streams and isolated lochs create a vision of glaciated upland scenery at its finest.

There is a splendid section between Tyndrum and Bridge of Orchy when the railway is forced to swing in two half circles (the Tyndrum Curve), first to cross a valley on a round-arched viaduct, and then to skirt the base of Beinn Dórain (3,524 feet), an awe-inspiring conical hill. The Tyndrum Curve is a famous spot for railway photographers, and one of the places where (if the traveller is seated near the end of the train)

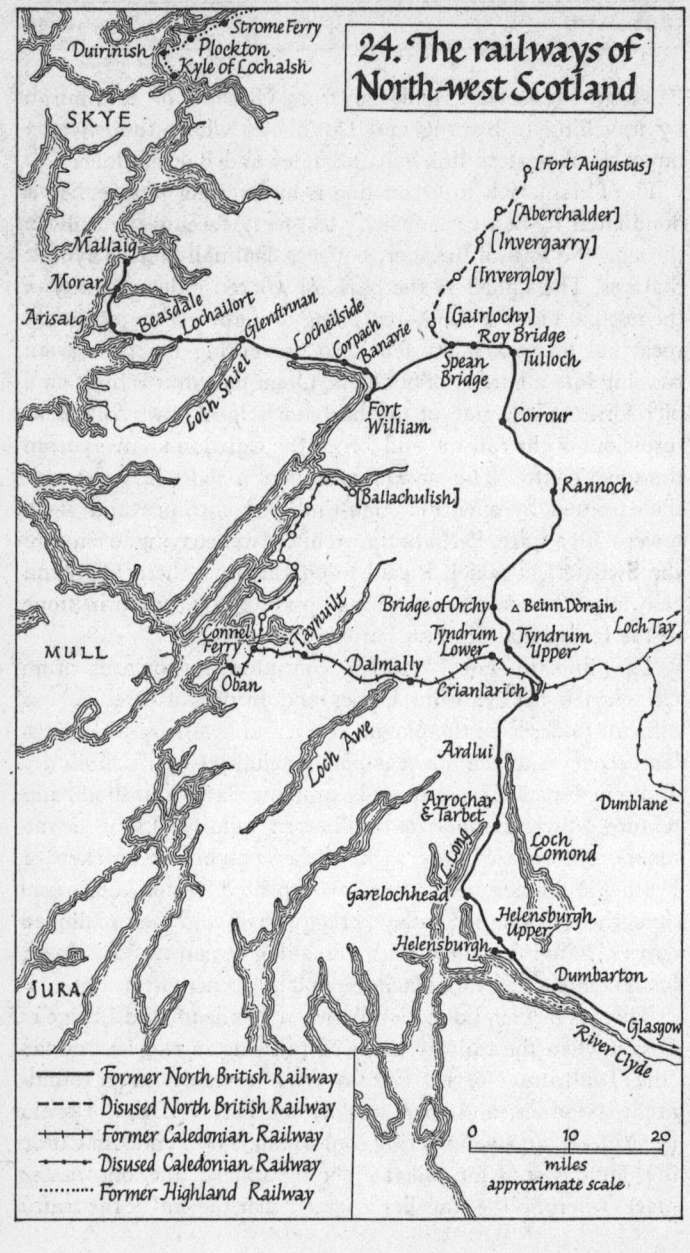

it is possible not only to look at the scenery but also see the engine and leading carriages tackle this impressive section – the best of both worlds.

It might seem a far cry from this Highland scenery to railway liveries, but there is a strong connection. The umber of the North British, the Highland's various greens, and the Caledonian's light blue (the colour of a loch on a clear day) are all in keeping with this upland panorama. These liveries are distinctive and distinctly Scottish. British Rail, with its emphasis on dull uniformity, might recall that Victorian railway companies selected their particular colour schemes for commercial reasons. Existing in an era of tough competition when passengers meant profits for the shareholders, their liveries were purposely designed to be eyecatching, to mark out their trains and associate them with particular districts. The present midblue and grey livery is not a powerful or imaginative combination and B.R. might be advised to reconsider the traditional regional liveries.

But to return to the West Highland line, Rannoch still has a small turntable, while Corrour is a typical island station, situated in the middle of a deserted and remote moor, with no road or habitation. There is, however, a track which leads to a house some miles away on Loch Treig (visible from the train) and another on Loch Ossian. Corrour was built as a private station and was officially opened to the public only in 1934, though it had been used by them for many years previously. Achnashellach, on the Kyle line, was originally a private station for Viscount Hill, as was Glencarron Halt (now closed) for Mr Shaw of Glencarron Lodge.

Between Tulloch and Roy Bridge the line runs through Monessie Gorge. The River Spean has cut a jagged verticalsided course and the railway has followed by means of a stone embankment. It is a splendid piece of engineering. At Spean Bridge, the station signs still proclaim, 'Change here for Fort Augustus'. There was indeed a North British branch running due north from Spean Bridge along Loch Lochy to Gairlochy,

Invergloy, Aberchalder and Fort Augustus, though it has since been closed and the track lifted. Ben Nevis (4,406 feet) is visible to the south on the approach to Fort William. The line also passes the town's ruined castle. Fort William is a terminus and has recently been rebuilt by British Rail, incorporating a buffet and tourist information office. Engines are changed here and sleeping cars detached for the journey to Mallaig.

Just after Banavie the railway crosses the Caledonian Canal by a swing bridge, which provides a direct view of the rising flight of locks and then curves around the end of Loch Eil on a stone viaduct offering a splendid sight of its 'U'-shaped profile. The stations on this later section all have double rather than island platforms. The line continues west beside Loch Eil, crossing the River Finnan at the head of Loch Shiel by the Glenfinnan viaduct (1897–1901), Britain's first concrete bridge, 90 feet high and consisting of twenty-one arches, and reaches the coast at Beasdale and Arisaig. These Highland lines make it easy to imagine what it was like to travel in the Victorian period. Trains composed of Mark I carriages have steam heating, compartments and corridors. Clouds of white steam drift around the windows, the wheels beat rhythmically over the metals, while the scenery is timeless and the stations have barely changed since they were built. All that is missing is the solid bark and hiss of a steam engine as it toils up the winding gradients.

Mallaig terminus has a simple grey-stone station master's house, a modern booking office and a disused engine-shed. The platform is empty and it looks as if the original awnings have been removed.

THE HIGHLANDS: EAST COAST

The former Highland Railway's line from Perth to Inverness is another magnificent upland journey. It too is single-track and trains are forced to pass at stations. The lowlands around Perth are soon left behind on the route north, fields being exchanged for forests and hills replacing the gently rolling farmland. Dunkeld Station retains the original cast-iron brackets and suspended between them are several large gas-lamps. Pitlochry, constructed from local grey-brown stone with honey-coloured dressings, is another pleasant station. The railway climbs towards Blair Atholl, the land becoming bleaker and more remote, and ascends Glen Garry, running through the Pass of Drumochter to Druimuachdar Summit, just beyond the now disused Dalnaspidal Station. The stone foundations of a watertower (lacking tank) survive at Dalwhinnie Station, provided to replenish locomotives which had just toiled through the Grampians.

The train descends into the picturesque Spey valley, its floor covered with clear green grass blending into the sienna valley sides, which in turn rise to umber bracken on the tops, alternating with areas of exposed grey rock. The lower slopes are further enlivened with short mauve-brown and dark viridian trees, producing a harmonious spectrum of natural colours.

Kingussie Station, a long stone building with stepped gables, displays the date 1894. Aviemore is a large weather-boarded station designed to cater for the seasonal tourist trade. The halt for the Strathspey Railway (see p. 341) is slightly to the north of the B.R. station, adjacent to the engine sheds. After Carr Bridge, there were stations at Tomatin and Moy, by the loch, while a magnificent round-arched stone viaduct carries the railway across the Nairn valley. The line swings around to approach Inverness from the east, descending to the coastal plain. Although Inverness is an important railway junction (with lines radiating in all directions), it is in fact a terminus, situated at the apex of an inverted triangular network of tracks. The Highland Railway's locomotive sheds, Lochgorm Works, were placed in the middle. Inverness still has considerable sidings and yards, while a number of industries are sited close by. The train-shed and the station façade have been modified, but the shields of the Highland Railway remain set in its walls.

The Station Hotel is an integral part of the terminus. An asymmetrical building in grey-ochre stone, it has a double-column entrance beneath a sadly truncated clock tower. Round-arched and pedimented Venetian windows, decorative balustrades, quoins and a dentil border make for a lively and interesting Italianate exterior, which contrasts sharply with the simplified and somewhat dull modern station façade.

Besides the Perth line, Inverness has routes to Aberdeen, Kyle of Lochalsh, Thurso and Wick. The last three are upland lines, while the former is confined to the lowlands of Aberdeen, its latter half being owned by the Great North of Scotland Railway. The H.R.'s line to Kyle was not completed till February 1897, though the section to Stromeferry had been opened in August 1870. The explanation for this delay lay with the cost and effort required to clear a level path for the track and terminus. The site for the goods yard, engine-shed and station itself had to be blasted out of solid rock and the cost of the gelignite alone was £6,000.

The section from Achanalt to Achnashellach, via Achnasheen, where the line crosses the North West Highland range, must be among the bleakest in Britain. Achnasheen Station, constructed as the mid-way watering point for locomotives, was also the passing point on this single-track railway. From here the line climbs to Luib Summit steadily between Loch Scaven and Loch Gowan. There follows a long descent down Glen Carron to Attadale, where the line skirts the southern coast of Loch Carron, winding along its shore to Stromeferry and Kyle. There is a ferry service from here to Kyleakin and Mallaig. Station masters are now only memories on the line, tickets being bought from the guard between Kyle and Dingwall.

Dingwall is also the point where the Kyle and Wick routes divide. The railway north to Georgemas Junction follows a tortuous course winding its way through the coastal hills, being forced inland where Dornoch Firth has flooded the valley as far as Culrain and Invershin. Between Rogart and Golspie, there was a station called The Mound from which a short branch ran south to Dornoch Terminus. At Helmsdale the railway turns inland, running along its valley to the flatter and damper moors of Caithness, and the line divides at Georgemas Junction, with the northern arm continuing to Thurso and the eastern arm to Wick. Again this route has been subjected to closures and a number of the remoter halts have been shut, as has the branch which ran from Wick along the coast to Lybster.

Finally, to return to Inverness and the coastal route to Aberdeen, the first section, as far as Keith, was owned by the Highland Railway and the second, from there to Aberdeen, was part of the Great North of Scotland Railway's network. There were originally fifteen stations on the H.R.'s half. Now there are only three. The first is at Nairn, which is a pleasant grey-stone building (similar to Kingussie) with step gabled pavilions and a central canopy. The chimneys and windows are executed in the Tudor manner. Forres is unusual in that it is situated on a sharp curve which forms part of a loop from the main line with goods yards in the middle. There was a Highland Railway branch running due south from here to Aviemore, and it is on its last section from Boat of Garten that the Strathspey Railway operates.

There were two stations at Elgin almost adjacent to one another. The first has been modernized, while the second on the G.N. of S.R.'s line north to Lossiemouth has been closed but can still be seen. Keith was the meeting place for the two companies. It has a much reduced station, its bay platforms having been infilled, though retaining the original stone buildings, iron columns and brackets. Huntly, Insch and Inverurie are the only other G.N. of S.R. stations still in operation. However, the route from Keith to Aberdeen is dominated by a large number of disused stone stations and the trackbeds of five defunct branch lines, which made up the bulk of the company's network. Aberdeen was the south-eastern terminus for their system (see p. 330).

PRESERVED STEAM RAILWAYS

The Glasgow Museum of Transport

This museum contains the finest display of vintage locomotives in Scotland, housed at the city's former tramway workshops in Albert Drive. With the closure of the tram service in 1962, a number of these historic vehicles were restored and put on display. Fortunately the museum was able to act when British Rail decided that there were to be no more steam runs on their network, taking four locomotives which had been maintained for special trains. These formed the nucleus of what has become an impressive transport collection.

There are two engines representing the Caledonian Railway. No. 123, a 4-4-2, is the oldest, having been built in 1886 to represent the company at the Edinburgh International Exhibition. The large driving wheels made No. 123 a swift engine and so it was used on the Carlisle to Edinburgh section of the West Coast Route. No. 828, an 0-6-0 tender goods locomotive, is the other C.R. engine on display. Completed in 1899 at the company's workshops at St Rollox, No. 828 hauled freight trains until 1963, when she was acquired by the Scottish Locomotive Preservation Trust, restored to Caledonian livery and then loaned to the museum.

The Highland Railway was responsible for designing the first British 4-6-0 locomotive in 1894. No. 103 was one of fifteen built that year. They were powerful engines with small driving wheels to enable them to haul heavy goods trains through the Scottish uplands. Withdrawn in 1934, No. 103 was thoroughly overhauled in 1959 and repainted in Stroudley's 'improved engine green', which is in fact a light yellowish-green.

No. 256, *Glen Douglas*, a 4-4-0 express locomotive, has been restored to the umber of the North British Railway. Built at Cowlairs in 1913, *Glen Douglas* worked for the L.N.E.R. and British Railways, not being withdrawn till 1959. Representing the Great North of Scotland Railway is No. 49, *Gordon Highlander*. This engine was built by the North British Loco

Company in 1920 and continued working until 1948, when it was restored and shedded for special tours. It has been repainted in the G.N. of S.R.'s mid-green livery and lined out in light yellow, black and red. The only surviving locomotive from the Glasgow & South Western is No. 9, an 0-6-0T, built in 1917. Although these shunters were hardly representative of their company, No. 9 does serve as a reminder of their style and livery.

Falkirk Railway Museum (S.R.P.S.)

In 1964 the Scottish Railway Preservation Society leased a transhipment shed in Springfield Goods Yard, Falkirk, for their musuem. From the fire-damaged buildings which they took over has emerged a well-housed collection of steam locomotives. One of their first acquisitions was No. 419, an 0-4-4T, the third Caledonian engine in preservation. Built in 1907, No. 419 had continued to work for B.R. until withdrawal in 1962. They were used throughout the Caledonian system for suburban and branch line trains, being efficient and reliable locomotives. One of their oldest engines is the former North British 0-6-0 tender goods engine, No. 673. Built in 1891 by Neilson & Co., No. 673 saw overseas service during the First World War and on returning was named *Maude*.

The Society has acquired two more modern engines, an ex-L.N.E.R. No. 246, *Morayshire* (1927), a general-purpose 4-4-0, and a B.R. standard 2-6-4T, No. 80105, which are both on display at Falkirk. There are a number of industrial saddle tanks, but possibly more interesting is the fine collection of coaches, including a royal carriage, originally built in 1898 and used by King Edward, a six-wheeled coach from the Highland Railway and two Caledonian carriages, restored to run behind No. 123. There is, in addition, a display of goods vehicles from the various Scottish railway companies.

The Strathspey Railway

The Strathspey Railway has about five miles of track between Aviemore and Boat of Garten Stations on the former Highland

Railway. The line had been built by the Inverness & Perth Junction Railway in 1865 and subsequently absorbed by the H.R. It was closed to passenger traffic in 1965, though Aviemore has remained a station on the line between Perth and Inverness. The scheme to re-open the railway for steam running was promoted by the S.R.P.S. and the Highlands and Islands Development Board. The engine shed at Aviemore has been restored and the track was re-laid in 1972.

There are a number of industrial saddle-tank engines at Aviemore, together with two main-line locomotives. No. 46464 is an Ivatt designed 2–6–0, built at Crewe in 1950. The company has bought another of these Mogul class, No. 46512, which is at present on the Severn Valley, being restored before the journey north. The 'Black Five' No. 45025 (L.M.S. No. 5025) has been thoroughly overhauled and moved to the Strathspey Railway, having worked on the Keighley & Worth Valley line.

Most of the carriages are of British Railways origin, but there are a few coaches of L.M.S. and Great North of Scotland ancestry. The station and signal boxes at Boat of Garten have been restored and a loop and sidings re-laid, while a new station at Aviemore is being built.

12 Conclusions: The New Age of Railways

The railways have exercised a profound influence on Britain and there can be few aspects of society which have not been affected in some way by their construction. Even politics felt the force of the steam engine. Gladstone, who had been responsible for much railway legislation under Peel in the 1840s, realized that a hired train could take him quickly and efficiently around Britain. His Midlothian campaign, conducted in 1879-80, was a novel countrywide programme of speeches based on a rail timetable. As a result, leading politicians were helped to become recognizable national figures in the latter part of the nineteenth century.

However, railways were built first and foremost for economic reasons. In the 1830s and 1840s expanding manufacturies, mills and mines needed a new transport system to augment the canals and roads, which could no longer cope with their growing orders. The railways, by making use of advances in steam technology, were an obvious answer to this problem. Permitting the cheap transport of bulky, low-value goods, they maintained the momentum of industrial expansion. For the first time perishables could be sent long distances, so that fish, milk and fruit trains became important aspects of freight working. The mails were switched from stage-coach to the railways and delivery times for letters and parcels fell.

People were the unforeseen element in early rail schemes. The stage-coach and the canal packet boat disappeared as the railways developed the passenger side of their operation. In this respect their influence has been long lasting. The Duke of

Wellington, a true Conservative, complained at the outset that the railways 'would encourage the lower classes to move about'. He had been present at the opening of the Liverpool & Manchester Railway in 1830, and had perceived some of the far-reaching effects of railway construction.

The railway was the truly modern element in Victorian England. Both Dickens and Macaulay saw trains not merely as a means of transport but also as emblems of a new era. Railways were a civilizing force, representing and causing moral improvement, slum clearance, higher wages, better education and above all 'Progress'. Hence, when Tennyson, as Victoria's poet-laureate, was searching for objects and notions to represent modern England, he wrote,

> There methinks would be more enjoyment than in
> the march of mind,
> In the steamship, in the railway, in the thoughts
> which shake mankind.

The Victoria and Albert Museum is partly housed in a group of buildings designed by Francis Fowke in 1866 to house a museum of science and art. It is rather surprising to look up in the main courtyard of this centre of antiquity to see a golden mosaic in the pediment featuring a railway engine. Along with books and figures of learning and government, it represents the most important features of Queen Victoria's England.

The railways exercised a wide-felt influence on England's social pattern. Increased leisure time and more cash combined with cheap, quick travel to produce a spread of coastal holiday resorts – in much the same way that southern Spain has developed after the introduction of the charter flight. Nationwide sporting leagues, in football, cricket and rugby, were again only made possible with the evolution of an efficient and fast railway network for players and supporters. The founding of so many sporting clubs in the 1860s and 1870s bears chronological witness to this fact.

CONCLUSIONS: THE NEW AGE OF RAILWAYS

The suburb is a railway phenomenon. Settlement patterns underwent a major re-orientation as a result first of industrialization and then the completion of the rail network. The railways encouraged the division of towns into business and residential districts by classes. Suburban train services permitted the better off to live away from their workplaces in more rural surroundings, while working-class terraces proliferated in the 1860s and 1870s as North London was linked to the City by railway lines both above and beneath ground.

The railways continued to be the major and unchallenged form of transport for people and goods until the First World War. However, the inter-war years saw the beginnings of the motor age. Cars began to be assembled on production lines from mass-produced components. For the first time they were cheap, fairly reliable and easily maintained. The outbreak of war in 1939 brought a temporary halt to their battle with the steam engine, as factories were diverted to manufacture tanks, lorries and aircraft parts. The 1950s witnessed the decline of British Railways as the natural means of travelling. Messrs Morris and Ford, an Englishman and an American, sold cars to a recovering and growing economy, and trains emptied as more and more cheap automobiles took to the road. Petrol was inexpensive and motoring fun. It was clear by 1960 that something had to be done. When the patient is sick the doctor is called and the Beeching Report was researched, published and implemented.

On 1 January 1948 Britain's railways were nationalized. Although many have complained about the switch from private to public ownership, for the passenger the initial effect was not significant, as the same locomotives hauled the same carriages to similar timetables. Nationalization in 1948 was a political and financial matter. Even in the late 1950s the traveller would have found it hard to detect any major changes in railway travel. Chocolate and cream Pullman cars still ran the length and breadth of England, steam engines designed by former companies continued to be manufactured by B.R. and were often painted in a similar livery, while there was little movement of stock around the regions. Indeed the Western, Southern, Midland and Eastern Regions' organization and daily operation scarcely differed from those of the old Great Western, Southern, London Midland Scottish, and London North Eastern Railway companies, though the creation of a separate Scottish Region (formerly divided between the L.M.S. in the west and the L.N.E.R. in the east) was a major advance. Externally, only the words 'British Railways' and the cream and maroon colours for their newest coaches were obviously novel.

It was not until the 1960s, when two major decisions were taken, that nationalization really made itself felt. In 1963 the Beeching Report was published and recommended that many of the smaller or less profitable branch lines should be shut, while duplication of routes was to be phased out. Consequently the former Great Central Railway from Manchester to Marylebone, via Loughborough and Leicester, closed in favour of the parallel Midland route to St Pancras. Britain's rail mileage was dramatically reduced from 17,500 in 1962 to 12,400 in 1968. Today there are only 11,100 miles of railways in the country.

The second significant innovation resulted from the decision to phase out steam running by 1968 and replace it either by diesel or electric traction. On Western Region, 'Castle', 'Hall' and 'King' class locomotives gradually disappeared and were replaced by 'Warships', 'Westerns', Sulzers and Brush diesel-electrics. Steam died and with it a number of well-loved local services.

These two major decisions were made purely on economic and technical grounds. The motor car had deposed the railway as the natural means of travelling short and even long distances. The new diesel-hydraulics were advanced mechanical beings, more powerful than the largest steam engines and required no back-breaking toil to keep them running, while their cabs, placed at each end of the locomotive, provided better protection for the crew and superior visibility. The diesel was simpler to run, if more complicated to maintain, and in the initial stages often less reliable. Any economist or engineer working purely on rational grounds would rightly have favoured the decisions to prune the network and abandon steam working.

Unfortunately, these developments were accompanied by a changed attitude towards the railways themselves. They were regarded by the government, and possibly the public as well, as inefficient and unpleasant beings which had to be forced to make a profit. Their losses were no longer to be tolerated. Politicians did not appreciate that it is impossible in an advanced economy for any railway system to create a surplus. Rising wage bills in a labour-intensive industry, the development of highly competitive alternatives (the aircraft and the automobile) and the need to up-date technical equipment meant that profitability was a fantasy in the 1960s. Nor was it realized that the railways performed a valuable social function. They kept juggernauts off the roads and enabled people in remote areas without motor cars to travel, without harming the environment.

During the late 1960s and until the mid-1970s, British Rail experienced a dark depression. They were criticized by the public for their shortcomings and badgered by successive governments concerned to see their accounts in the black. Fortunately the autumn of 1973 marked a turning point. There was a fundamental change in opinion and Parliament conceded that B.R. should not be judged solely by commercial criteria. It was recognized that the railways were unable to make a profit, particularly now that the Middle East crisis had boosted oil prices. Their social service was perceived and thought sufficiently valuable to merit a subsidy. The launching of an important investment programme resulted in the new High Speed Train, wider electrification of main-line and commuter routes, the development of freight transportation, and further improvements in track and signalling. As Richard

Marsh declared in 1973, 'we then told the government they must accept the fact that there were no benefits from cutting the system, and that it must be accepted that the social benefit to the community as a whole by keeping it intact was far greater than a book-keeping loss'. As a result British Rail's future seems secure and the developments of the last five years have witnessed the system's transformation. An expansive and adventurous policy has produced new trains, faster times and more passengers, rescuing B.R.'s tarnished image.

Mention has been made of nationalization's initial failure to affect the outward form of British Railways. This remained the case until the 1960s when, as a concomitant of the Beeching Plan and the end of steam, a new standardized and simplified public image was chosen for B.R. The fascinating differences and idiosyncrasies of the system, thrown up quite naturally as a result of its historical evolution, were regarded as unfashionable and unfortunate. Such distinctions were to be removed or concealed. British Rail deliberately set about standardizing every railway feature, with conformity as the keynote. Locomotives and carriages were to be painted in the same livery, blue and yellow for the former, blue and grey for the latter. The simplified double-arrow symbol replaced the more traditional lion, wheel and crown device. Station signs, formerly varied and distinct, were everywhere to be substituted by uncomplicated black and white enamelled boards. Victorian architectural features which did not harmonize with 1960s notions of simplicity were to be concealed or destroyed. Euston Station was rebuilt and the sublime arch unnecessarily destroyed. The contractor responsible for the demolition even offered to rebuild it at his own expense near by, but British Rail rejected the suggestion.

To be fair to British Rail, there was a rationale behind this policy. It was not a form of organized vandalism based on a hearty disrespect for the past, as some commentators have suggested. The image men at B.R. argued that the railways should be an unobtrusive, efficient, predictable and modern-looking transport system. The passenger should not have to think about his journey. He should neither delight in it, nor should it cause him any problems. Greater efficiency certainly had resulted from the introduction of improved diesels and electric locomotives produced in fewer classes than before. Accordingly British Rail felt that distinctions between various trains were now irrelevant and should be dropped. Famous names such as 'The Bristolian', 'The Golden Arrow' and 'The Devon Belle' have disappeared and engines, carriages and trains were all made anonymous. Today there remains but one Pullman service in Britain, to Manchester, and when its stock wears out this service will probably end for good. Even the 'Flying Scotsman' (the 10 am H.S.T. from King's Cross) has no external distinguishing features. Standardization and the suppression of difference is designed to support the image of reliability and efficiency. Does it also create an empty atmosphere of boredom?

However, owing to the efforts of pressure groups and a lot of public criticism, much of the momentum behind this policy has been reduced. The outcome of B.R.'s action may be questioned on two points. First, the results lack imagination and interest for traveller and employee alike. It is difficult to become committed to a system where there is no competition, no distinction and where a single standard is accepted. Secondly, British Rail may be seen to be fighting against potentially their greatest attraction. They have tried to deny their own history. Each company's distinctive style, its individuality, and the differences which this created, form some of the most interesting aspects of the railway system. The varied station buildings, the brightly coloured liveries with their decorative coats-of-arms, the famous expresses and the rivalries have all left their mark on the present network. They attract tourists and enthusiasts, while making travel more interesting for the regulars. Given that the new technology allows B.R. to operate a fast, reliable and cost-effective transport system, it would seem silly not to use their past as an additional attraction, thereby giving them the best of both worlds. Instead of trying to conceal or destroy the finer points of railway buildings, British Rail would be better advised to restore them to their original magnificence.

The major termini have been described by Sir John Betjeman as the cathedrals of the nineteenth century. Liverpool Street, with its magnificent vaulted train-shed and its double rows of lancet windows, certainly resembles a cathedral in scale and style. Betjeman's comparison based on architectural similarities may be pushed further. The terminus was as important for Victorian man as was the church for his medieval counterpart. In both cases the economy, the structure of society and the prevailing opinions were reflected and moulded by these two types of building. It is recognized, of course, that British Rail's funds are limited and that they cannot possibly afford to repair every Victorian station on their system. All that one asks is that they change their outlook and make due consultation before undertaking demolition. However, there are good indications that B.R. is now much more aware of their heritage and that the unnecessary destruction of outstanding buildings, such as the Euston arch, will not be repeated.

It would be unfair not to mention the achievements of the last twenty years. Not all modern architecture is without merit, and some is as good as that of previous centuries. The railways may lay claim to a number of fine designs. The stations at Bishops Stortford and Broxbourne on the former Northern & Eastern Railway (later the G.E.R.), like those at Bridgend, Basildon, Bedford and London Bridge, have been recently rebuilt with merit. Ian Nairn accurately describes Bishops Stortford as a 'sensitive marriage of old and new', where a traditional circular tower serves as the station master's office, carefully linked to a light, airy booking office of steel and glass. Euston itself is certainly no ugly building, though it may not better its nineteenth-century predecessor.

The High Speed Trains are another of British Rail's

CONCLUSIONS: THE NEW AGE OF RAILWAYS

achievements, being fast, comfortable and reliable. The old baggage problems have been solved by their wide end doors and adjacent luggage racks. The air conditioning, sound proofing, automatic doors and double-glazed windows have eradicated many of the worries of second-class travel, though the carriages resemble the inside of an aircraft rather than a corridor compartment coach of former years. But many will miss the steam heating (sometimes unreliable), the crowded seats facing one another, the cases blocking narrow passages, the awkward sliding doors, the jolting and swaying moquette-covered benches, the panelled walls, the sepia photographs of resorts, and the wide, clear windows letting in fresh air and gusts of smoke. They had a magic which seems to be lacking in the new streamlined carriages.

For the future, it is hoped that British Rail will be able to expand their freight business, as they have made great efforts to modernize their carrying services. It can only be left to firms to appreciate the advantages of having a private siding, without any of the environmental drawbacks associated with lorries. The increased use made of the railways as a result of the introduction of the High Speed Trains and the electrification of routes to the north-west represents a real step forward, while the arrival of the Advanced Passenger Train in 1980 has maintained this momentum. The general shift in public opinion, mirrored by the government, in favour of railway investment must mean that British Rail is entering a new 'Golden Age'.

The one thing lacking in our railway system is a magical element. The romance, the thrill of the special, the unusual and the different has been gradually worn down over the last twenty years. It would be fascinating to see it replaced. At present B.R. is considering closing the North London Line (see p. 71). Apart from the fact that it caters for a million commuters every year, this seems to be a negative step, as it remains one of the most interesting railway journeys in the capital. From stately Broad Street, it takes in Dickensian dwellings by viaducts, skirts distant King's Cross and St Pancras, touches the suburban villadom of Hampstead and Brondesbury and terminates on the other side of the Thames at rural Kew and Richmond. Possibly B.R. might be better advised to develop the line as an attraction for visitors. An off-peak steam service would certainly add to its glories. The success of the summer steam excursions from York and the popularity of the National Railway Museum are both clear indications of the public's interest. British Rail has all the potential necessary to revive its magical gene. Should this element of historical continuity be restored then Britain could rightly claim to have the finest railway system in the world.

Appendix 1 Steam, Diesel and Electric Wheel Arrangements

STEAM

Front	Rear	Notation	Name of type
		2-2-0	Planet
		2-2-2	Jenny Lind
		0-4-0	
		0-4-2	
		0-4-4	
		2-4-0	
		2-4-2	Columbia
		4-4-0	American
		4-4-2	Atlantic
		0-6-0	
		0-6-2	
		2-6-0	Mogul
		2-6-2	Prairie
		2-6-4	Adriatic
		4-6-0	
		4-6-2	Pacific
		0-8-0	
		2-8-0	Consolidation
		2-8-2	Mikado
		2-6-6-2	Garratt
		0-10-0	Decapod
		2-10-0	

DIESELS AND ELECTRICS

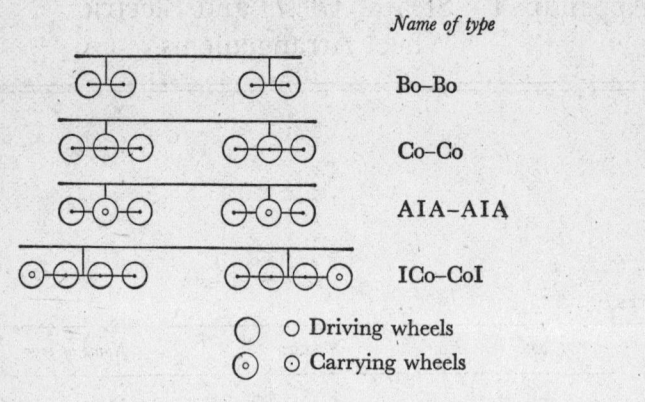

Letter Codes in Wheel Arrangements

Class letters:
P = Passenger (ie 6–P class)
F = Freight (ie 4–F class)
MT = Mixed Traffic (ie 4–MT class)

Wheel arrangement letters:
o–6–oT   Tank engine
o–6–oPT   Pannier-tank engine
o–4–oST   Saddle-tank engine
o–4–o WT   Well-tank engine
o–4–oVB   Vertical-boilered engine

Appendix 2 Railway Company Liveries

Company	Locomotives (passenger)		Carriages (main-line)	
	Main colour	Lining	Below waistline	Above
Barry	Dark lake	Yellow, black	Dark red	
Brecon & Merthyr	Lake	Black, yellow, vermilion	Chocolate	
Caledonian	Light blue	White, vermilion	Dark lake	White
Cambrian	Black	Blue-grey, vermilion	Dark green	White
Furness	Dark red	Black, vermilion	Dark blue	White/light blue
Glasgow & South Western	Dark green	Black, white	Crimson lake	
Great Central	Mid-green	Black, white	Brown	Cream
Great Eastern	Royal blue	Black, vermilion, white	Varnished teak or chocolate	
Great North of Scotland	Mid-green	Black, yellow, red		
Great Northern	Grass green	Dark green, black, white	Varnished teak	

Company	Locomotives (passenger) Main colour	Lining	Carriages (main-line) Below waistline	Above
Great Western	Swindon green	Black, orange chrome yellow	Chocolate	Cream
Highland Railway	Brunswick green	Black, white	Dark green	White
Lancashire & Yorkshire	Black	White, vermilion	Dark lake	Medium brown
L.B. & S.C.R.	Greenish/golden yellow[1]	Olive green, black, red, white	Red-brown	
L.C. & D.R.	Black	Grey, yellow, red	Varnished teak	
L.N.W.R.	Black	Light blue, white, vermilion	Dark chocolate	White
L.S.W.R.	Grass/pea green	Black, white, purple-brown	Dark brown	Light buff
L.T. & S.R.	Bright green	Chocolate, vermilion	Dark green	Salmon pink
Metropolitan & District	Dark olive green	Black, vermilion	Varnished teak	
			Varnished teak or dark brown	

[1] Otherwise known after the company's colour-blind engineer, William Stroudley, as his 'improved engine green'.
In fact, it is very definitely a yellow hue, more akin to yellow ochre.

Company	Locomotives (passenger) Main colour	Lining	Carriages (main-line) Below waistline	Above
Metropolitan	Dull red	Black, yellow	Varnished teak First class	White
Midland	Dark red	Black, yellow	Dark chocolate red Sleepers, dark umber brown	
North British	Dark brown	Red, yellow	Dark lake or teak	
North Eastern	Light/apple green	Black, white	Varnished teak, or lake	
North London	Black	Red, light blue, white	Varnished teak	
North Staffordshire	Dark chocolate	Vermilion, black, yellow	Dark brown	White
South Eastern	Green	Red, black, yellow	Dark lake	
S.E. & C.R.	Dark green	Light brown, lemon yellow	Maroon	
Taff Vale	Black	Red, yellow, white	Dark chocolate	Cream

POST-1923

Great Western	As before	
L.N.E.R.	As the N.E.R.	
L.M.S.	As the Midland	
Southern	Locomotives generally followed the L.S.W.R. pattern, though the malachite green for expresses and the carriage green were new	

POST-1948

British Railway	Swindon green	Maroon
Goods	Black, orange	Pullmans: chocolate and cream, or Nanking blue and white
	Red	
After 1965	Mid-blue	Mid-blue cream
	Yellow	grey
		(A line is painted along the carriage below the roof according to its class: first, yellow; second, blue; restaurant or buffet, red)

Railway companies regularly changed or modified their liveries. These are possibly the most representative, and have been selected from around 1900. For a fuller account of their histories, consult E. F. Carter, *Britain's Railway Liveries 1825–1948*, London (1952).

Appendix 3   Railway Museums

This is not an exclusive list of transport museums but comprises the main permanent collections. The reader should consult the index for wider coverage of other private and public railway collections mentioned in the text.

The National Railway Museum, York
The Museum houses the largest group of railway exhibits in Britain. Opened in 1975, it combined the earlier collection from Queen Street York with the railway section of the Clapham Museum of Transport. A wide selection of steam locomotives from a variety of companies have been fully restored and assembled here. Diesel and electric-powered engines, together with passenger and goods rolling stock, are also on display. In addition, signs, name plates, signals and all the smaller items of railway memorabilia are represented. The converted sheds with their two turntables provide direct access to the main line for stock movement and steam tours.

Glasgow Museum of Transport
Though this is a transport collection (embracing trams, buses, cars and carriages), it does offer a representative selection of exhibits from Scotland's railway history. There are locomotives from the five major companies. In addition, there are models, signs and furniture from early stations, while a new gallery has been opened to record the Glasgow Underground. The Museum is conveniently situated in a former tram shed adjacent to Pollokshields East Station.

London Transport Museum, Covent Garden
Originally housed in the grounds of Syon Park, the Museum moved to Covent Garden in 1980. There are both early steam and electrically powered locomotives, together with a number of passenger and motor cars. The exhibits depict every aspect of the Underground's develop-

ment, including station architecture, advertising and technical aspects such as signalling. There are also buses, trams and trolleybuses.

The Great Western Railway Museum, Swindon

Established in a former Wesleyan chapel not far from the main line and the famous railway works, the Museum contains a number of historic steam engines. There is a replica of the broad-gauge engine *North Star* built by Swindon apprentices. In addition, there are a variety of G.W. signs, name plates, ticket machines, lamps and models, while a number of exhibits are associated with Brunel, the company's eminent engineer.

The Science Museum, South Kensington

The Transport Galleries contain several locomotives, including the Deltic prototype, *Caerphilly Castle* and the original *Rocket*. There are mock booking offices, a signal box and a display showing track development. Models and diagrams illustrate the technical advances in locomotive and carriage design.

Darlington North Road Museum

North Road Station, formerly the terminus of the Middleton Railway, has been restored to house a number of historic locos connected with the north-east. Both *Derwent* and *Locomotion No. 1* are preserved here, together with two other vintage engines. In addition, there is a host of memorabilia from the region.

The Merseyside County Museum

The transport gallery contains *Lion*, a vintage 0-4-2 loco from the Liverpool & Manchester Railway, together with three replica coaches illustrating its three classes of travel. There is also a fully restored saddle-tank engine, No. 1 (1904), from the Mersey Dock & Harbour Board and an electric motor coach, No. 3 (1892), from the Liverpool Overhead Railway.

Glossary of Architectural Terms

ARROWLOOP   A vertical slot in a wall or battlement for the use of an archer, or purely decorative

BARGEBOARD   A wide decorated timber board fitted immediately below the roof, forming an overhanging border to a gable

CHAIR   The metal plate and socket screwed to each sleeper to support the rails

CLERESTORY   A row of windows in the upper part of a building, above a lower roof

COFFER   A recessed panel, usually ornamented, in the under surface of a ceiling or balcony

CUPOLA   A small, dome-like roof

DENTIL   A small, square block used in series to decorate a cornice

FAÏENCE   Glazed porcelain used as a decorative facing

FINIAL   An ornament placed on a gable, often an urn or obelisk

FLORIATION   Flower decoration

FLUTING   A series of regularly spaced grooves, mostly on columns

FOLIATION   Leaf decoration, usually on capitals

KEY   The wooden or metal wedge which holds a rail firmly in its chair

LANCET WINDOW   A narrow pointed window

OGEE ARCH   An 'S'-shaped arch

PEDIMENT   The triangular or curved gable end of a building situated above the frieze

PILASTER   A projecting square column, attached to a wall

PORTE COCHÈRE A projecting porch over an entrance to provide cover for carriages

PORTICO An imposing porch in classical or Renaissance manner

QUOIN Emphasized bricks or stones on the corners of a building

RUSTICATION Joints between stones emphasized by use of deep grooves or channels

STRAPWORK A form of Elizabethan decoration consisting of interlaced bands

TERRA-COTTA A kind of hard, unglazed pottery of fine texture, used in place of stone, popular in the late nineteenth century

TYMPANUM The triangular area above the frieze and below the inclined cornice often decorated with sculpture

VALANCING The decorative wooden border or canopy surrounding a platform awning

Guide to Further Reading

The railways are a subject which has been discussed at great length, covering its many aspects in breadth and detail. This guide could be doubled in size if every work or journal relating to Britain's railways were mentioned. The bibliography that follows has been deliberately restricted to include only standard texts and works which have proved most helpful in writing this study.

The finest general work is also the oldest, W. T. Jackman, *Transportation in Modern England*, 2 vols. (1916, reprinted 1962), while H. J. Dyos and D. H. Aldcroft's *British Transport* (1969) has updated the subject. Studies on railways alone include J. Simmons, *The Railways of Britain* (1968), H. Perkin, *The Age of the Railway* (1970) and C. H. Ellis, *British Railway History*, 2 vols. (1954–9). More specialized are J. R. Kellett, *The Impact of Railways on Victorian Cities* (1969), E. F. Carter, *An Historical Geography of the Railways of the British Isles* (1959), G. Biddle, *Victorian Stations* (1973) and M. Binney and D. Pearce (Editors), *Railway Architecture* (1979). A splendid impression of what the railways were like in their heyday may be obtained from J. Spence's companion volumes of historic photographs, *Victorian and Edwardian Railways* (1975) and *Railway Travel* (1977). Informative maps may be found in S. K. Baker, *Rail Atlas of Britain* (1977), while the *British Railways Pre-Grouping Atlas and Gazetteer* (1976) remains a standard work.

The technical side of railway history is also well documented. There are two classic works, Angus Sinclair's *Development of the Locomotive Engine* (1906, reprinted 1970) and E. L. Ahrons, *The British Steam Railway Locomotive 1825–1925*, with a supplement by O. S. Nock (1966). In addition, B. Reed, *150 Years of British Steam Locomotives* (1975), C. H. Ellis, *Railway Carriages in the British Isles* (1965), and L. T. C. Rolt, *Victorian Engineering* (1970) are all useful. J. G. Bruce's *Tube Trains under London* (1968) and *Steam to Silver* (1970) have covered the technical development of the Underground's rolling stock.

The regional framework to Britain's railway history has been assembled in the series edited by D. St John Thomas and J. A. Patmore, *A Regional History of the Railways of Great Britain*. This runs as follows: Vol. 1, D. St John Thomas, *The West Country* (1973); Vols. 2 and 3, H. P. White, *Southern England* (1961) and *Greater London* (1963); Vol. 4, K. Hoole, *The North East* (1965); Vol. 5, D. I. Gordon, *Eastern Counties* (1968); Vol. 6, J. Thomas, *Scotland, the Lowlands and the Borders* (1971); Vol. 7, R. Christiansen, *The West Midlands* (1973); Vol. 8, D. Joy, *South and West Yorkshire* (1975); Vol. 9, R. Leleux, *The East Midlands* (1976); Vol. 10, G. O. Holt, *The North West* (1978); and Vol. 11, P. E. Baughan, *North and Mid Wales* (1980).

More specifically, there are a number of works dealing with London: R. H. G. Thomas, *London's First Railway, the London & Greenwich* (1972), M. Robbins, *The North London Railway* (1953), A. A. Jackson, *London's Termini* (1969) and *London's Local Railways* (1978), J. Betjeman and J. Gay, *London's Historic Railway Stations* (1972), J. R. Day, *The Story of London's Underground* (1972), T. C. Barker and M. Robbins, *A History of London Transport*, 2 vols. (1963, 1974), and C. E. Lee's excellent studies of the various Underground lines, published by London Transport.

The south-west, or rather the Great Western, is one of the most comprehensively covered areas. These are a few of the histories: E. T. MacDermot and C. R. Clinker, *History of the Great Western Railway*, 2 vols. (1964), F. Booker, *The Great Western Railway* (1977) and R. Burdett Wilson, *Go Great Western* (1972). The Southern region is explored in O. S. Nock, *The London & South Western Railway* (1965) and *Southern Steam* (1966), J. H. Turner, *The London, Brighton & South Coast Railway* (1977), and C. F. Klapper, *Sir Herbert Walker's Southern Railway* (1973).

East Anglia and Lincolnshire is documented in C. J. Allen, *The Great Eastern Railway* (1955), O. S. Nock, *The Great Northern Railway* (1958), J. N. Young, *Great Northern Suburban* (1977) and R. S. Joby, *Forgotten Railways, East Anglia* (1977). H. D. Welch has written *The London, Tilbury & Southend Railway* (1951).

The Midlands have been treated in the histories of two of their largest companies, C. H. Ellis, *The Midland Railway* (1953) and George Dow, *History of the Great Central*, 3 vols. (1959–65). Unfortunately, there is no modern history of the L.N.W.R. Recent closures in the region have been covered by P. H. Anderson, *Forgotten Railways, the East Midlands* (1973).

Although there is as yet no comprehensive survey of Welsh railways, there are a number of good company histories. J. I. C. Boyd, *The Festiniog Railway*, 2 vols. (1975), D. S. Barrie, *The Taff Vale Railway* (1950) and *The Barry Railway* (1962), and R. Christiansen and R. W.

Miller, *The Cambrian Railways* (1977) are all useful works. R. Christiansen has also written *Forgotten Railways, North and Mid Wales* (1976).

Most of the north-west's railway history is dealt with in the relevant regional studies or in those dealing with the Midland and Great Central companies. In addition, there are a number of works detailing the development of the smaller railways: R. P. Griffiths, *The Cheshire Lines Committee* (1947), E. Mason, *The Lancashire & Yorkshire Railway in the Twentieth Century* (1954), and N. Coates and M. Walters, *The Lancashire & Yorkshire Album* (1971).

The north-east was much more of a one-company region, falling under the dominance of the North Eastern Railway, though the North British and the Midland made some inroads. Hence, the following studies are relevant; C. J. Allen, *The London & North Eastern Railway* (1966), J. Wrottesley, *The Great Northern Railway*, 2 vols. (1979), K. Hoole, *The Stockton & Darlington Railway* (1975) and *Forgotten Railways: North East England* (1973).

There are several histories dealing with Scotland. H. A. Vallance, *History of the Highland Railway* (1938), C. H. Ellis, *The North British Railway* (1955), and Sir M. Barclay-Harvey, *History of the Great North of Scotland Railway* (1949), are all valuable standard works.

It is difficult to keep abreast of developments in the area of preserved steam. Societies are expanding all the time and as locomotives are restored so others are acquired. The latest edition of H. C. Casserley's *Preserved Locomotives* (1976) and the Rev. W. Awdry and C. Cook's *Guide to the Steam Railways of Britain* (1979) offer a broad indication of this phenomenon.

Index

A–4 class, 269, 273, 275; *see also Mallard*
Aberdeen, 274, 316, 330–31, 339
Aberdour, 327
Aberystwyth, 223, 225, 231
Aberystwyth & Welsh Coast Railway, 223
Accidents, 9, 52, 124, 190, 239–40, 257, 275
Acton Central Station, 78–9, Plate 19
Advanced Passenger Train, 2, 12, 13, 14, 36–7, 51, 198–9, 351, Plate 8
Airport stations, 123, 178, 281
Aldgate Station, 58
Alton, Alresford & Winchester Railway, 147
American influence, 22–3, 30, 31, 33, 44, 45, 63, 117, 133, 252, 253
Amersham, 31, 206
Anderson, Sir Robert, 317
Andrews, George, 282, 300–301, 301–302, 303
Architecture, 221, 350; *see also* Hotels *and names of individual stations*
Arnold, Dr, 97
Arnos Grove Station, 70
Articulated carriages, 46, 171
Ashford, 119, 120, 135, 147
Atlantic class, 22–3, 102
Atmospheric railway, 107–8
Audley End Station, 155

Aylesbury, 31, 58, 64, 69, 177, 206, 207
Aylesbury & Buckingham Railway, 69
Ayr, 313–14

Bakerloo Line, 60–61, 66; locomotives, 32, 63, Plate 17
Baker Street Station, 56, 58, 60, 68, 196, 206
Baker, William, 71
Bala Lake Railway, 225, 233
Banbury, 208–9
Bangor, 216, 225
Barlow, William, 187–8, 251, 328
Barnes, Frederick, 153
Barnstaple, 104, 105–7
Barrow-in-Furness, 54, 261
Barry, Charles, 140, 150
Barry, E. M., 54, 137, 138, 150
Barry Railway, 220
Basingstoke, 128, 131, 132
Bath Station, 94–5, 254
Batley, 294
Battersea, 140
Battle of Britain class, 26, 133–4, 171; *see also* West Country class
Battle Station, 119–20
Bedford, 36, 98, 202, 350
Beeching Report, 1, 7, 110, 143, 212, 345, 346
Bell, William, 278, 281, 286, 301, 305
Bennett, Arnold, 184
Berwick, 6, 287–8

INDEX

Betjeman, Sir John, 137, 293, 350
Beyer, Peacock, 23, 41, 57, 211, 232, 264–5
Bicester, 98, 208
Birkenhead, 45
Birmingham, 3, 33, 34, 38, 178–81, 207, Plate 13; Moor Street, 179–181; New Street, 178–9; Snow Hill, 179, 181
Birmingham Railway Museum, Tyseley, 209–10
Birmingham, Wolverhampton & Dudley Railway, 181–2
Bishopsgate Station, 149
Bishops Stortford, 155, 161, 163, 350
'Black Five' class, 198, 235, 269, 271, 306, 342
Blackfriars Station, 141–2
Blackpool, 101, 254–6
Blaenau Ffestiniog, 224, 225, 230
Bletchley, 98, 203, 209
Bluebell Railway, 80, 143–4
Blythe Bridge Station, 185, 186
Blythe & Tyne Railway, 283–5
Bodmin Road Station, 109
Bogies, 22–3
Bournemouth, 128, 130
Bowen-Cooke, C. J., 25
Box tunnel, 94
Bradford, 290, 291, 292–3
Bressingham Live Steam Museum, 170
Bridgend, 218, 350
Bridgewater Canal, 2, 246
Bridgnorth, 234
Brighton, 11, 101, 122, 124–5, 254
'Brighton Belle', 117, 121–2
Bristol, 3, 85, 95–6, 102, 229; Temple Meads Station, 95, 228
Britannia Bridge, 213–14
Britannia class, 26, 170, 235
British Railways, 346–52, Plate 1; electrification, 35, 36, 168, 347; formation, 8, 345–6; locomotives, 26–7, 42, 168, 170, 210, 235, 271, 341, 346–7; rolling stock, 11, 46–7, 48–9; signalling, 52–3

British Transport Commission, 10, 66–7
Broad Street Station, 71, 73
Brookwood, 126–7
Broxbourne, 161, 163, 350
Brunel, Isambard, 50, 84, 85, 89, 93ff, 98, 105, 107–8, 109, 221
Bulleid, O. V., 26, 132–4
Bulmers Railway Centre, 100–101
Bury St Edmunds Station, 153–4

Caerphilly Railway Society, 236
Caledonian Railway, 6, 259; locomotives, 340, 341; rolling stock, 341
Cambrian Railways, 6, 222–4
Cambridge, 155–6
Camden, 62, 176
Canadian Pacific, 2, 146
Canals, 2, 6–7, 93, 94, 200, 204–5, 235, 239, 246, 273, 292, 294
Cannon Street Station, 137, 138, 154
Canterbury, 119, 121
Cardiff, 38, 218, 220, 221–2
Carnforth, 268
Carlisle, 259–60, 288, 289, 312
Carriages, 11, 15, 42–7, 136, 196, 204, 265, 266, 308, 341; slip, 104, 201–2
Carstairs, 313
Castle class, 2, 20, 90, 96, 104, 112, 209
Catering, 12–13, 93
Cathcart, 320
'Cathedrals Express', 98
Central Line, 60, 65–6, 162, 165, 167; locomotives, 31
Chappel and Wakes Colne Station, 171
Charing Cross Station, 119, 137
Chat Moss, 238–9, 241
Cheap Trains Act, 8–9, 101
Cheltenham Flyer, 2, 96
Cheshire Lines Committee, 8, 227, 240, 245, 252, 270
Chester, 227–8
Chester & Crewe Railway, 227

INDEX

Chester & Holyhead Railway, 6, 213–17, 225
Chiltern Court, 68
Churchward, George, 25, 88, 220
Churton, Edward, 86, 87
Circle Line, 30, 58–60; locomotives, 32, 34, Plate 23
City of Truro, 92–3
City & South London Railway, 2, 30, 31, 62–3, 66, Plate 6
Clacton, 151
Clapham Junction, 73, 113, 134, 135, 140, 142–3
Class 08, 42
Class 47, 41, Plate 9
Claughton, Sir Gilbert, 25
Clayton tunnel, 52, 124
Cockermouth, Keswick & Penrith Railway, 263, 264
Colchester, 151–3, 171
Collett, C. B., 20, 26, 88, 220, 223
Colne Valley Railway, 172
Colwyn Bay, 182, 216, 217
Conan Doyle, Sir Arthur, 58
Construction problems, 3–6, 224, 257, 276, 343
Conway, 214, 216
Cook, Thomas, 191
'Cornish Riviera', 101–5, Plate 25
Coronation class, 26, 198, 275
Coventry, 178
Cowlairs, 321
Cranmore, 112
Crewe, 54, 134, 182–3, 205, 227
Crewkerne, 132
Cricklewood, 201
Cromer, 154, 170
Cubitt, Lewis, 151, 157–8, 160, Plate 28

Darlington, 279–81
Darlington North Road Museum, 18, 360
Dart Valley Railway, 110–11, 112, 130
Dawlish, 107, 120
Deltic class, 39–41
Denmark Hill Station, 140

Departure boards, 126, 150, 243–4, 316–17, 330–31
Deptford, 138, 139
Derby, 39, 198–9, 295
Derwent, 281
Dickens, Charles, 52, 175, 182–3, 344
Didcot, 89–90, 97
Dinting Railway Centre, 198, 270
District Railway, 58–60, 61, 64–5, 66, 67–8, 73, 85, 141, Plate 21; locomotives, 32–4, 35, 136, Plates 15, 16
Dobson, John, 54, 277, 282
Dollis Hill Station, 71
Doncaster, 159–60, 298
Doré, Gustave, 138
Douglas, 264, 265
Dover, 118, 120–21
Downham Station, 157
Drummond, Dugald, 142, 209
Duke of Gloucester, 15, 17, 26–7, 210, Plate 4
Dumfries, 313
Dundee, 328–30
Durham, 281–2
Durham & Sunderland Railway, 305

Ealing Broadway, 56, 67
Earls Court Station, 62, 64, 73
East Anglian Railway, 7
Eastbourne, 125, 128
East Coast Route, 6, 158–60, 257, 269, 273–5, 312, 328, 330
East Croydon, 123
Eastern Counties Railway, 7, 81, 148, 149, 151, 153, 161
Eastern Region, 8, 277, 346
Eastern Union Railway, 7, 153, 154
Eastleigh, 128–30
East Somerset Railway, 112
Edge Hill Station, 241, 250–51
Edis, Colonel Robert, 150
Edinburgh, 6, 322–6; Haymarket, 322–3; Princes Street, 325–6; Waverley, 323–4
Edinburgh & Glasgow Railway, 6, 321–3

Edinburgh Suburban & Southside Junction Railway, 324–5
Electrification, 113–14, 121–2, 135, 252, 253
Ely, 156, 159
Embsay, 308
Epping Station, 165
Esher Station, 131
Eton College, 86
Euston: Arch, 174–5, 179; station, 56, 175, 350
Evening Star, 27, Plate 5
Excursions, 11, 101, 254–5, 265, 313–14, 344
Exeter, 102, 104–5, 132

Fairbourne Railway, 232–3
Farringdon Station, 56, 203
Faversham, 121
Fenchurch Street Station, 81, 168
Festiniog Railway, 230
Finsbury Park Station, 167, 203
Fishguard, 54, 218
Flying Scotsman, 93, 269
Folkestone, 119, 120
Forth Bridge, 1, 322, 327, Plate 40
Fort William, 332, 336
Fowler, Sir John, 56, 322, 327
Freight, 2, 13–14, 48–9, 176, 220, 240
Frith, W. P., 84
Furness Railway, 258, 259, 261–2, 263, 265–7

Gauges, 9, 50, 57, 81, 85, 108, 161, 218, 225, 309
Gillingham, 131, 132
Gladstone, William, 57, 59, 64, 343
Glasgow, 274, 313, 314–21; Buchanan Street, 314–15; Central, 314–15, 316–18, 331; Queen Street, 314–15, 321; Underground, 318–20; St Enoch, 314–315
Glasgow Museum of Transport, 311, 314, 319, 320, 340–41, 359
Glasgow & South Western Railway, 310ff; locomotives, 23, 311, 341
Gleneagles, 317, 326

Gloucester Road Station, 59, 64–5, Plate 18
Gloucester Station, 229
Golden Arrow, 12, 117–19, 269, 349
Gooch, Sir Daniel, 21, 57, 84, 88, 98–9
Goole, 299
Grand Junction Railway, 3, 7, 250, 312; locomotives, 21–2; rolling stock, 43
Grantham, 159
Great Central Railway, 82, 148, 160, 178, 191, 193, 194ff, 206–9, 228, 245, 299; locomotives, 198, 270, Plate 33
Great Eastern Railway, 7, 69, 80–81, 165, 167; locomotives, 24, 170, 171; rolling stock, 270
Great Grimsby & Sheffield Junction Railway, 297, 300
Great Northern Railway, 57, 148, 159, 187, 291, 293, 307; locomotives, 21, 22, 23, 25, 306; rolling stock, 211
Great Northern Railway of Ireland, 9
Great Northern suburban stock, 35, 36, 114, 168, 318, Plate 27
Great North of Scotland Railway, 6, 330–31, 339; locomotives, 340–341; rolling stock, 343
Great Western Railway, 7, 11, 50, 54, 57, 75, 131, 181, 204, 207–8, 228, 229, 231, 235–6; in Wales, 218, 220, 223, 224, 225–6, Plate 29; locomotives, 24, 25, 38–9, 100–101, 144, 209–10, 220, 223–4, 234–5, 269, Plate 30; pannier tanks, 24, 92, 101, 111, 112, 210, 211, 234–5, 307; Prairie locomotives, 111, 112; rolling stock, 44, 45, 46, 48, 111, 236, 270; signalling, 51, 52–3
Great Western Museum, Swindon, 25, 46, 92–3, 360
Great Western Society, Didcot, 46, 88, 90, 213, 220
Green, Benjamin, 287, 289

Green, Leslie, 61, 65, 301
Greenwich, 1, 137, 138, 139
Gresley, Sir Nigel, 25, 47, 132, 133, 146, 171, 269, 274
Grimsby, 155, 160, 302
Grouping, 8, 118, 198, 223, 311
Gwili Railway, 236

Hackney, 79, 161
Hackworth, Timothy, 24
Halifax, 290, 292, 307
Hall class, 90, 111, 209, 223, 269
Hammersmith & City Railway, 34, 67, 75
Hanwell viaduct, 53, 86
Hardwick, P. C., 84, 174
Hardwick, Philip, 54, 174, 179
Harlington Station, 202
Harrogate, 101
Harrow, 68, 69, 207
Harwich, 153
Hastings, 119-20
Haverthwaite Station, 266
Hawkshaw, Sir John, 137, 138, 229, 251
Hawksworth, F. W., 111, 235
Hedley, William, 18
Helensburgh, 332
Henley, 89
Hereford Station, 100-101, 226, 228-9
Hertford, 36, 161-5, 167
Hexham, 288, 289
Highland Railway, 6, 336-9; locomotives, 25, 340, Plate 39; rolling stock, 341
High Speed Train, 2, 13, 14, 37, 42, 51, 198-9, 221, 351, Plate 10
High Wycombe, 196, 207, 208
Hill, Sir Rowland, 56
Holborn Viaduct Station, 136, 141
Holiday Haunts, 103
Holmes, Sherlock, 58, 64
Holyhead, 216-17
Hope valley line, 298
Horne, E. E., 77ff
Horstead Keynes Station, 143, 144
Hotels, 2, 116, 183, 195; Aberdeen, Station Hotel, 331; Bradford, Midland Hotel, 293; Cardiff, Central Hotel, 221-2; Derby, Midland Hotel, 199; Edinburgh, Caledonian Hotel, 325-6, Plate 41; North British Hotel, 323-4; Glasgow, Central Hotel, 317; North British Hotel, 321; Gleneagles, 317, 326; Hull, Royal Station Hotel, 300, 301-2; Inverness, Station Hotel, 338; Liverpool, Adelphi Hotel, 253-4; Lime Street Chambers, 251; London, Charing Cross Hotel, 137; City Terminus Hotel, Cannon Street, 138; Great Eastern Hotel, 150-151; Great Northern Hotel, 158; Great Western Royal Hotel, Paddington, 84-5; Grosvenor Hotel, 116-17; Midland Grand, St Pancras, 188-9, Plate 32; Manchester, Midland Hotel, 245-6, Plate 34; Newcastle, Royal Station Hotel, 286-7, Plate 38; Peterborough, Great Northern Hotel, 159; Sheffield, Royal Victoria Hotel, 196-7; Stoke-on-Trent, North Stafford Hotel, 183-4; York, Royal Station Hotel, 278
Huddersfield, 290, 293-4
Huddersfield & Sheffield Junction Railway, 294-5
Hudson, George, 7, 276-7, 295, 299, 300, 302, 306
Hull, 298-302; Paragon terminus, 300-301
Hull & Selby Railway, 298-9
Hull, South & West Junction Railway, 300
Hymek class, 41-2

Industrialization and railways, 218-220, 238, 241-2, 247, 249, 290, 343
Inverness, 336, 337-8
Ipswich, 153
Ipswich & Bury Railway, 153

Irish Mail, 217, Plate 31
Isle of Man Railway, 264-5
Isle of Wight Steam Railway, 146-7

Jenny Lind class, 20-21
John Hampden, 64
Johnson, S.W., 211
Jones, David, 25
Joy, David, 20-21
Jubilee class, 209, 270
Jubilee Line, 60, 66, 207; *see also* Bakerloo Line

Keighley, 292, 307, 308
Keighley & Worth Valley Light Railway, 306-8
Kemble, 93
Kennet & Avon Canal, 94, 204
Kensington & Richmond Railway, 74-7
Kent & East Sussex Railway, 144-5
Kentish Town, 201, 210
Keswick, 263, 267
Kettering Station, 190, 194
Kew Station, 67, 68, 78
Kilmarnock, 313
King Arthur class, 118, 269
King class, 26, 100, 103, 112, Plate 25
King George V, 100
Kingsbury & Harrow Railway, 68
King's Cross Station, 56, 157-8, 167-8, 187, 188, Plate 28
King's Lynn, 156-7
Kirkcaldy, 327
Kirtley, Matthew, 24
Kyle of Lochalsh, 338

Ladbroke Grove Station, 207
Lake District, 263-4, 265-7
Lakeside & Haverthwaite Railway, 265-7
Lancashire & Carlisle Railway, 257, 258, 259
Lancashire & Yorkshire Railway, 135, 244, 251, 256, 270-71, 291, 293, 294, 299; locomotives, 35, 135, 210, 269, 307
Lancaster, 257-8, 268

Land ownership, 262
Lea valley, 163-4
Leeds, 45, 290-92, 295, 309
Leeds & Selby Railway, 3, 276, 290-91
Legislation, 8-10, 101
Leicester, 159, 191-3, 194, 195, 199, 281
Leicester & Swannington Railway, 3, 191
Lewes, 125
Lewes & East Grinstead Railway, 143
Lincoln, 148, 160-61
Liskeard, 109
Liveries, 47, 63, 64, 319, 335, 349, 355-8
Liverpool, 30, 237-8, 241, 248, 249-54; Central Station, 251, 252; Lime Street, 241, 251; Overhead Railway, 30, 249, 253; *see also* Edge Hill
Liverpool & Manchester Railway, 2-3, 7, 16, 49, 237, 238-41, 250, 253, 280, 322, 344; locomotives, 21, 360; rolling stock, 43, 360; signals, 51
Liverpool Street Station, 73, 149-51, 161, 350
Llanberis Lake Railway, 233
Llandudno Junction, 216, 217, 224
Llangollen Railway Society, 235-6
Llanidloes, 6
Locomotion, 15, 18-19, 279-80, 281
Locomotives: diesel, 37-42, 88, Plate 9; electric, 29-37, 135, 253, Plate 7; goods, 23-4, 220; steam, 16-29, 101
London & Birmingham Railway, 2, 3, 7, 174, 179, 204, 206, 277
London Bridge Station, 136, 137, 139-40
London, Brighton & South Coast Railway, 7, 11, 52, 116, 117, 118, 135, 138; locomotives, 24, 35, 144, 145, 170; rolling stock, 45
London, Chatham & Dover Railway, 117, 141-2

INDEX

London & Croydon Railway, 7
London & Greenwich Railway, 54, 137–8
London, Midland & Scottish Railway, 198, 217, 311, 313; locomotives, 26, 39, 42, 101, 170, 171, 209, 211, 235, 266, 269, 270, 274–5, 307, 342, Plate 35; rolling stock, 46, 47, 172, 342
London & North Eastern Railway, 12, 198, 297–8, 311; locomotives, 25–6, 36, 210–11, 236, 269, 274–5, 288, 309, 341; rolling stock, 46, 47, 266
London & North Western Railway, 11, 50, 53, 71, 73, 77, 209, 224–5, 226, 228, 237, 277, 291; locomotives, 22, 25; rolling stock, 46, 73, 144, 205, 211
London Passenger Transport Board, 9, 66
London & Southampton Railway, 3, 125–6, 142
London & South Western Railway, 51–2, 67, 73, 75, 105–7, 135, 147; locomotives, 22, 23, 35, 144, 147, 209; rolling stock, 136
London, Tilbury & Southend Railway, 23, 56, 81, 168–70; locomotives, 23, 170
London Transport, 9, 66–7, 113, 169; surface stock, 32–5, 101, 211, 234; tube stock, 30–32, 146
London Transport Museum, 23, 30, 31, 57, 63, 69, 143, 359–60
Longport, 184
Longton, 186
Loughborough, 193, 210
Loughton, 186
Lowestoft, 154–5
Ludgate Hill Station, 141
Luton, 201–2

Main Line Steam Trust, 193, 198, 210–11
Mallaig, 336, 338
Mallard, 2, 26, 273, Plate 3
Malvern, 99–100

Manchester, 12, 63, 240–49, 255, 291, 293; Central, 245; Exchange, 241, 244–5; London Road, 243; Piccadilly, 243–4, 247; Victoria, 244, 294
Manchester, Sheffield & Lincolnshire Railway, 82, 161, 171, 195, 196, 277, 297, 299; *see also* Great Central Railway
Manor class, 90, 111, 223–4
Mansion House Station, 67, 73
Market Harborough, 190–91, 206
Marsh, Sir Richard, 10
Marylebone Station, 82, 177, 195, 196, 206
Maryport & Carlisle Railway, 262
Matlock, 199–200
Maunsell, R. E. L., 118, 145, 269
Merchant Navy class, 26, 100, 119, 131, 132–3, Plate 26
Mersey Railway, 135, 249, 252
Merseyside County Museum, Liverpool, 43, 253, 360
Merthyr Tydfil, 218, 221
Metro-Cammell, 34, 122, 319
Metroland, 68–71
Metropolitan Railway, 56–8, 64, 66, 68, 75–6, 195, 203, 206–7; locomotives, 23, 31, 33, 34, 57–8, 63–4, 136, Plate 14; rolling stock, 44, 69–70
Middlesbrough, 304
Middleton Railway, 309
Mid-Hants 'Watercress' Railway, 147
Midland City Line, 202–3
Midland Counties Railway, 194
Midland & Great Northern Joint Railway, 8, 152, 154, 156, 170–71
Midland Railway, 53, 68, 98, 100, 154, 160, 169, 178, 190, 237, 277, 293, 297, 306–7, 314; locomotives, 20, 24, 199, 211, 307; rolling stock, 11, 44, 47, 136, 205, 211, 266
Midland Railway Centre, Butterley, 211
Mileage, 1, 11, 346
Miles Platting, 294

Minehead, 112
Ministry of Transport, 9, 67
Monkwearmouth Station, 305
Moorgate Station, 36, 58, 59, 148, 158, 203
Morecambe, 257, 258
Morden Station, 70
Morgan, Sir Charles, 116
Mumbles Railway, 222

Nationalization, 7, 8, 9–10, 345–6
National Railway Museum, York, 26, 43, 143, 205, 220, 279, 352, 359
Necropolis Station, 126–7
Newark, 159
Newcastle, 282–7; Metro system, 283–6
Newcastle & Berwick Railway, 287
Newcastle & Carlisle Railway, 3, 288
Newhaven, 118
Newmarket Railway, 7
Newport, 218, 221, 222
Newton Abbot, 105, 107, 108
Newton-le-Willows, 241
Newtown, 6, 223, 225
Nine Elms, 125–6, 128, 142, 209
Norfolk Railway, 7
Northampton, 191, 205–6
North British Railway, 6, 259, 273; locomotives, 340
North Dulwich Station, 140–41
North Eastern Railway, 11, 134, 259, 291, 299; locomotives, 35, 36, 38, 134–5, 306, 309; rolling stock, 48, 270, 308
Northern & Eastern Railway, 161
Northern Line, 30–31, 32, 62
North London Railway, 71–81, 177, 351–2; locomotives, 80; rolling stock, 45, 80, 211
North Midland Railway, 198
North Norfolk Railway, 170–71
North & South Western Junction Railway, 78–9
North Staffordshire Railway, 183–6; locomotives, 187
North Star, 21, 92

North Western Railway, 258
North Yorkshire Moors Railway, 305–6
Norwich, 153, 154
Nottingham, 194–5
Notting Hill Gate Station, 59, Plate 20
Novelty, 19

Oban, 332–4
Ongar, 165, 167
Oswestry, 223, 224
Oxford, 38, 97–8, 155, 156
Oxford, Worcester & Wolverhampton Railway, 98, 233–4

Paddington Station, 45, 50, 56, 57, 83–5
Paignton, 105, 108, 111
Parker, Sir Peter, 10
Passengers, 10–12, 136, 343–4
Paxton, Joseph, 84, 200, 282
Peachy, William, 277, 305
Peak class, 41
Peak Railway Society, 199–200
Pearson, Charles, 56
Peel, Sir Robert, 9, 101, 343
Penistone viaduct, 295
Penrith, 264
Penzance, 110
Perth, 326–7, 336
Peterborough, 158, 159, 160, 161, 171, 206
Peterborough & Nene Valley Railway, 171
Piccadilly Line, 60, 64–5, 66; locomotives, 31–2, 65
Planet, 21
Plymouth, 102, 104, 105, 109
Pontypridd, 225
Portsmouth, 128
Port Talbot, 218, 222
Preston, 247, 249, 257
Preston & Wyre Railway, 256
Priestley, J. B., 148
Priestman, W. D., 38
Princes Risborough, 38, 196, 207, 208

Princess class, 101, 211, 274
Prosser, Thomas, 277, 291
Puffing Billy, 17-18
Pullman services, 12, 42, 44-5, 47, 69, 171, Plate 22; 'Bournemouth Belle', 101, 127-8; 'Brighton Belle', 121-2; 'Devon Belle', 130-31, Plate 26; 'Eastern Belle', 151; 'Golden Arrow', 101, 117, 118-19; Manchester Pullman, 12, 204, 237; Midland Pullman, 237; 'Queen of Scots' Pullman, 46; South Wales Pullman, 221

Quainton Railway Society, 58, 80, 195, 211
Quainton Road, 196, 206, 211

Race to the North, 26, 47, 96-7, 273-5, 328, 330
Rainhill, 239
Ramsbottom, John, 21, 22
Ramsey, 264, 265
Ravenglass & Eskdale Railway, 267-8
Reading, 85, 86, 89
Red Dragon Express, 220-21
Red Hill tunnels, 194
Restaurant cars, 12-13, 45, 46, 73, 205, Plate 11
Retford, 158, 159
Ribbleshead viaduct, 260
Richmond, 56, 67, 68, 73, 75, 78
Riddles, R. A., 26, 210, 271
Rocket, 15, 18-21, 239, Plate 2
Rolt, L. T. C., 29
Romney, Hythe & Dymchurch Railway, 145-6
Royal Albert Bridge, Saltash, 53, 108
Royal Border Bridge, Berwick, 287, Plate 36
Royal George, 19, 24
Royal Scot class, 170, 270, 274, Plate 31
Rugby, 177-8, 182, 203, 206, 281

St Andrews, 328

St Pancras Station, 2, 116, 137, 157-158, 187-9, 200, 245
Salford, 241, 247
Salisbury, 131
Saltaire, 292
Sans Pareil, 19, 49
Scarborough, 11, 254, 303-4
Science Museum, London, 19, 30, 32, 39, 51, 63, 65, 104, 239, 279, 360
Scott, Sir George Gilbert, 54, 188, 189, 317
Scottish Region, 8, 311, 346
Sevenoaks, 119, 123, 141
Severn Beach, 95-6
Severn tunnel, 1, 3, 229
Severn Valley Railway, 220, 233-5
Settle, 260, 268
Settlements, railway-created, 54, 68-9, 70, 90, 92, 134, 183, 204, 205, 255, 261, 345
Sheffield, 196, 198, 290, 295-8
Sheffield, Ashton-under-Lyne & Manchester Railway, 297
Sheffield Park Station, 143, 144
Shepherds Bush Station, 60
Sherborne, 130, 131
Sherringham, 154, 170, 171
Shildon, 136, 280
Shrewsbury, 227, 228
Shrewsbury & Birmingham Railway, 181
Sible and Castle Hedingham Station, 172
Signalling, 51-3, 63, 122, 123, 268, 299-300, Plates 12, 13
Silver Link, 275
Skipton, 308
Sleeping carriages, 13, 44
Sloane Square Station, 59
Slough Station, 85, 86, 87
Snowdon Mountain Railway, 225, 232
Somerset & Dorset Railway, 306
Southall, 85, 88
Southampton, 128
South Eastern & Chatham Railway, 119, 120, 135, 138; locomotives, 145

Southend, 81, 169
Southern Railway, 35, 146; locomotives, 26, 100, 112, 119, 147, 269; rolling stock, 119, 122; *see also* Merchant Navy class and West Country class
Southern Region, 8, 80, 346
Southern Uplands, 311–14
Southgate Station, 71
South Hampstead Station, 176–7
South Kensington Station, 60
Southport, 270
South Wales Railway, 218
Spalding, 156, 161
Speedlink, 48
Sport, 60, 99, 128, 221, 246, 322, 344
Stafford, 181
Stanier, Sir William, 26, 198, 274
Steamport, the Southport Locomotive & Transport Museum Society, 270–71
Steamtown, Carnforth, 268–70
Stephenson, George, 16, 18, 191, 202, 238–9, 280, 306
Stephenson, Robert, 18–21, 161, 174, 199, 213–14, 280, 287
Stirling, James, 23
Stirling, Patrick, 22
Stockton & Darlington Railway, 2, 7, 18, 238, 279–81, 304; locomotives, 18–19, 24
Stockwell, 2, 62
Stoke-on-Trent, 183–4, 228
Stour Valley Railway, 171–2
Stranraer, 313–14
Stratford, 77, 79, 80, 161, 170, 171
Strathspey Railway, 337, 341–2
Stroud, 93–4
Stroudley, William, 45, 144, 356
Suburbia, 85–6, 134–5, 255, 345
Sunderland, 305
Swansea, 218, 220, 222
Swindon, 27, 54, 90–93, 99

Taff Vale Railway, 22, 212, 221, 224, 225–6, 236, 307
Talyllyn Railway, 230–31
Taunton, 104

Tay Bridge, 327, 328
Telegraph, 87–8
Tennyson, Lord, 344
Terrier class, 144, 145, 147, 170
Thompson, Francis, 155, 199, 214, 216, 227
Thurso, 338–9
Tite, Sir William, 87, 128, 132, 259–60, 264, 326–7
'Torbay Express', 104, 112
Torbay Steam Railway, 108, 111–12
Torquay, 11, 108
Track, 16, 49–51, 105, 203; *see also* gauges
Trevithick, Richard, 16–17
Trubshaw, Charles, 191, 245
Truro, 109, 110
Turner, J. M. W., 88
Tyndrum, 333
Tyseley, 181, 209

Ulverston Station, 261–2, 265
Urie, R. W., 147
Uttoxeter Station, 186

Vale of Rheidol Railway, 223, 231
Vauxhall, 131
Viaducts, 109, 110, 124, 137–8, 160, 193, 260, 295, 336
Victoria Line, 60, 66; locomotives, 32, Plate 24
Victoria Station, 73, 114–17, 118, 140

Wagons, 47–9
Wakefield, 290
Walker, Sir Herbert, 118, 121, 127, 132, 135
Ware, 163–4
Warrington, 3, 245, 247
Warship class, 41, 346
Waterhouse, Alfred, 241, 243, 251
Waterloo & City Line, 55, 127
Waterloo Station, 60, 119, 125–8, 142, 316
Water troughs, 193–4
Watford, 177, 204
Waverley Route, 312

Webb, Francis, 183
Wellington, Duke of, 239, 240, 343-4
Welshpool & Llanfair Railway, 231-2
Welwyn Garden City, 36
Wembley, 70, 204
West Acton, 54, 71
West Coast Route, 12, 257-9, 268, 273-5, 312-13, 325, 330
West Country class, 26, 133-4, 144, 210, 307; *see also* Battle of Britain class
Western class, 41, 346
Western Region, 8, 50, 56, 101, 221, 223, 346
West Highland Line, 314, 332-6
West London Extension Railway, 73, 74
West London Railway, 73-7
Westminster Station, 59
West Ruislip Station, 207
West Somerset Railway, 112
Weymouth, 104, 128
Wheels, 18-19, 21
Whitby & Pickering Railway, 306
White City Station, 65-6
Whitland & Cardigan Railway, 226

Whitley Bay Station, 283, 286
Wick, 338, 339
Willesden Junction, 73, 78, 177
Wimbledon, 68, 135
Windermere, 101, 263, 267
Windsor, 83, 87
Wolverhampton, 73, 98, 181-2
Wolverton, 54, 134, 203-4, 205
Woodford Station, 165
Woodhead tunnel, 53, 297-8
Wood Lane Station, 65, 66
Woolwich, 38, 80, 139, 147
Worcester, 98-9
Workington, 262
Wrexham, 228, 235
Wyatt, Matthew Digby, 84, 95

Yarmouth, 154
Yarmouth & Newport Railway, 147
Yarmouth & Norwich Railway, 52
Yeovil, 131-2
York, 101, 276-9, 291, 301, Plate 37; *see also* National Railway Museum
York & North Midland Railway, 272, 276, 295, 299, 302, 303, 306
Yorkshire Dales Railway, 308-9

More About Penguins and Pelicans

For further information about books available from
Penguins please write to Dept EP, Penguin Books Ltd,
Harmondsworth, Middlesex UB7 0DA.

In the U.S.A.: For a complete list of books available from
Penguins in the United States write to Dept CS, Penguin
Books, 625 Madison Avenue, New York, New York 10022.

In Canada: For a complete list of books available from
Penguins in Canada write to Penguin Books Canada Ltd,
2801 John Street, Markham, Ontario L3R 1B4.

In Australia: For a complete list of books available from
Penguins in Australia write to the Marketing Department,
Penguin Books Australia Ltd, P.O. Box 257, Ringwood,
Victoria 3134.